California

HARCOURT BRACE SOCIAL STUDIES

Series Authors

Dr. Richard G. Boehm

Claudia Hoone

Dr. Thomas M. McGowan

Dr. Mabel C. McKinney-Browning

Dr. Ofelia B. Miramontes

Dr. Priscilla H. Porter

Series Consultants

Dr. Alma Flor Ada

Dr. Phillip Bacon

Dr. W. Dorsey Hammond

Dr. Asa Grant Hilliard, III

HARCOURT BRACE & COMPANY

Orlando Atlanta Austin Boston San Francisco Chicago Dallas
New York Toronto London

 Visit The Learning Site at http://www.hbschool.com

Series Authors

Dr. Richard G. Boehm
Professor and Jesse H. Jones
Distinguished Chair in
Geographic Education
Department of Geography and
Planning
Southwest Texas State University
San Marcos, Texas

Claudia Hoone
Teacher
Ralph Waldo Emerson School #58
Indianapolis, Indiana

Dr. Thomas M. McGowan
Associate Professor
Division of Curriculum and
Instruction
Arizona State University
Tempe, Arizona

Dr. Mabel C. McKinney-Browning
Director
Division for Public Education
American Bar Association
Chicago, Illinois

Dr. Ofelia B. Miramontes
Associate Professor of Education
and Associate Vice Chancellor
for Diversity
University of Colorado
Boulder, Colorado

Dr. Priscilla H. Porter
Co-Director
Center for History–Social Science
Education
School of Education
California State University,
Dominguez Hills
Carson, California

Series Consultants

Dr. Alma Flor Ada
Professor
School of Education
University of San Francisco
San Francisco, California

Dr. Phillip Bacon
Professor Emeritus of Geography
and Anthropology
University of Houston
Houston, Texas

Dr. W. Dorsey Hammond
Professor of Education
Oakland University
Rochester, Michigan

Dr. Asa Grant Hilliard, III
Fuller E. Callaway Professor of
Urban Education
Georgia State University
Atlanta, Georgia

Media, Literature, and Language Specialists

Dr. Joseph A. Braun, Jr.
Professor of Elementary Social
Studies
Department of Curriculum and
Instruction
Illinois State University
Normal, Illinois

Meredith McGowan
Youth Services Librarian
Tempe Public Library
Tempe, Arizona

Rebecca Valbuena
Language Development Specialist
Stanton Elementary School
Glendora, California

California Consultants

Muncel Chang
Department of Geography
Butte College
Oroville, California
and
Department of Geography
California State University, Chico
Chico, California

Dr. William F. Deverell, Jr.
Associate Professor of History
California Institute of Technology
Pasadena, California

Dr. Jack Forbes
Professor Emeritus of Native
American Studies and
Anthropology
University of California, Davis
Davis, California

Dr. Dorothy Freidel
Assistant Professor of Geography
Sonoma State University
Sonoma, California

Dr. Susan W. Hardwick
Department of Geography
Southwest Texas State University
San Marcos, Texas
formerly Professor of Geography
California State University,
Chico
Chico, California

Rick Moss
History Curator
California African–American
Museum
Los Angeles, California

Mary Ruthsdotter
Projects Director
National Women's History Project
Windsor, California

Grade-Level Reviewers

Catherine Hinchman
Teacher
John Ehrhardt Elementary School
Elk Grove, California

Yvonne R. Magallanes
Bilingual Coordinator
Rowan Avenue Elementary School
Los Angeles, California

Mike McCrory
Teacher
Sequoia Middle School
Fresno, California

Federico Moncloa
Teacher
Freedom Elementary School
Freedom, California

Barbara F. Senneway
Teacher
Sequoia Middle School
Fresno, California

Sherrye Smith
Teacher
Elk Grove Unified School District
Sacramento, California

Helen B. Tross
Curriculum Resource Teacher
John Adams Elementary School
Santa Ana, California

Contents

John Muir

Marie Wilcox

Hernando Cortés

CHAPTER 4

Maria Concepcion Bustamente

California Joins the United States | 190

John C. Frémont

Emma Johnson

F.Y.I.

Building Basic Study Skills

Building Citizenship

Features

Maps

F.Y.I.

Time Lines

Charts, Graphs, Diagrams, and Tables

Atlas

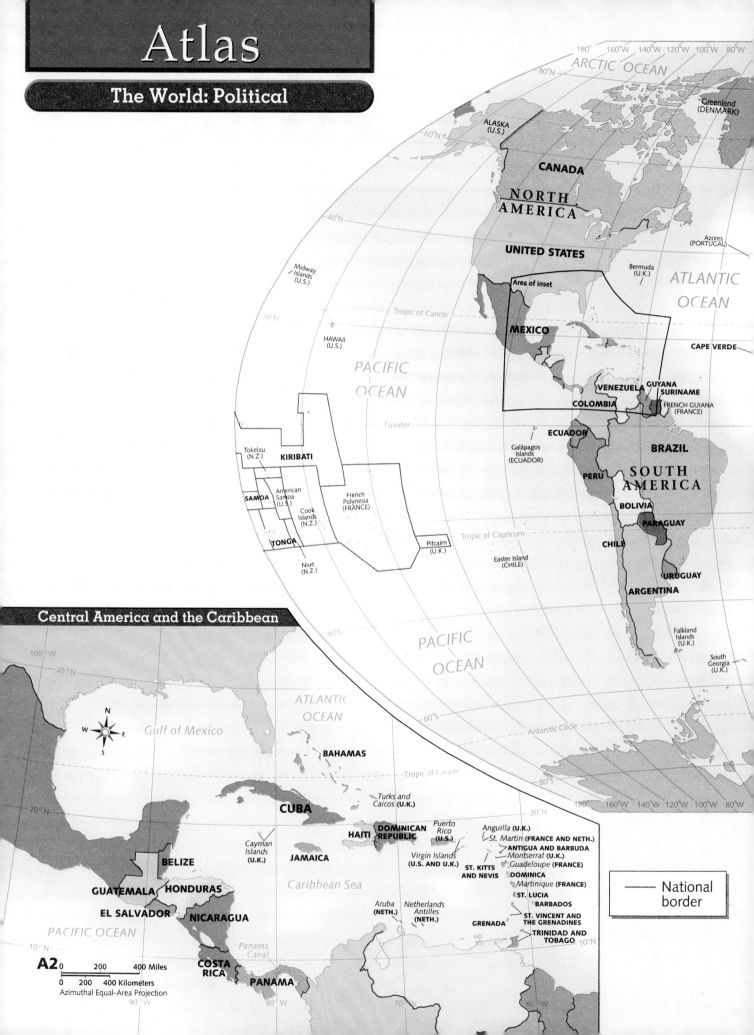

Atlas

The World: Political

Central America and the Caribbean

National border

A2

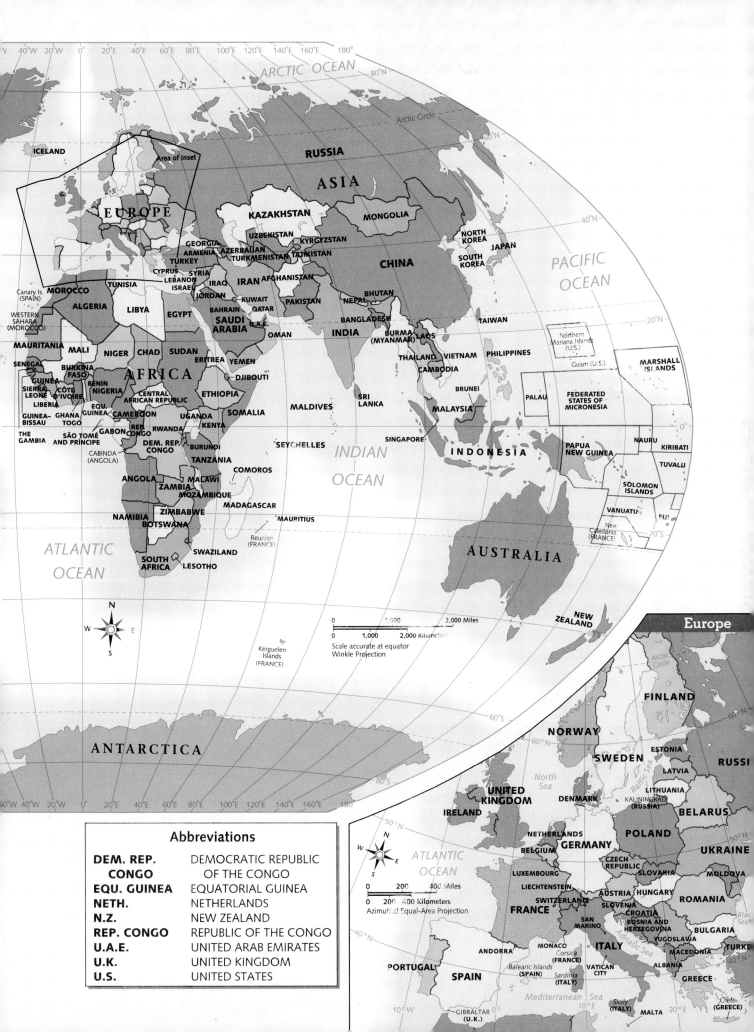

ARCTIC OCEAN

80°N

Arctic Circle

60°N

ICELAND

Area of inset

RUSSIA

ASIA

EUROPE

KAZAKHSTAN

MONGOLIA

40°N

UZBEKISTAN

KYRGYZSTAN

NORTH KOREA

JAPAN

GEORGIA
ARMENIA
TURKEY
AZERBAIJAN
TURKMENISTAN
TAJIKISTAN

CHINA

SOUTH KOREA

CYPRUS
LEBANON
ISRAEL

SYRIA
IRAQ
IRAN
AFGHANISTAN

JORDAN

Canary Is.
(SPAIN)

MOROCCO

TUNISIA

KUWAIT
BAHRAIN
QATAR

PAKISTAN

BHUTAN

NEPAL

20°N

ALGERIA

LIBYA

EGYPT

SAUDI ARABIA

U.A.E.

TAIWAN

WESTERN SAHARA (MOROCCO)

OMAN

INDIA

BANGLADESH

BURMA (MYANMAR)

LAOS

Northern Mariana Islands (U.S.)

MARSHALL ISLANDS

MAURITANIA

MALI

NIGER

CHAD

SUDAN

ERITREA

YEMEN

THAILAND

VIETNAM

PHILIPPINES

Guam (U.S.)

SENEGAL

BURKINA FASO

AFRICA

DJIBOUTI

CAMBODIA

0°

GUINEA

BENIN

NIGERIA

CENTRAL AFRICAN REPUBLIC

ETHIOPIA

BRUNEI

PALAU

FEDERATED STATES OF MICRONESIA

SIERRA LEONE

CÔTE D'IVOIRE

SRI LANKA

MALDIVES

GUINEA-BISSAU

GHANA TOGO

EQU. GUINEA

CAMEROON

UGANDA

SOMALIA

MALAYSIA

LIBERIA

THE GAMBIA

SÃO TOMÉ AND PRÍNCIPE

GABON

REP. CONGO

RWANDA

KENYA

SINGAPORE

NAURU

KIRIBATI

PAPUA NEW GUINEA

CABINDA (ANGOLA)

DEM. REP. CONGO

BURUNDI

TANZANIA

SEYCHELLES

INDONESIA

TUVALU

INDIAN OCEAN

ANGOLA

MALAWI

COMOROS

SOLOMON ISLANDS

ZAMBIA

MOZAMBIQUE

MADAGASCAR

VANUATU

FIJI

ATLANTIC OCEAN

NAMIBIA

ZIMBABWE

BOTSWANA

MAURITIUS

Reunion (FRANCE)

AUSTRALIA

New Caledonia (FRANCE)

20°S

SOUTH AFRICA

SWAZILAND

LESOTHO

N
W   E
S

0   1,000   2,000 Miles
0   1,000   2,000 Kilometers
Scale accurate at equator
Winkle Projection

NEW ZEALAND

Kerguelen Islands (FRANCE)

60°S

ANTARCTICA

80°S

40°W 20°W 0° 20°E 40°E 60°E 80°E 100°E 120°E 140°E 160°E 180°

Abbreviations

DEM. REP. CONGO	DEMOCRATIC REPUBLIC OF THE CONGO
EQU. GUINEA	EQUATORIAL GUINEA
NETH.	NETHERLANDS
N.Z.	NEW ZEALAND
REP. CONGO	REPUBLIC OF THE CONGO
U.A.E.	UNITED ARAB EMIRATES
U.K.	UNITED KINGDOM
U.S.	UNITED STATES

Europe

FINLAND

NORWAY

ESTONIA

SWEDEN

LATVIA

RUSSIA

North Sea

Baltic Sea

LITHUANIA

UNITED KINGDOM

DENMARK

KALININGRAD (RUSSIA)

BELARUS

IRELAND

NETHERLANDS

POLAND

BELGIUM

GERMANY

UKRAINE

ATLANTIC OCEAN

LUXEMBOURG

CZECH REPUBLIC

SLOVAKIA

MOLDOVA

LIECHTENSTEIN

AUSTRIA

HUNGARY

ROMANIA

FRANCE

SWITZERLAND

SLOVENIA

CROATIA

BOSNIA AND HERZEGOVINA

YUGOSLAVIA

BULGARIA

N
W   E
S

SAN MARINO

0   200   400 Miles
0   200   400 Kilometers
Azimuthal Equal-Area Projection

ANDORRA

MONACO (FRANCE)

Corsica (FRANCE)

ITALY

MACEDONIA

TURKE

PORTUGAL

SPAIN

Balearic Islands (SPAIN)

VATICAN CITY

Sardinia (ITALY)

Adriatic Sea

ALBANIA

GREECE

Mediterranean Sea

GIBRALTAR (U.K.)

Sicily (ITALY)

MALTA

Crete (GREECE)

Atlas

The World: Physical

ARCTIC OCEAN

Beaufort Sea
Queen Elizabeth Islands
Baffin Island
Greenland

Mt. McKinley
20,320 ft.
(6,194 m)

Bering Sea

Yukon R.
Mt. Logan
19,524 ft.
(5,951 m)

Great Bear Lake
Great Slave Lake
Mackenzie R.
Hudson Bay

Aleutian Islands

Gulf of Alaska

NORTH AMERICA

Vancouver Island

ROCKY MOUNTAINS
Columbia R.
Missouri R.
Mississippi R.
Ohio R.
Great Lakes
APPALACHIAN MTS.
Newfoundland

GREAT PLAINS

Mt. Whitney
14,495 ft.
(4,418 m)

Colorado R.

Azores

Bermuda

ATLANTIC OCEAN

Tropic of Cancer

Hawaiian Islands

Gulf of Mexico
Bahamas
Citlaltépetl
18,701 ft.
(5,700 m)
Yucatán Peninsula
Cuba
West Indies
Hispaniola
Cape Verde Islands

Caribbean Sea

PACIFIC OCEAN

Equator

Polynesia

Galápagos Islands

Orinoco River
Guiana Highlands
AMAZON BASIN
Amazon R.

SOUTH AMERICA

Brazilian Highlands

ANDES MOUNTAINS
Atacama Desert
Gran Chaco
Paraná River

Tropic of Capricorn

Mt. Aconcagua
22,831 ft.
(6,959 m)

Pampa

Patagonia

Falkland Islands

Strait of Magellan
Cape Horn
Tierra del Fuego

Antarctic Circle

Antarctic Peninsula

Ross Sea

Northern Polar Region

ASIA

EUROPE

Sea of Okhotsk

Kamchatka Peninsula

New Siberian Is.
Severnaya Zemlya
Novaya Zemlya
Barents Sea
Baltic Sea

0 400 800 Miles
0 400 800 Kilometers
Azimuthal Equidistant Projection

ARCTIC OCEAN
North Pole
Svalbard
Norwegian Sea
North Sea

Wrangel Island

Bering Sea

Bering Strait

Greenland Sea

British Isles

BROOKS RANGE

Beaufort Sea
North Magnetic Pole
Queen Elizabeth Islands
Greenland
Iceland

ATLANTIC OCEAN

A4

NORTH AMERICA

PACIFIC OCEAN

Baffin Bay
Arctic Circle

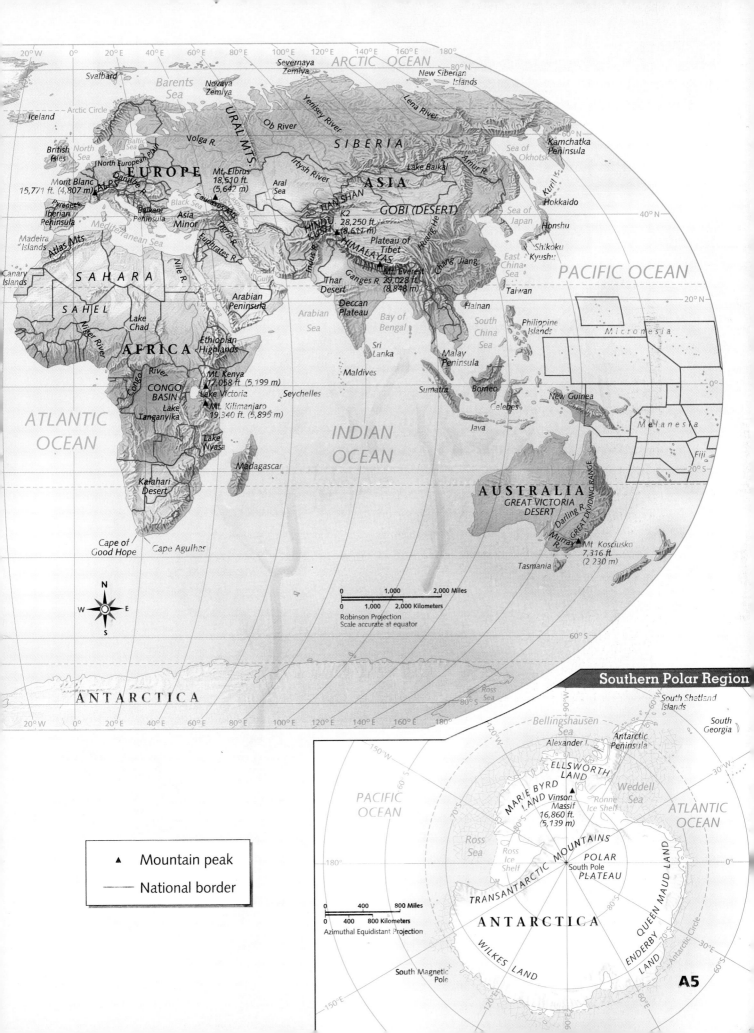

20°W 0° 20°E 40°E 60°E 80°E 100°E 120°E 140°E 160°E 180°

ARCTIC OCEAN

Svalbard
Severnaya Zemlya
New Siberian Islands
80°N

Iceland
Arctic Circle
Barents Sea
Novaya Zemlya

URAL MTS.

Yenisey River
Lena River
60°N
Kamchatka Peninsula

British Isles
North Sea
Baltic Sea
Volga R.
Ob River
Irtysh River
S I B E R I A
Lake Baikal
Amur R.
Sea of Okhotsk

North European Plain
EUROPE
Mont Blanc 15,771 ft. (4,807 m)
ALPS
Danube R.
Mt. Elbrus 18,510 ft. (5,642 m)
Aral Sea
A S I A
TIAN SHAN
GOBI (DESERT)
Huang He
Kuril Is.
Hokkaido

Pyrenees
Iberian Peninsula
Caucasus Mts.
Black Sea
Balkan Peninsula
Asia Minor
Tigris R.
Euphrates R.
HINDU KUSH
K2 28,250 ft. (8,611 m)
HIMALAYAS
Plateau of Tibet
Chang Jiang
40°N
Sea of Japan
Shikoku
Honshu
Kyushu

Madeira Islands
Atlas Mts.
Mediterranean Sea
Nile R.
Indus R.
Ganges R.
Mt. Everest 29,028 ft. (8,848 m)
East China Sea
PACIFIC OCEAN

Canary Islands
S A H A R A
Arabian Peninsula
Thar Desert
Taiwan
20°N

S A H E L
Lake Chad
Arabian Sea
Deccan Plateau
Bay of Bengal
Hainan
South China Sea
Philippine Islands
M i c r o n e s i a

Niger River
AFRICA
Ethiopian Highlands
Sri Lanka
Malay Peninsula

Congo River
CONGO BASIN
Mt. Kenya 17,058 ft. (5,199 m)
Lake Victoria
Mt. Kilimanjaro 19,340 ft. (5,895 m)
Maldives
Seychelles
Sumatra
Borneo
Celebes
New Guinea
M e l a n e s i a

ATLANTIC OCEAN
Lake Tanganyika
INDIAN OCEAN
Java
Fiji
20°S

Lake Nyasa
Madagascar
AUSTRALIA
GREAT VICTORIA DESERT
GREAT DIVIDING RANGE

Kalahari Desert
Darling R.

Cape of Good Hope
Cape Agulhas
Murray R.
Mt. Kosciusko 7,316 ft. (2,230 m)

Tasmania

0 1,000 2,000 Miles
0 1,000 2,000 Kilometers
Robinson Projection
Scale accurate at equator

N
W E
S

A N T A R C T I C A

20°W 0° 20°E 40°E 60°E 80°E 100°E 120°E 140°E 160°E 180°

▲ Mountain peak
— National border

South Shetland Islands
Bellingshausen Sea
South Georgia

Alexander I.
Antarctic Peninsula
ELLSWORTH LAND

PACIFIC OCEAN
MARIE BYRD LAND
Vinson Massif 16,860 ft. (5,139 m)
Ronne Ice Shelf
Weddell Sea
ATLANTIC OCEAN

Ross Sea
TRANSANTARCTIC MOUNTAINS
POLAR PLATEAU
South Pole
QUEEN MAUD LAND

Ross Ice Shelf
ENDERBY LAND

WILKES LAND
A N T A R C T I C A
Antarctic Circle

0 400 800 Miles
0 400 800 Kilometers
Azimuthal Equidistant Projection

South Magnetic Pole

A5

Atlas

Western Hemisphere: Political

ARCTIC OCEAN

Beaufort Sea

Viscount Melville Sound

Baffin Bay

Greenland **(DENMARK)**

Bering Strait

ALASKA (U.S.)
Fairbanks

Yukon River

Great Bear Lake

Foxe Basin

Arctic Circle

Anchorage

Whitehorse

Mackenzie River

Yellowknife

Hudson Strait

Davis Strait

60° N

Gulf of Alaska

Juneau

Liard River

Great Slave Lake

CANADA

Hudson Bay

Labrador Sea

Bering Sea

Peace River

Lake Athabasca

James Bay

Edmonton

Saskatchewan R.

Lake Winnipeg

St. Lawrence River

St. John's

Calgary

Saskatoon

Regina

Winnipeg

Thunder Bay

Ottawa

Quebec

Gulf of St. Lawrence

Vancouver

Seattle

UNITED STATES

Great Lakes

Toronto

Montreal

St. John

Halifax

Puget Sound

Portland

Columbia

Snake R.

Boise

Great Salt Lake

Salt Lake City

Missouri R.

Chicago

Detroit

Albany

Boston

St. Lawrence R.

New York City

Reno

San Francisco

Las Vegas

Denver

Colorado R.

St. Louis

Mississippi R.

Indianapolis

Cleveland

Philadelphia

Washington, D.C.

Richmond

Norfolk

Los Angeles

San Diego

Phoenix

El Paso

Memphis

Atlanta

Raleigh

Charleston

ATLANTIC OCEAN

Tucson

Hermosillo

Rio Grande

Dallas

Houston

New Orleans

Savannah

30° N

Chihuahua

San Antonio

Gulf of Mexico

Jacksonville

Tampa

Miami

BAHAMAS

Nassau

Tropic of Cancer

MEXICO

Monterrey

Durango

Havana

CUBA

HAITI

Port-au-Prince

Santo Domingo

Honolulu

León

Tampico

JAMAICA

PUERTO RICO (U.S.)

HAWAII (U.S.)

Guadalajara

Mexico City

BELIZE

Belmopan

Kingston

DOMINICAN REPUBLIC

PACIFIC OCEAN

Puebla

Veracruz

Acapulco

GUATEMALA

Guatemala City

HONDURAS

Tegucigalpa

San Salvador

Managua

EL SALVADOR

San José

Maracaibo

Caribbean Sea

NICARAGUA

COSTA RICA

Panama City

Caracas

GUYANA

SURINAME

PANAMA

Medellín

Cali

VENEZUELA

Georgetown

Paramaribo

Cayenne

COLOMBIA

Bogotá

Rio Negro

FRENCH GUIANA (FRANCE)

0°

Equator

Quito

ECUADOR

Guayaquil

Galápagos Islands **(ECUADOR)**

Iquitos

Manaus

Amazon R.

Belém

Fortaleza

Tapajós River

Xingu R.

Tocantins

São Francisco R.

Recife

Trujillo

PERU

BRAZIL

Lima

Cuzco

Brasília

Salvador

FRENCH POLYNESIA **(FRANCE)**

Lake Titicaca

La Paz

BOLIVIA

Goiânia

Belo Horizonte

Papeete

Arequipa

Sucre

Campo Grande

Rio de Janeiro

Tropic of Capricorn

Antofagasta

Paraguay R.

PARAGUAY

Asunción

São Paulo

Curitiba

Salta

San Miguel de Tucumán

CHILE

Córdoba

Paraná R.

Pôrto Alegre

Valparaíso

Rosario

URUGUAY

30° S

Santiago

Buenos Aires

Montevideo

Concepción

La Plata

Rio de la Plata

Mar del Plata

0   1,000   2,000 Miles

0 1,000 2,000 Kilometers

Miller Cylindrical Projection

Valdivia

Bahía Blanca

ARGENTINA

N

W   E

S

—— National border

⊛ National capital

• City

Falkland Islands **(U.K.)**

South Georgia **(U.K.)**

A6

Punta Arenas

150° W   120° W   90° W   60° W   30° W

Atlas

Western Hemisphere: Physical

ARCTIC OCEAN

North Magnetic Pole

Queen Elizabeth Islands

Ellesmere Island

Greenland

Melville Island

Devon Island

Baffin Bay

Viscount Melville Sound

Banks Island

Point Barrow

Beaufort Sea

Victoria Island

Brooks Range

Great Bear Lake

Baffin Island

Mt. McKinley 20,320 ft. (6,194 m)

Yukon River

Yukon Plateau

Mackenzie Mts.

Mackenzie River

Great Slave Lake

Foxe Basin

Hudson Strait

Davis Strait

Arctic Circle

Cape Farewell

60° N

Alaska Range

Liard R.

Peace River

Lake Athabasca

Athabasca R.

Hudson Bay

Labrador Sea

Gulf of Alaska

Mt. Logan 19,524 ft. (5,951 m)

Saskatchewan River

Lake Winnipeg

James Bay

Labrador

Kodiak Island

Alaska Peninsula

Coast Mountains

C A N A D I A N

S H I E L D

Aleutian Islands

Queen Charlotte Islands

Coast Ranges

R O C K Y

G R E A T

NORTH AMERICA

Great Lakes

St. Lawrence R.

Newfoundland

Gulf of St. Lawrence

Vancouver Island

Cascade Range

Snake R.

M O U N T A I N S

P L A I N S

Mississippi R.

Nova Scotia

Bay of Fundy

Puget Sound

Sierra Nevada

Black Hills

Missouri R.

INTERIOR PLAINS

Ohio R.

APPALACHIAN MTS.

Cape Cod

Long Island

Great Salt Lake GREAT BASIN

Colorado R.

Platte R.

Arkansas R.

Ozark Plateau

Mt. Whitney 14,495 ft. (4,418 m)

COASTAL PLAIN

Cape Hatteras

ATLANTIC OCEAN

Death Valley (lowest point in N.A.) -282 ft. (-86 m)

Sierra Madre Occidental

Rio Grande

Sonoran Desert

30° N

Baja California

Gulf of California

Sierra Madre Oriental

Gulf of Mexico

Bahamas

Hawaiian Islands

Tropic of Cancer

Cuba

Greater Antilles

Hispaniola

Puerto Rico

PACIFIC OCEAN

Citlaltépetl 18,701 ft. (5,700 m)

Yucatán Peninsula

Lesser Antilles

Lake Nicaragua

Caribbean Sea

Line

Isthmus of Panama

Lake Maracaibo

Orinoco R.

Llanos

Guiana Highlands

Islands

Equator

Chimborazo 20,561 ft. (6,267 m)

Rio Negro

Amazon R.

Galápagos Islands

AMAZON BASIN

Cape São Roque

Marquesas Islands

Tapajós River

Xingu River

Tocantins R.

São Francisco River

Huascarán 22,205 ft. (6,768 m)

Mato Grosso Plateau

Brazilian Highlands

Cook Islands

Society Islands

Tuamotu Archipelago

Lake Titicaca

Paraguay R.

SOUTH AMERICA

Tropic of Capricorn

A N D E S

Gran Chaco

Paraná R.

Iguazú Falls

Uruguay R.

30° S

0   1,000   2,000 Miles

0   1,000   2,000 Kilometers

Miller Cylindrical Projection

Mt. Aconcagua 22,831 ft. (6,959 m)

M O U N T A I N S

Rio de la Plata

Pampa

Valdés Peninsula (lowest point in S.A.) -131 ft. (-40 m)

▲ Mountain peak

▼ Point below sea level

— National border

≋ Waterfall

N
W   E
S

Patagonia

Falkland Islands

Strait of Magellan

Tierra del Fuego

Cape Horn

150° W   120° W   90° W   60° W   30° W

RUSSIA

60°N

Bering Sea

ALASKA
(AK)

180°

40°N

PACIFIC OCEAN

WASHINGTON
(WA)

OREGON
(OR)

NEVADA
(NV)

CALIFORNIA
(CA)

```
0          250          500 Miles
0     250     500 Kilometers
Modified Azimuthal Equal-Area Projection
```

—— National border
——— State border
⊛ National capital

N
W   E
S

160°W

Tropic of Cancer

HAWAII
(HI)

20°N

140°W

120°W

Atlas

United States: Political

RUSSIA

ARCTIC OCEAN

70° N

170° E

ALASKA

60° N

Yukon River

CANADA

Fairbanks

120° W

Bering
Sea

Anchorage

60° N

180°

0   250   500 Miles
0   250   500 Kilometers

Juneau

PACIFIC
OCEAN

50° N

170° W   160° W   150° W   140° W   130° W

CANADA

120° W   110° W

Seattle
Tacoma
Olympia   Spokane
WASHINGTON

Great Falls

Portland   Columbia River

Salem   Helena ★ MONTANA

Eugene   Billings

OREGON   IDAHO

Boise   WYOMING

Snake River   Casper

PACIFIC

OCEAN

Pocatello

40° N

NEVADA

Reno
Sacramento ★   Carson City

Great
Salt
Lake   Ogden
Salt Lake City ★
Provo

WYOMING

Cheyenne

San Francisco • Oakland
San Jose

UTAH   Denver

Colorado
Springs

Fresno   Colorado River

30° N

CALIFORNIA   Las
Vegas

COLORADO

Puebl

130° W

Bakersfield

Flagstaff   Santa Fe ★

Los Angeles   San Bernardino
Albuquerque

ARIZONA   NEW MEXICO

San Diego

Phoenix

Roswell

Tucson

El Paso

Rio Grande

MEXICO

	Northeast	⊛	National capital
	Southeast	★	State capital
	Middle West	•	Major city
	Southwest	—	National border
	West	—	State border

PACIFIC
OCEAN   155° W
160° W

Honolulu

HAWAII

20° N

Hilo

0   100   200 Miles
0   100   200 Kilometers

20° N

120° W

0   250   500 Miles
0   250   500 Kilometers
Albers Equal-Area Projection

N
W   E
S

110° W

A10

Atlas

United States: Physical

CANADA

Alaska inset
RUSSIA
ARCTIC OCEAN
170° E
120° W
70° N
Brooks Range
ALASKA
Seward Peninsula
Yukon River
CANADA
Mt. McKinley 20,320 ft. (6,194 m)
Alaska Range
Yukon River
St. Lawrence Island
60° N
60° N
Bering Strait
Bering Sea
Gulf of Alaska
Kodiak Island
50° N
Aleutian Islands
180°
170° W
160° W
150° W
140° W
130° W
0   250   500 Miles
0   250   500 Kilometers

Legend
Arid
Evergreen forest
Grassland
Mixed forest
Mountains
Tundra
— National border
— State border
▲ Mountain peak
△ Highest point
▼ Lowest point

Main map labels
WA
Mt. Rainier 14,410 ft. (4,392 m)
Mt. St. Helens 8,364 ft. (2,549 m)
Columbia River
Mt. Hood 11,235 ft. (3,427 m)
Coast Range
Cascade Range
Coast Ranges
OR
Columbia Plateau
Snake River
ID
Salmon River Mountains
Bitterroot Range
ROCKY
MT
Fort Peck Lake
Yellowstone River
Bighorn Mts.
Wind River Range
Teton Range
WY
Great Divide Basin
Front Range
Cape Mendocino
Pyramid Lake
Donner Pass
Lake Tahoe
NV
GREAT BASIN
Great Salt Lake
Wasatch Range
Uinta Mts.
Mt. Elbert 14,433 ft. (4,399 m)
MOUNTAINS
Sierra Nevada
Sacramento River
Central Valley
San Joaquin
Mt. Whitney 14,495 ft. (4,418 m)
Death Valley -282 ft. (-86 m)
Mojave Desert
UT
Lake Powell
Colorado River
San Juan Mts.
CO
Sangre de Cristo Mts.
CA
Grand Canyon
Lake Mead
Colorado Plateau
NM
Point Conception
Channel Islands
Salton Sea
Imperial Valley
Sonoran Desert
AZ
Baldy Peak 11,403 ft. (3,476 m)
Guadalupe Peak 8,749 ft. (2,667 m)
Rio Grande

PACIFIC OCEAN

120° W
110° W

30° N
130° W

MEXICO

Hawaii inset
160° W
155° W
PACIFIC OCEAN
Kauai
Niihau
Oahu
Molokai
Lanai
Maui
Kahoolawe
Hawaii
20° N
Mauna Kea 13,796 ft. (4,205 m)
HAWAII
0   100   200 Miles
0   100   200 Kilometers

N
W   E
S

0   250   500 Miles
0   250   500 Kilometers
Albers Equal-Area Projection

120° W
110° W

A12

Atlas

California: Political

State capital ★
County seat ●
Other city •
National border ▬
State border ▬
County border ▬

OREGON
IDAHO

Crescent City
Yreka
DEL NORTE
SISKIYOU
MODOC
Alturas

HUMBOLDT
LASSEN
Eureka
SHASTA
Weaverville
Redding
TRINITY
Susanville
TEHAMA
Red Bluff
PLUMAS
GLENN
Chico
Quincy
Willows
BUTTE
COLUSA
Oroville
SIERRA
Downieville
Colusa
YUBA
Nevada City
NEVADA
Ukiah
Lakeport
Yuba City
Marysville
Truckee
MENDOCINO
LAKE
SUTTER
PLACER
Auburn
Lake Tahoe
YOLO
Woodland
Placerville
Markleeville
SONOMA
NAPA
EL DORADO
Santa Rosa
Napa
SACRAMENTO
AMADOR
ALPINE
Sonoma
Fairfield
Jackson
Petaluma
SOLANO
CALAVERAS
MARIN
Martinez
Stockton
San Andreas
Bridgeport
NEVADA
San Rafael
Berkeley
CONTRA COSTA
TUOLUMNE
SAN FRANCISCO
Oakland
SAN JOAQUIN
Sonora
Mono Lake
San Francisco
ALAMEDA
MONO
Redwood City
STANISLAUS
Modesto
SAN MATEO
San Jose
MARIPOSA
SANTA CLARA
Merced
Mariposa
SANTA CRUZ
MERCED
MADERA
Santa Cruz
Madera
Hollister
FRESNO
Monterey Bay
Salinas
SAN BENITO
Fresno
Independence
Monterey
INYO
Hanford
Visalia
MONTEREY
Tulare
KINGS
TULARE
SAN LUIS OBISPO
Ridgecrest
Lake Mead
San Luis Obispo
Bakersfield
KERN
Santa Maria
SANTA BARBARA
Barstow
Lompoc
SAN BERNARDINO
Needles
Santa Barbara
VENTURA
Santa Clarita
Ventura
LOS ANGELES
San Bernardino
Oxnard
Glendale
Pasadena
Los Angeles
Riverside
Torrance
Anaheim
Palm Springs
Long Beach
Santa Ana
Blythe
Huntington Beach
ORANGE
RIVERSIDE
PACIFIC OCEAN
Salton Sea
Oceanside
IMPERIAL
Escondido
El Centro
San Diego
SAN DIEGO
San Diego Bay
MEXICO
ARIZONA

Pacific Ocean

0   75   150 Miles
0   75   150 Kilometers
Albers Equal-Area Projection

A14

42°N
41°N
40°N
39°N
38°N
37°N
36°N
35°N
34°N
33°N
32°N

124°W
123°W
122°W
121°W
120°W
119°W
118°W

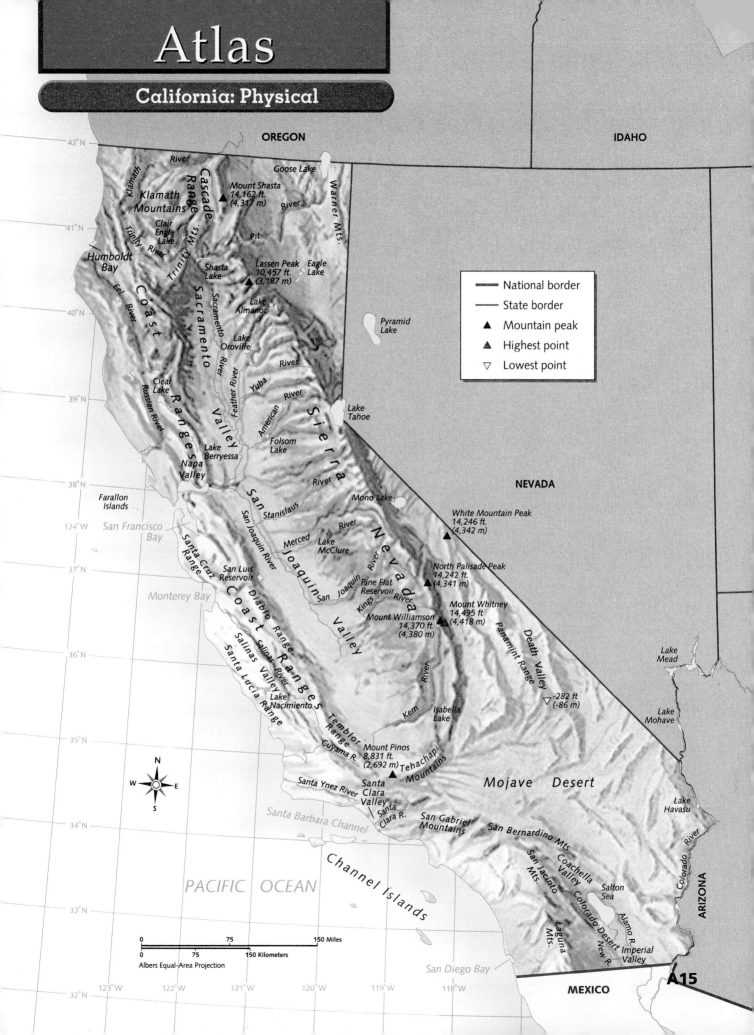

Atlas

California: Physical

OREGON

IDAHO

NEVADA

ARIZONA

MEXICO

River

Goose Lake

Klamath River

Cascade Range

Klamath Mountains

Mount Shasta 14,162 ft. (4,317 m)

Warner Mts.

Clair Engle Lake

Trinity River

Trinity Mts.

Pit River

Humboldt Bay

Shasta Lake

Lassen Peak 10,457 ft. (3,187 m)

Eagle Lake

Coast

Eel River

Sacramento River

Lake Almanor

Lake Oroville

Pyramid Lake

Sacramento Valley

Feather River

River

Clear Lake

Russian River

Yuba

American River

Sierra

Lake Tahoe

Folsom Lake

Lake Berryessa

Napa Valley

River

Farallon Islands

San Francisco Bay

Stanislaus

Mono Lake

White Mountain Peak 14,246 ft. (4,342 m)

Santa Cruz Range

San Joaquin River

Merced River

Lake McClure

Nevada

North Palisade Peak 14,242 ft. (4,341 m)

Monterey Bay

San Luis Reservoir

Pine Flat Reservoir

Kings River

San Joaquin

Mount Whitney 14,495 ft (4,418 m)

Diablo Range

San Joaquin Valley

Mount Williamson 14,370 ft. (4,380 m)

Death Valley

Lake Mead

Coast Ranges

Salinas River

Salinas Valley

Kern River

Isabella Lake

Panamint Range

−282 ft (−86 m)

Lake Mohave

Santa Lucia Range

Lake Nacimiento

Temblor Range

Mount Pinos 8,831 ft. (2,692 m)

Tehachapi Mountains

Mojave Desert

Lake Havasu

Cuyama R.

Santa Ynez River

Santa Clara Valley

Santa Clara R.

San Gabriel Mountains

San Bernardino Mts.

Colorado River

Santa Barbara Channel

Channel Islands

PACIFIC OCEAN

San Jacinto Mts.

Coachella Valley

Colorado Desert

Salton Sea

Laguna Mts.

Alamo R.

New R.

Imperial Valley

San Diego Bay

Legend

━━━	National border
───	State border
▲	Mountain peak
▲	Highest point
▽	Lowest point

0   75   150 Miles
0   75   150 Kilometers
Albers Equal-Area Projection

Atlas

Geography Terms

Timberline

Slope

MOUNTAIN RANGE

Sea level

Glacier

VALLEY

Inlet

PLATEAU

Canyon

Mesa

Fall line

PLAIN

COASTAL PLAIN

Coast

Mouth of river

Lake

Sea level

Channel

Isthmus

Peninsula

Cape

OCEAN

---

basin bowl-shaped area of land surrounded by higher land

bay body of water that is part of a sea or ocean and is partly enclosed by land

bluff high, steep face of rock or earth

canyon deep, narrow valley with steep sides

cape point of land that extends into water

channel deepest part of a body of water

cliff high, steep face of rock or earth

coast land along a sea or ocean

coastal plain area of flat land along a sea or ocean

delta triangle-shaped area of land at the mouth of a river

desert dry land with few plants

dune hill of sand piled up by the wind

fall line area along which rivers form waterfalls or rapids as the rivers drop to lower land

floodplain flat land that is near the edges of a river and is formed by the silt deposited by floods

foothills hilly area at the base of a mountain

glacier large ice mass that moves slowly down a mountain or across land

gulf body of water that is partly enclosed by land but is larger than a bay

harbor area of water where ships can dock safely near land

hill land that rises above the land around it

inlet a narrow strip of water leading into the land from a larger body of water

island land that has water on all sides

isthmus narrow strip of land connecting two larger areas of land

lake body of water with land on all sides

marsh lowland with moist soil and tall grasses

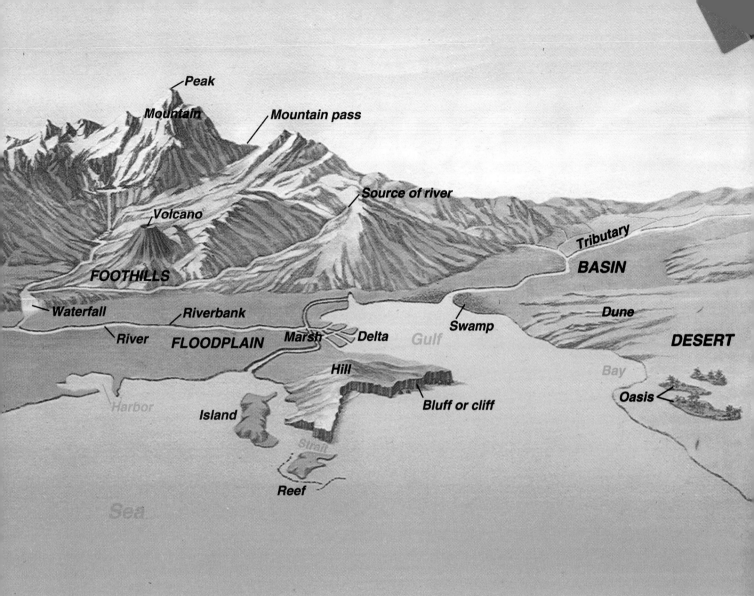

mesa flat-topped mountain with steep sides

mountain highest kind of land

mountain pass gap between mountains

mountain range row of mountains

mouth of river place where a river empties into another body of water

oasis area of water and fertile land in a desert

ocean body of salt water larger than a sea

peak top of a mountain

peninsula land that is almost completely surrounded by water

plain flat land

plateau area of high, flat land with steep sides

reef ridge of sand, rock, or coral that lies at or near the surface of a sea or ocean

river large stream of water that flows across the land

riverbank land along a river

sea body of salt water smaller than an ocean

sea level the level that is even with the surface of an ocean or sea

slope side of a hill or mountain

source of river place where a river begins

strait narrow channel of water connecting two larger bodies of water

swamp area of low, wet land with trees

timberline line on a mountain above which it is too cold for trees to grow

tributary stream or river that empties into a larger river

valley low land between hills or mountains

volcano opening in the Earth, often raised, through which lava, rock, ashes, and gases are forced out

waterfall steep drop from a high place to a lower place in a stream or river

WHY STUDY SOCIAL STUDIES?

"Every one of you already holds the important office of citizen. Over time you will become more and more involved in your community. You will need to know more about what being a citizen means. Social studies will help you learn about citizenship. That is why social studies is important in your life."

The authors of
Harcourt Brace Social Studies

The Themes of Social Studies

A good nickname for California is "the Golden State." After all, it was for gold that thousands of settlers came to California in 1849. Since then California's golden sunshine has brought millions of other citizens to our state. A **citizen** is a member of a country, a state, or a city or town. *Harcourt Brace Social Studies* will help you learn what it means to be a citizen of the Golden State.

To help you think, feel, and act as a citizen, *Harcourt Brace Social Studies* begins every lesson with a question. The question helps you focus your thinking on one or more themes, or key topics, of social studies. Citizens need to understand these themes in order to make decisions. The themes help you think clearly and understand what you read. They also help you see how the lesson connects to your own life.

These students are being good citizens. What actions make you a good citizen?

Commonality and Diversity

In some ways people everywhere are alike. We all need food, clothing, and homes. We all laugh, get angry, and have our feelings hurt. These things show our commonality (kah•muh•NAL•uh•tee), or ways we are alike. At the same time, we all have different ways of thinking, feeling, and acting. That is our diversity (duh•VER•suh•tee).

Places, too, can be both the same and different. Many places on Earth have the same kinds of landforms. A **landform** is one of the shapes that make up the Earth's surface—for example, mountains, hills, and plains. Yet every place on Earth is different in some way.

California has people from many diverse backgrounds.

These people are cooperating with each other to clean up this beach.

Conflict and Cooperation

Because all people have different needs and wants, they may have conflicts, or disagreements. But people can often work out their conflicts by cooperating, or working together. In social studies you will learn about many of the ways people in California have found to settle their disagreements.

Telephones have changed over the years. In what ways have they stayed the same?

Continuity and Change

Most things change over time, but some things stay the same. Things that have stayed the same for years and will likely stay the same for a long time have continuity (kahn•tuh•NOO•uh•tee). Understanding continuity and change can help you see how things in California and other parts of the world came to be as they are.

Individualism and Interdependence

Sometimes citizens act as individuals (in•duh•VIJ•wuhlz), or on their own, to change things in the world. What they do as individuals may be helpful or harmful to others. Much of the time, however, people do not act on their own. They depend on one another for help. Such interdependence (in•ter•dih•PEN•duhns) can help citizens do more together than each could do alone.

Interaction Within Different Environments

People behave in ways that affect not only other people but also their **environment** (in•VY•ruhn•muhnt), or surroundings. This is true of their home environment, their school environment, and other environments they may be a part of. In turn, environments affect people. Understanding such interactions, or ways people and places affect one another, is important. It helps you see why things happened in the past and why things happen today.

REVIEW **What are the five themes of social studies?**

The individuals on this soccer team must learn to work together. Members of a team depend on one another.

How are these surfers interacting with their environment?

Read Social Studies

1. Why Learn This Skill?

Social studies is made up of stories about people, places, and events. An **event** is something that happens. Sometimes you read these stories in library books. At other times you read them in textbooks like this one. Knowing how to read social studies can make it easier to study and do your homework. It can help you find important ideas and learn about people, places, and events.

2. Getting Started

Your book is divided into five units. At the beginning of each unit, you will find several pages that will help you preview the unit and predict what it will be about.

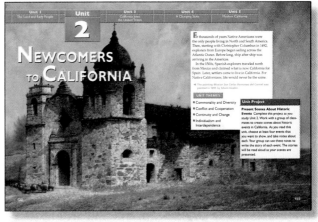

▲

Each unit begins with a short overview of the unit and a list of the social studies themes it teaches. You will also read about a project you can complete as you study the unit.

▲

The Unit Preview has a map that shows where some of the important events you will read about took place. It also has a time line that shows the order in which the events happened. There may be a story line that shows some of the people, places, or events.

▲

Each unit has at least one literature selection that helps you understand the time and place you are studying. The literature selection may be a story, or it may be a poem or a song.

3. The Parts of a Lesson

Each unit has two chapters, and each chapter is divided into lessons. The beginning and end of a lesson are shown below.

The time line shows the period of time in which the events in the lesson took place.

This question helps you see how the lesson relates to life today.

This statement gives you the lesson's main idea. It tells you what to look for as you read the lesson.

These are the new terms you will learn in this lesson.

The first time a vocabulary term appears in the lesson, it is highlighted in yellow.

Each lesson, like each chapter and each unit, ends with a review. A time line may show the order of some of the events in the lesson. The review questions and activities help you check your understanding and show what you know.

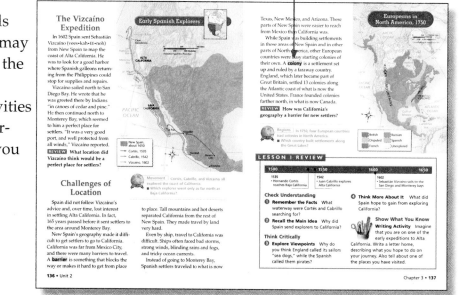

4. Understand the Process

You can follow these steps to read any lesson in this book.

1 Preview the whole lesson.

- Look at the title and the headings to find out what the lesson is about.
- Look at the pictures, the captions, and the questions to get an idea of what is most important in the lesson.
- Read the Focus question at the beginning of the lesson to see how the lesson relates to life today.

- Read the Main Idea statement to find out the main idea of the lesson.
- Look at the Vocabulary list to see what new terms you will learn.

2 Read the lesson to learn more about the main idea. As you read, you will come to a number of questions with the label **REVIEW**. Be sure to answer these questions before you continue reading the lesson.

3 When you finish reading the lesson, say in your own words what you have learned.

4 Look back over the lesson. Then answer the Lesson Review questions from memory. These questions will help you check your understanding of the lesson. The activity at the end of the review will help you show what you know.

5. Some Other Parts of Your Book

Your textbook has many other features to help you learn. Some of them are shown on this page.

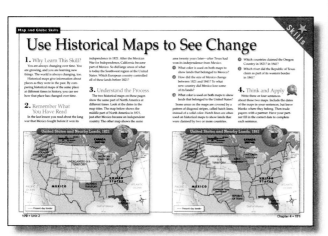

▲ Skill lessons help you build basic study skills. They also help you build citizenship skills as you work with others.

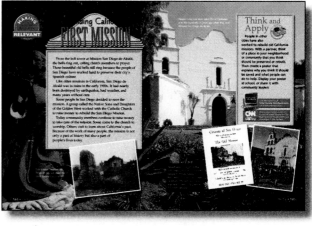

▲ The feature called Making Social Studies Relevant helps you see how social studies is connected to your life and the lives of other people.

At the back of your book is a section called For Your Reference. It includes the following reference tools.

- How to Gather and Report Information
- Almanac
- Some Famous People in California History
- Gazetteer
- Glossary
- Index

6. Think and Apply

Use the four steps in Understand the Process each time you read a lesson in *Harcourt Brace Social Studies*.

▲ The Counterpoints pages help you understand the different points of view people may have about certain issues.

History

One of the subjects you will learn about in social studies is **history**—the study of the past. Studying history helps you see links between the past and the present. It places people and their activities in time. As you read about the past in *Harcourt Brace Social Studies*, ask yourself the questions that follow. They will help you think like a **historian**, a person whose work is to study the past.

What Happened?

To find out what really happened in the past, you need proof that it happened. You can find proof by studying paintings, photographs, and films. You can also find proof by studying what people have written or said. They may have written down their thoughts in a journal or diary. They may have told their story in a letter or a poem.

Some records of the past are made by people who saw or took part in an event. Each of these records gives the people of today a direct link to a past event. Other records, however, were made later by people who only heard or read about the event.

History places people and their activities in time. What might a historian ask about this girl?

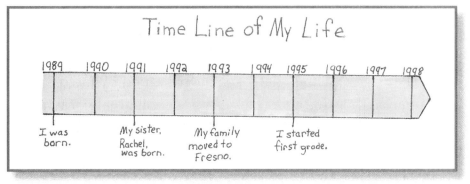

Time Line of My Life

1989 1990 1991 1992 1993 1994 1995 1996 1997 1998

I was born.

My sister, Rachel, was born.

My family moved to Fresno.

I started first grade.

You can list the important events of your life on a time line.

When Did It Happen?

One way to understand a story of the past is to put events in the order in which they happened. The dates in a story can help you do this. So can a time line. A **time line** is a diagram that shows the order in which events took place and the amount of time that passed between them. Time lines can help you understand how one event may have led to another.

Who Took Part in It?

To understand the stories of the past, you need to know about the people in the stories and the times in which they lived. By learning more about these people, you can better understand the actions and feelings of people from other times and places.

History lets you come face to face with people from the past.

A good way to learn about people is to read their own words. By reading the words of people, you can come to understand their point of view. A person's **point of view** is his or her set of beliefs that have been shaped by factors such as whether that person is old or young, male or female, rich or poor. A person's point of view is also shaped by a person's race and **culture**, or way of life. Your understanding of history will grow when you study the many points of view of the people who took part in different events.

How and Why Did It Happen?

Many events in history are linked to other events. To find links between events, you need to analyze them. When you **analyze** an event, you break it down into its parts. Then you look closely at how those parts are connected. You also look at who took part in the event and what life was like at that time.

REVIEW **What questions should you ask yourself when you read about the past?**

What does this photograph tell you about how people in the past thought about conserving nature?

Geography

Every story has a setting, and part of the setting is the place where the story happens. Knowing about places is an important part of **geography**—the study of the Earth's surface and the way people use it. **Geographers**, the people whose work is to study geography, think about five questions or topics when they study a place. These five topics are so important that many people call them the five themes of geography.

- **Location**
  (Where is it?)
- **Place**
  (What is it like there?)
- **Human-environment interactions**
  (How does this place affect the lives of people living there? How do people living there affect this place?)
- **Movement**
  (How and why do people, ideas, and goods move to and from this place?)
- **Regions**
  (How is this place like other places? How is it different?)

Thinking about these themes or asking yourself these questions when you study geography will help you understand the setting of a story.

1. Location

Everything on the Earth has its own location. A **location** is where something can be found. You can describe location in many ways. You can use numbers and street names to give the location of a building. You can also tell what the building is near. You might say that your school is located near a shopping mall or across the street from a park.

The Big Sur area extends along the coast of California from near Monterey to San Luis Obispo County.

2. Place

Geographers look at what makes one place different from another place. As you know, every place on Earth has certain features that make it different from all other places. Some of these are its **physical features**, or features that have been formed by nature. The physical features of a place include its landforms, bodies of water, and other natural resources. A **natural resource** is something found in nature that people can use.

Many places also have **human features**, or features that have been made by people. Human features include buildings, farms, airports, bridges, and freeways. What people do and the number of people who live in an area are human features, too.

3. Human-Environment Interactions

Geographers also study how humans and the environment interact, or affect each other. Sometimes people change their environment. They may clear land to grow crops or to build houses and highways. The environment can also affect people. It may affect the kinds of jobs they have, foods they eat, clothes they wear, and homes they live in.

The city of San Francisco is an example of place.

4. Movement

Each day people in California interact with each other and with people in different parts of the United States and around the world. They travel, and they send goods from place to place in cars, trucks, trains, ships, and airplanes. They send ideas from one place to another by newspaper, television, radio, telephone, and computer. Geography helps you understand how people, goods, and ideas got to where they are.

By airplane is one way people and goods move from one place to another.

5. Regions

To study a place more closely, geographers sometimes divide the Earth into regions. A **region** is a place with at least one feature that makes it different from other places. A region can be a city, a state, or a part of a country. A region could be a place with a certain kind of landform or plant life. It could also be a place where people share a language or a way of life.

REVIEW **What are the five themes of geography?**

Redwood trees (above) grow only in certain regions in California, and people can ski (left) only in certain regions of California.

Read a Map

Maps
by Dorothy Brown Thompson

High adventure
    And bright dream—
Maps are mightier
    Than they seem:

Ships that follow
    Leaning stars—
Red and gold of
    Strange bazaars—

Ice floes hid
    Beyond all knowing—
Planes that ride where
    Winds are blowing!

Train maps, maps of
    Wind and weather,
Road maps—taken
    Altogether

Maps are really
    Magic wands
For home-staying
    Vagabonds!

1. Why Learn This Skill?

Knowing how to read maps is an important skill both for learning social studies and for acting as a citizen. Maps tell you about the world around you through the five themes of geography—location, place, movement, human-environment interactions, and regions.

2. The Parts of a Map

A map is a drawing that shows the Earth or part of the Earth on a flat surface. Most maps include a title, a key or legend, a compass rose, a scale, and a locator.

The **map title** tells you the subject of the map. Look at the map shown on page 33. What is its title?

The title may also help you understand what kind of map it is. There are many kinds of maps. One kind is a physical map. A physical map shows mostly landforms and bodies of water. Sometimes it uses shading to help you see where hills and mountains are located.

Another kind of map is a political map. It shows mostly the locations of cities and the boundaries of states or countries. A **boundary** is a border, or the outside edge, of a place. What two countries share a national border with the United States?

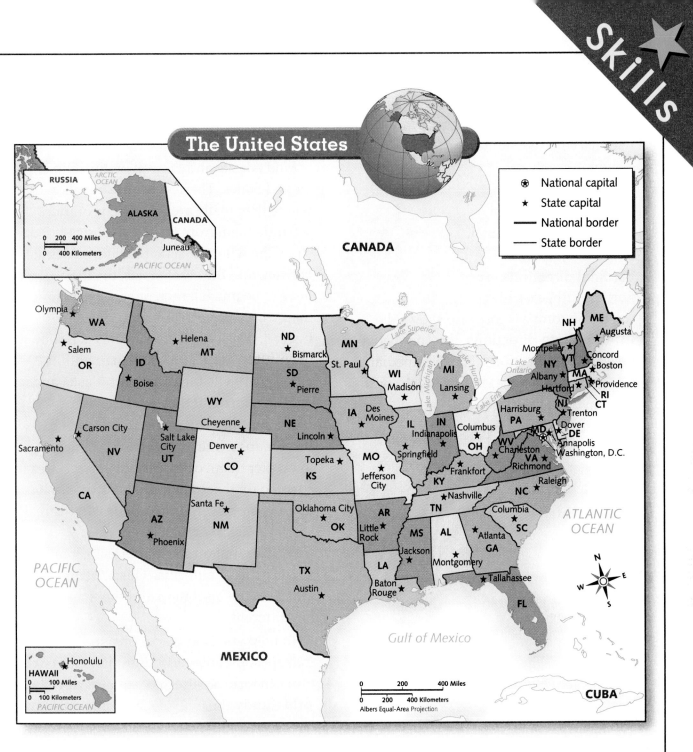

The United States

RUSSIA
ARCTIC OCEAN

ALASKA

CANADA

0   200   400 Miles
0   400 Kilometers

Juneau

PACIFIC OCEAN

Map Key

⊛ National capital
★ State capital
— National border
— State border

CANADA

Olympia ★ **WA**

★ Salem
OR

ID ★ Helena
★ Boise **MT**

★ Helena

ND
Bismarck ★

MN

St. Paul ★

Lake Superior

WI
Madison ★

MI
Lansing ★

Lake Michigan

Lake Huron

Lake Ontario

Lake Erie

NH **ME**
★ Augusta

Montpelier ★ **VT** Concord ★
NY ★ Boston
Albany ★ **MA**
Hartford ★ Providence
RI
CT

SD
Pierre ★

WY
Cheyenne ★

NE
Lincoln ★

IA Des
Moines ★

IL **IN**
Indianapolis ★

Springfield ★

OH
Columbus ★

Harrisburg ★
PA

NJ
★ Trenton
Dover ★
MD **DE**
Annapolis
⊛ Washington, D.C.

★ Carson City
NV

Sacramento ★

Salt Lake
City ★
UT

Denver ★
CO

Topeka ★
KS

MO
Jefferson
City ★

Springfield ★

KY
Frankfort ★

WV
Charleston ★

VA
Richmond ★

Raleigh ★
NC

★ Nashville
TN

Columbia ★
SC

CA

Santa Fe ★
NM

AZ
★ Phoenix

Oklahoma City ★
OK

AR
Little ★
Rock

MS
Jackson ★

AL
Montgomery ★

Atlanta ★
GA

ATLANTIC OCEAN

PACIFIC OCEAN

TX
Austin ★

LA
Baton ★
Rouge

Tallahassee ★

FL

N
W   E
S

HAWAII
Honolulu ★

0   100 Miles
0   100 Kilometers

PACIFIC OCEAN

MEXICO

Gulf of Mexico

0   200   400 Miles
0   200   400 Kilometers
Albers Equal-Area Projection

CUBA

Introduction • 33

Many of the maps in this book are historical maps that show California as it was in the past. Historical maps often have dates in their titles.

The **map key**, sometimes called a map legend, explains what the symbols on the map stand for. A **symbol** is something that stands for something else. Symbols on maps

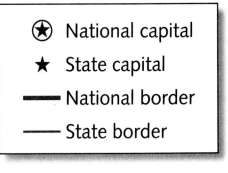

⊛ National capital
★ State capital
— National border
— State border

may be colors, patterns, lines, or other kinds of marks. On the map on page 33, a star within a circle is used to show the national capital.

The **compass rose**, or direction marker on a map, shows the cardinal, or main, directions. The **cardinal directions** are north, south, east, and west. The compass rose also shows the **intermediate directions**, the ones between the cardinal directions. The intermediate directions are northeast, southeast, southwest, and northwest.

The **locator** is a small map or globe. It shows where the place on the main map is located within a state, a country, or a continent, or in the world. On the map of the United States, the locator is a globe that shows the continent of North America. The United States is shown in red.

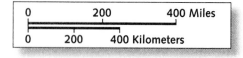

The **map scale** compares a distance on a map to a distance in the real world. A map scale helps you find the real distance between places on a map. Each map in this book has a scale that shows both miles and kilometers.

Find Alaska and Hawaii on the map of the United States. These states are not shown where they really are. Hundreds of miles separate them from the other 48 states. To show the whole area that includes Alaska, Hawaii, and the other states, the map would have to be much larger, or each part of the map would have to be much smaller. Instead, Alaska and Hawaii are each shown in an **inset map**, or a small map within a larger map. The boxes around Alaska and Hawaii show that they are inset maps.

An inset map often has its own scale. Inset maps make it possible to show places in greater detail or places outside the area covered on the main map. Look at Alaska on the map of the United States. In the real world, Alaska is much larger than California, but on the map Alaska looks smaller than California. This is because the scales on the inset map and the main map are different.

To help you find places on a map, mapmakers sometimes add lines that cross each other to form a pattern of squares called a **grid**. Study the map of California on page 35. Around the grid are letters and numbers. In this grid the columns, which run north and south, have numbers. The rows, which run east and west, have letters. Each square on the map can be named by its letter and number.

A map with a grid may have an index like the one above the map of California. The index helps you find the names of the places you are looking for. It lists them in alphabetical order. The index also gives the grid letter and number for each place.

3. Understand the Process

1. Look at the map on this page. What states share a border with California?

2. Find the map key on the map. What symbol is used to show the state capital?

3. Find Sacramento, California's capital, in the map index. What are Sacramento's grid letter and number?

4. Find the letter B and the number 2 on the grid. Put a finger of one hand on the letter B and a finger of your other hand on the number 2. Then move your fingers toward each other, along row B and column 2. You will find Sacramento in the square where your fingers meet. In what square is it located?

5. What city is located in square C-3? Check your answer with the map index.

4. Think and Apply

Look at the map of California with a partner. Together, name the parts of the map. Then talk about what the map tells you about California. Take turns using the map grid to find different places in the state.

California

Index to Cities

Bakersfield.......C-3
Eureka.............A-1
Fresno.............C-2
Long Beach.....D-3
Los Angeles.....D-3
Monterey........C-2
Oakland..........B-2
Palm Springs....D-3
Redding...........A-2
Sacramento......B-2
San Diego........D-3
San Francisco...B-2
San Jose...........B-2
Stockton..........B-2

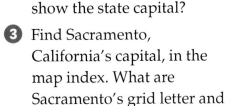

★ State capital

100   200 Miles
100   200 Kilometers
Albers Equal-Area Projection

Humboldt Bay
Eureka
Redding
Klamath R.
Trinity R.
Sacramento River
Feather River
American River
Eel River
Lake Tahoe
Sacramento
Stockton
San Francisco
Oakland
San Jose
San Francisco Bay
Monterey Bay
Monterey Fresno
San Joaquin R.
Bakersfield
Los Angeles
Long Beach
Palm Springs
San Diego
San Diego Bay
PACIFIC OCEAN
Salton Sea
Colorado R.
OR
ID
UT
NV
AZ
MEXICO

N W E S

Civics and Government

The subject of civics and government is the study of citizenship and the ways citizens govern themselves. A **government** is a system for deciding what is best for a group of people. It protects the group members and settles disagreements among them. The main job of government is to make laws and see that they are carried out. Laws help people live together in order and safety.

Citizens have an important part in making the government work. The laws that guide people are written and carried out by citizens. In *Harcourt Brace Social Studies*, you will learn how the government of California works. You will also learn how people and events have affected the state's government.

Economics

An **economy** is the way people in a state, a region, or a country use resources to meet their needs. The study of how people do this is called **economics**. In *Harcourt Brace Social Studies*, you will read about how people in California make goods and buy and sell them. You will also learn how California's economy has changed over time.

Culture

In *Harcourt Brace Social Studies*, you will learn about people of the past who have made California what it is today. You will find out who these people were and what they said and did. You will learn about their beliefs and their ways of thinking and of showing their ideas. You will look at their families and communities and at how they make their living. All these things make up their culture. In *Harcourt Brace Social Studies*, you will discover the many cultures in California's story, past and present.

REVIEW **What kinds of things do you learn when you study civics and government, economics, and culture?**

Work Together in Groups

1. Why Learn This Skill?

Many of the projects you will do in your social studies class would be hard for one person to do alone. If you work with a partner or in a group, however, each of you can work on just part of a project.

To carry out group projects, each group member needs to cooperate with the others. Knowing how to work together is an important skill for students and for all citizens.

2. Understand the Process

Suppose that you and some other students in your class are asked to do a project, such as putting on a class play, painting a large mural, or cleaning up a park. You might find it helpful to follow a set of steps for working as a group.

1 Organize and plan together.
  - Set your goal as a group.
  - Share your ideas.
  - Cooperate with others to plan your work.
  - Make sure everyone has a job.

2 Act on your plan together.
  - Carry out your jobs.
  - Help one another.
  - If there are conflicts, talk until you settle them.
  - Show your group's finished work to the rest of the class.

3 Talk about your work.
  - Talk about how well you worked together and what you learned.

3. Think and Apply

Follow the above steps for working together as you take part in the activities in *Harcourt Brace Social Studies*.

To carry out group projects, each group member needs to cooperate with the others.

The Golden State

Unit

1

Unit 2
Newcomers to
California

Unit 3
California Joins
the United States

THE LAND AND EARLY PEOPLE

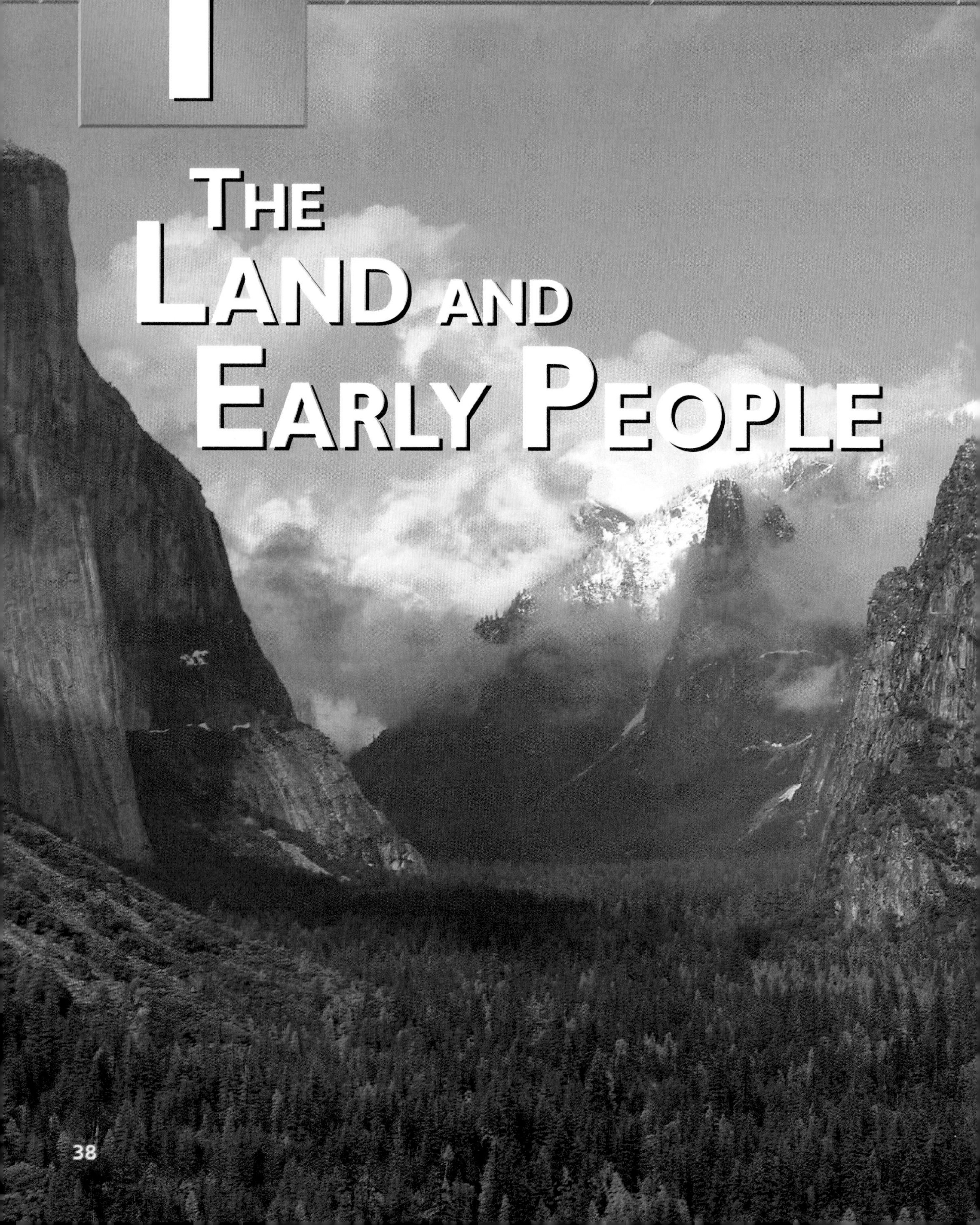

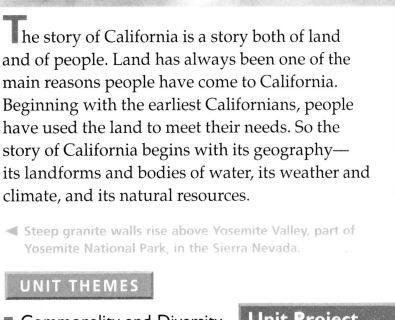

The story of California is a story both of land and of people. Land has always been one of the main reasons people have come to California. Beginning with the earliest Californians, people have used the land to meet their needs. So the story of California begins with its geography— its landforms and bodies of water, its weather and climate, and its natural resources.

◄ Steep granite walls rise above Yosemite Valley, part of Yosemite National Park, in the Sierra Nevada.

UNIT THEMES

- Commonality and Diversity
- Continuity and Change
- Individualism and Interdependence
- Interaction Within Different Environments

Unit Project

Build a Diorama Complete this project as you study Unit 1. Choose one of the four natural regions of California. Then make a diorama that shows how the early people who lived there used the region's natural resources to meet their needs. As you read this unit, take notes about the region you choose. List its major landforms, bodies of water, and other natural resources. Also write down how different groups of early people used those natural resources. You can then use these notes when you are ready to work on your diorama.

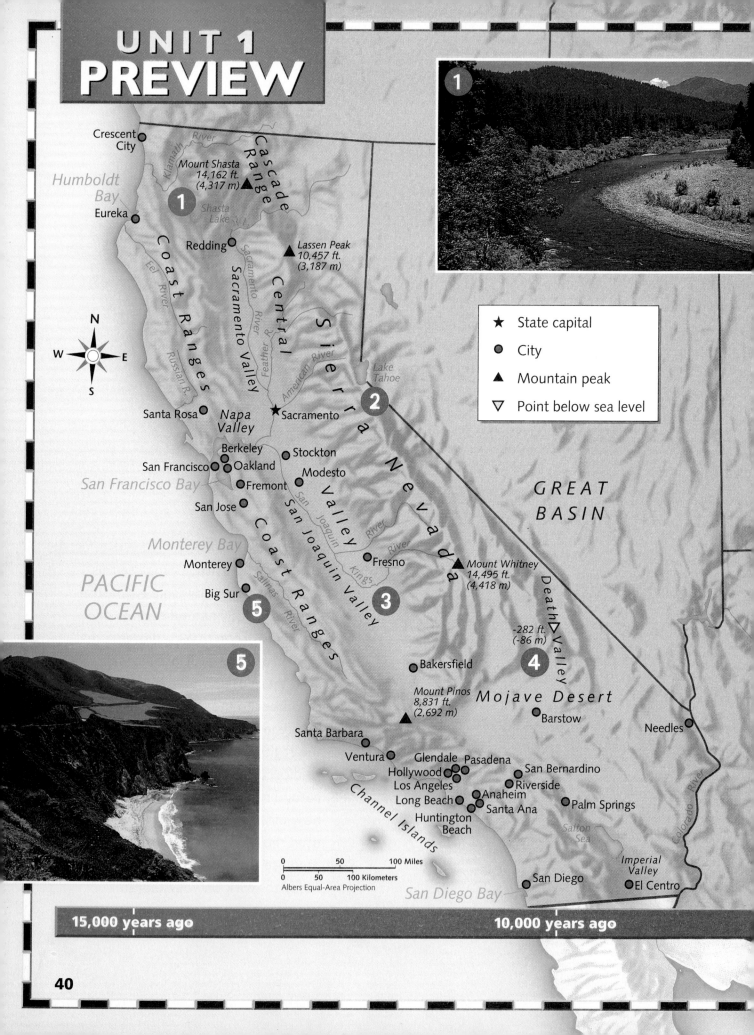

Crescent City

Humboldt Bay

Klamath River

Cascade Range

Mount Shasta 14,162 ft. (4,317 m) ▲

1

Shasta Lake

Eureka

Redding

Lassen Peak 10,457 ft. (3,187 m) ▲

Sacramento River

Eel River

Coast Ranges

Sacramento Valley

Feather R.

Central

Sierra

American River

Lake Tahoe

2

★	State capital
⬤	City
▲	Mountain peak
▽	Point below sea level

Santa Rosa

Napa Valley

★ Sacramento

Berkeley

San Francisco • Oakland

Stockton

Modesto

San Francisco Bay

Fremont

San Jose

Nevada

GREAT BASIN

Monterey Bay

Coast Ranges

San Joaquin Valley

San Joaquin River

Kings River

Fresno

Mount Whitney 14,495 ft. (4,418 m) ▲

Death Valley

Monterey

Big Sur

5

Salinas River

3

-282 ft. (-86 m) ▽

4

PACIFIC OCEAN

Bakersfield

Mount Pinos 8,831 ft. (2,692 m) ▲

Mojave Desert

Barstow

Needles

Santa Barbara

Ventura

Glendale Pasadena

Hollywood

Los Angeles

Long Beach

Anaheim

Santa Ana

Huntington Beach

San Bernardino

Riverside

Palm Springs

Colorado River

Salton Sea

5

Channel Islands

Imperial Valley

San Diego

El Centro

0	50	100 Miles
0	50	100 Kilometers

Albers Equal-Area Projection

San Diego Bay

California

The Yuroks

The Chumash

The Yokuts

The Mojaves

3

2

4

5,000 years ago   Present

GRANDMOTHER OAK

by Rosi Dagit

illustrated by Steve Adler

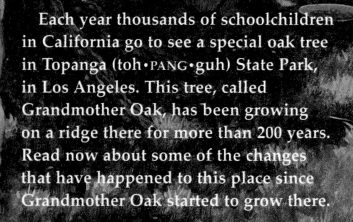

Each year thousands of schoolchildren in California go to see a special oak tree in Topanga (toh•PANG•guh) State Park, in Los Angeles. This tree, called Grandmother Oak, has been growing on a ridge there for more than 200 years. Read now about some of the changes that have happened to this place since Grandmother Oak started to grow there.

Long ago, before there were people in Southern California, the Santa Monica Mountains rose out of the sea. Thousands of years later, a lovely oak tree grew up tall and strong on a ridge. Its branches reached to the sky. The birds made it their home. The grizzly and deer ate the acorns. The wind blew through the branches, making a beautiful sound.

One day, a fierce thunderstorm hit the ridge, and lightning struck the tree. A huge branch came crashing down. Tears of sap oozed down the trunk. The remaining branches wept as the storm shook their leaves. But the tree stood strong.

Many years slipped by, and a group of Tongva people came to the ridge. A village of several families made their home near the oak. Even the youngest children could climb her low branches and shake down the acorns. Older children perched in the high branches, calling to the birds. The elders leaned against her trunk, seeking the strength to lead well and the wisdom to understand the ways of the world.

Year after year, families from the village returned to the gnarled tree. She became known as Grandmother Oak. The people gathered under her canopy to celebrate life and sang songs in praise of her strength and spirit. Sighs of contentment whispered with the wind.

One year, the Tongva families set a fire to clear the brush. A powerful gust fanned the flames. The fire rushed up the ridge, and the people ran away in terror. Grandmother Oak stood strong, but a burning ember lodged in the hole where the huge branch had fallen. For months, the heartwood inside smoldered and burned, leaving the trunk hollow to the ground. Puffs of smoke curled in the fading breeze.

Later, the families returned to the site of the fire. Only Grandmother Oak remained. The children shouted with joy when they found a way to climb into the trunk, up through the heart of the tree and out the branch hole. Sometimes they would nestle inside, feeling the smooth heartwood. The wind lifted laughter from the branches now!

acorn a nut that is a seed of an oak tree

wisdom knowledge

gnarled (NARLD) twisted

canopy (KA•nuh•pee) the top branches of a tree

heartwood the older wood at the center of a tree's trunk

Time crept slowly for Grandmother Oak. Each year her branches spread further to reach the sun. Spaniards came to live on the ridge. Grandmother Oak reminded them of the large oaks of their homeland far away. She provided cool shade for the cattle when the sun shone hot. When the wind rustled her leaves, her spirit reached out to touch the new-comers. But they did not understand.

Their large ranch stretched across the hills and brought many changes. Cattle ate all the grass, chasing away the deer and birds. The grizzly no longer roamed the hills. Grandmother Oak stood lonely. Her strong branches still reached for the sky, moaning when the wind blew through the hollow trunk.

Many years have passed since the Tongva families and the Spaniards went away. The cattle are gone now, too. Grandmother Oak watches from the top of the ridge as houses and roads fill the open land. Her heavy limbs droop toward the ground.

Recently, another large branch fell after heavy winter rains. Beetles bore holes in her bark. The scrub jays scold as they gather her acorns. Hummingbirds dance amid the sunlit leaves. The wind makes the tree creak with age, sigh with wisdom.

Different people come now. People like you and me. Some stand in awe, or silently touch her chiseled bark. Children race to hide within her. They climb through her trunk and sing with glee. Sometimes they sit quietly, feeling her strength seep into them, giving them visions of what went before, and what is yet to come. Even those who have never known a tree, find strength in her ancient spirit. Once again, laughter rings out with the winds. Grandmother Oak stands strong.

chiseled
(CHIH•zuhld)
carved as by
a sharp knife

CALIFORNIA'S GEOGRAPHY

"None can escape its charms. Its natural beauty cleans and warms like a fire, and you will be willing to stay forever in one place like a tree."

John Muir (MYOOR), a writer and naturalist, describing the beauty of Yosemite Valley

Where Is California?

FOCUS
Why might you need to find out where a place is located?

Main Idea Read to find out some of the different ways to describe California's location.

Vocabulary
continent
hemisphere
equator
relative location
mountain range
Pacific Rim
crossroads

You can describe the location of a place in many ways. You can use a number and a street name to give the location of the house or building in which you live. Your home address also has the name of your community and your state, California. California has an address, too—a global address.

California's Global Address

If someone asked you to describe the location of California, what would you say? You could say that California is part of the United States of America. But you could say more. The United States is part of the land area of North America, so you could also say that California is in North America.

The Earth's largest land areas are called **continents**. There are seven continents—Africa, Antarctica, Asia, Australia, Europe, North America, and South America. Some geographers group Europe and Asia together and call them Eurasia (yu•RAY•zhuh).

The Earth is shaped like a sphere, or ball, so half of the Earth is called a **hemisphere**. *Hemi* means "half." North America and South America are two continents that are in the Western Hemisphere. Now you can describe California as being in the United States, in North America, and in the Western Hemisphere.

The Earth also has a northern half and a southern half. The **equator** is the imaginary line between the Northern Hemisphere and the

You could use this globe to learn where California is located.

Where on Earth Is California?

CALIFORNIA

THE UNITED STATES

NORTH AMERICA

WESTERN HEMISPHERE

LEARNING FROM DIAGRAMS California is a state in the western part of the United States.
■ Which usually covers a larger area, a country or a continent?

Southern Hemisphere. On a map or a globe, you can see the equator halfway between the North Pole and the South Pole. Where on Earth is California? You can now give this answer. California is in the United States, in North America, in the Western Hemisphere, and in the Northern Hemisphere.

REVIEW **How is a continent different from a hemisphere?**

A Western State

"In the west" is a good way to describe California's relative location in the United States. The **relative location** of a place is where it is, compared to one or more other places on Earth. The location of California in relation to most of the other states in the United States is in the west.

As you know, the United States is made up of 50 states. Geographers often group states into larger regions. California is one of the 11 states that make up the region of the United States called the West.

The states in a region are alike in many ways. For example, they are all in the same part of the United States. They may also have the same kinds of landforms and natural resources. The people who live in those states often earn their living in the same ways.

The West is one of five regions that make up the United States. The other four regions are the Southwest, the Middle West, the Northeast, and the Southeast.

Regions of the United States

Regions The 50 states are often grouped into five regions.
■ Which states are in the West region?

The West is the largest of the five regions of the United States. It has the wettest and driest places and the warmest and coldest places in the United States. The West also has the country's lowest valley and its highest mountains. In fact, the West region has more mountains than any other region. The country's largest **mountain range**, or group of connected mountains, is the Rocky Mountains. They cover much of the western United States.

Four states make up the Southwest region—Arizona, New Mexico, Texas, and Oklahoma. All except Oklahoma share a border with Mexico. The Southwest is a region of wide-open spaces. Much of it is dry land or desert. Yet there are also thick pine forests, mountains capped with snow, grassy plains, and river valleys.

The Middle West region stretches across the middle of the United States. The land there is mostly flat or rolling,

The Rocky Mountains are about half as old as the Appalachian Mountains and twice as high

and it is good for farming. Mighty rivers flow across this region, too. The largest are the Mississippi, Ohio, and Missouri rivers. Four of the Great Lakes—Lake Superior, Lake Michigan, Lake Huron, and Lake Erie—border states in the Middle West. Lake Erie and the fifth Great Lake—Lake Ontario—border the Northeast region.

The Northeast is the smallest region of the United States. It stretches along the Atlantic Ocean from Maine to Maryland and west to the Great Lakes.

Along the coast are rocky shores and narrow, sandy beaches. Farther inland are the tree-covered Appalachian (a•puh•LAY•chee•uhn) Mountains. This low mountain range covers much of the eastern United States.

The Southeast region reaches from the Atlantic Ocean west to Arkansas and Louisiana and from the Gulf of Mexico north to the Ohio River. Along the Atlantic and Gulf coasts, the land is mostly flat. Farther inland, however, these low plains give way to the Appalachian Mountains.

REVIEW **In which of the five regions of the United States is California located?**

A Crossroads

California is a large state. In fact, only Alaska and Texas are larger. Rhode Island, the smallest state, could fit inside California nearly 30 times!

California lies between Oregon on the north and the country of Mexico on

Many scientists believe that the Appalachian Mountains were once taller and more rugged than the Rocky Mountains.

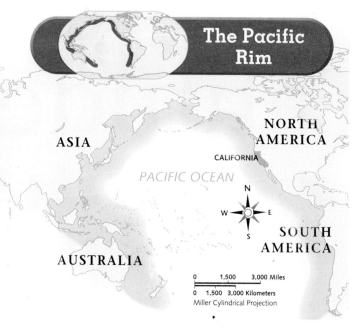

The Pacific Rim

ASIA

NORTH AMERICA

CALIFORNIA

PACIFIC OCEAN

N
W · E
S

SOUTH AMERICA

AUSTRALIA

0   1,500   3,000 Miles
0 1,500 3,000 Kilometers
Miller Cylindrical Projection

Region The Pacific Rim region includes all the places that border the Pacific Ocean.
■ On which edge of the rim is California located?

MAP THEME

the south. To the east are Nevada and Arizona. To the west is the Pacific Ocean. California is one of five states in the West region that touch the Pacific Ocean. The others are Oregon, Washington, Alaska, and Hawaii.

The Pacific Ocean also borders countries on three other continents—Asia, Australia, and South America. California and the other states and countries that border the Pacific Ocean are part of a world region known as the **Pacific Rim**.

Because California is located on the edge of the Pacific Ocean, it has become an important crossroads. A crossroads was once a place where two roads crossed and people met to buy and sell goods. Now a **crossroads** is any place that connects people, goods, and ideas.

Today, people, goods, and ideas go from California to places all over the world. Other people, goods, and ideas also come to California from all over.

REVIEW What large body of water does California share with other states and countries?

LESSON 1 REVIEW

Check Understanding

1 **Remember the Facts** In which region of the United States and in which hemisphere is California located?

2 **Recall the Main Idea** What are three different ways to describe California's location?

Think Critically

3 **Link to You** How would you describe the relative location of your home? your school? your community?

4 **Think More About It** Some people group California and the other states that border the Pacific Ocean in a separate region called the Pacific states. Why might people do that?

Show What You Know

Writing Activity Find California on a globe or a world map. Write and share a paragraph describing its relative location compared to each state around it and to Mexico.

Use Latitude

1. Why Learn This Skill?

There are many ways to describe the relative location of a place, but there is a more exact way to tell where the place is. You can describe its **absolute location**, or exact position on the Earth, using latitude and longitude.

Latitude and longitude are lines that mapmakers draw on maps and globes. One set of lines runs east and west. These are called **lines of latitude**. Because lines of latitude are always the same distance apart, they are also called **parallels** (PAIR•uh•lelz). Parallel lines never meet.

Lines of latitude are measured in degrees (°) north and south from the equator. They go from 0° at the equator to 90° at each of the poles. Lines of latitude north of the equator are marked *N* for *north*. Lines south of the equator are marked *S* for *south*.

A second set of lines on maps and globes runs north and south from the North Pole to the South Pole. These lines are called **lines of longitude** (LAHN•juh•tood), or **meridians** (muh•RIH•dee•uhnz).

The **prime meridian**, which passes near London, England, is the starting point for the lines of longitude. Lines of longitude go

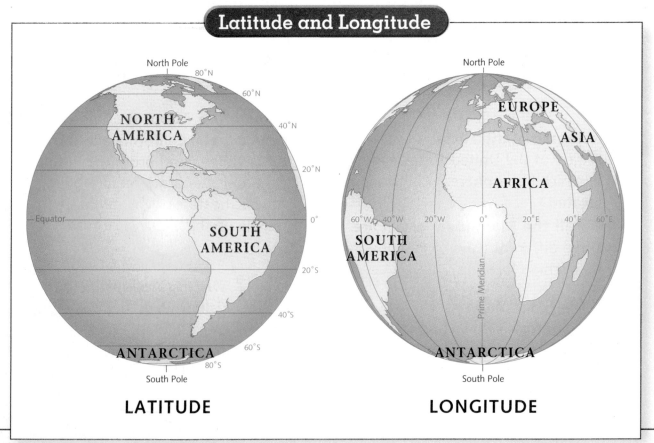

Latitude and Longitude

LATITUDE

North Pole
80°N
60°N
40°N
20°N
Equator — 0°
20°S
40°S
60°S
80°S
South Pole

NORTH AMERICA
SOUTH AMERICA
ANTARCTICA

LONGITUDE

North Pole
60°W 40°W 20°W 0° 20°E 40°E 60°E
Prime Meridian
South Pole

EUROPE
ASIA
AFRICA
SOUTH AMERICA
ANTARCTICA

and Longitude

from 0° at the prime meridian to 180° halfway around the globe. Lines of longitude west of the prime meridian are marked *W* for *west*. Lines east of the prime meridian are marked *E* for *east*.

2. Understand the Process

Lines of latitude and longitude on a map or globe form a grid. This grid can help you locate any place on the Earth. You can give the absolute location of a place by naming the line of latitude and the line of longitude closest to it. Look at the map of California on this page, and answer these questions.

❶ On which line of latitude is the border between California and Oregon located?

❷ Find Los Angeles on the map of California. Near which line of latitude is Los Angeles? Near which line of longitude is it? To give the location of Los Angeles, name its latitude first and then its longitude. Los Angeles is located near 34°N, 118°W.

❸ Which city is near 37°N, 122°W?

❹ Which lines of latitude and longitude best give the location of Stockton?

3. Think and Apply

Use latitude and longitude to tell where you live or where someone else lives in California. Write a note to a friend that tells how you found the location on the map.

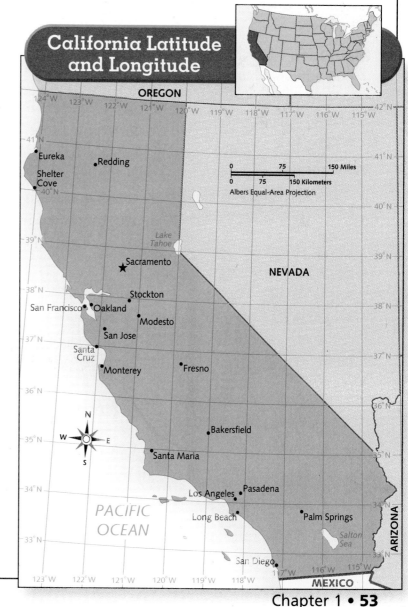

California Latitude and Longitude

California's Natural Regions

FOCUS

What does the land look like where you live?

Main Idea
Read to find out what makes each of California's natural regions different.

Vocabulary

natural region
coastal plain
fault
volcano
lava
fertile
irrigation
sea level
basin
plateau

The writer John Muir (MYOOR) was a young man working in Indiana when he injured his eyes in a factory accident. He promised himself that if he became able to see again, he would look at nature, not at machines. He did get his sight back, and he kept his word.

Beginning in 1867 John Muir traveled mostly on foot through many parts of Africa, Asia, Europe, and North America. But Muir fell in love with California. "The whole State," he wrote, ". . . is one block of beauty." Muir made his home in California and spent his life studying the state's four natural regions. A **natural region** is a region made up of places that share the same kinds of physical, or natural, features, such as plains, mountains, valleys, or deserts.

The Coast

California's Coastal region stretches for more than 800 miles (1,287 km) north and south along the Pacific Ocean. People have lived along this coast for thousands of years. Today, this region has more large cities than any of the state's other natural regions. In fact, more people live in the cities and surrounding areas of San Francisco, Los Angeles, and San Diego than in all the rest of the state.

Low mountains follow the California coast and reach north into Oregon and Washington. These mountains, called the Coast Ranges, are made up of several small mountain ranges. Among the mountain ranges that make up the Coast Ranges in California are the Klamath (KLA•muhth), the Diablo (dee•AH•bloh), the Santa Cruz, and the Santa Lucia (loo•SEE•uh).

The Coast Ranges are California's lowest mountains. However, many of their peaks are more than 4,000 feet (1,219 m) high. The tallest, Mount Pinos (PEE•nohs), is 8,831 feet (2,692 m) high.

The Coast Ranges give much of California's coast a rocky, rugged look. In northern California, the Coast Ranges drop sharply into the Pacific Ocean, forming steep cliffs like rock walls. In southern California, however, the mountains give way to a wider coastal plain with sandy beaches along the shore. A **coastal plain** is an area of low land that lies along the ocean.

People from all over the world have moved to this part of the state in order to enjoy its sunny weather and world-famous beaches.

Up and down the coast, wide valleys lie between the mountains of the Coast Ranges. North of San Francisco is the Napa Valley. To the south are the Santa Clara and Salinas (sah•LEE•nahs) valleys.

Two groups of islands are also part of California's Coastal region. West of San Francisco are the small, rocky Farallon (FAIR•uh•lahn) Islands. Off the coast of southern California are the eight Channel Islands. Santa Catalina, the best known of the Channel Islands, draws many visitors each year.

Another important physical feature marks California's Coastal region. It is

In the Big Sur area of northern California, the Pacific Coast Highway winds along the rocky coastline.

the San Andreas (an•DRAY•uhs) Fault. A **fault** is a crack in the Earth's surface along which underground layers of rock can move. The San Andreas Fault is more than 600 miles (966 km) long. It begins off the coast of northwestern California and runs to the southeast.

When the rock along a fault moves, it causes an earthquake. Each year many small earthquakes shake the Coastal region. Often people do not even feel them. Large earthquakes, however, can cause great damage. The shaking can cause buildings and bridges to fall.

In recent years powerful earthquakes have shaken several California cities, including San Francisco, Los Angeles, and Santa Cruz. Buildings and bridges in California are built extra strong to protect them against earthquakes, but damage still happens. A woman who lived in a second-floor apartment told about the earthquake that shook

The San Andreas Fault (left) is one of 63 major faults in California. These buildings (below) were damaged by an earthquake that hit southern California in January 1994.

southern California in 1994. First she heard a loud crack. Then the dining area of her apartment moved downward. "I felt a sensation of falling," she said. "But until I actually saw what was on the outside, I really was not aware that it had totally crushed the first floor."

REVIEW How is the coast in northern California different from the coast in southern California?

The Mountains

The Coast Ranges are just one of California's chief mountain ranges. In fact, mountains cover more than half the state. "Go where you may within the bounds of California," wrote John Muir more than 100 years ago, "mountains are ever in sight, charming and glorifying every landscape." John Muir spent much of the first six years he was in California exploring the state's mountain ranges. California's largest mountain range, the Sierra Nevada (see•AIR•ah neh•VAH•dah), stretches north and south across much of the eastern part of the state. *Sierra Nevada* means "snowy mountain range" in Spanish. This mountain range is more than 400 miles (644 km) long and about 70 miles (113 km) wide. Several mountain peaks in the Sierra Nevada

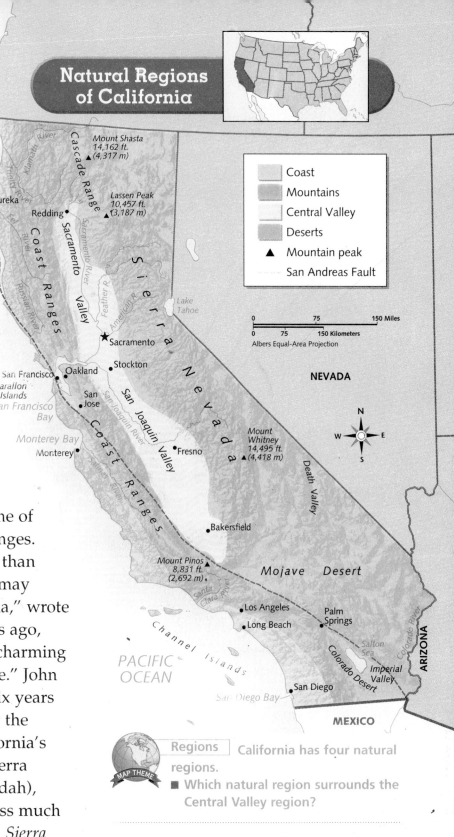

Natural Regions of California

Coast
Mountains
Central Valley
Deserts
▲ Mountain peak
San Andreas Fault

0   75   150 Miles
0   75   150 Kilometers
Albers Equal-Area Projection

Mount Shasta 14,162 ft. ▲ (4,317 m)
Lassen Peak 10,457 ft. ▲ (3,187 m)
Eureka
Redding
Klamath River
Trinity River
Eel River
Russian River
Cascade Range
Sacramento River
Feather R.
American R.
Sacramento Valley
Coast Ranges
Lake Tahoe
★ Sacramento
Stockton
San Francisco
Farallon Islands
San Francisco Bay
Oakland
San Jose
Monterey Bay
Monterey
San Joaquin River
San Joaquin Valley
Fresno
Sierra Nevada
Mount Whitney 14,495 ft. ▲ (4,418 m)
NEVADA
Death Valley
Bakersfield
Mount Pinos 8,831 ft. ▲ (2,692 m)
Coast Ranges
Salinas River
Santa Clara River
Mojave Desert
PACIFIC OCEAN
Channel Islands
Los Angeles
Long Beach
Palm Springs
Salton Sea
Imperial Valley
Colorado Desert
Colorado River
ARIZONA
San Diego
San Diego Bay
MEXICO

Regions California has four natural regions.
■ Which natural region surrounds the Central Valley region?

rise more than 14,000 feet (4,267 m)— almost twice the height of those in the Coast Ranges. Among the Sierra Nevada's peaks is Mount Whitney, which is 14,495 feet (4,418 m) high. The

The Sonora Pass cuts through the Sierra Nevada at an elevation of 9,624 feet (2,933 m).

only mountain peaks in the United States that are higher are in Alaska.

Between the towering peaks of the Sierra Nevada are deep valleys. Many of these valleys are known for their great beauty. One of the most beautiful is Yosemite (yoh•SEH•muh•tee) Valley, which is part of Yosemite National Park in the central Sierra Nevada.

Yosemite National Park draws thousands of visitors every year. They go to see the rocky peaks and the high waterfalls. Yosemite Valley has North America's highest single waterfall,

Ribbon Falls. It drops 1,612 feet (491 m). Ribbon Falls is almost two times higher than the Transamerica Pyramid building in San Francisco! Another of the valley's waterfalls, Yosemite Falls, drops a total of 2,425 feet (739 m), but it is actually made up of two large falls—the Upper Falls and the Lower Falls—and a series of smaller falls between them.

Other mountains lie north of the Sierra Nevada. These are the Cascade Range. Like the Coast Ranges, the Cascades reach north into Oregon and Washington.

The two most famous mountain peaks in the Cascades of California are Mount Shasta and Lassen Peak. Both are volcanoes. A **volcano** is an opening in the Earth's surface from which hot gases, ashes, and lava may pour. **Lava** is hot, melted rock from deep inside the Earth. Of the two volcanoes, only Lassen Peak has erupted, or poured out lava, in the 1900s. And the last time it was active was from 1914 to 1921. During those years it threw out hot gases and tons of ash and lava. Today Lassen Peak is part of Lassen Volcanic National Park.

REVIEW Which mountain is California's highest?

GEOGRAPHY

The Ring of Fire

California and many other places along the Pacific Rim lie in a region sometimes called the Ring of Fire. The Ring of Fire stretches along the western coast of the Americas and the eastern coast of Asia and into the southern Pacific Ocean. It has many active volcanoes, or volcanoes that are erupting or are likely to erupt. Thousands of others are dormant (DAWR•muhnt), or not in danger of erupting.

Large eruptions rocked Lassen Peak in 1914 and 1915.

▲ Major volcano
Ring of Fire

ARCTIC OCEAN

ASIA

▲ Mt. Fuji

▲ Mt. Pinatubo

▲ Krakatau

AUSTRALIA

Mt. St. Helens
Mt. Hood
Mt. Shasta
Lassen Peak

NORTH AMERICA

Paricutin ▲▲
Popocatépeti

PACIFIC OCEAN

SOUTH AMERICA

Mt. Aconcagua ▲

N
W E
S

0   1,500   3,000 Miles
0   1,500 3,000 Kilometers
Miller Cylindrical Projection

The Central Valley

The Central Valley of California is a large, lowland area of great natural beauty sometimes called the Great Valley. It lies west of the Sierra Nevada and east of the Coast Ranges. Fertile soil has washed down from the mountains into the valley below. Soil that is **fertile**, or good for growing crops, is needed for farming. Many of California's largest farms are in the Central Valley. So are many of its cities.

The Central Valley stretches for more than 450 miles (724 km) from Redding in the north to Bakersfield in the south. In fact, it is really two valleys. The San Joaquin (wah•KEEN) River flows through the southern part, which is called the San Joaquin Valley. In the northern part, the Sacramento River gives its name to the Sacramento Valley.

REVIEW Which two valleys make up the Central Valley of California?

The Deserts

Deserts stretch across most of southeastern California. The Mojave (moh•HAH•vay) Desert covers a large area between the southern Sierra Nevada and the Colorado River. The Colorado Desert lies farther south.

Within California's Desert region are several large valleys. Near the Mexican border are the Imperial and Coachella (koh•CHEL•uh) valleys. People have used irrigation to turn these valleys into rich farmland. **Irrigation** is the use of canals, ditches, or pipes to carry water to dry places.

Some parts of the Desert region are too hot and dry for farming or for large cities. Death Valley, near the Nevada border, is one of the hottest and driest places in the United States. It is also the lowest point in California and in all of the Western Hemisphere. One place in Death Valley lies 282 feet (86 m) below

California is the nation's top farming state. Most farming in the state takes place in the Central Valley.

sea level, or land that is level with the surface of the ocean.

Death Valley and much of California's Desert region are part of a larger region called the Great Basin. A **basin** is a low, bowl-shaped land area with higher ground all around it. The Great Basin extends into parts of six western states.

In the Great Basin are other landforms, including mountains and plateaus (pla•TOHZ). A **plateau** is an area of high, flat land. The part of the Great Basin that is in northeastern California is a lava plateau. Thousands of years ago lava from volcanoes flowed across this area.

REVIEW What two deserts stretch across southeastern California?

Visitors to the Joshua Tree National Park (above right), in California's Desert region, can see cactuses (right) and many other interesting desert plants.

LESSON 2 REVIEW

Check Understanding

① **Remember the Facts** What are the four natural regions of California?

② **Recall the Main Idea** How is each natural region in California different from the others?

Think Critically

③ **Link to You** In which natural region of California do you live? Tell why you like living there or why you might like to live in one of the state's other natural regions.

④ **Think More About It** How do California's four different natural regions help to make the state an interesting place in which to live?

Show What You Know

Riddle Activity Write four riddles, one about each of the natural regions in California. One example might be, "I am the natural region that has both beaches and mountains." Ask a partner to answer your riddles.

Use an Elevation

1. Why Learn This Skill?

The height of the land in California changes greatly. In some places, mountain peaks reach high into the clouds. In other places, valleys lie far below sea level. But how do you know how high or low the land is? And how do you know how much higher or lower one place is than another place? To answer these questions, you need to be able to use a map that shows elevation (eh•luh•VAY•shuhn). **Elevation** is the height of the land above sea level.

The elevation of all land is measured from sea level, or the surface of the ocean. The elevation of land at sea level is zero. Mount Whitney's elevation is 14,495 feet (4,418 m). That means that the top of Mount Whitney is 14,495 feet (4,418 m) higher than sea level.

2. Understand the Process

The elevation map of California on page 63 uses color to show elevation. To find elevations, you must know what each color stands for. You can find this in the map key.

The map does not give exact elevations. Instead, each color stands for a range of elevations. That is, each color stands for an area's highest and lowest elevations and all of the elevations in between.

The top of Mount Whitney is the highest point in California.

1 Find the Central Valley on the map. Most of the Central Valley is colored light green. That tells you that much of the land in the Central Valley is from 0 to 655 feet (0 to 200 m) above sea level. What is the elevation of the land around Lake Tahoe?

2 What range of elevations is shown by the color dark purple?

3 Which city has a higher elevation, Palm Springs or Fresno?

3. Think and Apply

Imagine that you and your family are planning a trip between any two cities on the map on page 63. Lay a ruler across the map to connect the two cities. Then write the name and elevation of each city, and tell the elevation of the highest and lowest land you will cross on your trip.

Map

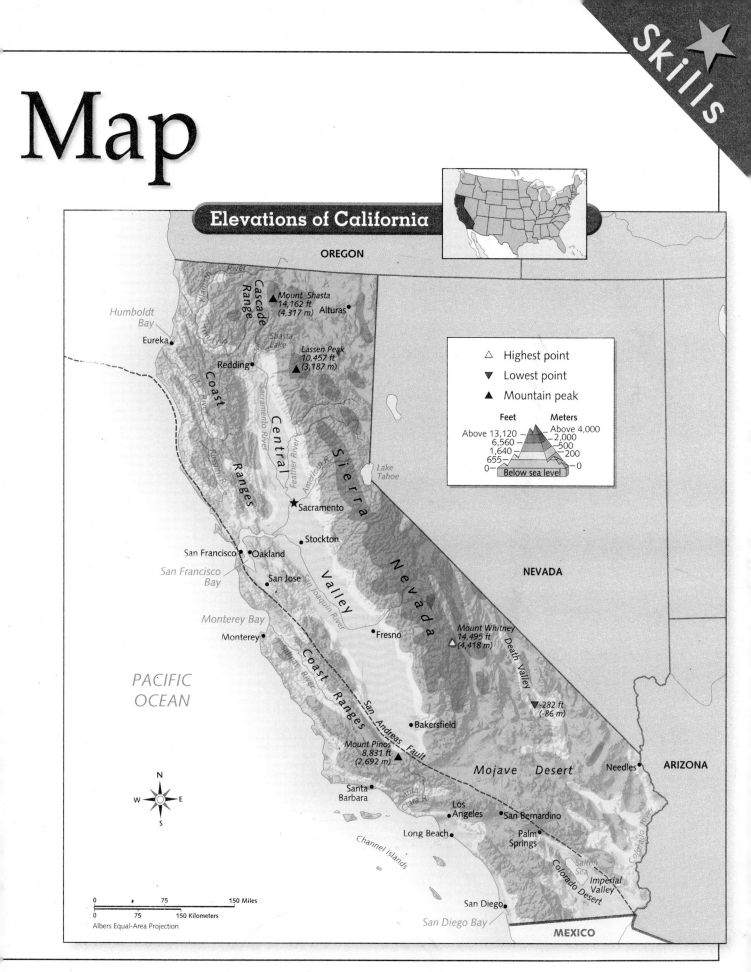

Elevations of California

OREGON

Humboldt Bay

Klamath River

Cascade Range

Mount Shasta
14,162 ft
(4,317 m)

Alturas

Eureka

Shasta Lake

Trinity River

Redding

Lassen Peak
10,457 ft
(3,187 m)

Coast Ranges

Eel River

Sacramento River

Russian R.

Feather River

Central

American R.

Sierra

Lake Tahoe

NEVADA

Highest point
Lowest point
Mountain peak

Feet	Meters
Above 13,120	Above 4,000
6,560	2,000
1,640	500
655	200
0	0

Below sea level

★ Sacramento

Stockton

San Francisco • Oakland

San Francisco Bay

San Jose

Valley

San Joaquin River

Monterey Bay

Nevada

Monterey

Fresno

Mount Whitney
14,495 ft
(4,418 m)

Death Valley

PACIFIC
OCEAN

Coast Ranges

Salinas River

San Andreas Fault

-282 ft
(-86 m)

Bakersfield

Mount Pinos
8,831 ft
(2,692 m)

Mojave Desert

Needles

ARIZONA

Santa Barbara

Santa Clara R.

Los Angeles

San Bernardino

Long Beach

Palm Springs

Colorado River

Channel Islands

Salton Sea

Colorado Desert

Imperial Valley

San Diego

San Diego Bay

MEXICO

N
W   E
S

0   75   150 Miles
0   75   150 Kilometers
Albers Equal-Area Projection

LESSON 3

California's Bodies of Water

Water is important to everything that lives in California. Rivers and lakes provide fresh water for wildlife, and for people and their farms, factories, and cities. The ocean links California with countries of the Pacific Rim and the rest of the world. The state's many bodies of water are also used by the people of California for fishing, swimming, surfing, diving, and boating.

Inlets and Bays

California's coastline stretches for more than 840 miles (1,352 km). At many places the shoreline juts sharply into the land to form inlets. An **inlet** is a narrow strip of water leading into the land from a larger body of water.

The California coast has two large natural harbors, one at San Francisco Bay and the other at San Diego Bay. A **harbor** is a place on a coast—often in a bay—where ships can dock and be safe from storms. There are smaller natural harbors at Humboldt Bay and Monterey Bay.

REVIEW What are California's two largest natural harbors?

FOCUS
What bodies of water do you live nearest to?

Main Idea Read to find out about California's important bodies of water and to learn how they are alike and different.

Vocabulary
inlet	channel
harbor	floodplain
tributary	delta
river	reservoir
system	hydroelectric
erosion	power

Many large cities, such as San Diego (below), have been built along California's bays. Many Californians enjoy kayaking (above).

Rivers

The state's two longest rivers are the San Joaquin and the Sacramento. From its source, or beginning, in the Sierra Nevada, the San Joaquin River flows north through the Central Valley. The Sacramento River flows from the Cascades south through the Central Valley.

Northeast of San Francisco, the San Joaquin joins the Sacramento. At its mouth, the Sacramento River flows into San Francisco Bay. The mouth of a river is the place where it flows into a larger body of water.

On their journeys through the Central Valley, the San Joaquin and Sacramento rivers are joined by a number of tributaries (TRIH•byuh•tair•eez). A **tributary** is a smaller river that flows into a larger river. Smaller rivers, such as the American and the Feather, are tributaries of the Sacramento River. The Merced River is a tributary of the San Joaquin.

Together, a river and its tributaries make up a **river system**. All river systems drain, or carry water away from, the land around them. The Sacramento river system drains much of northern California. The San Joaquin river system drains much of the center of the state.

In southern California, the Colorado River is very important. It provides water for large cities and desert farms.

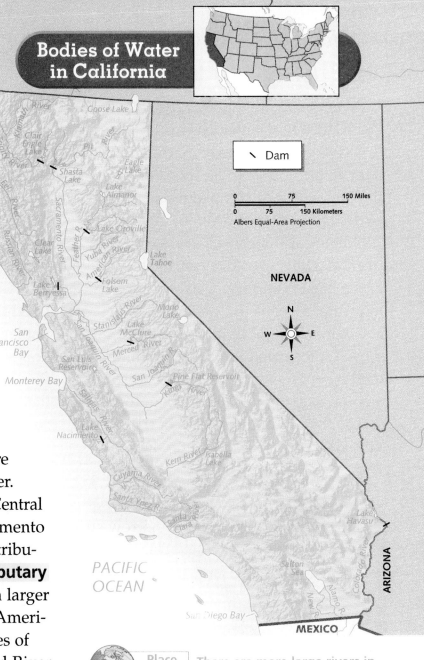

Bodies of Water in California

Dam

0   75   150 Miles
0   75   150 Kilometers
Albers Equal-Area Projection

NEVADA

ARIZONA

MEXICO

PACIFIC OCEAN

Place There are more large rivers in northern California than there are in southern California.

■ What river forms part of the eastern border of California?

The southern part of the state has few other large rivers. Most of the water in desert rivers dries up very quickly because there is little rain.

REVIEW What are California's two longest rivers?

Wearing Down and Building Up the Land

Rivers have great power to shape the Earth. As one scientist has said, "There is no force on this planet more powerful than water flowing over time." In fact, flowing water has formed many of the Earth's physical features.

Flowing water causes **erosion** (ih•ROH•zhuhn), or the wearing away, of the Earth's surface. A river's moving water sweeps the land's rocks and sand along with it. The river also moves soil carried into it by rain and melting snow. As rocks, sand, and soil are bounced and tumbled along, they scrape the bottom and sides of the river. This scraping carves a deeper and wider **channel**, or path, for the river to flow through.

In the mountains, where many of California's rivers start, the land is steep. Rivers flow swiftly in narrow channels, rushing downhill in low waterfalls and rapids.

When the rivers reach the flat land of the plains and valleys, they flow more slowly. They drop some of the rocks, sand, and soil they have been carrying. This adds new soil to their floodplains. A **floodplain** is the low, flat land along a river. When a river floods, water spreads out over the floodplain. As the water soaks into the ground or flows back into the river's channel, it leaves silt behind. Silt is fine sand and soil. It builds up

At 12 miles (19 km) wide and 22 miles (35 km) long, Lake Tahoe is the largest mountain lake in North America.

The Salton Sea lies below sea level. How is the land around the Salton Sea different from the land around Lake Tahoe?

from many floods to form soil that is good for farming.

A river drops silt at its mouth, too. If there is no strong current, or moving water, to carry the silt away, it begins to build up. Over time the silt can form a delta. A **delta** is land built up at a river's mouth. A large delta has formed in the Central Valley, where the San Joaquin River joins the Sacramento River.

REVIEW In what ways do rivers change the land?

Lakes and Reservoirs

California has more than 8,000 lakes. Most are natural lakes, or lakes formed by nature. The deepest natural lake in

California is Lake Tahoe (TAH•hoh). Located high in the Sierra Nevada on the California-Nevada border, Lake Tahoe is more than 1,500 feet (457 m) deep. When the writer known as Mark Twain first saw this lake more than 100 years ago, he described it as

> 66 walled in by a rim of snow-clad mountain peaks. . . . I thought it must surely be the fairest picture the whole earth affords. 99

Lake Tahoe is one of California's two largest lakes. The other is the Salton Sea. The Salton Sea is salty, like the ocean, but it is really a large lake. It is in the south, in the Imperial Valley.

Lake Tahoe and the Salton Sea are very different. Not only is one fresh and the other salty, but they were formed in different ways and at different times. Melting ice formed Lake Tahoe thousands of years ago. The Salton Sea was formed between 1905 and 1907 when the Colorado River flooded. Since that time, water from farms in the nearby Imperial and Coachella valleys has slowly added to the lake's size.

California also has some lakes made by people. Dams have been built across many rivers and streams to help control flooding. A dam can protect against flooding by not letting too much water flow through the river at one time.

When a dam is built across a river, the flowing water collects behind it. Soon the water floods the land behind the dam, forming a lake. A lake made

How Waterpower Is Used to Make Electricity

1 Water is stored in a reservoir.

2 Pipes carry water to the power plant.

Generator

3 Water turns the machines that make electricity.

Turbine

4 Water returns to the river.

by people to collect and store water is called a **reservoir** (REH•zuh•vwahr).

A dam can also help people make electricity. Water rushing through a dam can be used to turn large machines that make electricity. Electricity made by using the power of rushing water, or waterpower, is called **hydroelectric power**. Hoover, Davis, Glen Canyon, and Parker dams on the Colorado River make electricity this way. The electricity is used in California and in other states of the West and Southwest regions of the United States.

REVIEW What is the difference between a natural lake and a reservoir?

LEARNING FROM DIAGRAMS Water rushing through dams provides the waterpower needed to make electricity.

■ What two kinds of machines are used to make electricity?

5 Power lines carry electricity to users.

LESSON 3 REVIEW

Check Understanding

1 Remember the Facts What are California's two largest lakes?

2 Recall the Main Idea How is each kind of body of water in California different from the others?

Think Critically

3 Link to You Do you live near a body of water? Do you like living there? Would you like to live near a certain body of water? Explain your answer.

4 Think More About It How do California's different bodies of water help make the state an interesting place in which to live?

Show What You Know

Observation Activity Flowing water wears down the land. Look at photographs in books and magazines, or look around your home, your school, or your neighborhood. What examples of water erosion do you see? Write a description of each one. Use your descriptions to explain the different examples of erosion to family members.

FOCUS

What is the weather like most of the time where you live?

Main Idea Read to find out why different places in California have different climates.

Vocabulary

temperature
precipitation
climate
air mass
humidity
rain shadow
drought
Santa Ana winds
canyon

Weather and Climate

How would you describe today's weather where you live? You might talk about the **temperature** (TEM•per•cher), or the measure of how warm or cold something is. You might also talk about wind and precipitation (prih•sih•puh•TAY•shuhn). **Precipitation** is water, in the form of rain, sleet, or snow, that falls to the Earth's surface. Temperature, wind, and precipitation are all features of weather.

The kind of weather a place has most often, year after year, makes up its **climate**. People often claim that you can choose any climate you like and find it in California.

Temperature

The temperature of the air depends partly on the latitude of a place. California, like the rest of the United States, is located between the equator and the North Pole. This means that temperatures in California fall between the year-round heat of most places at the equator and the year-round cold of the North Pole. However, temperatures in northern California are generally cooler than temperatures in the southern part of the state.

Temperature also depends on elevation. Generally, the higher the land is above sea level, the lower the temperature will be.

In the warm climate of southern California, people can enjoy the beach all year round.

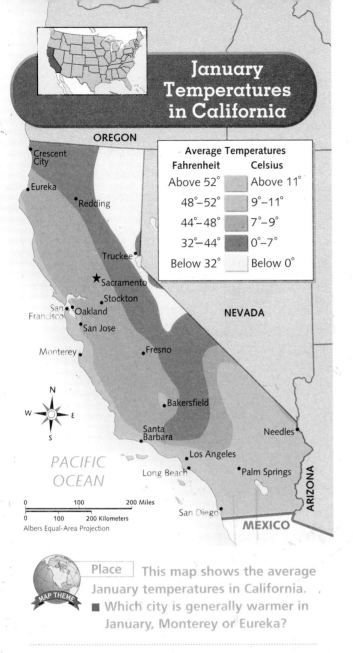

January Temperatures in California

Average Temperatures	
Fahrenheit	Celsius
Above 52°	Above 11°
48°–52°	9°–11°
44°–48°	7°–9°
32°–44°	0°–7°
Below 32°	Below 0°

OREGON

Crescent City
Eureka
Redding
Truckee
Sacramento
Stockton
San Francisco
Oakland
San Jose
Monterey
Fresno
Bakersfield
Santa Barbara
Needles
Los Angeles
Long Beach
Palm Springs
San Diego

NEVADA
ARIZONA
MEXICO

PACIFIC OCEAN

N W E S

0   100   200 Miles
0   100   200 Kilometers
Albers Equal-Area Projection

Place This map shows the average January temperatures in California.
■ Which city is generally warmer in January, Monterey or Eureka?

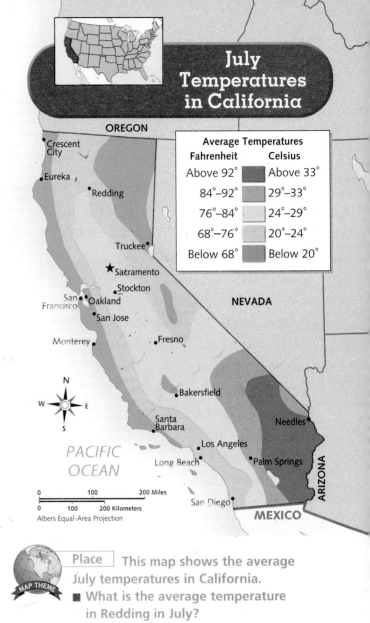

July Temperatures in California

Average Temperatures	
Fahrenheit	Celsius
Above 92°	Above 33°
84°–92°	29°–33°
76°–84°	24°–29°
68°–76°	20°–24°
Below 68°	Below 20°

OREGON

Crescent City
Eureka
Redding
Truckee
Sacramento
Stockton
San Francisco
Oakland
San Jose
Monterey
Fresno
Bakersfield
Santa Barbara
Needles
Los Angeles
Long Beach
Palm Springs
San Diego

NEVADA
ARIZONA
MEXICO

PACIFIC OCEAN

N W E S

0   100   200 Miles
0   100   200 Kilometers
Albers Equal-Area Projection

Place This map shows the average July temperatures in California.
■ What is the average temperature in Redding in July?

Temperatures usually drop about 3°F (almost 2°C) for every 1,000 feet (305 m) that the elevation increases. So temperatures are most often cooler in the mountains than in the valleys and deserts of California, no matter what the latitude is.

The lowest temperature ever recorded in California was −45°F (−43°C). It was recorded high in the Sierra Nevada on January 20, 1937, at Boca. The highest temperature ever recorded in California, or anywhere else in the United States, was 134°F (57°C). It was recorded in Death Valley on July 10, 1913.

REVIEW How does elevation affect temperatures in California?

Wind

Winds move clouds and warm or cool air from one place to another. This, too, affects weather. In California, as in the rest of the United States, winds generally move from west to east, bringing changing weather with them. Most changes in the weather are brought about by large, moving bodies of air called **air masses**. An air mass is described as warm or cold if it is warmer or colder than the air around it. Air masses take their temperature and moisture from the land or ocean over which they form.

Air masses that form over the northern Pacific Ocean are generally cool and wet because the temperature is low and the **humidity** (hyoo•MIH•duh•tee), or amount of moisture in the air, is high. Cold air masses from the Pacific Ocean make much of California's northern coast rainy and foggy.

These same cold air masses sometimes bring snow to the mountains—lots of snow! In January 1911, 390 inches (991 cm) of snow fell in Alpine County, high in the Sierra Nevada. That is the greatest amount of snow for a single month ever recorded in the United States.

In California, and in most other places in the West region of the United States, rain and snow fall mostly on the western side of the mountains. As wet air blows in from the Pacific Ocean, it is pushed up the mountains. As the air rises, it cools quickly, forming clouds. From the clouds, rain or snow falls. By the time the air reaches the eastern side of the mountains, little moisture is left in it. Places there receive little precipitation. They lie on the drier side of the mountains, in the **rain shadow**.

REVIEW How do mountains affect precipitation?

Precipitation

The yearly precipitation in a place is measured as rainfall, even though not all of it falls as rain. In most years, cold air masses drop more than 80 inches (203 cm) of rain on the northern coast of California near Crescent City. Farther south, however, the climate is drier. San

The Rain Shadow

③ Winds push clouds up the Coast Ranges, and cooler temperatures cause rain or snow.

④ Winds push clouds across the Central Valley.

② Moist air forms clouds.

① Air picks up moisture from the ocean.

Place California receives very different amounts of precipitation in different parts of the state.

■ Which city usually receives more precipitation, Eureka or Palm Springs?

Francisco gets about 22 inches (56 cm) of rain, while Los Angeles gets about 16 inches (41 cm), and San Diego gets about 10 inches (25 cm). Places in the rain shadow of the mountains get even less precipitation. Death Valley once went without rain for 760 days. That is the longest time without rain ever recorded in the United States.

Most parts of California have a wet season, when most of the year's precipitation falls, and a dry season. The dry season generally lasts from April to October in the north. In the south it lasts from March or April to November.

REVIEW How does the amount of precipitation change from north to south along the California coast?

Precipitation in California

OREGON

Crescent City

Eureka

Redding

Truckee

★ Sacramento

Stockton

San Francisco • Oakland

San Jose

Monterey

Fresno

NEVADA

N
W E
S

Bakersfield

Santa Barbara

Needles

PACIFIC OCEAN

Los Angeles

Long Beach

Palm Springs

ARIZONA

San Diego

MEXICO

Average Yearly Precipitation	
Inches	Centimeters
More than 64	More than 163
32–64	81–163
16–32	41–81
8–16	20–41
Less than 8	Less than 20

0   100   200 Miles
0   100   200 Kilometers
Albers Equal-Area Projection

6 Remaining clouds have little moisture.

5 Winds push clouds up the Sierra Nevada, and cooler temperatures cause more rain or snow.

LEARNING FROM DIAGRAMS
Places in a rain shadow receive little precipitation.
■ What happens after winds push clouds up mountains?

Brush fires sometimes burn out of control and destroy buildings in their paths, such as these apartments in Oakland.

Too Little, Too Much

Sometimes California has dry spells that last longer than the normal dry season. A long time with little or no rain is called a **drought** (DROWT). Because of droughts, Californians have to save water. They know how important water is to the future of the state.

Droughts can cause great problems, especially for farmers. Crops can dry up and die, and the soil can blow away.

California writer John Steinbeck described how farmers felt when there was too little rainfall. He wrote,

66 I have spoken of the rich years when the rainfall was plentiful. But there were dry years too, and they put a terror on the valley. 99

When there is too little rain, brush fires can also be a problem, both in northern

This sign featuring Smokey Bear could have described the conditions on the day this brush fire in Marin County broke out.

SMOKEY

SMOKEY

FIRE DANGER

HIGH

TODAY!

and southern California. In 1991 a huge brush fire destroyed parts of Oakland and the area around it. The fire killed 25 people and did a lot of damage.

Brush fires happen often in southern California, especially from late summer to early winter, when the land is driest. In the Los Angeles area the fires are sometimes spread by the **Santa Ana winds**. These hot, dry winds were named by the early settlers of Santa Ana, near Los Angeles. The winds form in the Great Basin and blow westward across southern California. At times the winds sweep through the canyons in the Coast Ranges at more than 40 miles per hour (64 kmph). A **canyon** is a deep, narrow valley with steep sides.

Too much rain can cause death and damage, too. In most years the Feather River valley in northern California gets less than 32 inches (81 cm) of rainfall.

Yuba City was one of many cities affected by floods in northern California in January 1997.

But in January 1997 the area received an average of 25 inches (64 cm) of rainfall in just a few days. In the floods that followed, 8 people died and crops and animals were destroyed. Many bridges and roads were washed out.

Preventing brush fires and floods in California has become very important as more and more people move to the state.

REVIEW What can happen when a place does not get enough rain?

LESSON 4 REVIEW

Check Understanding

❶ **Remember the Facts** Explain how weather and climate are different.

❷ **Recall the Main Idea** Why do different parts of California have different climates?

Think Critically

❸ **Think More About It** What are some ways that climate affects how people live?

❹ **Link to You** What physical features affect the climate where you live?

Show What You Know

Charting Activity Each day for a week, record the temperature and precipitation in your area. Then make a chart showing the high and low temperatures as well as the inches of rain or snow. Share your chart with your family.

LESSON 5

Natural Resources

Early settlers in what is now California found a land that was not only beautiful but also rich in natural resources. As you know, a natural resource is something found in nature that people can use. Soil, rocks, water, plants, and animals are all natural resources.

People throughout time have used natural resources in many ways to help meet their wants and needs, but resources are limited. *Limited* means there is only so much of something. People's wants and needs, however, are not limited. If people are to meet most of their wants and needs, it is important for them to use all resources wisely.

FOCUS

How do people use the natural resources found in your part of the state?

Main Idea Read to find out how people in California use the state's many natural resources.

Vocabulary

product
growing season
mineral
manufacturing
fuel
petroleum
nonrenewable
 resource
renewable
 resource
habitat
extinct

Soil

Many parts of California have fertile soil. California's most fertile farmland, however, is in the Central Valley. In fact, the Central Valley has three-fifths of California's farmland.

California is the leading farming state in the United States. California farmers grow more than 200 kinds of farm products, including fruits, vegetables, and nuts. A **product** is

More strawberries are grown in California than in all the rest of the United States. They grow well in the state's fertile soil.

76

20-Mule Teams

In the 1800s most of the world's borax came from Death Valley. Huge wagons were built to carry the borax out of Death Valley. The wagons were pulled by teams of mules. Although the actual number of mules in a team varied from 12 to 20, these teams became known as 20-mule teams. Borax still comes from deserts in southern California, but most of it is now mined outside of Death Valley, where it is easier for people to live and work. Today, trucks and railroads are used to haul the borax.

A 20-mule team

something that people make or grow, usually to sell.

There are many different reasons for California's farming success. One is the state's fertile soil. Another is a long **growing season**, the length of time when the weather is warm enough for crops to grow. Still another is irrigation, which allows farmers to grow crops in drier parts of the state.

Many parts of the state also provide grazing land for cattle, horses, and other livestock. California leads the United States in the production of eggs and milk and other dairy products. It is also among the leaders in the raising of sheep and turkeys.

REVIEW In which natural region is most of California's farmland?

Minerals and Fuels

California is rich in mineral resources, too. A **mineral** is a natural substance found in rocks. Among the state's mineral resources are gold, silver, copper, tungsten, boron, and borax.

Most of the state's mineral resources are used in building and in manufacturing (man•yuh•FAK•chuh•ring). **Manufacturing** is the making of goods. Tungsten, for example, is used in making electrical equipment. Boron is used for an eye wash, and borax is used to manufacture cleaning products.

California is also rich in fuels. A **fuel** is a natural resource used to make heat or energy. Coal, natural gas, and petroleum (puh•TROH•lee•uhm) are all fuels. **Petroleum** is another name for oil.

California does not have coal, but the state does have large amounts of petroleum. In fact, petroleum is California's most valuable fuel resource. It is pumped from deep wells. Most of California's petroleum is found near Los Angeles and off the coast near Santa Barbara and Long Beach.

People once thought that the petroleum in California would never run out. Now they know that one day it will be gone. Petroleum is a nonrenewable resource. A **nonrenewable resource** is a resource that cannot be made again by nature or by people.

REVIEW What is California's most valuable fuel resource?

California's most valuable fuel resource—petroleum— is found mainly in the southern part of the state.

Water

Many Californians believe that water is the state's most important natural resource. In fact, water is so important that it is sometimes called "California's liquid gold."

Like many natural resources, water is not spread evenly around the state. The northern and eastern mountain areas have plenty of water from rain and melted snow, but California's deserts and most of its southern valleys are dry.

Southern California is generally dry, yet the area has plenty of farmland and more people than other parts of the state. This is made possible because water is brought into the area from other places. Los Angeles, for example, gets much of its water from the Owens River valley more than 200 miles (322 km) to the northeast. The water

How Much Water?

USE	AMOUNT
Brushing teeth	1 to 2 gallons (4 to 8 L)
Flushing a toilet	5 to 7 gallons (19 to 26 L)
Running a dishwasher	9 to 12 gallons (34 to 45 L)
Taking a shower	15 to 30 gallons (57 to 114 L)
Washing dishes by hand	20 to 30 gallons (76 to 114 L)

- The average amount of water used by one person in a day is 123 gallons (466 L).
- The average amount of water used by a household in a year is 110,000 gallons (416,394 L).

LEARNING FROM TABLES This table gives the average amount of water used for some common household activities.
■ How much more water does it take to wash dishes by hand than to run a dishwasher?

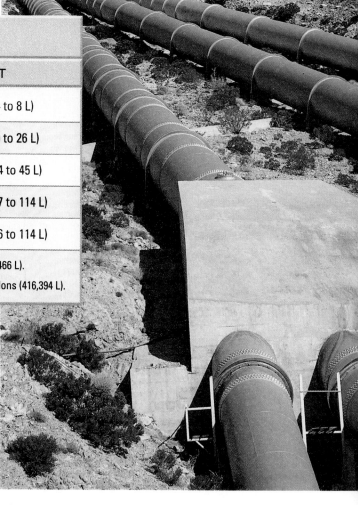

Giant pipes like these carry water to places that need it.

is held in reservoirs there until it is needed. Then it is sent hundreds of miles through ditches and giant pipes to Los Angeles and other places.

REVIEW Which parts of the state have the most and the least water?

Forests

Forests cover about two-fifths of California. Only Alaska has more land covered with trees. Pines are the most common trees in the Cascades, the Sierra Nevada, and the Coast Ranges. Many Douglas firs and redwoods also grow along the Coast Ranges. Other common trees in the state include hemlocks, cedars, and oaks.

Many trees in the California forests are cut down for lumber. In fact, only Oregon and Washington produce more lumber than California does. As trees are cut down for their wood, new trees are often planted. Trees are a renewable resource. A **renewable resource** is a resource that can be made again by nature or by people.

The most famous kinds of trees in California are redwoods. The California redwood is California's state tree. California redwoods, also called coast redwoods, are the world's tallest trees. They often grow 300 feet (91 m) into the sky—about as high as a 30-story building! Giant sequoias, also called Sierra redwoods, do not grow nearly as tall as coast redwoods. However, their trunks may be as large as 40 feet (12 m) across. Once, after a giant sequoia was cut down, its leveled-off stump became a dance floor for 24 couples!

Giant sequoias are among the Earth's largest and oldest living things. Many of these trees are more than 2,000 years old. But another kind of tree in California lives even longer. The Great Basin bristlecone pine can live for more than 4,000 years. One tree in California is more than 4,600 years old!

People were once allowed to cut down as many trees as they wanted. But now laws protect many of California's oldest and largest trees. Giant sequoias and many other redwoods are protected from being cut down, and so are many Great Basin bristlecone pines.

REVIEW What are the tallest trees in the world?

The General Sherman, a giant sequoia, is the world's largest tree. It is 275 feet (84 m) tall and 103 feet (31 m) around. It grows in Sequoia National Park.

Animals

Animals have always been an important natural resource in California. Early people used animals for food and for making clothing and tools. Later settlers also depended on California's animals.

Where people have not settled in large numbers, many animals have their **habitats**, or places where they find food and shelter. California has many different kinds of habitats, including water, deserts, and mountain forests.

Ocean waters along California's Pacific coast are the habitat of whales, seals, otters, and other sea animals. The ocean is also home to many kinds of fish and shellfish, including abalones, clams, crabs, shrimps, and scallops. The state's freshwater rivers and lakes have bass, salmon, and trout.

Snakes, lizards, rabbits, and mice are just a few of the animals that live in the deserts. Others are coyotes (ky•OH•teez), foxes, and deer. California's state reptile, the desert tortoise, is there, too.

Mountain forests are the habitat of bears and wildcats. Deer, minks, muskrats, rabbits, and mountain sheep live there, too. Elk and pronghorns, a kind of antelope, live in the northern part of the state.

Birds in California include doves, grouse, geese, turkeys, and quail. The California valley quail is the state bird.

Animal habitats are sometimes harmed or destroyed by people. Less than 100 years ago, huge condors flew in the California sky. By 1987, however, condors could be found only in zoos. The condors had nearly died out, or become **extinct** (ik•STINGT). Many had been crowded out of their habitats by all the growth of cities. But many people worked to save the birds. Today, their numbers are growing, and condors are once again living in the wild.

REVIEW What are three kinds of animal habitats in California?

The desert tortoise is the state reptile of California.

Sea lions hunt for food in the waters off California's coast.

LESSON 5 REVIEW

Check Understanding

1 **Remember the Facts**   What is the difference between a renewable and a nonrenewable resource?

2 **Recall the Main Idea**   How do people in California use the state's many natural resources?

Think Critically

3 **Think More About It**   In what ways do you think early settlers depended on California's natural resources?

4 **Cause and Effect**   How do people sometimes affect animal habitats? What can people do to protect animal habitats?

Show What You Know

Poster Activity   Make a poster about one of California's natural resources. Describe how it is used and why it is important to people or to the environment. Add pictures to your poster and give it a title. Then display it in your classroom.

Use a Land Use

1. Why Learn This Skill?

Where do the products that you use come from? Where are most goods in California manufactured? Where are the natural resources found that are used to make those goods? Where are most of the farms and ranches in California located? To find the answers to questions like these, you need a map that shows where some resources are found and how the land is used to produce others.

2. Understand the Process

The map on page 83 is a land use and resource map of California. It uses colors to show **land use**, or how most of the land in a place is used. However, the map does not show every forest or every farming or manufacturing area in California. It shows only the main ones. Look at the map key to see which color stands for each kind of land use.

1 Which color shows areas where manufacturing is the most important land use? Where in California does most manufacturing take place?

Most of the lumber produced in California comes from forests in the Coast Ranges and the Sierra Nevada.

and Resource Map

② How is most of the land along the San Joaquin River used? How is that different from the way most land in northwestern California is used?

③ Where is most of California's little-used land? Why do you think this land is not used much?

The map on this page uses picture symbols to show where some natural resources of California are found. To find out what resources each symbol stands for, look at the map key again.

④ Near which river is most of the oil and natural gas in northern California found?

⑤ What minerals might you see being mined if you were to travel east from Bakersfield?

3. Think and Apply

Draw a land use and resource map of the area near your community. Use the map on this page and encyclopedias and other library books to find out how people use the land in that area and what natural resources are found there.

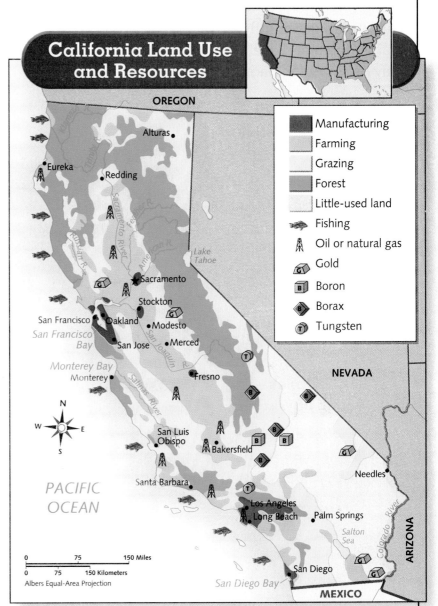

California Land Use and Resources

Map key:
- Manufacturing
- Farming
- Grazing
- Forest
- Little-used land
- Fishing
- Oil or natural gas
- Gold
- Boron
- Borax
- Tungsten

0   75   150 Miles
0   75   150 Kilometers
Albers Equal-Area Projection

Make a map key to explain the colors and symbols that you used for your map. Compare your map with the maps drawn by other students in your class.

CONNECT MAIN IDEAS

Use this organizer to show what you have learned about California's geography. Write one or two sentences to summarize the main idea of each lesson. A copy of the organizer may be found on page 16 of the Activity Book.

Where Is California?

_____

_____

_____

_____

California's Natural Regions

_____

_____

_____

_____

California's Geography

California's Bodies of Water

_____

_____

_____

_____

Weather and Climate

_____

_____

_____

_____

Natural Resources

_____

_____

_____

_____

WRITE MORE ABOUT IT

Write a Descriptive Letter Imagine that you have a friend who lives in another state. You want your friend to visit California. In a letter, describe each of California's natural regions.

Compare and Contrast Suppose that you have been asked to write a story about rivers in California for a nature magazine. In your story, explain how rivers can both wear down and build up the land.

USE VOCABULARY

For each pair of vocabulary terms, write one or two sentences explaining how the terms are related.

1 hemisphere, equator

2 relative location, absolute location

3 tributary, river system

4 temperature, climate

5 nonrenewable resource, renewable resource

CHECK UNDERSTANDING

6 What is the Pacific Rim?

7 What happens when the rock along a fault moves?

8 Which natural region has many of California's largest farms?

9 What are California's two largest natural harbors?

10 What are California's two longest rivers?

11 Why are temperatures most often cooler in the mountains than in the valleys?

12 What is California's most valuable fuel resource?

THINK CRITICALLY

13 **Personally Speaking** Which of California's natural resources do you think is the most important? Explain.

14 **Explore Viewpoints** Why do you think someone from another state might want to move to California?

APPLY SKILLS

Use Latitude and Longitude
Use the map on page 53 to answer these questions.

15 Which city is located nearest to 37°N, 122°W?

16 Which city is located nearest to 40°N, 124°W?

17 Which lines of latitude and longitude best give the location of Stockton?

18 Which lines of latitude and longitude best give the location of Eureka?

Use an Elevation Map Imagine that you and your family are traveling from Fresno to Santa Barbara. Use the elevation map on page 63 to describe the landforms you pass along the way.

Use a Land Use and Resource Map Look at the map on page 83. Describe how land use generally changes as you travel east from the Sacramento River to Lake Tahoe.

READ MORE ABOUT IT

Sierra by Diane Siebert. HarperCollins. This beautifully illustrated book describes the Sierra Nevada.

Visit the Internet at
http://www.hbschool.com
for additional resources.

THE EARLIEST CALIFORNIANS

"My words are
tied in one
With the great
mountains,
With the great
rocks,
With the great
trees,
In one with
my body
And my heart."

from a Yokuts prayer

Marie Wilcox is one of
the Yokuts people who
live in California today.

Early People of California

| 10,000 years ago | 5,000 years ago | Present |

FOCUS
How do people today change as the world around them changes?

Main Idea Read to find out how the earliest people of California changed their ways of life as their environment changed.

Vocabulary

glacier   civilization
nomad   religion
vegetation
tribe
nation
culture
legend
artifact
archaeologist

Many thousands of years ago, a large part of the Earth experienced an Ice Age. During this time the Earth's climate turned very cold. It was so cold that glaciers (GLAY•sherz) covered much of the land. A **glacier** is a huge, slow-moving mass of ice.

So much of the Earth's water was trapped in glaciers that the water level in the oceans dropped. This caused a "bridge" of dry land to appear at several different times between the continents of Asia and North America. It connected present-day Russia and Alaska. People from Asia may have traveled across this land bridge into North America.

Land and People Long Ago

The earliest people who came to North America were most likely nomads (NOH•madz). A **nomad** is a person who keeps moving from place to place. These nomads followed roaming herds of animals, which they hunted for food. They likely gathered plants for food, too.

Glaciers, such as this one in Alaska, are now found only in very cold places. But during the Ice Age, glaciers covered even parts of California.

Routes of Early People

Movement Early people may have followed these routes from Asia to the Americas.

■ In what general direction did people travel to reach California from what is now Alaska?

Mastodons were important resources for early people.

These first Americans, or Native Americans, probably traveled in small groups of families that lived and worked together. For thousands of years their children and their children's children slowly spread out all over North America and South America. They became the first Californians, or Native Californians, when they reached what is now California. They likely reached California at least 10,000 years ago.

When the earliest people arrived in California, the climate was much cooler and more humid than it is today. Rich **vegetation**, or plant life, provided food for very large animals. Some of these animals weighed thousands of pounds. Giant mastodons and mammoths roamed the valley grasslands and the mountain forests.

Mastodons and mammoths were huge animals like hairy elephants. Many were as tall as 14 feet (4 m) and had tusks up to 14 feet long. From one mammoth, early hunters could get enough meat to last for months. The people used the skin to make clothing and shelters. They used the bones to make tools and weapons.

REVIEW What giant animals did early people hunt in what is now California?

A Time of Great Change

Over thousands of years the environment of California slowly changed. The climate became warmer and drier. Much of the vegetation the giant animals ate could no longer grow. Because of this the mammoths and other giant animals became extinct.

Some people moved on to new lands as the environment changed. Others stayed but changed their ways of life. Since there were no giant animals to provide food, the people hunted smaller animals and began to fish. They also began to gather more nuts and berries and eat more plants.

In time the people learned where certain plants grew best. They also learned at what times of the year nuts, berries, and other plant parts became ripe. Each season the people traveled to places where they could both gather food and hunt.

REVIEW Why did mammoths and other giant animals in California become extinct?

The California Tribes

About 5,000 years ago people began to gather in villages for at least part of each year. Some people formed what today are called tribes. **Tribe** is a term often used to describe Native American groups that share the same language or

Major Tribes

Present-day border

0   75   150 Miles
0   75   150 Kilometers
Albers Equal-Area Projection

Location Indian tribes lived in all parts of California.
■ Which tribes lived close to where you live now?

have the same leaders. Today we know them as the Chumash (CHOO•mash), the Miwoks (MEE•wahks), the Mojaves (moh•HAH•vayz), and many others.

Often these large groups are known as nations. A **nation** is a group of people that share land and a common way of life. A nation can include several tribes.

Over time the Native Californians came to have many different ways of speaking, behaving, and dressing. Each tribe also came to have its own beliefs. Together, these ways of living made up a **culture**. A tribe's culture made it different from other tribes.

Native Californians spoke more than 130 different languages. Sometimes the language spoken by one group was not at all like the language spoken by a neighboring group. However, most Native Californians could speak two, three, or more languages.

Each California tribe had its own culture, yet the Native Californians were alike in many ways. They all believed that people needed to respect all living things. They believed that if the animal spirits were happy, people would have a good hunt.

All the Native Californians also used legends to tell about important events and people in their history. A **legend** is a story handed down over time. The Native Californians also used legends to explain the animals, plants, and other physical features around them.

One legend told by the early people of California explains why moles cannot see well. Moles are small animals that live underground. They use their front paws, which turn outward, to dig tunnels.

Children listened carefully as their parents and grandparents told them legends. Then the children repeated each line of the legend until they had learned it for themselves. In that way the legend was handed down from adults to children over many years.

REVIEW In what ways were Native Californians alike?

Mole and the Sun

One day back in the Beforetime, Sun decided that it would be easier to roll along the ground than across the sky. So, soon after he rose, when he thought no one was watching, he dropped down from the sky.

But Mole, who had gone out hunting early, saw, and ran to catch Sun as he fell.

"Hai, help!" squeaked Mole, shutting his eyes against Sun's great brightness. "The Sun has fallen!"

"What?" said some.

"Who called?" asked others.

"Hai, hai! Help me!" cried Mole again. "Sun has fallen, and he is heavy!"

All of the animals ran to help, and soon they had shoved Sun back into the sky, where he has stayed ever since.

But Mole's eyes still squint against the light, and his front paws to this day are bent back from holding up the Sun.

from *Back in the Beforetime: Tales of the California Indians* by Jane Louise Curry

Using Resources

California was rich in natural resources. Yet Native Californians wasted very little. They could make food from a few months of hunting last a full year. They gathered seeds, especially acorns, and pounded them into flour.

The early people of California made everything they used from the natural resources they found around them. Because they lived in different regions, however, there were different kinds of resources for them to use. People in some tribes carried water in tightly woven reed baskets, while those in other tribes used clay pots. Some tribes made rope and clothing from animal hair. Other tribes used plant fibers. Some used wood from trees to build shelters and make tools. Others used branches and animal bones and skins.

REVIEW **Why were natural resources important to California's early people?**

Clues from the Past

Native Californians did not have written languages. They left no written story for people today to read. What we know today about California's early people comes from the artifacts (AR•tih•fakts) they left behind. An **artifact** is any object made by people in the past. Pots, baskets, weapons, and tools all help tell a tribe's story.

Scientists called **archaeologists** (ar•kee•AH•luh•jists) study artifacts to learn about what life was like long ago. To an archaeologist, spear points tell

Archaeologists carefully clean and label the artifacts they find. The artifacts help them learn more about what life was like long ago.

something about how people hunted and where they hunted. Piles of shells are clues that people ate clams and mussels and that they may have built a village nearby.

Some early cultures left behind more and different kinds of artifacts than others. Between 2,500 and 500 years ago, people who lived far to the south of California built great civilizations (sih•vuh•luh•ZAY•shuhnz). A **civilization** is a culture that usually has cities and highly developed arts and sciences.

This carved Mayan artifact shows a woman with children.

In Mexico and Central America, the Mayas (MY•uhz) and the Aztecs both formed great civilizations. They built large cities with beautiful palaces, gardens, and bridges. Roads paved with stones connected all these places.

Because of the many artifacts left by these cultures, archaeologists know that they each made art and music. They

Rancho La Brea Tar Pits

The Rancho La Brea (BRAY•uh) Tar Pits lie in Hancock Park in Los Angeles. These tar pits are one of the world's best sources of Ice Age fossils. The gooey tar pits hold the remains of many animals and plants that got stuck in them and died there long ago. The remains of at least one person have also been found. Many of the animals and plants are thousands of years old and belong to groups that are now extinct. Today people go to the tar pits to visit the museum there. It is filled with clues about California long, long ago.

Los Angeles

Exhibits at the Rancho La Brea Tar Pits show visitors how animals got stuck in the tar.

Sunset Blvd.

West Hollywood

Santa Monica Blvd.

Sunset Blvd.

Santa Monica Blvd.

Hollywood Freeway

Hollywood

101

N
W E
S

Beverly

Fairfax Ave.

La Brea Ave.

Blvd.

Beverly Hills

RANCHO LA BREA TAR PITS

Wilshire Blvd.

Olympic Blvd.

Western Ave.

Pico Blvd.

0   1 Mile
0   1 Kilometer

Los Angeles

10

Santa Monica Freeway

also followed a **religion**, or set of beliefs about God or gods.

Artifacts and other clues from the past tell archaeologists that many people lived in California long ago. In fact, more people lived in California than in any other place in what is now the United States. Five hundred years ago, more than 1 of every 10 Native Americans, or American Indians, in the United States lived in California.

REVIEW How do archaeologists learn about people in the distant past?

This scene of the Aztec city of Tenochtitlán (tay•nawch•teet•LAHN) is a detail of a mural painted by Mexican artist Diego Rivera. The Aztec artifact (above left) is a frog made of gold.

LESSON I REVIEW

10,000 years ago	5,000 years ago	Present

10,000 years ago	5,000 years ago	500 years ago
• Early people may have reached what is now California	• People began to gather in villages	• More than 1 of every 10 American Indians in what is now the United States lived in California

Check Understanding

1 Remember the Facts How did Native Californians tell about important events and people in their history?

2 Recall the Main Idea How did the early people of California change their ways of life when their environment changed?

Think Critically

3 Think More About It Why do you think early people formed tribes?

4 Cause and Effect How did living in different regions affect the California tribes?

Show What You Know

Art Activity Suppose you have written a book called *The Early People of California*. Draw a cover for your book. Show the lives of people who hunted animals and gathered nuts, berries, and plants. Add your book cover to a bulletin board display in your classroom.

Use Tables to

1. Why Learn This Skill?

How many ways can you think of to describe yourself? You might give your height, your weight, and your age. You might also describe yourself by making comparisons with other people you know. To make a comparison is to say how two or more things are the same and how they are different.

When you make comparisons, a table is a good way to show the information. A table lets you compare numbers, facts, and other information quickly. Before you can show the information, however, you must decide how you want to **classify** it, or group it. A table shows information in a pattern.

2. Understand the Process

Native Californians spoke more than 130 different languages. Many of the languages, however, belonged to the same **language group**. All the languages in a language group are alike in some way.

The tables on these pages show to which language group the language of each tribe listed belonged. Both tables give the same information, but they classify it in different ways.

Table A: Language Groups	
LANGUAGE GROUP	**TRIBE**
Algonquian (al•GAHN•kwee•uhn)	Wiyot (WY•aht)
	Yurok (YOOR•ahk)
Athapascan (a•thuh•PAS•kuhn)	Hoopa (HOOP•uh)
	Kato (KAY•toh)
	Tolowa (TAHL•uh•wah)
Hokan (HOH•kahn)	Chumash (CHOO•mash)
	Karok (KAR•ahk)
	Mojave (moh•HAH•vay)
	Pomo (POH•moh)
	Shasta (SHAS•tuh)
Penutian (puh•NOO•chuhn)	Maidu (MY•doo)
	Miwok (MEE•wahk)
	Modoc (MOH•dahk)
	Yokuts (YOH•kuhts)
Uto-Aztecan (YOO•toh AZ•tek•uhn)	Paiute (PY•yoot)
	Shoshone (shuh•SHOH•nee)
Yukian (YOO•kee•uhn)	Wappo (WAH•poh)
	Yuki (YOO•kee)

A Pomo grinding basket

Group Information

1 Study Table A. Which tribes listed in the table spoke a language that belonged to the Hokan language group? to the Algonquian language group?

2 Now study Table B. Table B gives the same information as Table A, but the information is classified in a different way. How are the tribes in Table B listed?

3 Which table makes it easier to find out which tribes spoke a language belonging to a certain language group? Which table makes it easier to find out to which language group a certain tribe's language belonged? Explain your answers.

3. Think and Apply

Make a table that shows how the Native Californians were alike and how they were different. You can use what you read about them in the last lesson. You may also want to find other information in library books and encyclopedias. Compare your table with those of classmates. Did you classify the information in the same way? Explain.

Table B: Language Groups	
TRIBE	LANGUAGE GROUP
Chumash	Hokan
Hoopa	Athapascan
Karok	Hokan
Kato	Athapascan
Maidu	Penutian
Miwok	Penutian
Modoc	Penutian
Mojave	Hokan
Paiute	Uto-Aztecan
Pomo	Hokan
Shasta	Hokan
Shoshone	Uto-Aztecan
Tolowa	Athapascan
Wappo	Yukian
Wiyot	Algonquian
Yokuts	Penutian
Yuki	Yukian
Yurok	Algonquian

Maidu ceremonial hair ornaments

The Coast

FOCUS

How can the natural resources of a region affect how people live?

Main Idea
Read to find out how the Native Californians who lived in the Coastal region used the natural resources around them.

Vocabulary

shaman
weir
trade
wealth
tradition
ceremony
government
ancestor

The Yuroks built their houses (below) and canoes (above) from redwood and cedar trees.

The very first Californians may have lived in California's Coastal region. They built their villages along the coast and the region's rivers. Like people today, they used the region's rich natural resources to meet their needs. They cut down trees and fished in ocean inlets and rivers. They dug for clams and other kinds of shellfish. They gathered seaweed and hunted sea lions, deer, and other animals.

The Yuroks

The Yuroks (YOOR•ahks) lived in the northwestern part of what is now California, along the Pacific coast and the Klamath River. Ocean winds bring heavy rains to this part of California, so the forests grow tall and thick. Huge redwoods and giant cedars towered above the Yuroks' villages. The Yuroks used wooden planks split from those trees to build rectangular homes. Their houses had slanted roofs that allowed the water to run off in rainy weather. To protect their wooden houses from fires, they removed all the brush, or low bushes, in and around their villages.

The Yuroks also used the trees to make their canoes. Using stone tools, they hollowed out the insides of giant logs. Sometimes they burned out the insides of the logs. They used their canoes to travel up and down the coast and to hunt sea animals.

The forests also provided food for the Yuroks. In summer and fall some Yuroks left their villages to gather berries and nuts. For the Yuroks, as for most California Indians, acorns were an

The Yuroks and other groups in the northern Coastal region probably used fishing weirs like the one shown above in this 1923 photograph. They used weirs to catch salmon (left).

important food. Their most important food, however, was the salmon from the rivers.

REVIEW What are two ways the Yuroks used the large trees that grew around them?

Catching Salmon

"Ne-peg-wuh! Ne-peg-wuh!" The Yuroks waited every year to hear this call. It meant that a **shaman** (SHAH•muhn), or religious leader, had caught the year's first salmon. The salmon season had begun.

Each spring, salmon left the Pacific Ocean and swam up the rivers in northern California to spawn, or lay their eggs. It was said that there were so many salmon, a person could walk across the rivers on their backs.

To catch the salmon, the Yuroks made weirs (WIRZ). A **weir** is a fence built across a river in order to trap fish. To make their weirs, the Yuroks built fences from sticks and attached them to long poles. They stretched the weirs across rivers. Then the men of the village could spear the trapped fish as the fish swam up the rivers.

Women prepared the salmon so that it could be kept for many months. First, they cleaned the salmon and dried it in the sun. Then, they cooked it slowly over fires, turning it often and moving it from the flames into the smoke. Day after day they repeated this work until there was enough salmon to last until the next time they heard *"Ne-peg-wuh!"*

REVIEW How did the Yuroks catch salmon?

Symbols of Wealth

The Yuroks fished for salmon into the early summer. In any season, however, there were always animals for the Yuroks to hunt and plants for them to gather. In fact, food was so easy to get that the Yuroks had spare time. They used it to collect objects they thought were beautiful and valuable.

Like many Native Californians, the Yuroks collected shells and strung them like beads. These strings of shells were used as money in trade. **Trade** is the exchanging, or buying and selling, of goods. The Yuroks traded the strings of shells for things they could not make from the natural resources around them.

The Yuroks and other groups in the northern Coastal region allowed families and individuals to use some lands only for themselves. In other groups, land was something to be shared by the whole tribe. However, some things, such as oak and pine nut trees, could belong to a certain family and were cared for by them.

Gaining the use of land and other forms of **wealth**, or riches, was important to the Yuroks. A person who owned several strings of shells was thought to be very wealthy. Some men even wore special marks on their arms for measuring the length of their shell strings. Wealthy women wore beautiful fur skins and jewelry and owned finely woven baskets.

REVIEW How were the Yuroks different from some other groups in the way they thought about land?

CULTURE

Pomo Basket Makers

Most of the California tribes made baskets for every possible use and purpose, from birth to death. The Pomos, who live along the northern coast, are still known for their basket-making skills. As they make their baskets from plant materials, they often weave designs made with feathers and beads. Susan Billy is a Pomo basket maker. She says that when she weaves baskets, she feels connected to "all the grandmothers who have gone before me."

Susan Billy and some of her baskets

The Hoopas

Not far from the Yuroks, along the Trinity River, lived the Hoopas (HOOP•uhz). The Hoopas lived in small villages upstream from the Yuroks, in the valleys of the Coast Ranges. The Hoopas and Yuroks spoke different languages, but their cultures were alike. They both felt that gaining wealth was important. Their environments were also alike, and they used natural resources in much the same way. Salmon and acorns provided most of their food.

The Yuroks, the Hoopas, and many other tribes in the Coastal region, such as the Tolowas, used beads made from shells (below) for trading and as jewelry. The Tolowa woman in this photograph from the early 1920s (right) is showing her wealth by wearing necklaces made from shells.

Present-day border

Siskiyou Mts.

Klamath River

Scott River

Klamath

Red Mountain
▲ 4,265 ft.
(1,300 m)

PACIFIC OCEAN

Klamath River

YUROK

Mountains

N
W E
S

HOOPA

Redwood Creek

New River

Humboldt Bay

Trinity River

South Fork Trinity River

0   10   20 Miles
0   10   20 Kilometers
Albers Equal-Area Projection

Region The Yuroks and Hoopas lived in what is now northwestern California.
■ Which tribe's lands bordered the Pacific Ocean?

The Hoopas, too, built rectangular wooden houses with slanted roofs. In their villages were sweat lodges. Fires burning inside these buildings kept them very hot. The men gathered there to think and pray. When they finished, they would jump into the river next to the village to cool and clean themselves.

Hoopa women did most of the gathering of plants for food and basket making. They also took care of the sick, often using medicines made from plants. The men were hunters, fishers, and woodcarvers.

The fall was a time for giving thanks. Each year the Hoopas took part in two celebrations—the White Deerskin Dance and the Jump Dance. During these celebrations children learned the traditions of their tribe. A **tradition** is an idea or a way of doing something that has been handed down from the past.

These celebrations are still held every September. Today there are about 2,500 Hoopas and 4,200 Yuroks living in northern California.

REVIEW Why were sweat lodges important places in Hoopa villages?

The Chumash

The Chumash (CHOO•mash) lived along the southern part of the Coastal region, from what is now Topanga and Malibu to San Luis Obispo (oh•BIS•poh). Some lived in the Cuyama and San Joaquin valleys. They also lived on such nearby Channel Islands as Santa Cruz, Santa Rosa, and San Miguel (mee•GAYL).

In this part of the Coastal region there were fewer salmon, so acorns were the main food. The Chumash also fished, caught crabs, dug for clams, and hunted seals and sea otters.

Where the Chumash lived, the climate was too warm and dry for many redwoods or giant cedars to grow. Instead of building their houses from wooden planks, the Chumash drove long poles into the ground. Then they bent the poles and tied them together. This frame of poles was covered with thick layers of grasses.

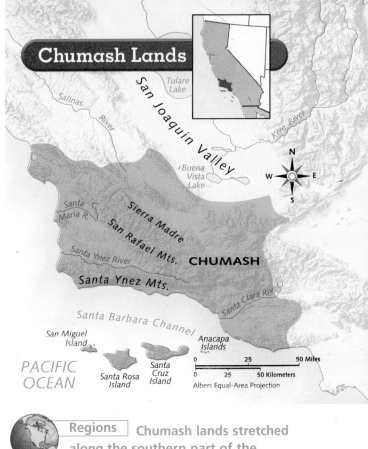

Chumash Lands

Regions Chumash lands stretched along the southern part of the Coastal region.

■ Which three mountain ranges are part of what were Chumash lands?

Some Chumash houses were 50 feet (15 m) wide and could hold as many as 70 people. One Spanish explorer wrote,

    ❝ They arrange their houses in groups. The houses are well constructed, round like an oven, spacious and fairly comfortable; light enters from a hole in the roof. . . . In the middle of the floor they make a fire for cooking seeds, fish, and other foods, for they eat everything boiled or roasted. ❞

Some Chumash villages had as many as 1,000 people. Each village had several houses, a sweat lodge, buildings for storing food, and an area for ceremonies. A **ceremony** is a series of actions performed during a special event. At different times of the year, the Chumash held ceremonies to give thanks for the plants and animals around them.

The Chumash had their own system of government, as did other California tribes. A **government** is a system for deciding what is best for a group of people. It protects the group members and settles disagreements among them. A government has its own rules and leaders.

In Chumash villages the main leader was called the *wot*. The wot's son usually became the next leader. If the wot had no son, however, a daughter, a brother, or a sister might become the leader. The wot decided who could hunt and gather in each area. He or

she also talked about problems with the leaders of other Chumash villages so that they could all work together.

The Chumash were expert canoe builders. They called their canoes *tomols* (TOH•mohlz). They built them from wooden planks split from logs that washed up along the shore. Sometimes they traveled north to the mountains to get the wood. They split the wood with a whale bone or a deer antler and smoothed the edges with a clam shell or a stone knife. Then they sewed the pieces of wood together with ropes made from animal skins.

The Chumash had a natural resource that other tribes in the Coastal region did not have. On some of their lands, thick tar bubbled up from the ground. The Chumash used this tar to seal the seams on their canoes and make them waterproof. Then they decorated the

Chumash homes (below) were round in shape. When present-day Chumash people built this canoe (left), they used the same materials their people have used for hundreds of years— wooden planks sealed with thick tar.

sides with shells. "Like a flower on the water" was the way a Chumash man once described a Chumash canoe.

In these strong canoes the Chumash were able to travel long distances to trade. They paddled their canoes across the choppy waters of the Santa Barbara Channel to reach the Channel Islands. They even traveled as far as San Nicolas Island, 65 miles (105 km) from the coast!

About 3,000 Chumash live in California today. Many things that their ancestors (AN•ses•terz) created can still be seen. An **ancestor** is an early family member. Archaeologists have found such artifacts as baskets, stone cooking pots, and wooden bowls. They have also found large mounds of shells along the shore. These shells were from the shellfish the Chumash ate.

The early Chumash also left behind their rock art, which can still be seen today in several places in California.

Chumash rock paintings, like these in Kern County, can still be seen in some places in California.

They often painted pictures of fish, birds, and other animals, as well as stars and plants. They used ground-up rocks to make their paints.

REVIEW **What did the ancestors of the Chumash leave behind?**

LESSON 2 REVIEW

Check Understanding

1. **Remember the Facts** In which parts of the Coastal region did the Yuroks, the Hoopas, and the Chumash live?

2. **Recall the Main Idea** How did the Indians who lived in California's Coastal region use the natural resources around them?

Think Critically

3. **Link to You** What are some ways of doing things that have been handed down from your ancestors?

4. **Think More About It** Why might the Yuroks have moved around more in summer than in winter?

Show What You Know

Simulation Activity Imagine that you and a partner are members of two different tribes in the Coastal region. Role-play a conversation in which you describe to each other the ways your tribes use natural resources to meet your needs. Practice your role-play and then share it with the class.

Identify Causes and Their Effect

1. Why Learn This Skill?

Suppose you get up late and miss your school bus. Getting up late is the cause of your missing the bus. A **cause** is something that makes something else happen. Missing your bus is the effect of your getting up late. An **effect** is what happens as a result of something else happening.

Sometimes an effect has more than one cause. Besides getting up late, you may have read the comics or watched TV before you got dressed.

Understanding causes and their effects can help you make better decisions. It can also help you understand why things happen.

2. Remember What You Have Read

In the last lesson you read about the Yuroks, who lived in northern California.

1 What natural resources did the Yuroks use to build their homes?

2 What were the roofs on Yurok homes like? Why were they built that way?

3. Understand the Process

You can use the following steps to help you find all the causes of an effect.

- Identify the effect.
- Look for all the causes of that effect.

Causes

Ocean winds bring heavy rains to California's northern coast.	Redwoods and giant cedars grow along California's northern coast.

Effect

The Yuroks used wood from redwoods and giant cedars to build homes with slanted roofs.

- Think about how the causes relate to each other and to the effect. Ocean winds bring heavy rains to California's northern coast, so forests grow tall and thick. To build their homes, the Yuroks split wooden planks from the redwoods and giant cedars that grew in the forests. They built their homes with slanted roofs so that the rain would run off.

4. Think and Apply

History is full of causes and effects. Interview your parents, grandparents, or other adults in your community. Ask them questions about how your community has changed over time. Then use the steps from Understand the Process to identify an effect and look for all the causes of it. Share your findings with classmates.

FOCUS

How might the way of life in one region be different from the way of life in another region? How might they be the same?

Main Idea Read to compare the ways of life of the Native Californians who lived in the Central Valley and the mountains of California.

Vocabulary

granary
division of labor
specialize
foothill
cooperate

The Central Valley and the Mountains

Today most people in California live near the coast in large cities. That was not true hundreds of years ago. At that time most people lived in the Central Valley and on the western slopes of the Sierra Nevada.

The Native Californians who lived in these regions had cultures that were much the same. Most of them spoke languages of the same language group, and they used the same kinds of natural resources to meet their needs. As in the Coastal region, there were many animals to hunt and plenty of plants, berries, and nuts to gather. Like the Indians who lived in the other regions of California, the Indians of the Central Valley and the mountains traded with nearby tribes to get any goods that their own environment did not provide.

The Maidus

The Maidus (MY•dooz) lived along the tributaries of the Sacramento River, including the Feather and American rivers. The Maidus lived in village groups. These village groups were made up of a circle of villages with another village in the center. The village in the center had a large building where members of the tribe could meet and hold ceremonies. Together, these villages owned and shared a hunting and fishing area.

This headdress was worn by a Maidu shaman. Acorns (above) were important foods for the Native Californians who lived in the Central Valley and the mountains of California.

With a seed beater, this Maidu woman knocks grass seeds into a large collecting basket.

Next to the earth lodges stood open grass-roofed porches. People spent much of their time on the porches in warm weather. Another kind of building was the barrel-shaped **granary** (GRAY•nuh•ree), which was used for storing acorns. Guards stood watch on nearby hillsides to protect the villages and the granaries from outsiders.

Acorns were the main food of the Maidus. The people sang a song they believed would help them have a bigger harvest:

> 66 The acorns come down from
>   heaven.
>   I plant the short acorns in
>   the valley.
>   I plant the long acorns in
>   the valley.
>   I sprout, I, the black acorn,
>   sprout, I sprout. 99

Besides acorns, the Maidus gathered pine nuts and seeds from other plants, such as wild rye grasses. Women and children gathered nuts by hand, but they used a tool called a seed beater to collect seeds. The seed beater was used to hit tall grasses, causing the seeds to fall off into a basket held below it.

The Maidus gathered food in spring, summer, and fall and stored the extra food for winter. They made good use of all the natural resources around them and wasted very little. They even roasted and ate grasshoppers and other kinds of insects!

The Maidus were skilled hunters, too. The men hunted deer and elk as well as smaller animals, such as squirrels and

Each Maidu village group probably had from three to five villages. A village may have had as many as 50 houses. Some Maidus lived in houses made of tree branches that were bent, gathered together, and covered with grasses. Others lived in large mound-shaped shelters built of wood and covered with dirt. These earth lodges were as much as 40 feet (12 m) across. The floors were dug into the ground to a depth of about 4 feet (1 m). In the center of the floor was a deep pit for the fire.

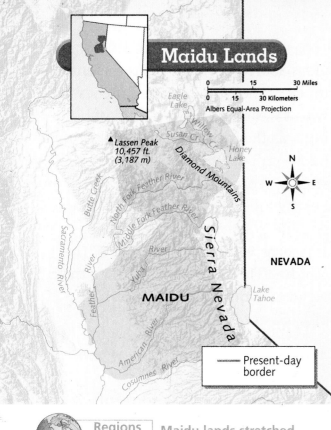

Maidu Lands

Eagle
Lake

0   15   30 Miles
0   15   30 Kilometers
Albers Equal-Area Projection

▲ Lassen Peak
10,457 ft.
(3,187 m)

Willow Cr.

Honey
Lake

Susan Cr.

Diamond Mountains

North Fork Feather River

Middle Fork Feather River

Butte Creek

Sacramento River

River

Feather

River

Yuba

MAIDU

American River

Cosumnes River

Sierra Nevada

NEVADA

Lake
Tahoe

N
W   E
S

Present-day
border

Regions Maidu lands stretched across what is now the northeastern part of California.

■ What mountain range formed much of the eastern boundary of what were Maidu lands?

rabbits. They also fished along the rivers, using logs to make rafts and canoes.

People from different Maidu villages would gather for events such as the Bear Dance, which celebrated good feelings between the people of the villages. Dancers carried sweet-smelling tree branches, which stood for peace and friendship.

REVIEW How were Maidu village groups arranged?

The Miwoks

The Miwoks (MEE•wahks) lived in different regions of California. Some groups lived along the Pacific coast. Others lived at Clear Lake and near San Francisco Bay. The largest group, however, lived on the western slopes of the Sierra Nevada and in the San Joaquin Valley.

These Miwoks lived in more than 100 different villages. They made their homes with wooden poles that were bent and gathered together. Bark, leaves, grasses, or plants covered the houses.

A Miwok village could have hundreds of houses. A large, round building in the center of the village was used as a meeting place, and each village had a sweat lodge.

As in most California tribes, the labor, or work, of a Miwok village was divided among different workers. Dividing the work among different workers is called **division of labor**. Division of labor made it easier for the village to meet its needs.

This round house at Indian Grinding Rock State Historic Park in Amador County is built to look like the ones used by the Miwoks.

In a division of labor, people often specialize (SPEH•shuh•lyz). To **specialize** is to work at one kind of job a person can do well. While some men in Miwok villages made arrow points from stone, others made bows or fish traps. Women used the grasses and reeds they gathered near rivers to weave baskets.

As in other California tribes, games were an important part of Miwok life. The games were fun, but they also taught children important skills they would need when they grew up. For example, there were relay races in which children passed a rock or stick to the next runner. This helped them learn to work together and to try hard. It made them fast and strong.

In one game two hoops made of willow branches were rolled from different sides of a field. At the very moment the hoops lined up with each other, a player would try to throw a long pole through both hoops at once. Being able to throw a stick at just the right time would make it easier to learn to spear a fish.

REVIEW How did games help Miwok children?

The Yokuts

"My words are tied in one with the great mountains . . . with the great trees." These words are part of an old Yokuts (YOH•kuhts) prayer. Trees were an important part of life for the Yokuts. Many large

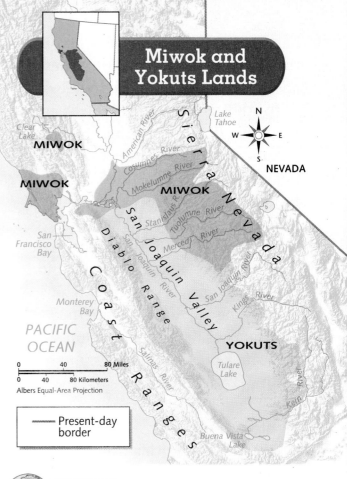

Miwok and Yokuts Lands

Region The Miwoks and Yokuts lived on neighboring lands in central California.

■ In which tribe's lands was Tulare Lake?

Like most other California tribes, the Yokuts made baskets for many purposes. Many of the baskets had interesting designs.

oak trees grew in the areas where they lived—the San Joaquin Valley and the foothills of the Sierra Nevada. A **foothill** is a low hill at the base of a mountain or a range of mountains. The Yokuts used the oak trees to build their homes, and they depended on acorns from these trees for food.

The houses of the Yokuts were built by the women of the village. To make the houses the women had to **cooperate**, or work together. They bent young oak branches and tied the branches together at the top. Then they stuck the tied branches into the ground. Grass or brush mats covered one side of the house, blocking out the strong sun.

Like most California tribes, the Yokuts used acorns as their main food.

Acorns, however, are too bitter to be eaten just as they are. Most California tribes followed the same steps to take away the bitter taste.

Each fall the Yokuts gathered thousands and thousands of acorns. They took off the shells and used stone tools to grind the acorns into flour. Then they soaked the acorn flour with hot water. This step was done as many times as it took to wash away the bitter taste. After that, they set the flour out to dry in the sun. It could then be cooked into hot cereal, baked into bread, made into pudding, or added to soups. Nuts and berries were added for flavor.

The Yokuts divided themselves into smaller groups. Each group lived in its own village and had its own leader and shaman. The people believed that the

Making Acorn Flour

1 Gather acorns from under oak trees.

2 Crush the acorns with rocks and take off the shells.

3 Use stone tools to grind the acorns into flour.

shaman had the power to heal them when they were sick.

The Yokuts had a way of getting news to the people in every village. A runner carried messages to nearby villages. Then, in each village, a village crier called out the news to the village's people.

Sometimes the news would be about a celebration, such as a good harvest of acorns, a birth, or a marriage. Then the people of the villages would gather to dance and sing.

REVIEW How did the Yokuts get news to the people in every village?

LEARNING FROM DIAGRAMS Like other Native Californians, the Yokuts used acorn flour to make cereal, bread, pudding, and soup. To improve the taste of these foods, they often added berries, nuts, and herbs.

■ Why did the Yokuts pour hot water over the acorn flour?

④ Sift the flour through a basket to get rid of any large pieces.

⑤ Pour hot water over the acorn flour to take away the bitter taste. Do this until the bitter taste is gone.

⑥ Dry the flour in the sun.

LESSON 3 REVIEW

Check Understanding

❶ **Remember the Facts** What were some important foods that tribes in the Central Valley ate?

❷ **Recall the Main Idea** How were the ways of life of the Native Californians who lived in the Central Valley and the mountains of California alike? How were they different?

Think Critically

❸ **Personally Speaking** Think of some of the games you like to play. Name some skills you are learning when you play those games.

❹ **Think More About It** It is very difficult to make acorns taste good. How do you think people figured out how to make a bitter food useful?

Show What You Know

Game Activity Think about an important skill that children need to learn. Then invent a game that teaches that skill. Your game can use only the natural resources around you. Teach your game to a group of classmates.

FOCUS

How do people today solve the problem of living in very dry, hot climates?

Main Idea Read to find out how the desert environment of the Mojave Indians affected how they lived.

Vocabulary

adapt
agriculture
spring
scarce

The Desert

Early people were able to **adapt**, or fit their ways, to living in every region of California. The land and its resources affected where they lived and the kinds of shelters they built. They ate what they could gather or catch. They made their clothing from what they could find.

The Mojaves (moh•HAH•vayz) lived in what is now called the Mojave Desert, on land that lies in the present-day states of California, Arizona, and Nevada. Much of this area has a very dry, hot climate. To adapt to their desert environment, the Mojaves developed a way of living that was different from that of most other California tribes.

Desert Farming

There was not as much food in the desert as in the other regions of California. The Mojaves did not have as many trees and grasses as the tribes of the Central Valley and the foothills of the Sierra Nevada did. They did not have seafood, as the tribes of the Coastal region did. To meet their need for food, the Mojaves learned to do something that most other

The Colorado River was the Mojaves' most important source of water. With water from the river, the Mojaves were able to grow such crops as corn (above).

Native Californians did not need to do. They developed **agriculture**, (A•grih•kuhl•cher), or farming.

Deserts are very dry places, but there are streams and even a few rivers. In fact, the name *Mojave* means "people who live on the river." The Mojave Indians built their homes along the banks of the Colorado River. It was the river that allowed them to grow crops in the desert.

The Colorado River was the Mojaves' most important source of water, but they did have other sources. They knew how to get water from cactuses and yucca plants. They also got water from desert springs. A **spring** is an opening in the Earth's surface through which water flows from under the ground.

It was the Colorado River, however, that made agriculture possible in the desert. The river begins high in the Rocky Mountains. It flows southwest to the Mojave Desert and then south into the Gulf of California. In spring, as the mountain snows melted and the spring rains began to fall, the river usually flooded. The Mojaves depended on the fine layer of silt left behind by the floods. In the fertile soil of the floodplain, they planted squash, watermelons, pumpkins, beans, and corn.

REVIEW Why did the Mojaves develop agriculture?

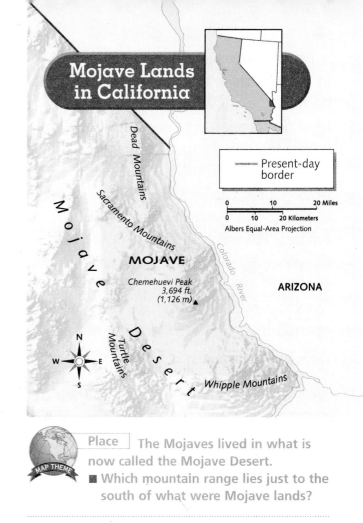

Mojave Lands in California

Present-day border

0   10   20 Miles
0   10   20 Kilometers
Albers Equal-Area Projection

Dead Mountains

Sacramento Mountains

Mojave Desert

MOJAVE

Chemehuevi Peak
3,694 ft.
(1,126 m)▲

Turtle Mountains

Whipple Mountains

Colorado River

ARIZONA

Place   The Mojaves lived in what is now called the Mojave Desert.
■ Which mountain range lies just to the south of what were Mojave lands?

Mojave Culture

The Mojaves did not get all of their food from agriculture. They also fished and hunted for food. They caught fish in the Colorado River by using nets, scoops, and fishing lines. They hunted small animals, such as rabbits, raccoons, and skunks. They also ate the meat of rattlesnakes and lizards.

Food sources are **scarce**, or limited, in the desert, so the Mojaves often traveled over a wide area to gather food. From season to season, they went where they could find berries, figs, and roots. They gathered the fruits of the prickly pear cactus and the bean pods of the honey mesquite (muh•SKEET) bushes. They also gathered nuts from the piñon (PIN•yohn) pine tree. They shook the pine cones down from the trees and roasted them. The heat opened the pine cones, freeing the pine nuts inside.

Mojave houses were large rectangles with mud-covered grass roofs to keep out the hot desert sun. The sides of the houses were often left open. This allowed any breezes to blow through. Some houses were large enough for many families to live together.

Most of the California Indians made baskets for storing items and for cooking. The Mojaves, however, did not have much grass for making baskets. But they did have plenty of clay for making pottery. They used clay pots for cooking as well as for storing food.

CULTURE

California Native Americans Today

More than 240,000 Native Americans whose ancestors lived in what is now the United States live in California today. They belong to more than 100 different tribes. In fact, only the state of Oklahoma has more Native Americans than California has.

Many of California's Native Americans live and work in cities and towns or on ranches. Others live on special lands set aside by the government for use by Indians. On these lands, Indians have their own government. No matter where they live, however, Indian people are working hard to preserve their cultures. Many still follow the ways of their ancestors and study their native languages.

Many tribes participated in this powwow, or celebration, in San Francisco.

The Mojaves used their resources carefully and well, but they could not make everything they needed. More than most other groups, they used trade to meet many of their needs. They traded things they grew or made, such as yellow squash, corn, pumpkins, and clay pots, for shell beads, wooden bowls, and other things they could not grow or make in their own lands.

The Mojaves traveled about 150 miles (241 km) on foot through the desert to trade with the Chumash. To get there faster, they ran most of the way. Today people still follow some of the paths the Mojaves traveled. Interstate 40 and the Burlington Northern Santa Fe Railroad both run along old Mojave trails in California.

About 400 years ago the Mojaves saw Europeans for the first time. These people were from Spain. Over time more Europeans arrived, bringing great changes to all of California.

REVIEW Besides farming, how else did the Mojaves meet their needs?

Very few examples of Mojave buildings remain today. Archaeologists have found pottery artifacts like the one above in what were Mojave lands.

LESSON 4 REVIEW

Check Understanding

1 Remember the Facts How did the Mojaves use the Colorado River for agriculture?

2 Recall the Main Idea How did the Mojaves adapt their ways of life to their desert environment?

Think Critically

3 Think More About It Why might builders of highways and railroads decide to follow old Native American trails?

4 Link to You How have the people where you live adapted to their environment?

Show What You Know
Storytelling Activity
Make up a legend about how the Mojaves learned to adapt their way of life to their desert environment. Use animals from the region as characters in your story. When you have finished your story, tell it to the class.

CHAPTER 2 REVIEW

10,000 years ago

10,000 years ago
• Early people may have reached what is now California

CONNECT MAIN IDEAS

Use this organizer to show that you understand how Native Californians used natural resources to meet their needs. Write one way the people of each Indian group used the natural resources around them. A copy of the organizer may be found on page 24 of the Activity Book.

The Earliest Californians

The Coast

Yuroks

Hoopas

Chumash

The Desert

Mojaves

The Central Valley and the Mountains

Maidus

Miwoks

Yokuts

WRITE MORE ABOUT IT

Write a Report Imagine that you are an archaeologist who has found an artifact made by Native Californians. Write a report that explains what the artifact is and how it was used.

Write an Imaginative Narrative Imagine that you are a Chumash boy or girl. Write about a day in your village. Describe your village, and tell how people there meet their needs.

5,000 years ago
• People began to gather in villages

500 years ago
• More than 1 of every 10 American Indians in what is now the United States lived in California

USE VOCABULARY

Use each vocabulary term in a sentence that helps explain its meaning.

1. culture
2. religion
3. trade
4. tradition
5. government
6. ancestor
7. division of labor
8. specialize
9. agriculture
10. scarce

CHECK UNDERSTANDING

11. How did the early peoples of California meet their needs after the giant animals became extinct?

12. How did the Yuroks use the large trees that grew around them?

13. What natural resource did the Chumash have that other tribes in the Coastal region did not have?

14. What was the main food for the Maidus and for most other California tribes?

15. Why were games an important part of Miwok life?

16. How were the Mojaves different from most other California tribes?

THINK CRITICALLY

17. **Past to Present** How did the division of labor help Native Californians meet their needs? How does it help Californians meet their needs today?

18. **Explore Viewpoints** How might the way the Mojaves thought about water have been different from the way the Yuroks thought about it?

APPLY SKILLS

Use Tables to Group Information
Make a table that compares the foods of the Indian tribes in the four natural regions of California.

Identify Causes and Their Effect
Think about something that has happened at school—maybe you got a good grade, made a team, won an award, or met a new friend. List the causes of that effect.

READ MORE ABOUT IT

Fire Race: A Karuk Coyote Tale About How Fire Came to the People retold by Jonathan London with Lanny Pinola. Chronicle Books.
This Karuk legend is like one told by many other groups in northwestern California.

HARCOURT BRACE

Visit the Internet at **http://www.hbschool.com** for additional resources.

PRESERVING CULTURES

Today many Native Americans in California are working to preserve, or keep alive, their cultures. Ahmium (ah•MY•uhm) Education is an organization that runs cultural programs for Indian groups in southern California. One of its goals is to help young Native Americans learn their traditional languages and music.

In 1998, Ahmium members performed at the Super Bowl in San Diego. Girls and boys sang and danced to traditional songs. The songs are called bird songs, says Michael Mirelez, a Cahuilla (ka•WEE•ah) Indian, because "the people used to follow the migration [seasonal journey] of the birds."

Paul Cuero, a Kumeyaay (KOO•mee•eye) Indian, is a well-known bird singer. He teaches the young singers and dancers. "Our songs are a link to the past, to who our ancestors are, and it's important that we carry that on." Ten-year-old Jessica of the Kumeyaay tribe says, "The dancing makes me feel good inside, and it helps to keep us together."

Drums (right) and rattles (above) are often used in Native American music.

Paul Cuero (left) teaches young people the traditional songs and dances of his tribe.

Think and Apply

Think about how the Ahmium members are working to preserve Native American cultures in southern California. Then think about the many cultures that are represented in your classroom and in your community. Brainstorm some ways you and others could learn about and help preserve these cultures.

HARCOURT BRACE
Visit the Internet at **http://www.hbschool.com** for additional resources.

CNN Turner Le@rning
Check your media center or classroom video library for the Making Social Studies Relevant videotape of this feature.

These young people are performing a traditional Native American dance at a rally in Jamul, California. By learning Native American dances, they, and the members of Ahmium who performed at the 1998 Super Bowl in San Diego, are helping to preserve their cultures.

UNIT 1 REVIEW

Summarize the Main Ideas
Study the pictures and captions to help you review what you read about in Unit 1.

Draw Another Scene
Choose one of the California Indian tribes described in Unit 1 but not shown here. Draw a scene showing how the people used natural resources in their daily life. Tell where your scene would go on the visual summary.

1 California has four natural regions—the Coastal region, the Mountain region, the Central Valley region, and the Desert region.

3 The Chumash lived in the Coastal region of southern California. They made their homes by bending poles, tying them together, and covering them with layers of grasses. The Chumash used tar to make their canoes waterproof.

2 The Yuroks lived in the Coastal region of northern California. They used redwood and cedar planks to build their homes. They built **weirs** to catch salmon.

4 The Yokuts lived in the San Joaquin Valley and the foothills of the Sierra Nevada. They used stone tools to grind acorns, their main food, into flour.

5 The Mojaves lived in the Desert region. Because there was little food and water there, the Mojaves learned to farm near the Colorado River.

UNIT 1
REVIEW

USE VOCABULARY

Write the term that correctly matches each definition.

artifact   drought

delta   irrigation

1. the use of canals, ditches, or pipes to carry water to dry areas

2. land that builds up at a river's mouth

3. a long time with little or no rain

4. any object made by people in the past

CHECK UNDERSTANDING

5. Why is California an important crossroads?

6. What are California's four natural regions? In which one of these regions do most Californians live today?

7. Which two river systems drain most of the Central Valley?

8. Why did trade develop among the California tribes?

9. Why did the Mojaves develop a way of life that was different from that of most other Native Californians?

THINK CRITICALLY

10. **Cause and Effect** How do California's location and its different elevations affect the climate in different parts of the state?

11. **Think More About It** In what ways were the early peoples of California alike? In what ways were they different?

APPLY SKILLS

Use a Land Use and Resource Map The map below uses color to show how the land in central California is used. It uses picture symbols to show where certain resources are found. Use the map to answer these questions.

12. How is most of the land between Oakland and San Jose used?

13. How is most of the land near the San Joaquin River used?

14. Near which central California city is boron mined?

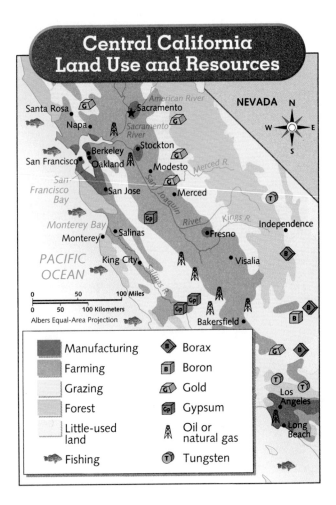

Central California Land Use and Resources

REMEMBER

- Share your ideas.
- Cooperate with others to plan your work.
- Take responsibility for your work.
- Help one another.
- Show your group's work to the class.
- Discuss what you learned by working together.

ACTIVITY

Make a Relief Map

Work in a group to make a relief map of California. First, draw an outline map of the state on a sheet of posterboard, and color the major bodies of water. Then, use construction paper, clay, papier-mâché, or foam egg cartons to show the Sierra Nevada, the Cascades, and the Coast Ranges. Color your map to show different elevations, and create a map key. Display your group's map in the classroom.

ACTIVITY

Paint a Mural

Work with a group of classmates to paint a mural about California's four natural regions. Show a scene from each, using pictures in your textbook and in library books for ideas. When the mural is complete, each group member should write facts about a place or an activity it shows. Present the mural and the facts to your class.

ACTIVITY

Perform a Simulation

With a group of classmates, role-play a scene about catching and preparing salmon. Think about all the steps that must be followed, and decide how to show each one. During the role-play, each performer should explain what he or she is doing and why.

Unit Project Wrap-Up

Build a Diorama Work with a partner to finish the Unit Project described on page 39. First, review the notes that you and your partner took as you read this unit. Next, decide what you will show in your diorama. Remember that it should show how early people used natural resources to meet their needs. Then, build your diorama inside a box. Add your diorama to a classroom display.

NEWCOMERS
TO CALIFORNIA

For thousands of years Native Americans were the only people living in North and South America. Then, starting with Christopher Columbus in 1492, explorers from Europe began sailing across the Atlantic Ocean. Before long, ship after ship was arriving in the Americas.

In the 1500s, Spanish explorers traveled north from Mexico and claimed what is now California for Spain. Later, settlers came to live in California. For Native Californians, life would never be the same.

◀ The painting *Mission San Carlos Borromeo del Carmel* was painted in 1895 by Edwin Deakin.

UNIT THEMES

- Commonality and Diversity
- Conflict and Cooperation
- Continuity and Change
- Individualism and Interdependence

Unit Project

Present Scenes About Historic Events Complete this project as you study Unit 2. Work with a group of classmates to create scenes about historic events in California. As you read this unit, choose at least four events that you want to show, and take notes about each. Your group can use these notes to write the story of each event. The stories will be read aloud as your scenes are presented.

130°W

40°N

ROCKY MOUNTAINS

GREAT PLAINS

Missouri River

Mississippi River

Snake River

Coast Ranges

San Francisco Bay

San Francisco (Yerba Buena)

San José

Monterey Bay

Monterey

ALTA CALIFORNIA

Sierra Nevada

Sacramento River

San Joaquin River

GREAT BASIN

Great Salt Lake

Colorado River

Platte River

Arkansas River

Los Angeles

Mojave Desert

San Diego Bay

San Diego

30°N

Santa Fe

PACIFIC OCEAN

Tucson

Tubac

El Paso del Norte

Rio Grande

Los Adaes

BAJA CALIFORNIA

Gulf of California

Loreto

MEXICO

Tropic of Cancer

120°W

La Paz

Mexico City

| 1500 | 1550 | 1600 | 1650 |

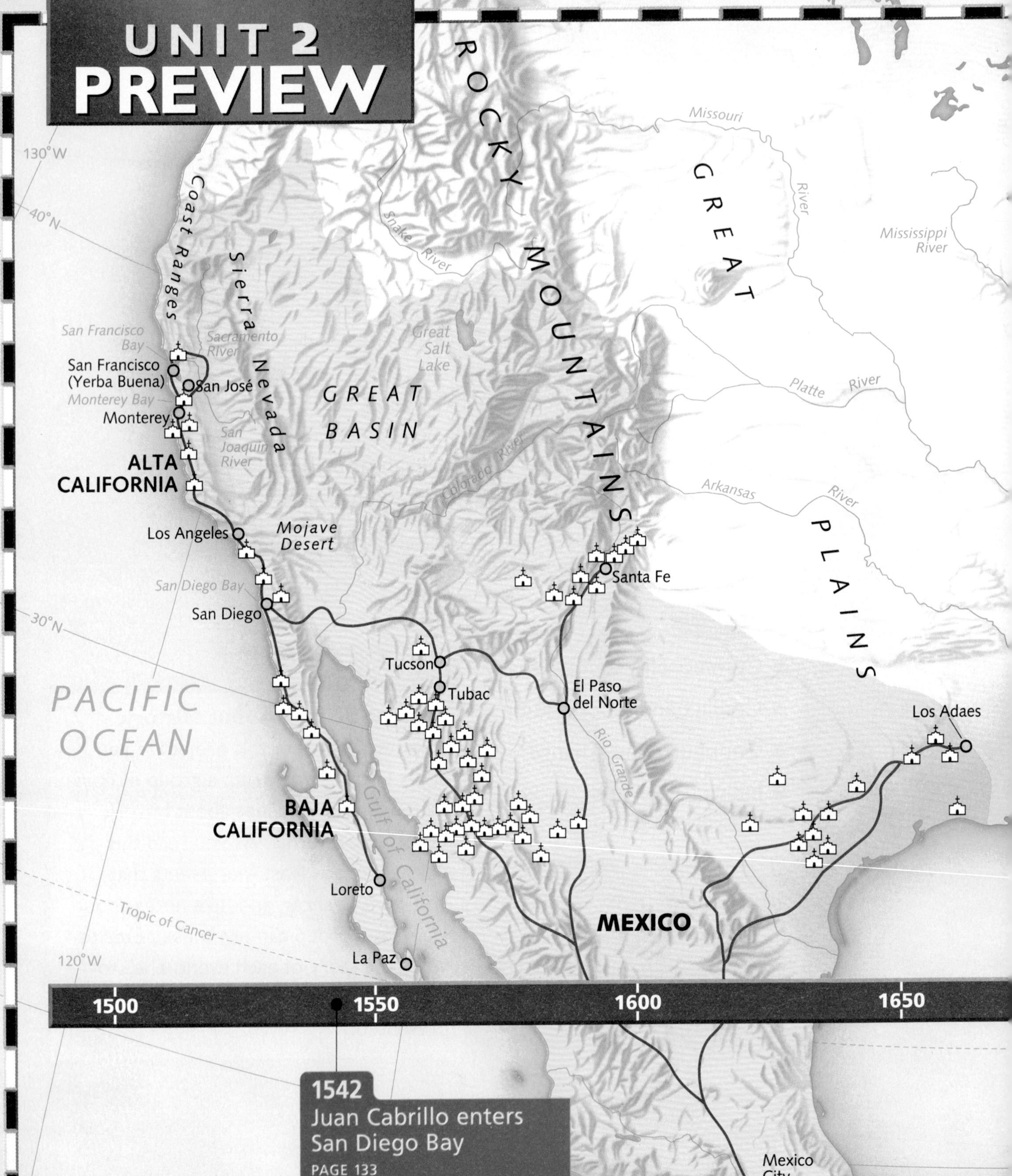

1542
Juan Cabrillo enters San Diego Bay
PAGE 133

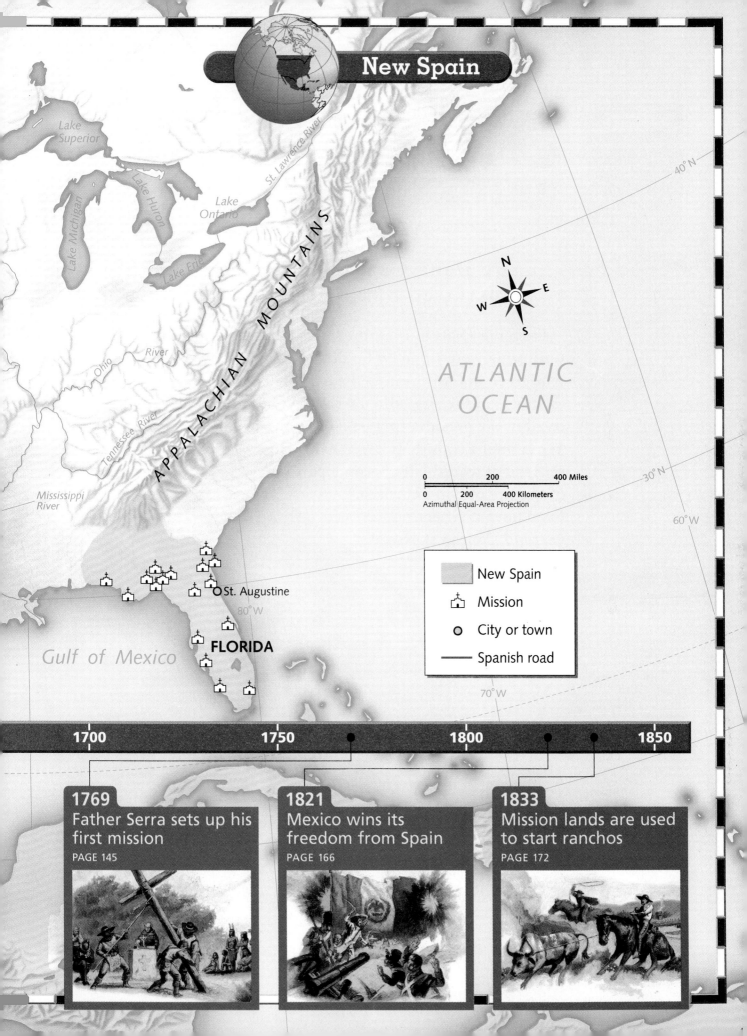

New Spain

ATLANTIC OCEAN

40° N

30° N

60° W

70° W

80° W

Lake Superior
Lake Michigan
Lake Huron
Lake Ontario
Lake Erie
St. Lawrence River
APPALACHIAN MOUNTAINS
Ohio River
Tennessee River
Mississippi River
Gulf of Mexico
St. Augustine
FLORIDA

0   200   400 Miles
0   200   400 Kilometers
Azimuthal Equal-Area Projection

Legend
New Spain
Mission
City or town
Spanish road

Timeline
1700 — 1750 — 1800 — 1850

1769
Father Serra sets up his first mission
PAGE 145

1821
Mexico wins its freedom from Spain
PAGE 166

1833
Mission lands are used to start ranchos
PAGE 172

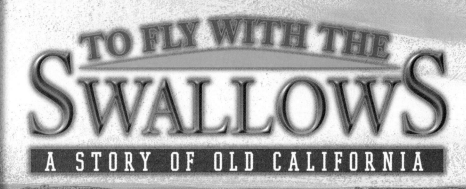

TO FLY WITH THE SWALLOWS

A STORY OF OLD CALIFORNIA

by Dana Catharine de Ruiz
illustrated by Lori Lohstoeter

From the 1500s to 1821, the lands that now make up California were ruled by Spain. Among the few settlers who lived in California in the early 1800s were the members of the Argüello (ar·GWAY·yoh) family. They lived in the presidio (pray·SEE·dee·oh), or fort, at Yerba Buena (YAIR·bah BWAY·nah). This settlement would later become part of the city of San Francisco. Read now as fifteen-year-old Concha starts another day at the lonely presidio.

Concha stirred in her bed as the morning birds chirped and sang. The sunlight filtered in through the cracks in the wooden shutters. It was April of 1806. Fifteen-year-old Concha—María de la Concepción Marcela Argüello y Moraga—stretched out her arms and yawned. She climbed out of bed carefully so as not to disturb the sleep of her little sisters. She smoothed the dark curls from Ana Paula's forehead and kissed Gertrudis's damp brow.

There were 15 Argüello children. Two were no longer at home. But still there was not much room, so Concha shared a room and a bed with two of her sisters. Even though their father was *comandante*—commander—of the presidio of Yerba Buena, the Argüello house was not much grander than its neighbors.

Once out of bed, Concha ran softly to the little window cut into the thick adobe wall. She threw open the

adobe
(ah•DOH•bay)
a kind of clay that can be dried into bricks

shutters and leaned so far out that her feet were no longer touching the floor. Swinging her feet back and forth reminded her of being a little girl in a big chair, unable to reach the floor. She smothered a laugh with her hand.

From her window, Concha could see over the thatched roofs of the other houses of the presidio to the bay. This was the border of Alta California, the northernmost point of the Spanish Empire in North America. This was the end of the world, she thought. There was the Pacific Ocean. Its blue waters, stretching endlessly west, carried frail ships to faraway places—Japan and China and Russia! But that was another world away.

thatched
covered with grass

Concha looked down on the nearby homes of the soldiers of her father's command. They and their families lived beneath the thatched roofs of the presidio houses. The soldiers in Yerba Buena were there to protect Spain's claim to this land. The British and French were interested in this land. So were the Russians.

Right next door to Concha's house, in the center of the presidio, was the church. It was [at] the center of their lives as well.

Concha could see the sun as it rose over San Francisco Bay. The bay was named by the Spanish for St. Francis. Concha thought that St. Francis would have been pleased. The bay area was a wonderful place for animals, and the saint had loved animals greatly.

She could see small groups of deer coming down through the woodlands to look for food along the water's edge. Playful sea otters romped and frolicked in the bay. Concha knew that their fur was very valuable and that many traders would come to Yerba Buena if the government of Spain allowed it. But it did not.

Spain did not even encourage visitors from other countries. It had been a very long time since any ship had sailed into the bay. This was partly because of Spanish policy, but mostly it was because Alta California was such a long way from Europe or Asia.

Concha looked up. The *golondrinas*—the swallows that had returned barely two weeks ago—were joyfully diving and swooping above the water. How graceful they were!

Oh! To be like the swallows! Free and able to fly away to distant lands when they were tired of the too quiet life of Alta California! Perhaps they had flown to Mexico City. Perhaps they had nestled in the eaves of the houses of her cousins who dressed in fine silks and danced the elegant new European dance steps. How long would it take the swallows to fly to Mexico City? To travel overland, Concha knew, would take close to eight months.

frolicked played

policy a plan of action

eaves the part of the roof that hangs over the walls of a building

SPANISH CALIFORNIA

"[The Aztecs]
live almost
like those
in Spain, . . .
it is truly
remarkable to
see what they
have achieved
in all things."

Hernando Cortés
(er•NAN•doh
kawr•TEZ), Spanish
explorer, 1521

Explorers Arrive from Mexico

| 1500 | 1550 | 1600 | 1650 |

The lives of Native Californians were changed forever by an explorer who never saw California. In August 1492 Christopher Columbus set sail from Spain, a country in Europe. He was looking for a new way to reach Asia, where he wanted to trade for silk, gold, and spices. The trip from Europe to Asia by land was long and dangerous. Columbus hoped to reach Asia easier and faster by sailing west across the Atlantic Ocean.

On October 12 Columbus finally reached land. He thought he had landed in Asia, but he was really at a small island off North America. Europeans did not know about North and South America then.

When Columbus returned to Spain, he told of the lands he had found. Soon other explorers sailed to the Americas. Some of them dreamed of finding riches. Others wanted to change the beliefs of the Native Americans, or convert them, to Christianity. "We came here to serve God and the King and also to get rich," said one Spanish explorer.

Hernando Cortés

In the 1500s Spanish explorers claimed large areas of North and South America for Spain. These explorers became known as **conquistadors** (kahn•KEES•tuh•dawrz), "conquerors."

FOCUS
Why do people explore new places today?

Main Idea Read to learn why Spain sent explorers to what is now California.

Vocabulary
conquistador
strait
peninsula
expedition
port
galleon
ocean current
barrier
colony

To protect themselves in battles, Spanish conquistadors wore metal armor (left). Tools such as an astrolabe (above) helped explorers find their location by the position of the stars.

Chapter 3 • **131**

Cortés and his soldiers were amazed by the Aztecs (above) and their treasures, like this gold ring (right).

One of the best known conquistadors was Hernando Cortés (er•NAN•doh kawr•TEZ). Cortés had heard stories of great wealth among the Aztec Indians in Mexico. In 1519 he and more than 500 soldiers set out to conquer the Aztecs.

After landing on the east coast of Mexico and defeating the Indians there, Cortés and his followers set out for Tenochtitlán (tay•nohch•teet•LAHN), the Aztec capital. Along the way they were joined by large numbers of Indians who were enemies of the Aztecs.

In Tenochtitlán the Spaniards found the treasures of gold and jewels they were seeking. They tore down the Aztec temples and later destroyed the city. On the ruins of Tenochtitlán they built Mexico City, which became the capital of New Spain. New Spain included Mexico and parts of what is today the Southwest region of the United States. By the middle 1500s, California was also part of New Spain.

Spanish explorers had heard stories of a body of water that connected the Atlantic and Pacific oceans. They called this waterway the Strait of Anián (ah•nee•AHN). A **strait** is a narrow channel that connects two larger bodies of water. The explorers hoped the Strait of Anián would be a shortcut to Asia. If they could find this strait, Spanish ships would not have to sail all the way around South America to reach Asia.

Cortés sailed north from Mexico's west coast in search of the Strait of Anián. In 1535 he reached Baja (BAH•hah) California, which is now part of Mexico. *Baja* means "low" in Spanish. At the time, the Spanish thought Baja California was an island. Later they learned that it is really a peninsula (puh•NIN•suh•luh). A **peninsula** is land that has water almost all around it.

Cortés claimed the land of Baja California for Spain, but this was his last journey to the Americas. He returned to Spain in 1540 without ever finding the Strait of Anián.

REVIEW **What people did Cortés conquer?**

The Cabrillo Expedition

The next Spanish expedition to look for the Strait of Anián was led by Juan Rodríguez Cabrillo (roh•DREE•gays kah•BREE•yoh). An **expedition** is a trip made for a special reason, such as to explore a place or find a treasure.

In June 1542 Cabrillo's expedition set out to explore the area Spain called Alta California. *Alta* means "high" in Spanish. The region is "higher," or farther north, than Baja California.

Cabrillo sailed north from the Mexican port of Navidad. A **port** is a trading center where ships are loaded and unloaded. In September 1542 Cabrillo entered what is now called San Diego Bay.

HISTORY

California's Name

Several years before the conquistadors came to the Americas, a popular book in Spain described a fictional island ruled by a queen named Calafia. The island was said to be full of "gold and precious stones." Many Spanish explorers dreamed of finding such an island and becoming rich.

When explorers reached the Baja Peninsula, they thought it was an island and called it California for Queen Calafia. Soon the whole area north and west of Mexico was called California.

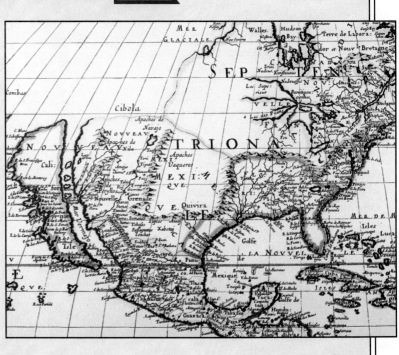

When this map was drawn in 1650, mapmakers thought that California was an island.

Farther north, Cabrillo met the Chumash Indians. While on San Miguel Island, Cabrillo fell and hurt himself. Still in pain, he sailed farther north, searching for the Strait of Anián. But bad weather forced the expedition to return to San Miguel Island. There Cabrillo died from his injury, which had never healed.

Spain learned much about the land and people of Alta California from Cabrillo's expedition. But these explorers found no treasures and no shortcut to Asia.

REVIEW **What part of California did Cabrillo explore?**

Cabrillo's expedition is still remembered in California. This painting (below) in the Santa Barbara County Courthouse shows Cabrillo landing in Alta California. The statue of Cabrillo (right) is part of Cabrillo National Monument in San Diego.

Spanish Trading Ships

In the 1560s Spain began sending large trading ships across the Pacific Ocean from New Spain to the Philippine (FIH•luh•peen) Islands in Asia. These **galleons** (GA•lee•uhnz) carried silver that had been mined in New Spain. They returned from the Philippines carrying spices, silk, and jewels. They also carried people from China and the Philippines. These people worked in Mexico as sailors and servants.

The galleons sailed for the Philippines every year from Mexico. On their return trips, the sailors steered the galleons north and east to use the winds and ocean currents that would bring them across the Pacific to Alta California. An **ocean current** is a stream of water that moves through the ocean.

This long, difficult voyage took seven to nine months. The sailors often ran out of fresh water, and their food spoiled. The Spanish needed a port in California where the sailors could get fresh food and water and repair the galleons. This would make it possible for more ships to return safely to Mexico.

Soon Spain had another reason to want to settle California. In the 1570s England sent ships to attack Spanish ports and ships. England called its sailors "sea dogs," but the Spanish called them pirates. One of the most feared English sailors was Francis Drake.

A Spanish Galleon

LEARNING FROM DIAGRAMS Galleons were about 140 feet (43 m) long and 36 feet (11 m) wide. Every bit of space was used to house sailors and to store supplies and goods for trade.
■ How many levels are shown below this ship's deck?

In 1577 Drake crossed the Atlantic Ocean. Battling terrible storms, he sailed through the Strait of Magellan at the southern tip of South America to reach the Pacific Ocean. He became the first English sailor to reach the west coast of the Americas.

Along the way Drake captured treasure from several ports in New Spain. From one galleon alone he took 80 pounds (36 kg) of gold. What a surprise it must have been for the Spanish to find an English ship in the Pacific! Until then, no other European countries except for Spain had sailed there.

Drake continued north to the California coast. He wrote that he had sailed through fogs north of what is now San Francisco and found a "convenient and fit harbor." He said that he had left a marker there, claiming the land for England's Queen Elizabeth.

Many historians today do not believe that Drake sailed as far north along the California coast as he claimed. However, his attack on Spanish trading ships in the Pacific Ocean was a strong challenge to Spain's power.

REVIEW How did Francis Drake threaten Spain?

The Vizcaíno Expedition

In 1602 Spain sent Sebastián Vizcaíno (vees•kah•EE•noh) from New Spain to map the coast of Alta California. He was to look for a good harbor where Spanish galleons returning from the Philippines could stop for supplies and repairs.

Vizcaíno sailed north to San Diego Bay. He wrote that he was greeted there by Indians "in canoes of cedar and pine." He then continued north to Monterey Bay, which seemed to him a perfect place for settlers. "It was a very good port, and well protected from all winds," Vizcaíno reported.

REVIEW What location did Vizcaíno think would be a perfect place for settlers?

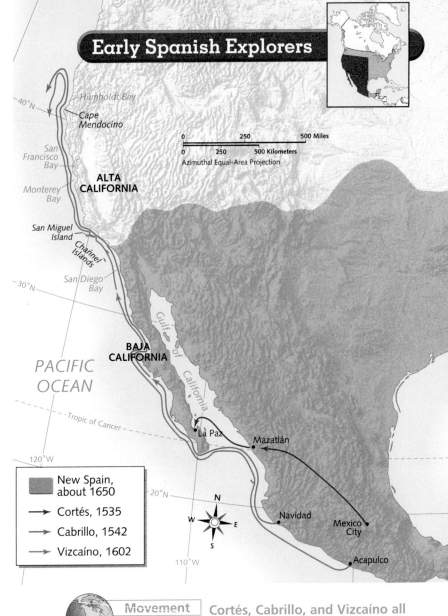

Early Spanish Explorers

Legend:
- New Spain, about 1650
- → Cortés, 1535
- → Cabrillo, 1542
- → Vizcaíno, 1602

Movement Cortés, Cabrillo, and Vizcaíno all explored the coast of California.
■ Which explorer went only as far north as Baja California?

Challenges of Location

Spain did not follow Vizcaíno's advice and, over time, lost interest in settling Alta California. In fact, 165 years passed before it sent settlers to the area around Monterey Bay.

New Spain's geography made it difficult to get settlers to go to California. California was far from Mexico City, and there were many barriers to travel. A **barrier** is something that blocks the way or makes it hard to get from place to place. Tall mountains and hot deserts separated California from the rest of New Spain. They made travel by land very hard.

Even by ship, travel to California was difficult. Ships often faced bad storms, strong winds, blinding rains and fogs, and tricky ocean currents.

Instead of going to Monterey Bay, Spanish settlers traveled to what is now

Texas, New Mexico, and Arizona. These parts of New Spain were easier to reach from Mexico than California was.

While Spain was building settlements in those areas of New Spain and in other parts of North America, other European countries were busy starting colonies of their own. A **colony** is a settlement set up and ruled by a faraway country. England, which later became part of Great Britain, settled 13 colonies along the Atlantic coast of what is now the United States. France founded colonies farther north, in what is now Canada.

REVIEW How was California's geography a barrier for new settlers?

MAP THEME Regions In 1750, four European countries had colonies in North America.
■ Which country built settlements along the Great Lakes?

Europeans in North America, 1750

ARCTIC OCEAN

60°N

500   1,000 Miles
500   1,000 Kilometers
Azimuthal Equal-Area Projection

60°N

50°W

140°W

Hudson Bay

ROCKY MOUNTAINS

PACIFIC OCEAN

30°N

APPALACHIAN MTS.

13 BRITISH COLONIES

30°N

N
W   E
S

Gulf of Mexico

ATLANTIC OCEAN

110°W

Caribbean Sea

80°W

0°

British   Russian
Disputed   Spanish
French   Unexplored

LESSON 1 REVIEW

1500	1550	1600	1650

1535
• Hernando Cortés reaches Baja California

1542
• Juan Cabrillo explores Alta California

1602
• Sebastián Vizcaíno sails to the San Diego and Monterey bays

Check Understanding

1 Remember the Facts What waterway were Cortés and Cabrillo searching for?

2 Recall the Main Idea Why did Spain send explorers to California?

Think Critically

3 Explore Viewpoints Why do you think England called its sailors "sea dogs," while the Spanish called them pirates?

4 Think More About It What did Spain hope to gain from exploring California?

Show What You Know

Writing Activity Imagine that you are on one of the early expeditions to Alta California. Write a letter home, describing what you hope to do on your journey. Also tell about one of the places you have visited.

Follow Routes on

1. Why Learn This Skill?

A historical map gives information about a place as it was in the past. It may show where cities or towns, now long gone, were once located. It may show where an important event took place. It may also show the **route**, or path, that people followed as they traveled from one place

to another. Knowing how to follow a route on a historical map can help you better understand the past and gather information about it.

2. Understand the Process

The title of a historical map often tells you the subject and the time period the map

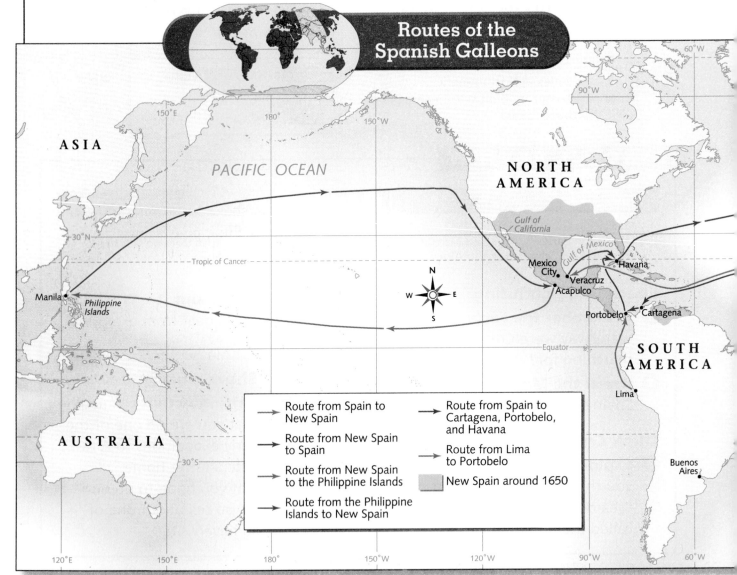

Routes of the Spanish Galleons

Legend:
- → Route from Spain to New Spain
- → Route from New Spain to Spain
- → Route from New Spain to the Philippine Islands
- → Route from the Philippine Islands to New Spain
- → Route from Spain to Cartagena, Portobelo, and Havana
- → Route from Lima to Portobelo
- New Spain around 1650

a Historical Map

shows. The map below shows some of the main routes the Spanish galleons sailed in the 1500s.

Many Spanish galleons traveled across the Atlantic Ocean from Spain to New Spain and other parts of the Americas. They carried goods from Spain, which they traded for silver and other riches found in New Spain.

Other galleons sailed all the way around the tip of South America to reach ports on New Spain's west coast. From there the galleons could sail west across the Pacific Ocean to trade in the Philippine Islands. They carried silver from New Spain and traded it for spices, silk, and jewels. Then they took these goods back to New Spain to be sold. Some of the goods were shipped to Spain and sold in Europe.

Look at the map key to learn what the symbols stand for. Then use these questions to help you learn more about the Spanish galleons' routes.

❶ What color shows the route from Spain to New Spain?

❷ In what direction did the galleons sail to reach New Spain from Spain?

❸ What color shows the route from New Spain to the Philippine Islands? from the Philippine Islands to New Spain?

3. Think and Apply

Review the map showing the routes of Cortés, Cabrillo, and Vizcaíno on page 136. Write five questions about their routes that this map can answer. Then exchange papers with a partner. You and your partner can answer each other's questions and explain how you used the map to answer each one.

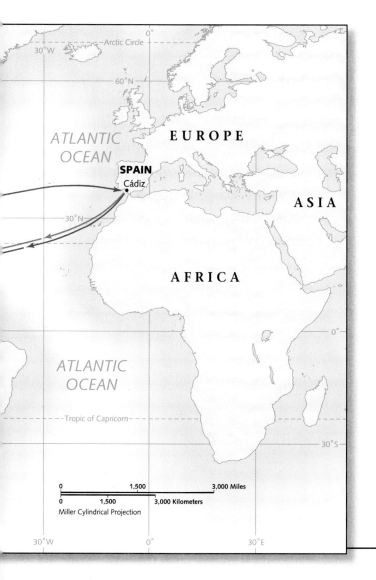

How Should Mars

Long ago, people came to explore California by land and water. Today, Californians are still exploring. They are helping people everywhere learn about new places—places in outer space.

On July 4, 1997, a spacecraft called *Pathfinder* landed on Mars. Out of the door of the spacecraft and onto the planet's surface rolled a rover named *Sojourner*. A rover is a robot machine that moves around and gathers information. *Sojourner* took photographs of Mars and beamed them back to Earth. This amazing machine was built by scientists at Pasadena's Jet Propulsion Laboratory.

Now many people are asking what the next step should be in exploring space. Some people say that astronauts should be sent to Mars. They believe that humans today need to continue to explore the unknown, just as they did long ago. Some even imagine a time when people will live on Mars.

Other people say that humans do not need to go to Mars. Information can be gathered by machines like *Sojourner*. These people believe that sending humans to Mars is too expensive and too dangerous.

Story Musgrave

Story Musgrave is a retired astronaut who flew in space six times. He says,

> "I would like to see programs that do not devour [use up] our resources on space. . . . We don't have to fly humans."

The rover *Sojourner* (right) explored and took photographs of the surface of Mars (below).

Be Explored?

Bruce Murray

Bruce Murray is a professor at the California Institute of Technology. He reminds people about the *Challenger* accident in 1986, when seven astronauts were killed. He says,

66 *Challenger's* sad legacy [lesson] was to remind us that humans should *not* be sent into space except for purposes worth risking lives for. 99

Carl Sagan

Carl Sagan was a scientist who believed that human travel to Mars would be a good idea. He said,

66 A human mission to Mars would provide a sense of adventure. It would help to stimulate [excite] a new generation of scientists, and it would make all people feel a little more optimistic [hopeful] about what we can do as a planet. 99

Compare Viewpoints

1. What is each person's point of view about space exploration?

2. Does Story Musgrave agree with Carl Sagan's viewpoint? How do you know?

3. Is it possible to tell from what Bruce Murray said whether he believes in sending humans to Mars? Explain your answer.

4. Which viewpoint do you agree with? Give reasons for your answer.

Think and Apply

Imagine two people who disagree about whether or not it is important to send people to Mars. Work with a partner to write a dialogue in which the two people discuss their different points of view. Then act out their discussion for the class.

FOCUS
Why might people today start new settlements?

Main Idea Read to learn about the different kinds of settlements Spain built in Alta California.

Vocabulary
mission
missionary
presidio
pueblo

Settling Alta California

1760	1775	1790

Spain paid little attention to Alta California until the 1760s. Then King Carlos III of Spain heard that other countries, such as Russia, had started to explore the Pacific coast of North America. To protect Spanish claims, King Carlos ordered that settlements be built in Alta California.

The Spanish Return

King Carlos gave this order after he heard that Russia had set up a colony in Alaska. The king worried that Russian fur traders would move south from Alaska. They might try to set up a colony in California.

Starting a Spanish colony in Alta California was not easy, however. Travel to California was difficult, and few people wanted to move so far away. Spain decided

The Spanish flag (above) was already flying over colonies in what is now Texas, New Mexico, and Arizona when Spain built its first mission in Alta California, San Diego de Alcalá (below).

The *San Carlos* sailed from the town of La Paz, in Baja California, for San Diego Bay on January 9, 1769. In later years the ship sailed back and forth between Alta and Baja California, carrying supplies.

that the best way to start a colony was to build **missions**, or religious settlements.

Missions were run by missionaries. A **missionary** is a person who teaches his or her religion to others. In California the missionaries were Catholic priests or other church workers who believed it was their duty to teach the Native Californians about Christianity.

The missions had many uses. Their main goals were to convert the Indians to Christianity and to teach them Spanish ways. But the missions also brought in people for the new colony in Alta California. Spain hoped the missions would raise crops and make money for the colony, too.

REVIEW What did Spain decide was the best way to start a colony in Alta California?

The Search for Monterey

In 1769 José de Gálvez (GAHL•ves), the chief government official in New Spain, planned four expeditions to settle the San Diego and Monterey bay areas. His plan called for two of the expeditions to travel by land across the Baja Peninsula. The other two would travel to Alta California by sea. All four expeditions were to meet at San Diego Bay, which Sebastián Vizcaíno had visited in 1602.

Gálvez chose Gaspar de Portolá (pawr•toh•LAH), an army captain and government official, as the leader of one land expedition. Traveling with Portolá were several soldiers, many Native Americans, and a priest named Junípero Serra (hoo•NEE•pay•roh SEH•rah).

Spanish soldiers, like the one pictured here, went along on land expeditions to Alta California to protect the travelers.

Father Serra was in charge of setting up the missions.

The other land expedition was led by Fernando Rivera y Moncada (ree•VAY•rah ee mohn•KAH•dah), an army captain. Traveling with him were more soldiers and Indians and a priest named Juan Crespi (KRAYS•pee).

Life on the trail was difficult. Many of the travelers got sick, and some died. Each day brought many new problems—crossing hot, sun-baked plains or climbing steep hills. Often the travelers had little water. In his diary Father Crespi described the land as "lacking grass and water, and abounding in stones and thorns."

By April 1769 the sailing expeditions sent by Gálvez had reached San Diego Bay. The first ship to arrive, the *San Antonio*, sailed into the bay on April 11, just 54 days after leaving Mexico. But the second ship, the *San Carlos*, did not arrive until April 29. It had sailed from Mexico first, but it had been blown off course. It took 110 days to reach San Diego Bay. Most of those on board were sick or dying because they had run out of food and water.

Then in May, Captain Rivera's land expedition arrived at San Diego Bay.

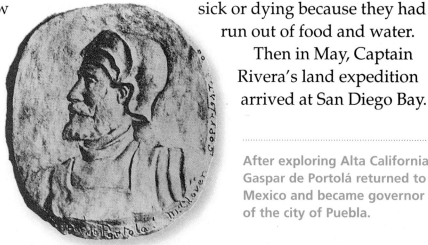

After exploring Alta California, Gaspar de Portolá returned to Mexico and became governor of the city of Puebla.

"Thanks be to God," wrote Father Crespi. "I arrived here at the Port of San Diego. It is beautiful to behold. . . ."

Portolá's group did not reach San Diego Bay until the end of June. During the trip Father Serra's left leg was painful. Years earlier he had been bitten by a snake or an insect, and his leg had never healed. "Where distances are so great," he wrote, "hardships must be faced."

When enough of the soldiers were well, Portolá set out over land to find Monterey Bay. The Indians they came across were friendly and provided food. Portolá looked for a bay that was "well

Father Junípero Serra (right) founded the mission of San Diego de Alcalá on July 16, 1769. It was the first of nine missions started by Father Serra in Alta California.

protected from all winds," as Vizcaíno had described it. But Portolá passed by the bay without knowing it was the place he was looking for. He went as far north as San Francisco Bay before returning to San Diego Bay in January 1770.

In March, Portolá tried again. He found Monterey Bay on May 24.

REVIEW What bay was Portolá searching for?

Building Missions

While Portolá was searching for Monterey Bay, Father Serra stayed at San Diego Bay. There, on July 16, 1769, he set up the first mission in Alta California. He named it San Diego de Alcalá (ahl•kah•LAH).

Father Serra then sailed to Monterey Bay, where he set up Mission San Carlos de Monterey. Father Serra and the people with him celebrated by hanging bells from an oak tree and raising a giant cross. Father Serra wrote,

66 We shouted at the top of our voices: 'Long live the Faith! Long live the King!' All the time the bells were ringing, and our rifles were being fired. 99

Father Serra remained in California for 16 years. Before he died in 1784, he had set up a chain of nine missions. Each of the missions was a day's walk from the next—about 30 miles (48 km).

A Spanish Presidio

Church or chapel

Commander's house

Guards' quarters

Soldiers' quarters

Storerooms

Workshops

Ditch

LEARNING FROM DIAGRAMS Officers, soldiers, and their families lived inside the presidios.

■ Why would storerooms be important in a presidio?

Most of the missions were set up in valleys, along trails used by Native Californians. Father Serra chose locations that had rich soil for farming and plenty of fresh water, usually next to an Indian town or village. That way, he could have workers, and he could bring the Indians into the Catholic religion. Each mission had a church, houses for the priests and the Indians, workshops, farmland, and pastures for cattle and sheep.

Today Father Serra is sometimes called the Father of the California Missions. The missions he founded helped the new California colony grow.

REVIEW **Where was the first mission in Alta California?**

Presidios for Protection

The Spanish built **presidios** (pray•SEE•dee•ohz), or forts, near the missions to protect them. The presidios were often built next to harbors, where they could defend the missions against attacks by ships from other countries. The first presidio in Alta California was built at San Diego in 1769. Other presidios were built at San Francisco, Monterey, and Santa Barbara.

All the presidios were built by Indian workers, and all the presidios were built in much the same way. A wall protected a square fort. Outside the wall was a ditch. Inside the wall stood a church and houses for the officers and soldiers and their families. Food for the people in the presidios came from the missions.

REVIEW Why were presidios built?

The Arrival of New Settlers

In the years after Father Serra died, the number of missions in Alta California grew to 21. With so many missions in Alta California, Spain wanted to find an easier way for new settlers and supplies to get there.

Juan Bautista de Anza (bow•TEES•tah day AHN•sah), a soldier, was chosen to find a new route. In 1774 he crossed northern Mexico and present-day Arizona to reach Alta California.

The next year, in October 1775, Anza made another trip to Alta California. He set out from Tubac (TOO•bahk), a presidio in northern Mexico. With him were about 240 men, women, and children and hundreds of cattle, mules, and horses. Anza's route took them through the Sonoran (soh•NAWR•ahn) Desert and over the San Jacinto (hah•SEEN•toh) Mountains—a distance of more than 1,600 miles (2,575 km). They finally reached Monterey in March 1776.

Because of the desert and the mountains, Anza's route proved to be no easier than the others. Land travel to Alta California remained very difficult, and most supplies still had to be sent by ship.

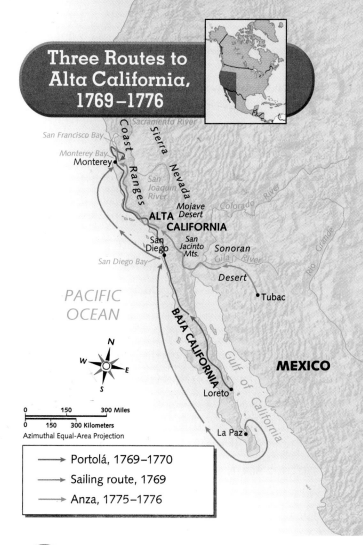

Three Routes to Alta California, 1769–1776

→ Portolá, 1769–1770
→ Sailing route, 1769
→ Anza, 1775–1776

Movement Portolá's and Anza's expeditions were in search of routes to Alta California.
■ Whose expedition crossed the Colorado River?

After traveling north to explore San Francisco Bay, Anza returned to Mexico. Late in 1776, however, the Spanish built a presidio on a windy beach that he had explored. Inland, near Dolores Creek, they built the Mission San Francisco de Asís (ah•SEES). These settlements were the beginning of the city of San Francisco.

REVIEW How was Anza's route different from the routes followed by earlier explorers?

The Pueblos

Before long, other people from Mexico were asked to go to California to start **pueblos** (PWEH•blohs). In Spanish, *pueblo* means "village." These farming communities were the first Spanish settlements in California that were not run by priests or soldiers. Many were started by people of mixed Spanish, Indian, and African backgrounds.

In 1777 a few settlers, mostly soldiers and their families, built California's first pueblo at the southern end of San Francisco Bay. This small pueblo of mud houses and farmland grew into the city called San Jose.

In 1781 other settlers built a pueblo farther south, near the Los Angeles River. That one grew to become Los Angeles. Of its first 44 settlers, 22 were children. Almost half of the settlers had Native American ancestors. Twenty-six of the settlers also had African ancestors.

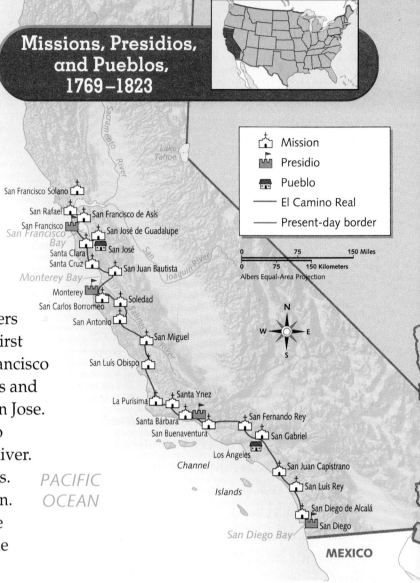

Missions, Presidios, and Pueblos, 1769–1823

Mission
Presidio
Pueblo
El Camino Real
Present-day border

San Francisco Solano
San Rafael
San Francisco de Asís
San Francisco
San José de Guadalupe
San Francisco Bay
Santa Clara
San José
Santa Cruz
San Juan Bautista
Monterey Bay
Monterey
Soledad
San Carlos Borromeo
San Antonio
San Miguel
San Luís Obispo
La Purísima
Santa Ynez
Santa Bárbara
San Fernando Rey
San Buenaventura
San Gabriel
Los Ángeles
Channel
San Juan Capistrano
Islands
San Luís Rey
San Diego de Alcalá
San Diego
San Diego Bay
MEXICO

PACIFIC OCEAN

Sacramento River
Lake Tahoe
San Joaquin River
Salinas River

0   75   150 Miles
0   75   150 Kilometers
Albers Equal-Area Projection

N S E W

Movement El Camino Real connected the missions, presidios, and pueblos in Alta California.

■ If it took one day to walk from one mission to the next, about how many days would it take to walk from San Juan Capistrano to San Luis Obispo?

HISTORY

1776

In 1776, as the Spanish were building San Francisco de Asís, important events were taking place on the other side of the continent. On July 4, 1776, thirteen of the British colonies had approved the Declaration of Independence. It said that the 13 colonies were the United States of America. The United States was fighting a war to win its freedom from Britain.

The United States Declaration of Independence

IN CONGRESS. JULY 4, 1776.
The unanimous Declaration of the thirteen united States of America.

But even with pueblos being built, the California colony grew very slowly. By 1781 only 600 newcomers, mostly men, lived in all of Alta California.

REVIEW How were pueblos different from other Spanish settlements in California?

El Camino Real

Priests, soldiers, Indians, and other travelers all used a trail that connected the missions, the presidios, and the pueblos. The dusty path soon grew into a well-traveled road. It was called El Camino Real (ka•MEE•noh ray•AHL), the Royal Road.

El Camino Real was Spain's first road in California. In time it stretched from

Like El Camino Real, U.S. Highway 101 follows the coast in some places.

San Diego in the south to Sonoma in the north. Travelers along the road stopped at the missions for food and rest. Today part of U.S. Highway 101 follows the same route as El Camino Real did.

REVIEW How did El Camino Real help people travel in California?

LESSON 2 REVIEW

1760 — 1775 — 1790

1769
• Father Junípero Serra builds the first mission in Alta California at San Diego Bay

1776
• A presidio is built at San Francisco Bay

1777
• The first Spanish pueblo is built where San Jose is now

1781
• A pueblo is built where Los Angeles is now

Check Understanding

1 Remember the Facts Why did King Carlos III of Spain order that settlements be built in Alta California?

2 Recall the Main Idea What kinds of settlements did Spain build in Alta California?

Think Critically

3 Explore Viewpoints What do you think the Indians thought about the arrival of settlers from Mexico?

4 Past to Present How do you think Highway 101 is different from El Camino Real in Father Serra's day?

Show What You Know

Writing Activity Imagine that the king of Spain has asked you to travel to Alta California. You are to report on the three different kinds of settlements there. Write a report that describes some of the settlements you visit. Share your report with a partner.

Read and Use a

1. Why Learn This Skill?

To understand the history of California, you need to know when important events happened. A time line can help you with that.

As you know, a time line is a diagram that shows some of the important events that took place during a certain period of time. It shows the order in which the events happened and the amount of time that passed between them. A time line can also help you see how events are connected to one another.

2. Understand the Process

The time line below shows when some important events in the early history of California took place. The earliest date is at the left, and the latest date is at the right.

Like a map, a time line has a scale. But the marks on a time line's scale show units of time, not distance.

Time lines can show different units of time. Some time lines show events that took place during one day, one month, or one year. Others show events that took place during a **decade**, or a period of ten years.

On the time line below, the space between two marks stands for one **century**, or a period of 100 years. The first part of the time line shows events that happened during the sixteenth century. The sixteenth century includes the years from 1501 to 1600. The next part of the time line shows the seventeenth century—from 1601 to 1700.

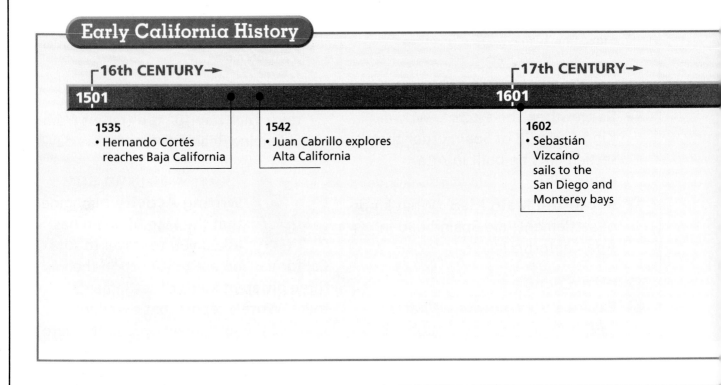

Early California History

16th CENTURY →
1501

1535
• Hernando Cortés reaches Baja California

1542
• Juan Cabrillo explores Alta California

17th CENTURY →
1601

1602
• Sebastián Vizcaíno sails to the San Diego and Monterey bays

Time Line

What century does the last part of the time line show?

Now use the time line to answer these questions about California's history.

1 In which year did Hernando Cortés reach Baja California?

2 How many years after Hernando Cortés reached Baja California did Juan Cabrillo explore Alta California?

3 When did Sebastián Vizcaíno sail to the San Diego and Monterey bays? In which century was that?

4 How long after Juan Cabrillo explored Alta California did Father Junípero Serra set up the first mission there?

5 Which two events happened in 1769? Where did both events take place?

6 Who reached Monterey Bay first, Gaspar de Portolá or Juan Bautista de Anza?

7 What is the latest event shown on the time line? In which century did that event happen?

3. Think and Apply

Make a time line that shows the twentieth and twenty-first centuries. Label the first and last years of both centuries, the year you were born, and every 5 years since then. Mark the year you will graduate from high school and some other important years for you in the past and in the future. Add photographs or drawings, and display your time line on a bulletin board.

◄18th CENTURY►

1701 — **1801**

1769
- Father Junípero Serra sets up San Diego de Alcalá, the first mission in Alta California
- The first presidio is built at San Diego

1770
- Gaspar de Portolá reaches Monterey Bay

1776
- Juan Bautista de Anza reaches Monterey Bay
- The presidio is built at San Francisco Bay

1777
- Alta California's first pueblo is built near the southern end of San Francisco Bay

1781
- Settlers build a pueblo in an area that grew to become Los Angeles

Life in the Missions

These bells (above and right) from California missions once called people to prayer, work, and meals.

Some settlers lived in the pueblos and the presidios, but it was mostly the missions that helped the California colony grow. At first the missions worked hard just to survive. In time, however, they began to do well as more and more Native Californians were put to work.

Prayer and Work

Imagine that the time is 200 years ago in California. A visitor from Mexico is walking along El Camino Real. A bell rings out from a nearby mission church to announce the visitor's arrival.

The padre (PAH•dray) welcomes the visitor. *Padre*, which means "father" in Spanish, is another name for a priest. He explains that the mission is teaching Christianity and Spanish ways to the Indians living there.

The visitor sees that everyone is busy. Indian women are weaving cloth, and Indian men are setting out adobe (ah•DOH•bay) bricks to dry in the sun. **Adobe** is a mixture of clay, straw, and water that is dried into bricks. All the mission buildings are made of adobe bricks. The padre explains that the thick adobe walls keep the buildings warm in winter and cool in summer.

Two boys are herding goats from the hills toward the mission gate. Other children are busy chasing birds away from crops in the fields and weeding the gardens. The sound of a hammer hitting metal comes from the blacksmith's workshop.

Mission Santa Barbara was founded on December 4, 1786. People at a mission in California used this olive press (right) to get oil from the olives they grew.

Before long the mission bell rings to call the people to prayer. Bells ring many times during the day at the mission. They call the people to eat. They announce the time to begin work and to stop work. Bells even tell the people when to wake up and when to go to sleep.

When missionaries came to California, they brought with them farm animals, fruit trees, and seeds for crops. They showed the Indians how to grow crops such as wheat, corn, beans, and barley. They taught them how to take care of horses, cattle, sheep, goats, and chickens. They also taught them how to use metal plows and many other new kinds of tools.

Most of the work was done by Indians. They grew the crops, cared for the animals, and worked as weavers, cooks, carpenters, and metalworkers.

The Indians at the missions were supposed to give up their old ways. They were not allowed to follow their own religions or customs. A **custom** is a usual way of doing things. Indians at

A Spanish Mission

Field

River

Field

Workshops

Indian village

Irrigation ditch

Priest's quarters

Olive trees

Church

Well

LEARNING FROM DIAGRAMS At the center of a typical Spanish mission in California was a courtyard. In the courtyard workers did chores such as weaving cloth, grinding corn, and making candles, and missionaries gave the Indians lessons about Christianity.

■ How was water brought from the river to the fields?

a mission could no longer hold the celebrations of their tribes or wear Indian clothing. If they tried to keep their customs, they were often punished.

The missionaries were very strict with the Indians. There were rules for every

Storerooms

Central kitchen

Pasture for cattle,
sheep, and goats

Blacksmith's
workshop

activity, and the Indians were sometimes beaten if they did not obey them. Indians were forced to work very hard to keep the missions going.

REVIEW How did the lives of Indians change when they came to the missions?

Some Indians Resist

By the late 1700s more than 20,000 Indians lived in the California missions. Some chose to live there because they wanted to learn Spanish ways. Others, however, were forced by soldiers to leave their homes and move to the missions.

Once the Indians got to the missions, they often were not allowed to leave. The missionaries were afraid that the Indians would not return if they left. They also worried that those who left would give up Christianity.

Some Indians tried to **resist**, or act against, the Spanish. Some ran away from the missions. If they were caught, however, they were often taken back and punished.

Other Indians started revolts. A **revolt** is an action against people in charge. In the 1770s Indians burned the missions at San Diego and San Luis Obispo. In 1785 a Tongva Indian woman who was named Toypurina (toy•poo•REE•nuh) led a revolt at the San Gabriel Mission. The revolt failed, and Toypurina was forced to leave her people forever.

In 1824 Indians started revolts at several other missions, including one at Santa Barbara. It took the Spanish several weeks to stop that revolt.

Although the Indian revolts did not succeed, they did make people think about the missions. In 1825 the governor of California reported to the Mexican government about the problems of Indians at the missions.

REVIEW How did some Indians resist Spanish rule at the missions?

A Way of Life Ends

Before the Spanish arrived, most Native Californians had hunted and gathered their food. At the missions they became farmers. If the crops failed, the Indians went hungry. At times they were treated as slaves. A **slave** is a person who is owned by another person and made to work. A French explorer who visited the missions in the late 1700s wrote that the missions had made the Indians "too much a child, too much a slave."

Many Indians died from diseases brought by the Spanish. Measles, for example, was unknown in North America before Spanish explorers and missionaries brought the disease with them without realizing it. By the late 1800s much of the Indian way of life had also died out.

REVIEW How did diseases affect the California Indians?

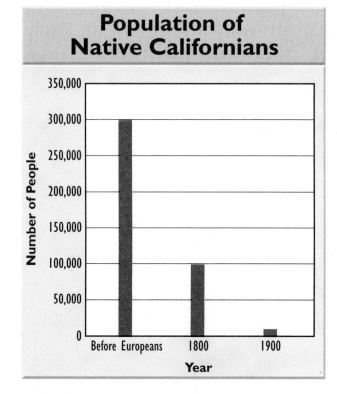

Population of Native Californians

Number of People / **Year**

LEARNING FROM GRAPHS No one knows for sure how many Indians lived in California before the arrival of Europeans. Some historians believe there were as many as 300,000 Indians. Others believe there were about 130,000 to 150,000.
■ About how many Indians were in California in 1800?

LESSON 3 REVIEW

Check Understanding

❶ **Remember the Facts** What kind of bricks were used to build missions?

❷ **Recall the Main Idea** How did the missions change the ways of life of the California Indians?

Think Critically

❸ **Think More About It** Why do you think some Indians wanted to learn Spanish ways? Why do you think others wanted to escape?

❹ **Past to Present** Many people today visit the missions of California.

Why do you think they are interested in places built so long ago?

❺ **Link to You** What missions are closest to where you live? Have you visited a mission? If so, what was it like?

Show What You Know

Art Activity Make a diorama of a California mission. Build your diorama in an empty box turned on its side. In your box, show the different buildings and some of the activities of the people. Share your diorama with classmates.

A True Story of Early California
VALLEJO
and the Four Flags
Esther J. Comstock

VALLEJO AND THE FOUR FLAGS

A True Story of Early California

BY ESTHER J. COMSTOCK
ILLUSTRATED BY CARLOS OCHAGAVIA

Mariano G. Vallejo (mar•ee•AHN•oh vah•YAY•hoh) was born in California in 1808. When he was a young boy, he and his family lived at Monterey. One day French pirates attacked and destroyed the presidio and village there. Many of the people had to go to live at the San Antonio Mission while their village was rebuilt. Read now about what life at the Spanish mission was like for ten-year-old Mariano Vallejo and his friend Juan Alvarado (HWAHN ahl•vah•RAH•doh).

governor a leader of a colony or a state

refugee (ref•yoo•JEE) a person who flees from danger

revolving turning

vat a large pot
tallow the fat from cattle

Almost a year passed before Mariano's family and the others could move back to Monterey. The governor sent many of them to the San Antonio Mission. The boys and girls, who had been used to army life, liked this new way of living. Even Mariano forgot the pirates in the excitement of so much that was new to see and do.

The Mission Indians at Monterey provided many services for the army post and its families. They made the candles and soap. They spun and wove the coarse wool into blankets. They tended the gardens and cattle.

Here, the refugee families lived in this beautiful San Antonio Mission. The visiting children begged the Indian servants to teach them some of these skills.

One day Mariano and one of his sisters tried making candles. The candle wicks hung from the spokes of a large revolving horizontal wheel. The worker could lower and lift the wheel, dipping several candles at a time into the vat of hot tallow.

"Turn the wheel slower," he told her. "Your tallow drips all over and the candles aren't even."

"They look all right. You're just too fussy," she retorted. "If I do it your way, it'll take all day."

"But you splash the tallow out of the kettle."

"You do it then," his sister said. "I'd sure hate to work for you. I'm going to watch them weave the blankets."

Sometimes the older children tried the carding,

or combing, and spinning of the wool. However, none of them were actually allowed to weave.

The boys preferred to gather at a large round basin, dug two feet deep in the ground. Water and fine *adobe* soil were poured into the cavity. Chopped weeds and reeds were added as needed, to thicken the mud.

The Indian workers laughed as the boys galloped around the basin, churning the mud and reeds into a thick mixture. The boys loved the feel of the soupy mud oozing between their toes. They yelled and squealed as they splashed each other.

When the overseer decided that the mud was thick enough, it was poured into wooden molds. These were about twelve by twenty-two inches in size. The sun finished the job, drying the bricks that now lay in rows. Mariano and the others each put his own mark on the hardening *adobe*.

But all of them stayed away from where the Indians soaked the cattle hides. Mariano and Juan and all the others held their noses as they ran past the smelly hides, drying on fences.

vaqueros (vah•KAY•rohs) cowhands
reata (ray•AH•tah) a lasso

There was no school here and none of the children missed it. As the mild winter passed, they had lots of time for horseback riding. Mariano, like other Spanish boys and girls, learned to ride before he could walk.

He and Juan trailed the *vaqueros*. Over and over Mariano practiced throwing his *reata* until he was the best of all the boys his age. With whoops and yells, they kept the new spring calves on the run.

These sun- and fun-filled days ended too soon for some. Word came it was time to move back to Monterey. When they arrived, many families had a sad homecoming. The homes were repaired, it was true, but many family treasures and pieces of furniture had been stolen or destroyed.

At the sight of still-damaged buildings, Mariano remembered his vow. When he grew up, he'd never let this happen again.

Soon the school reopened, to the disgust of many. Others,

like Mariano Vallejo and Juan Alvarado, and a younger friend named José Castro, were glad. Mariano told himself he must learn all that he could. Someday, some way, he'd make his country strong and safe.

Mariano Vallejo kept his vow. When he grew up, Vallejo become an important leader in the Mexican Army, helping to protect California when it was ruled by Mexico. And when California became part of the United States in 1850, Vallejo remained an important leader for the new state.

vow a promise

LITERATURE REVIEW

1 What services did the Mission Indians provide for the army post and its families?

2 How do you think you would have felt about having to leave your home at Monterey to live at the San Antonio Mission?

3 Imagine that you lived at the San Antonio Mission. Use the information in the story to help you write a journal entry that describes one kind of job that people did there. Tell how this work was important to the mission.

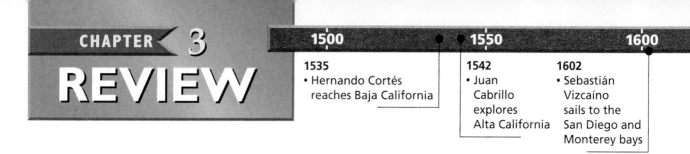

1500   1550   1600

1535
• Hernando Cortés reaches Baja California

1542
• Juan Cabrillo explores Alta California

1602
• Sebastián Vizcaíno sails to the San Diego and Monterey bays

CONNECT MAIN IDEAS

Use this organizer to show that you understand why Spain first settled Alta California and how its settlements affected Native Californians. Complete it by writing three details about each main idea. A copy of the organizer may be found on page 32 of the Activity Book.

Spanish California

Spain sent explorers to what is now California.

1. _____
_____
_____

2. _____
_____
_____

3. _____
_____
_____

Spain built different kinds of settlements in Alta California.

1. _____
_____
_____

2. _____
_____
_____

3. _____
_____
_____

Missions changed the ways of life of California's Indians.

1. _____
_____
_____

2. _____
_____
_____

3. _____
_____
_____

WRITE MORE ABOUT IT

Write a News Report Imagine that you are a news reporter traveling with a land expedition sent to Alta California. Write a report that tells the *Who? What? When? Where?* and *Why?* of your trip.

Express a Viewpoint Imagine that you are a Native Californian. Describe the changes that you see taking place because of the missions. How is your life changing? What do you think of those changes?

1769
• Father Junípero Serra builds the first mission in Alta California at San Diego Bay

1776
• A presidio is built at San Francisco Bay

1777
• The first Spanish pueblo is built where San Jose is now

1781
• A pueblo is built where Los Angeles is now

USE VOCABULARY

Write the definitions of the words below. Then use the words to make a crossword puzzle on a sheet of graph paper. Use the definitions as *ACROSS* and *DOWN* clues. Give your puzzle to a partner to solve.

1 galleon

2 barrier

3 colony

4 adobe

5 custom

6 revolt

CHECK UNDERSTANDING

7 What were Cortés and Cabrillo searching for when they sailed north from Mexico?

8 Why did the Spanish want a port in Alta California?

9 Why was it hard to get to Alta California from the rest of New Spain?

10 What did Spain decide was the best way to start a colony in Alta California?

11 How were missions different from presidios? from pueblos?

12 What was El Camino Real?

13 How did some Native Californians at the missions resist the Spanish?

THINK CRITICALLY

14 **Cause and Effect** In the 1760s Russia started to explore the Pacific coast of North America. How did this affect the Spanish settlement of Alta California?

15 **Explore Viewpoints** How might a missionary's point of view about missions be different from that of a Native Californian?

APPLY SKILLS

Follow Routes on a Historical Map Use the map on page 147 to answer these questions.

16 Which explorer started from Tubac?

17 Which explorer's route passed through San Diego?

Read and Use a Time Line Use the time line on pages 150–151 to answer these questions.

18 In which century did Juan Cabrillo explore Alta California?

19 Which two events happened in 1776?

READ MORE ABOUT IT

Spanish Missions by Bobbie Kalman and Greg Nickles. Crabtree. This book uses photographs and illustrations to describe the daily activities at the Spanish missions.

HARCOURT BRACE

Visit the Internet at
http://www.hbschool.com
for additional resources.

MEXICAN CALIFORNIA

"One afternoon a horseman from the Peraltas, where Oakland now stands, came to our ranch, and told my father that a great ship, a ship 'with two sticks in the center,' was about to sail from Yerba Buena. . . ."

Prudencia Higuera, the daughter of a ranch owner, describing how her family heard about a trading ship in 1840

Maria Concepcion Bustamente (right) lived in Alta California in the 1800s.

Mexico Wins Independence

| 1810 | 1820 | 1830 |

By 1800 Spain had been building colonies in the Americas for almost 300 years. However, it was beginning to have a problem with its colonists—the people living in its colonies. Many of them were beginning to want **independence**, or freedom, from Spanish rule. Just as the 13 British colonies had become the United States of America, many of the colonies in New Spain wanted to become their own countries.

Many people in Mexico had read the American Declaration of Independence. They dreamed of freedom for Mexico, too. Like the people of the United States, the people of Mexico also had to fight a long war to win their independence.

Because Alta California was so far from Mexico, people there heard little about this war for independence. Yet it was to change California forever.

FOCUS
How can events that happen in other places affect you and your family?

Main Idea Read to discover how events in Mexico during the early 1800s affected the people of Alta California.

Vocabulary
independence
Creole
Californio
economy
society

Independence for Mexico

The colonists who spoke out most against Spanish rule in Mexico were the **Creoles** (KREE•ohlz). Creoles were people of Spanish background who had been born in New Spain. Because they had not been born in Spain, they were not allowed to hold the best jobs in the government or the Church.

Many Indians, Africans, and people of mixed backgrounds also wanted an end to Spanish rule. They were Mexico's poorest people.

The Mexican flag (above) was first flown in 1821. To the left is a Mexican military uniform from the 1800s.

This part of *The Independence Mural* painted by Juan O'Gorman shows Father Miguel Hidalgo calling on the Mexican people to revolt against Spain.

They had even fewer chances for good jobs than the Creoles did.

In 1810 a priest named Miguel Hidalgo (mee•GAYL ee•DAHL•goh) called on the Mexican people to join in a revolt against Spain. In the early morning of September 16, he rang the church bells in the town of Dolores. People hurried to the church to find out what was happening.

No one wrote down what Father Hidalgo said that day, but many remembered his words. Mexico had been ruled badly, Hidalgo said. He asked the people to fight for freedom. "Long live America!" he cried. "Death to bad government!"

Hidalgo's speech became known as the *Grito de Dolores*, or Cry of Dolores. It marked the beginning of the Mexican War for Independence. This war lasted for 11 years. But in 1821 the people of Mexico won their independence at last.

No fighting took place in Alta California during the Mexican War for Independence. For years, however, the soldiers in the presidios there received no supplies from Spain. That was because Spain was too busy with the war in Mexico to pay much attention to far-off California. In fact, it was not until 1822, almost a year after the end of the war, that the people of Alta California even learned that Mexico had won its independence.

As a result of the Mexican War for Independence, California became part of the new country of Mexico. Most **Californios**, as the Spanish-speaking people of Alta California called themselves, welcomed Mexican rule.

REVIEW **Who was Miguel Hidalgo?**

Changes Come to California

The new Mexican government brought several important changes to California. The country's leaders wanted to get rid of any laws that reminded them of the old Spanish government. Some of those laws had to do with trade with other countries.

Under Spanish law the colonies in New Spain were not allowed to trade with other countries. But Spain had trouble making sure this law was followed. Russia, Britain, and the United States all sent trading ships to California. The first United States ship to arrive was the *Otter*, which reached Monterey in 1796.

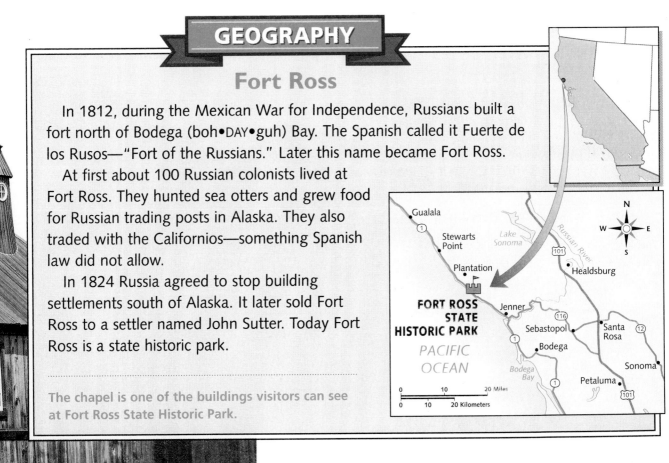

GEOGRAPHY

Fort Ross

In 1812, during the Mexican War for Independence, Russians built a fort north of Bodega (boh•DAY•guh) Bay. The Spanish called it Fuerte de los Rusos—"Fort of the Russians." Later this name became Fort Ross.

At first about 100 Russian colonists lived at Fort Ross. They hunted sea otters and grew food for Russian trading posts in Alaska. They also traded with the Californios—something Spanish law did not allow.

In 1824 Russia agreed to stop building settlements south of Alaska. It later sold Fort Ross to a settler named John Sutter. Today Fort Ross is a state historic park.

The chapel is one of the buildings visitors can see at Fort Ross State Historic Park.

Before Mexico won its independence, trading ships from other countries took a chance on being captured if they sailed along the California coast. The new Mexican government quickly changed that. Unlike Spain, it wanted to trade with other countries.

Soon ships from many countries, including the United States, sailed into the harbors at San Francisco, Monterey, and San Diego. The trade that took place there helped California's economy grow. An **economy** is the way people in a state, a region, or a country use resources to meet their needs.

The Mexican government also made two important changes that affected the Indians of California. It made the Indians citizens, and it decided to close the missions.

REVIEW What changes did the new Mexican government bring to California?

The Missions Close

The Mexican government wanted to close the missions for several reasons. The missions had grown very powerful, and they reminded people of Spanish rule. Revolts against the missions also had caused both Indians and Californios to be killed. The Mexican government hoped that if it closed all the missions, the Indians would become part of the Mexican society. A **society** is a group of people who live in the same place and have many things in common.

Perhaps the main reason for closing the missions had to do with land. The missions owned some of the best land, and the new government wanted this land and the money it could provide.

In 1833 Mexico passed a law to take the land from the missions over the next 15 years. The missions would become pueblos. The mission church would be

When this photograph was taken in 1894, the Mission San Antonio de Padua, like most other missions in California, was in ruins. It has since been rebuilt.

the pueblo's church. Half the land would be given to the Indians. The rest would be controlled by local governments.

In a few years most of the mission churches were in ruins. One person who later visited the old San Fernando Mission described what he saw.

66 It is terrible to see San Fernando Mission going to ruin so fast. . . . The big court on which the church fronts in the rear is now a farm yard, and half filled with wagons, a threshing machine, and hay and grain racks. Hogs are everywhere. 99

Government leaders had thought that closing the missions would help the Indians. But closing the missions really made life harder for the Indians. Often they did not get any of the mission lands. Many were tricked out of their land by settlers. Others chose to sell their land rather than keep it. Most mission lands ended up in the hands of Californios and new settlers.

Some Indians returned to their old villages, but they found that their lands there had also been taken by settlers. Others had lived their whole lives on a mission and did not know any other way of life. Many Indians had no choice but to go to work for the new owners of the mission lands.

REVIEW **Why did the Mexican government want to close the missions?**

LESSON I REVIEW

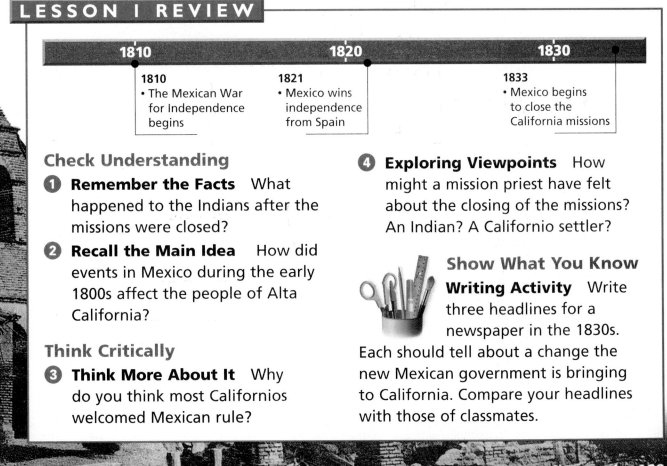

1810	1820	1830
1810 • The Mexican War for Independence begins	**1821** • Mexico wins independence from Spain	**1833** • Mexico begins to close the California missions

Check Understanding

1 **Remember the Facts** What happened to the Indians after the missions were closed?

2 **Recall the Main Idea** How did events in Mexico during the early 1800s affect the people of Alta California?

Think Critically

3 **Think More About It** Why do you think most Californios welcomed Mexican rule?

4 **Exploring Viewpoints** How might a mission priest have felt about the closing of the missions? An Indian? A Californio settler?

Show What You Know

Writing Activity Write three headlines for a newspaper in the 1830s. Each should tell about a change the new Mexican government is bringing to California. Compare your headlines with those of classmates.

Use Historical Maps

1. Why Learn This Skill?

You are always changing over time. You are growing, and you are learning new things. The world is always changing, too.

Historical maps give information about places as they were in the past. By comparing historical maps of the same place at different times in history, you can see how that place has changed over time.

2. Remember What You Have Read

In the last lesson you read about the long war that Mexico fought before it won its independence in 1821. After the Mexican War for Independence, California became part of Mexico. So did large areas of what is today the Southwest region of the United States. Which European country controlled all of these lands before 1821?

3. Understand the Process

The two historical maps on these pages show the same part of North America at different times. Look at the dates in the map titles. The map below shows the middle part of North America in 1821, just after Mexico became an independent country. The other map shows the same

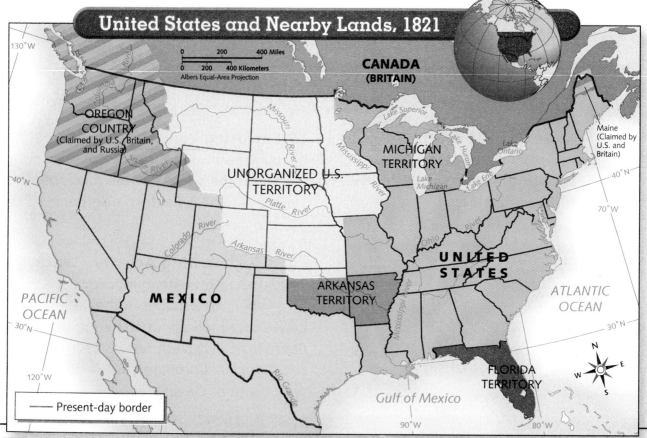

United States and Nearby Lands, 1821

130°W

0   200   400 Miles
0   200   400 Kilometers
Albers Equal-Area Projection

Columbia River

OREGON COUNTRY
(Claimed by U.S., Britain, and Russia)

Snake River

40°N

Missouri River

UNORGANIZED U.S. TERRITORY

Platte River

Colorado River

Arkansas River

PACIFIC OCEAN

30°N

120°W

M E X I C O

Rio Grande

CANADA (BRITAIN)

Lake Superior

MICHIGAN TERRITORY

Lake Huron
Lake Michigan
Lake Ontario
Lake Erie

Mississippi River

Ohio River

U N I T E D S T A T E S

ARKANSAS TERRITORY

Mississippi River

FLORIDA TERRITORY

Gulf of Mexico

Maine (Claimed by U.S. and Britain)

40°N

70°W

ATLANTIC OCEAN

30°N

N
W   E
S

90°W   80°W

—— Present-day border

to See Change

area twenty years later—after Texas had won its independence from Mexico.

1 What color is used on both maps to show lands that belonged to Mexico?

2 How did the size of Mexico change between 1821 and 1841? To what new country did Mexico lose some of its lands?

3 What color is used on both maps to show lands that belonged to the United States?

Some areas on the maps are covered by a pattern of diagonal stripes, called hatch lines, instead of a solid color. Hatch lines are often used on historical maps to show lands that were claimed by two or more countries.

4 Which countries claimed the Oregon Country in 1821? in 1841?

5 Which river did the Republic of Texas claim as part of its western border in 1841?

4. Think and Apply

Write three or four sentences about these two maps. Include the dates of the maps in your sentences, but leave blanks where they belong. Then trade papers with a partner. Have your partner fill in the correct date to complete each sentence.

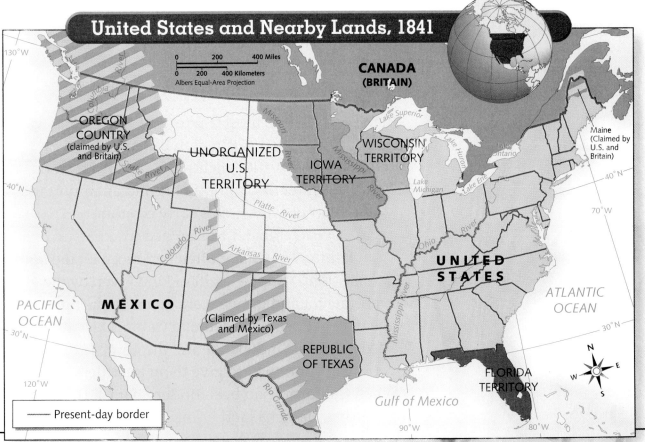

United States and Nearby Lands, 1841

This Corriente bull is much like the kind of cattle raised on California ranchos in the 1800s. Rancho workers used lariats, or lassos, like the one above when rounding up cattle.

The Growth of Ranchos

1830   1840   1850

In describing Alta California in 1771, the Spanish priest Juan Crespi wrote, "The country is delightful for it is covered with beautiful grass which affords excellent pasture for the animals." Settlers soon discovered that California's wild grasses made it a good place for raising cattle.

Before the Spanish came, there were no cattle or horses in the Americas. The Spanish brought the first ones with them from Spain. When the Spanish settled new lands, they took cattle and horses with them.

In the late 1700s, missionaries and colonists from Mexico brought cattle and horses to California. Their herds grew quickly. By 1830 there were about 500,000 cattle and many thousands of horses in California.

The Ranchos

In the early 1800s, most Californios lived along the coast. Some lived in pueblos, but most lived on **ranchos**, or large cattle ranches. These ranchos soon became the center of California life and an important part of California's early economy.

Each rancho was owned by a person or a family. The owner often had received the land as a **land grant**—a gift of land given by the government. Land grants were given by the Spanish as a way to get people to settle in California. After Mexico gained its independence, the new Mexican government continued to give them to settlers.

When California had been under Spanish rule, it had not been easy to get a land grant. Often the grants were given only to people who were already wealthy or had friends or family members in the government. Presidio officers also received land grants.

At first the number of ranchos in California grew slowly. In 1824 there were only about 20. As the Mexican government began closing the missions in 1833, it gave land grants to divide up the mission lands. It also gave the new rancho owners cattle from the missions. Between 1834 and 1846, more than 700 new ranchos were started.

Many of these ranchos were very large. Some covered 50,000 acres or more—an area larger than the city of San Francisco. On some ranchos the owners built large estates, or houses, called **haciendas** (ah•see•EN•dahs).

Ranchos needed a lot of land to provide enough grass for the cattle to eat. The animals roamed freely on the rancho land, eating most of the wild grasses in one place and then moving to another place. These cattle destroyed much of California's wild grasses.

Under Mexican rule, only Mexican citizens could receive a land grant. However, people could easily become Mexican citizens if they agreed to obey Mexican laws and to follow the Catholic religion. People from other countries

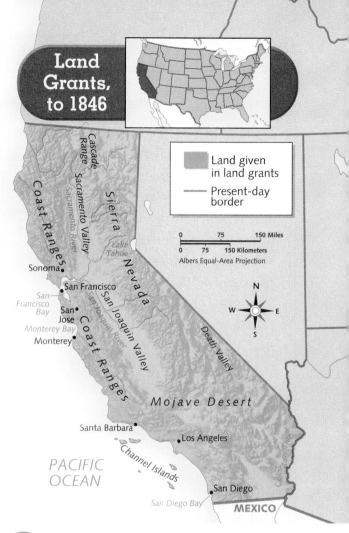

Land Grants, to 1846

Land given in land grants

Present-day border

 Location   The Mexican government gave settlers land in California so that they could start ranchos.

■ Where were most ranchos located?

Lachryma Montis, which in Latin means "tear of the mountain," was the name of the hacienda owned by Mariano Vallejo, one of the wealthiest and most powerful Californio rancho owners.

Juana Briones de Miranda, 1802?–1889

Juana Briones de Miranda (bree•OH•nays day meer•AHN•dah) was just one of the women in California who owned a rancho. She owned Rancho La Purísima Concepción (poo•REE•see•mah kohn•sep•see•OHN), a rancho of nearly 4,500 acres near San Jose.

Like many women of the time, Juana Briones married at an early age and had a large family. But her husband did not help take care of their children, so Juana had to care for them alone. She grew vegetables for the family to eat and sell. She also made clothes for others, took care of sick people, and ran a small restaurant. By 1844 she had earned and saved enough money to buy a rancho. She bought it from an Indian who had

received it as a land grant. She and her children built a larger house on the rancho and raised cattle. Today her rancho is a state landmark.

Juana Briones de Miranda lived in this house at Rancho La Purísima Concepción.

who moved to California were able to get land grants this way.

Women as well as men owned ranchos. Unlike women in the United States at that time, married women in Mexico could own land. They could also run their own businesses and sign contracts, or legal agreements.

REVIEW Why did both the Spanish and the Mexican governments give land grants?

The *Diseño*

To get a land grant, citizens usually had to write a letter to the government.

The letter had to tell what land they wanted. In one such letter, dated March 24, 1837, a citizen named Ignacio Palomares (ig•NAH•see•oh pal•oh•MAR•uhs) wrote, "The Citizen Ignacio Palomares and Ricardo Vejar before you in due form appear and say: . . . our families [are] now living within a very small space and . . . the land or place known as San Jose is vacant land. . . . In the most humble manner we now pray to you to grant to us [this] land."

The letter also had to include a *diseño* (dih•SAYN•yoh). A **diseño**, or "design," was a hand-drawn map that showed what the boundaries of the rancho would be. A *diseño* showed the whole land grant, including features such as trees, hills, and ponds. However, these maps were not always correctly drawn. Often there were problems later when people disagreed over the exact boundaries of their ranchos.

REVIEW What was a *diseño* for?

LEARNING FROM ILLUSTRATIONS This *diseño* shows part of the 22,136-acre Rancho San Miguelito owned by José Rafael Gonzalez. The river shown in the *diseño* is the Nacimiento (nah•see•me•EN•toh) River.
■ Why do you think *diseños* were often not correct?

LESSON 2 REVIEW

1830	1840	1850

1833
• Mexico begins to give land grants from mission lands

1846
• More than 700 ranchos have been set up in California

Check Understanding

❶ Remember the Facts How did cattle and horses first come to California?

❷ Recall the Main Idea How did the Mexican government get more people to settle in California?

Think Critically

❸ Past to Present How do people today get land for their homes and businesses? How is that different from how rancho owners got land?

❹ Think More About It *Diseños* were not always correctly drawn. What kinds of problems might have come about because of this?

Show What You Know

Map Activity Draw a *diseño* of your backyard, a neighborhood playground, or your school's grounds. Show the boundaries and features such as trees, playground equipment, and buildings. Display your *diseño* for others to see.

Life in Mexican California

FOCUS

How is trade important to you and your family?

Main Idea Read to learn how cattle ranching and trade were connected in Mexican California.

Vocabulary

fiesta
self-sufficient
labor
vaquero
rodeo
tallow
plaza
service
barter

A folding fan (top) and a Mexican guitar (above)

In Mexican California most people's jobs were connected with cattle ranching. There were no large cities, and there was almost no manufacturing. Even in the pueblos, most businesses had to do with the trading of goods produced from cattle.

Rancheras and Rancheros

Imagine that you are visiting a hacienda in 1840. You see a woman sitting on a fine horse. She is wearing high leather boots, a loose shirt tucked into a long full skirt, and a short jacket. She is a *ranchera*, an owner of a large California rancho. Both she and her husband, a *ranchero*, learned to ride horses as children.

Today the ranchera is taking part in a horse-riding contest. With a quick move, she sets her horse into a fast gallop. Suddenly she leans down to scoop up a coin from the ground!

The watching crowd cheers her skill. The people have gathered at the hacienda for a **fiesta**, or party. They are celebrating the wedding of the rancho owners' daughter. After the contest there will be special foods to enjoy. Guests will listen to musicians play guitars. There will be singing and dancing.

Wealthy rancho owners were known for the way they welcomed people. A guest might be treated to a week-long fiesta. One visitor to California wrote, "If I must be cast [thrown] . . . on the care of the stranger, let it be in California."

This painting, *Californios at Horse Roundup* by James Walker, shows rancho workers at the Mission de San Fernando Rancho trying to catch wild horses with lariats, or lassos.

Ranchos were nearly **self-sufficient**—they made almost everything needed by the people living on them. With the nearest pueblo or rancho often more than a day's ride away, people had to grow or make most of what they used. They grew their own food, raised their own cattle and sheep, and wove their own wool into cloth.

On large ranchos, much of the work was done by Indians. One ranchero said,

> 66 Indians farmed our soil, tended our cattle, sheared [cut wool from] our sheep, cut our lumber, built our houses, made tiles for our homes, ground our grain, slaughtered our cattle, and made our bricks. Indian women cared for our children and made all our meals. 99

In return for their **labor**, or work, the Indians were given food, a few clothes, and a hut near the main ranch house. Some lived in small villages, called *rancherias*, that were built on the rancho. But they received no money and had nowhere to go if they wanted to leave the rancho.

Not all rancho owners were wealthy, however. On poorer ranchos, families lived in small houses with dirt floors. They had little furniture and used the hides, or skins, of cattle to cover doors and windows. They did not have as many Indian workers to take care of their cattle. They did most of the work themselves.

There were usually many children living on a rancho. Families were large, and grandparents, parents, cousins, aunts, and uncles often lived together.

A California Rancho

Main house

Oven

LEARNING FROM DIAGRAMS

Every day on a rancho was filled with work.

❶ Women ground corn to make tortillas.

❷ Vaqueros rounded up and tended to the cattle, as this detail of a painting by William Hahn shows.

❸ Fiestas brought people from surrounding ranchos together.

■ Why do you think the oven was outside of the rancho house?

Most people living on ranchos had little chance to learn to read or write. There were no public schools on the ranchos. The children of some wealthy rancho owners, however, learned from a traveling teacher. Such teachers went from rancho to rancho, spending a few weeks in each home.

REVIEW **Why did ranchos need to be self-sufficient?**

Working on the Ranchos

On the ranchos the work with the cattle and the horses was done by **vaqueros** (vah•KAY•rohs), or cowhands. Both the Californios and the Indians worked as vaqueros. While living at the missions, many Indians had become expert riders who could rope cattle and tame horses.

Tannery

Vaqueros used all their skills during **rodeos**, the cattle roundups that took place each year. The cattle had to be brought together from all parts of the rancho to be counted and sorted. The vaqueros could tell if some of the cattle belonged to another rancho by looking at their brands. The brand was a special mark that each rancho burned into the skin of its cattle. Vaqueros branded the calves with their rancho's symbol during the rodeo.

Rodeos were part work and part fun. Rancho owners often turned cattle roundups into fiestas with contests and games like those of today's rodeos. Neighbors came from miles around.

In the summer and fall, some of the cattle were killed. After removing the meat, the vaqueros scraped and cleaned the hides and set them on racks to dry. Once they were dried, the hides could be used to make leather.

The fat scraped from the hides was melted in large metal tubs over low heat to make tallow. The **tallow**, the purest part of the melted fat, was used to make soap and candles.

REVIEW Who worked with the cattle and the horses on ranchos?

Living in the Pueblos

Not all people in California at this time lived on ranchos. Some people lived in pueblos. The **plaza**, an open square at the center of the pueblo, was the gathering place for people. On one side of the plaza stood the pueblo's church, where people came to worship.

Each pueblo had a government elected by the town's citizens. The leaders included a town council and a mayor, called an *alcalde* (ahl•KAHL•day). The *alcalde* also served as a judge.

In pueblos, people had different kinds of jobs. Soldiers settled there. So did skilled workers such as blacksmiths and saddlemakers. There were often stores and inns. This meant that people in pueblos had a greater choice of goods and services than people on ranchos had. A **service** is an activity that someone does for others for pay, such as cutting hair or repairing shoes.

REVIEW What was the gathering place in pueblos?

Growing Trade

Some pueblos were visited by traders from the United States. These traders came to California on ships that were like floating department stores. The ships were filled with goods that people in California wanted but could not grow or make themselves.

In 1834 Richard Henry Dana sailed to California from Massachusetts on one of those ships. In his book *Two Years Before the Mast*, he listed some of the goods the ship had brought to California. He wrote,

> **"** Our cargo was an assorted one; that is, it consisted of everything under the sun. We had . . . teas, coffee, sugar, spices, raisins, molasses, hardware, crockery-ware, tin-ware, cutlery, clothing of all kinds, boots and shoes. . . . **"**

When Californios saw a ship's sails in the harbor, they got ready to barter. To **barter** is to trade one kind of good for another without using money. The rancho owners, whose wealth was mostly in land and cattle, did not have much money. Bartering allowed them to trade what they produced for what they wanted.

Trading ships brought to California such goods as this rocking chair from New England (left), these Chinese boxes (center), and this Chinese-style jar (right).

The American traders wanted hides and tallow. Ships took the hides from California to factories in the United States. There the hides were used to manufacture shoes and boots. The traders sold the tallow to soap and candle manufacturers, mostly in South America.

In return for the hides and tallow, the traders offered cotton cloth and other manufactured products from the United States. They also brought teas and silks from China.

San Diego became the center of the hide and tallow trade in California. Many places along the coast, however, did not have good harbors. Ships had to remain at sea while small boats were sent to get the hides. Dana described throwing the hides from high cliffs into the sea for the small boats to pick up.

66 Down this height we pitched the hides, throwing them as far out into the air as we could; . . . the wind took them, and swayed them about, plunging and rising in the air, like a kite when it has broken its string. 99

Dana remained in California for less than two years, but other Americans stayed longer. They lived in the pueblos and worked for the United States trading companies.

The trading ships were a sign of change. Soon more people would be coming to California, and many of them would stay.

REVIEW **What products did Californios and traders exchange?**

LESSON 3 REVIEW

Check Understanding

1 **Remember the Facts** What happened at a rodeo?

2 **Recall the Main Idea** How were cattle ranching and trade connected in Mexican California?

Think Critically

3 **Link to You** Cattle ranching was the most important business in Mexican California. What kinds of businesses are important where you live?

4 **Personally Speaking** Would you rather have lived on a rancho or in a pueblo? Explain your answer.

5 **Past to Present** How is the way children on ranches learned like or different from the way children learn today?

Show What You Know

Poster Activity Imagine that you are a trader who has come to California on a trading ship. Make a poster that shows some of the items you have brought with you and what you want to trade them for. When you have finished, use your poster to explain to classmates how cattle ranching and trade were connected.

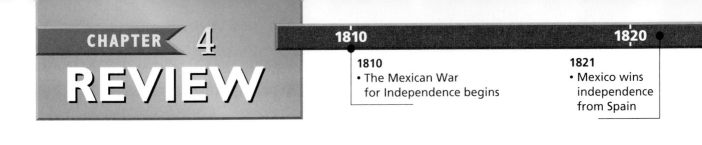

CHAPTER 4

REVIEW

1810

1810
• The Mexican War for Independence begins

1820

1821
• Mexico wins independence from Spain

CONNECT MAIN IDEAS

Use this organizer to show that you understand how the chapter's main ideas are connected. Complete it by writing two sentences about each main idea. A copy of the organizer may be found on page 40 of the Activity Book.

Mexican California

Events in Mexico during the early 1800s affected the people of California.

1. _____
2. _____

The Mexican government got more people to settle in California.

1. _____
2. _____

Cattle ranching and trade were connected in Mexican California.

1. _____
2. _____

WRITE MORE ABOUT IT

Write a Persuasive Letter Imagine that you are living in Alta California in the 1830s. Write a letter to the Mexican government asking for a land grant. Describe the land you want, and tell why.

Write a Journal Entry Imagine that you are a vaquero. Write a journal entry describing a day in your life. Be sure to describe the rancho where you work and the jobs that you do.

182 • Chapter 4

1830		1840		1850

1833
• Mexico begins to close the California missions
• Mexico begins to give land grants from mission lands

1846
• More than 700 ranchos have been set up in California

USE VOCABULARY

Write the term that correctly matches each definition.

barter   plaza

economy   service

independence

1. freedom

2. the way people in a state, a region, or a country use resources to meet their needs

3. an open square at the center of a pueblo

4. an activity that someone does for others for pay

5. to trade one kind of good for another without using money

CHECK UNDERSTANDING

6. What role did Father Miguel Hidalgo play in the struggle for Mexican independence?

7. How did Mexican independence affect trade in California?

8. What two changes did the new Mexican government make that affected the Indians of California?

9. Why were land grants given to people?

10. Why could the ranchos of California be called self-sufficient?

11. What two products from California ranchos did American traders want?

THINK CRITICALLY

12. **Think More About It** Ranchos were once the center of California life. What do you think is the center of California life today? Explain.

13. **Personally Speaking** Would you have enjoyed living on a California rancho? Why or why not?

APPLY SKILLS

Use Historical Maps to See Change Use the maps on pages 170–171 to answer these questions.

14. What happened to the land in the Florida Territory between 1821 and 1841?

15. What happened to the land in the Arkansas Territory between 1821 and 1841?

READ MORE ABOUT IT

Anita of Rancho Del Mar by Elaine O'Brien. Fithian Press. Learn about life on a California rancho in the 1830s through the adventures of young Anita and the Lorenzana family.

HARCOURT BRACE

Visit the Internet at **http://www.hbschool.com** for additional resources.

Rebuilding California's FIRST MISSION

From the bell tower at Mission San Diego de Alcalá, the bells ring out, calling church members to prayer. These beautiful old bells still ring because the people of San Diego have worked hard to preserve their city's Spanish culture.

Like other missions in California, San Diego de Alcalá was in ruins in the early 1900s. It had nearly been destroyed by earthquakes, bad weather, and many years without care.

Some people in San Diego decided to save the mission. A group called the Native Sons and Daughters of the Golden West worked with the Catholic Church to raise money to rebuild the San Diego Mission.

Today community members continue to raise money to take care of the mission. Some come to the church to worship. Others visit to learn about California's past. Because of the work of many people, the mission is not only a part of history but also a part of people's lives today.

This is what Mission San Diego de Alcalá looked like in 1900, before it was rebuilt.

San Diego Mission Built A.D. 1769.

Passmore

People today can learn what life in California was like hundreds of years ago when they visit Mission San Diego de Alcalá.

Think and Apply

People in other cities have also worked to rebuild old California missions. With a partner, think of a place in your neighborhood or community that you think should be preserved or rebuilt. Then create a poster that explains why you think it should be saved and what people can do to help. Display your poster at school, or share it with community leaders.

HARCOURT BRACE
Visit the Internet at **http://www.hbschool.com** for additional resources.

CNN Turner Le@rning
Check your media center or classroom video library for the Making Social Studies Relevant videotape of this feature.

Advertisements (right) in the *San Diego Union* in 1919 asked people to donate money to help restore Mission San Diego de Alcalá. The restored mission was rededicated on September 13, 1931 (far right).

Citizens of San Diego:

Will you help to save your rarest Historical Gem

The Old Mission

Mail what funds you can spare to

PHILIP MORSE, Treasurer
172 SIXTH STREET, CITY.

It should be our duty to save the first Mission from crumbling to ruins.

RIDE OUT AND SEE IT

UNIT 2 REVIEW

Summarize the Main Ideas
Study the pictures and captions to help you review the events you read about in Unit 2.

Tell More of the Story
Prepare a short oral report about one of the events shown in this visual summary. Be sure to tell at least one important effect of the event.

1 Juan Rodríguez Cabrillo entered San Diego Bay in September 1542.

3 Over time, many missions, presidios, and pueblos were built. They changed forever the ways of life of California's Indians.

4 In 1810 Father Miguel Hidalgo called on the Mexican people to join in a revolt against Spanish rule.

6 In 1833 the Mexican government began closing the California missions. The Mexican citizens who received mission lands often used the land to start ranchos.

2 In 1769 Father Junípero Serra set up the first Spanish mission in Alta California. He named the mission San Diego de Alcalá.

 5 Mexico won its independence from Spain in 1821. It also gained control over California.

7 Rancho owners traded hides and tallow for manufactured products from the United States and for teas and silks from China.

USE VOCABULARY

Write a term from this list to complete each of the sentences that follow.

expedition   society

peninsula   tallow

❶ Baja California is a _____.

❷ Cabrillo's _____ set out to explore Alta California.

❸ A group of people who live in the same place and have many things in common is called a _____.

❹ _____ was used to make candles.

CHECK UNDERSTANDING

❺ Why did early Spanish explorers hope to find the Strait of Anián?

❻ Who was in charge of setting up the first missions in Alta California? Where was the first mission built?

❼ Why were presidios built?

❽ What did the new Mexican government do with the California missions? with the mission lands?

❾ How were ranchos important to California's early economy?

THINK CRITICALLY

❿ **Think More About It** What skills and abilities do you think early explorers needed?

⓫ **Link to You** Describe some Spanish or Mexican traditions that affect your life as a Californian.

APPLY SKILLS

Use Historical Maps to See Change The Spanish brought horses with them to North America. Some horses got away, and over time, Native Americans began to use horses, too. The map below shows when horses reached different areas. It also shows some of the Native American groups in each place.

⓬ When did horses first reach northern California?

⓭ Which Indian group got horses first, the Navajo or the Nez Perce?

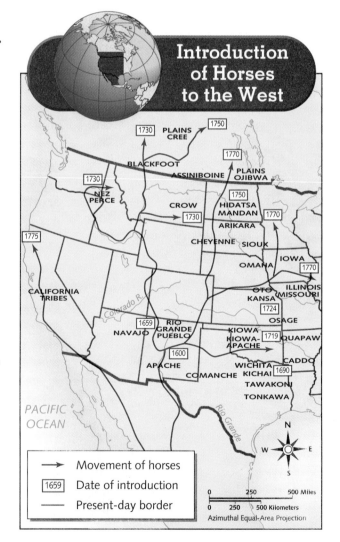

Introduction of Horses to the West

→ Movement of horses
1659 Date of introduction
— Present-day border

0 250 500 Miles
0 250 500 Kilometers
Azimuthal Equal-Area Projection

REMEMBER

- Share your ideas.
- Cooperate with others to plan your work.
- Take responsibility for your work.
- Help one another.
- Show your group's work to the class.
- Discuss what you learned by working together.

ACTIVITY Have Your Own Fiesta

Work with classmates to plan a classroom fiesta like the fiestas celebrated on the ranchos. First, do some research to find out more about fiestas. Then, decide which activities to include in your fiesta. You may want to make colorful costumes, prepare special foods, and sing old Mexican songs.

ACTIVITY Make a Poster

Imagine that you and some of your classmates have been hired by the Spanish government to create posters advertising for new settlers to come to California. Decide how your poster will try to get people to move to a land far away. Write an advertising slogan. Then create your poster and display it for other groups to see.

Unit Project Wrap-Up

Present Scenes About Historic Events Work with a group of classmates to finish the Unit Project described on page 123. Together, decide which events your group will present. Write the story of each event, choose roles, and design any costumes or backgrounds you will need. For each scene, the narrator will read aloud the story of the event as the people in the scene pose. Perform your scenes for invited guests from your school or from the community.

CALIFORNIA JOINS THE UNITED STATES

In the 1820s people from the United States started using new routes to reach California. These routes took them overland, across the Rocky Mountains and the Sierra Nevada. The first to come were fur trappers. They were followed by settlers looking for fertile land to farm.

Many people in the United States believed that their country should reach all the way to the Pacific Ocean. They got their wish when California became part of the United States following a war with Mexico. It was not until after the discovery of gold, however, that California became the thirty-first state.

◀ *Miners in the Sierras* was painted by Charles Nahl and Frederick A. Wenderoth.

UNIT THEMES

- Commonality and Diversity
- Conflict and Cooperation
- Continuity and Change
- Individualism and Interdependence

Unit Project

Make a 3-D Time Line Complete this project as you study Unit 3. Choose five important events to show on a three-dimensional time line. Take notes on when and where each event took place, who was there, and why the event was important to California's history. You can use these notes when you are ready to build your time line.

191

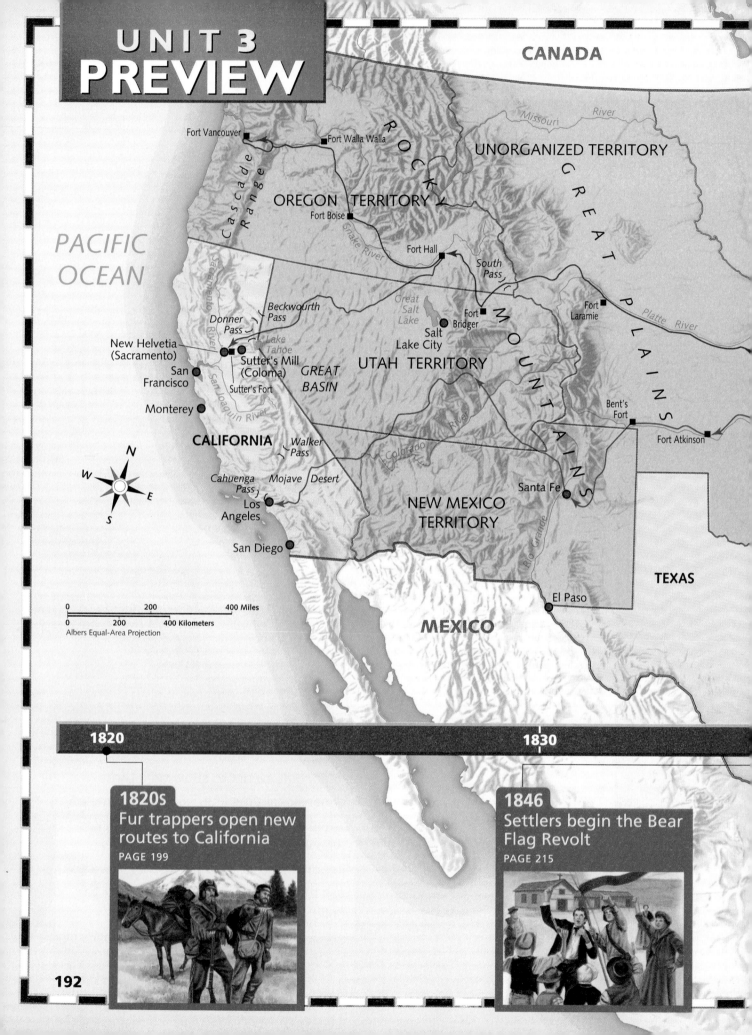

UNIT 3
PREVIEW

CANADA

UNORGANIZED TERRITORY

PACIFIC
OCEAN

Fort Vancouver

Fort Walla Walla

ROCKY

OREGON   TERRITORY

Fort Boise

Snake River

Fort Hall

South Pass

GREAT PLAINS

Missouri River

Platte River

Fort Laramie

Cascade Range

Sacramento River

Beckwourth Pass

Donner Pass

Lake Tahoe

New Helvetia (Sacramento)

Sutter's Mill (Coloma)

Sutter's Fort

San Francisco

Monterey

CALIFORNIA

GREAT BASIN

Walker Pass

San Joaquin River

Great Salt Lake

Salt Lake City

Fort Bridger

UTAH TERRITORY

MOUNTAINS

Colorado River

Bent's Fort

Fort Atkinson

Santa Fe

Cahuenga Pass

Mojave Desert

Los Angeles

San Diego

NEW MEXICO TERRITORY

Rio Grande

TEXAS

El Paso

MEXICO

N
W   E
S

| 0 | 200 | 400 Miles |
| 0 | 200 | 400 Kilometers |

Albers Equal-Area Projection

1820

1830

1820s
Fur trappers open new routes to California
PAGE 199

1846
Settlers begin the Bear Flag Revolt
PAGE 215

192

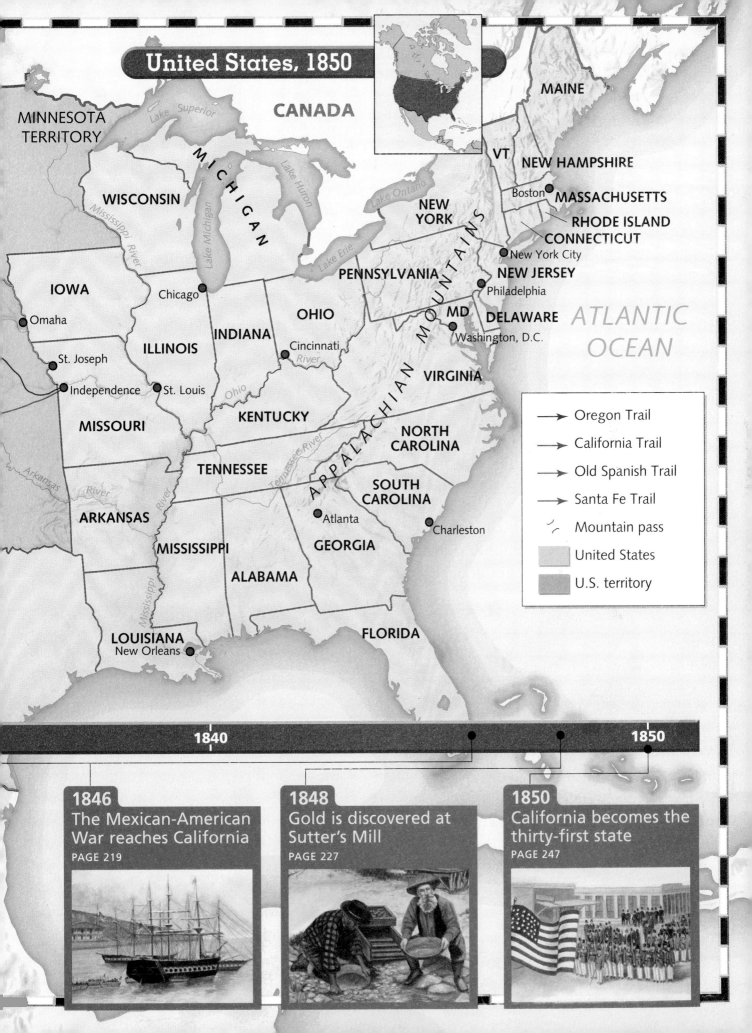

United States, 1850

CANADA

MINNESOTA TERRITORY

MAINE

VT

NEW HAMPSHIRE

WISCONSIN

MICHIGAN

Lake Superior

Lake Huron

Lake Michigan

Lake Ontario

Lake Erie

Boston • MASSACHUSETTS

RHODE ISLAND

CONNECTICUT

NEW YORK

IOWA

Mississippi River

Chicago •

• Omaha

St. Joseph •

• Independence

• St. Louis

ILLINOIS

INDIANA

OHIO

Cincinnati •

Ohio River

PENNSYLVANIA

APPALACHIAN MOUNTAINS

New York City •

NEW JERSEY

Philadelphia •

MD

Washington, D.C.

DELAWARE

ATLANTIC OCEAN

MISSOURI

KENTUCKY

VIRGINIA

Arkansas River

TENNESSEE

Tennessee River

NORTH CAROLINA

ARKANSAS

• Atlanta

SOUTH CAROLINA

• Charleston

MISSISSIPPI

GEORGIA

ALABAMA

Mississippi

LOUISIANA
New Orleans •

FLORIDA

→ Oregon Trail
→ California Trail
→ Old Spanish Trail
→ Santa Fe Trail
⌒ Mountain pass
▢ United States
▢ U.S. territory

1840   1850

1846
The Mexican-American War reaches California
PAGE 219

1848
Gold is discovered at Sutter's Mill
PAGE 227

1850
California becomes the thirty-first state
PAGE 247

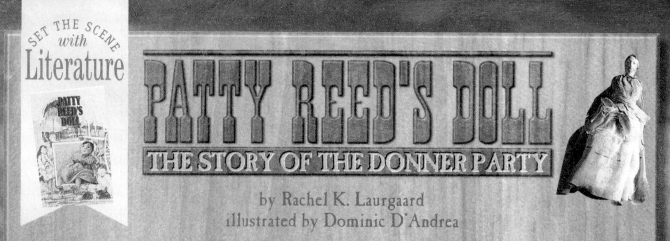

PATTY REED'S DOLL
THE STORY OF THE DONNER PARTY

by Rachel K. Laurgaard
illustrated by Dominic D'Andrea

Early visitors to California returned with stories of vast lands and great opportunities. But the trip west was not easy. To get to California people had to walk, ride a horse, or drive a covered wagon. There were many dangers and few comforts along the way.

Still, thousands of families decided to go. One group of people to travel west was the Donner Party. Among the people who made up the Donner Party was the Reed family, which included eight-year-old Patty Reed, her older sister Puss, and their younger brothers, Tommy and Jimmy. Traveling with the Reeds was the family dog, Cash.

The Donner Party set out for California from Springfield, Illinois, in the spring of 1846. By November of that year they had reached the Sierra Nevada. There, Indian guides, one of them named Salvador, joined the group. Patty's father had gone ahead through the mountains to California. Read now as Patty's doll tells what happened to the Donner Party as they tried to cross the mountains.

As we traveled up toward Truckee Lake, snow began to fall. When the clouds lifted from the summits of the mountains and the folks saw that they were covered with white, I could tell that they were frightened.

"Oh, it will be awful if we are snowed in," Patty said to Puss.

"We won't be. Papa will be coming any day now to meet us," her sister answered confidently.

Along the edge of Truckee Lake the mules plodded through soft, deep snow.

"Why, there's a cabin," Patty called out. The mule and Indian we were clinging to proved to be the best trail breakers, so we were somewhat ahead of the rest.

"It was built by a party that got marooned up here a few years ago, they told me," Mr. Stanton said. "We are close to the summit—only three miles or so."

We struggled on under a full moon, until the Indians made it known to Mr. Stanton that the snow had covered the trail and they were lost. We turned back and, arriving at the cabin we had passed, we found the Breen family already in possession.

However, they weren't much better off than the rest of us, crowded in the remaining wagons. Rain poured down in the night and leaked through the cabin roof of pine boughs just as it did through the tattered canvas of the wagon tops.

"The rain will melt the snow, won't it?" Patty's mother asked.

"It may not be rain up on the pass," Mr. Stanton answered in a worried tone. "When it rains lower down, it snows up above, they say."

summits
mountain peaks

confidently
with a sure feeling

marooned
left behind without hope of help

possession
ownership or control

boughs
branches of trees

floundering struggling

drifts piles of snow heaped up by the wind

advance to go forward

consultation discussion

provisions supplies of food

wallowing rolling about, as in mud

salvage to save

He was right. Floundering through the drifts next day, we were able to advance only a mile or two before nightfall. Wet and cold from plunging into the deep snow, the folks gathered around a blazing log fire that night in frightened consultation.

"We'll have to abandon the wagons, there's no doubt of that," someone said. "If we strap our provisions to the backs of the oxen, we may be able to pack through."

"It will be slow going with all the children," someone else said. "Every grownup will have to carry a child. The snow's much too deep for the little ones to make it alone."

The next day they tried to carry out this plan. The oxen were not very co-operative. The children laughed to see them buck and try to throw off the packs by wallowing in the snow. But it was no laughing matter to the men who were trying to salvage enough food to get their families safely across the mountains.

It was late afternoon when we started, and Patty and I were in the lead, with Salvador and the donkey making a road for the struggling line of people behind us. In some places the snow was waist-deep and, carrying children and driving unruly oxen, they were able to move only at a snail's pace. Finally the snow got so deep that the mule we were clinging to kept falling head first into gullies filled with snow. Patty was taken off, and Mr. Stanton and the Indians tried to ride ahead and find the road, while the rest waited behind.

By the time they returned, the wet, discouraged families were huddled around a roaring campfire in a dead pine tree filled with pitch. The oxen had rubbed off their packs against trees, and everyone was too exhausted to struggle on.

Mr. Stanton tried to persuade them that they must. They could get through, he thought, if it didn't snow any more. But his words went unheeded. Weary men and women remained crouched by the fire, with their children bundled up in blankets and buffalo robes on the snow beside them.

Patty, Puss, and the boys slept in their strange, cold bed, with little Cash and their mother watching over them. The wind sighed in the pine trees and the snow fell softly. By morning they were buried under mounds of white, for a foot of new snow had fallen in the night.

Grimly we turned back. It was useless to go ahead. Near the abandoned cabin, the men built log houses, roofing them with branches, hides, and wagon canvasses. At least we should be protected from the weather, and there was plenty of firewood to keep us warm.

"Do you think Papa will find us here?" Jimmy kept asking.

"If we can't get over the pass, neither can Father," his mother was forced to tell him.

"Will we be snowed in till spring?" Patty wanted to know.

pitch
the sticky sap of pine trees

unheeded
not listened to

MORE SETTLERS ARRIVE

"One might travel the world over without finding a valley . . . more alive with birds and animals, more bounteously watered [provided with plenty of water], than we had left in the San Joaquin."

John C. Frémont, mapmaker and explorer, about his 1844 trip through California

Trappers and Trailblazers

1825	1830	1835

For nearly 25 years California remained a part of Mexico. It also remained a hard place to get to. Sun-baked deserts and steep mountains separated it from both Mexico and the United States. Because of these barriers, few people came to California to settle.

Among those who did come to California were a few people from the United States. Like other settlers, they had to make a long journey to reach California. From the United States, ships had to sail down the Atlantic coast, around the tip of South America, and up the Pacific coast.

Trappers Open Up the West

For years this long, dangerous sea route was the only way for people from the United States to get to California. In the 1820s, however, fur trappers began to open up new overland routes through the West. They discovered these routes while looking for new places to trap beavers and other animals.

Beaver furs were used to make hats and other kinds of clothing. There was a great demand for these products in both Europe and the United States. A **demand** is a need or a desire for a good or service by people willing to pay for it.

In time, too much trapping used up most of the supply of beavers in the eastern United States. A **supply** is an amount of a good or service that is offered for sale. When the supply of something is not enough to meet the demand for it, prices rise.

FOCUS
Why might people look for new ways to get to places?

Main Idea Read this lesson to learn how new trails were opened up from the United States to California.

Vocabulary
demand
supply
governor
trailblazer
pass

Beaver skins like this one were turned into hats (above) and other kinds of clothing.

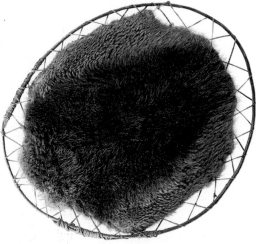

Chapter 5 • **199**

As beaver skins became even more valuable, trappers pushed westward to the Rocky Mountains to find more animals to trap. They trapped the animals along streams and rivers and sold the skins to fur traders. The traders in turn sold the skins to manufacturers.

REVIEW Why did fur trappers explore the West?

Jedediah Strong Smith

Over time the fur trappers began to move farther west into the rich lands of California. The first American to travel overland from the United States to California was Jedediah Strong Smith. Smith was an owner of the Rocky Mountain Fur Company. He hoped to explore California and find new places to trap animals.

In August 1826 Smith left his camp near the Great Salt Lake. With him were several other trappers. As Smith later wrote, the expedition crossed "barren, rocky, and mountainous" country to the Colorado River. With the help of Native American guides, the trappers crossed the Mojave Desert. There was little shade from the blazing sun, and there were few places to find water. Smith wrote that the men traveled "from morning until night without water."

By November the group had crossed the San Bernardino Mountains and reached the San Gabriel Mission. The head of the mission, Father José Sanchez, was surprised to see the ragged strangers. He welcomed them and gave them food, clothing, and a place to rest. The group later traveled south to San Diego.

California's governor, José María Echeandía (eh•chay•ahn•DEE•ah), did not welcome Smith. A **governor** is a leader of a colony or a state. Echeandía saw the Smith expedition as a danger. After all, the trappers had entered California without Mexico's permission. Echeandía worried that other people from the United States might do the same. The governor put Smith in jail but let him go when he promised to leave California.

Smith left, but he did not return the way he had come. He wanted to explore more of California, so he crossed the San Gabriel Mountains and headed north to the San Joaquin Valley.

The trappers knew that to return home they had to cross the Sierra Nevada. When they tried to cross those high mountains, however, they had to turn back. They could find no food in the deep snow for their horses.

The fur trappers who opened up the West were also known as mountain men because they were at home in the forests and mountains. Many had learned from Native Americans how to survive in the wilderness.

Smith decided to try to cross the mountains again. In May 1827 he and a few other trappers set out. With some horses and mules, they struggled through the Sierra Nevada's freezing temperatures and howling winds.

After several days, the tired travelers finally saw the flatlands of the Great Basin below them. They had become the first people from the United States to cross the Sierra Nevada. When Smith arrived back at the Great Salt Lake, he learned that the other members of the expedition had eventually made their way across the mountains, too.

REVIEW Why did Governor Echeandía not welcome Smith?

Fur trappers often needed to wear snowshoes when the snow was deep. How do you think snowshoes work?

More Trails West

Other trailblazers soon followed Smith to California. A **trailblazer** is a person who makes a new trail for others to follow. In 1827 Sylvester Pattie and his son, James Ohio Pattie, traveled through New Mexico into California. Like Smith, the Patties were jailed by Governor Echeandía for entering California without permission. Sylvester Pattie died in jail, but James was freed when a disease that may have been smallpox broke out. He told Mexican leaders that he had a vaccine (vak•SEEN) that would protect against smallpox. The governor freed Pattie and had him give the medicine to people in California.

Ewing Young also traveled to California. Later, in the 1830s, he helped start the Old Spanish Trail. It led from Santa Fe, in New Mexico, into southern California. This trail became an important trade route.

In 1834 Joseph Reddeford Walker found a route through a mountain pass in the Sierra Nevada. A **pass** is an opening between high mountains.

"He was one of the best leaders I have ever met, a good hunter and trapper, . . . and possessed of good knowledge of the mountains," someone wrote of Joseph Reddeford Walker.

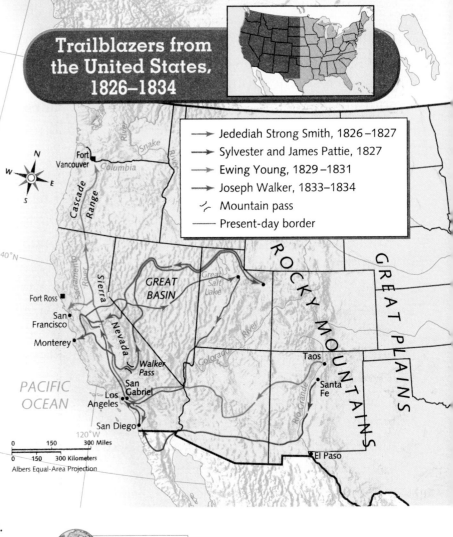

Trailblazers from the United States, 1826–1834

- → Jedediah Strong Smith, 1826–1827
- → Sylvester and James Pattie, 1827
- → Ewing Young, 1829–1831
- → Joseph Walker, 1833–1834
- ⌐ Mountain pass
- — Present-day border

Movement Several trailblazers opened up new trails to California in the 1820s and 1830s. ■ Who opened the trail that went farthest south before reaching California?

Walker Pass later became the main route for many settlers traveling to California.

Several years later James Beckwourth found another pass through the Sierra Nevada. Beckwourth had traveled to the West from the United States when he was just 18 years old. He became a fur trapper and trader. Beckwourth became friendly with several

Native American groups, and he often lived for long periods with the Indians. He made several trading trips to California in the 1830s and 1840s. There, he later wrote, he "did a very profitable business for several months."

All of these trailblazers helped open up California to people from the United States. Before long, other

Americans were heading west, hoping to begin new lives in California.

REVIEW How did Joseph Reddeford Walker and James Beckwourth help later settlers?

James Beckwourth discovered a pass through the Sierra Nevada that led into the American Valley. The cabin that he built near present-day Portola became a busy trading post.

LESSON 1 REVIEW

1825	1830	1835

1826
• Jedediah Smith reaches California overland

1827
• Jedediah Smith crosses the Sierra Nevada

1834
• Joseph Reddeford Walker finds Walker Pass

Check Understanding

❶ **Remember the Facts** What trail did Ewing Young help develop?

❷ **Recall the Main Idea** How were new trails opened up from the United States to California?

Think Critically

❸ **Cause and Effect** What happens to prices when supply is not enough to meet demand? What if supply is greater than demand?

❹ **Think More About It** How were earlier explorers, such as Portolá

and Anza, also trailblazers? Explain your answer.

Show What You Know

Table Activity Make a table titled *California Trailblazers*. Divide a sheet of paper into two columns. In the first column, list all the trailblazers you read about in this lesson. In the second column, describe what each trailblazer did. Then use your table and a large map of the United States to explain to classmates how each trailblazer helped open up new trails to California.

Compare Distances

1. Why Learn This Skill?

A map that shows a large land area cannot show as many details as a map that shows a small area. Maps that show different amounts of land in the same amount of space must have different scales. That is, the same distance on different maps shows different real distances on the Earth. Understanding this idea will help you use maps.

2. Understand the Process

Look at the two historical maps on these pages. Both maps show the route taken by Jedediah Strong Smith on his second expedition to California. Map A shows all of Smith's route through California, while Map B shows only the part that went through central California. Because Map B shows a smaller area, it can show more details about Smith's trip than Map A can.

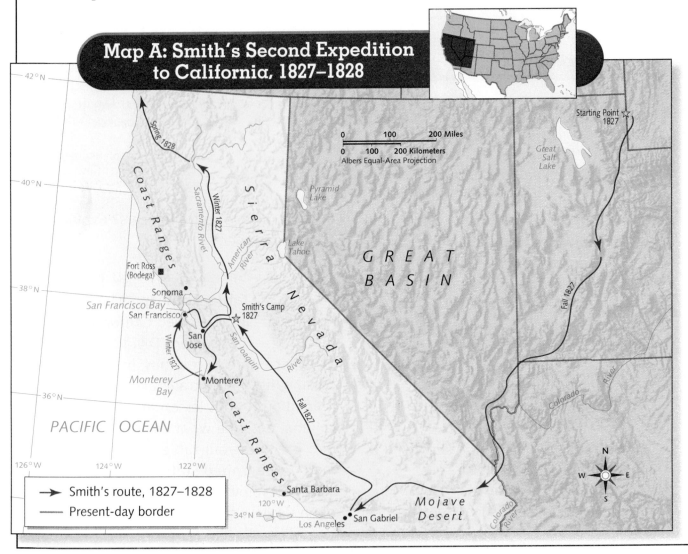

Map A: Smith's Second Expedition to California, 1827–1828

0   100   200 Miles
0   100   200 Kilometers
Albers Equal-Area Projection

42°N
40°N
38°N
36°N
34°N

126°W   124°W   122°W   120°W

Spring 1828
Winter 1827
Fall 1827
Winter 1827
Fall 1827

Coast Ranges
Sacramento River
American River
Sierra Nevada
San Joaquin River
Coast Ranges

Starting Point 1827
Great Salt Lake
Pyramid Lake
Lake Tahoe
GREAT BASIN
Colorado River
Colorado River

Fort Ross (Bodega)
Sonoma
San Francisco Bay
San Francisco
San Jose
Smith's Camp 1827
Monterey Bay
Monterey
PACIFIC OCEAN
Santa Barbara
Los Angeles
San Gabriel
Mojave Desert

N
W   E
S

→ Smith's route, 1827–1828
—— Present-day border

on Maps

1 Use your ruler to measure the distance between Fort Ross and San Jose on Map A. Then use the map scale to find how many miles that distance stands for. About how many miles is it from Fort Ross to San Jose?

2 Now measure the distance between Fort Ross and San Jose on Map B. Use the map scale. How does this distance compare with the distance on Map A?

You can use either map to find the distance between any two places shown.

3. Think and Apply

Find two maps that show the same area. Find the distance between the same two places on each. Is the real distance the same? What kinds of details are shown on one map but not on the other?

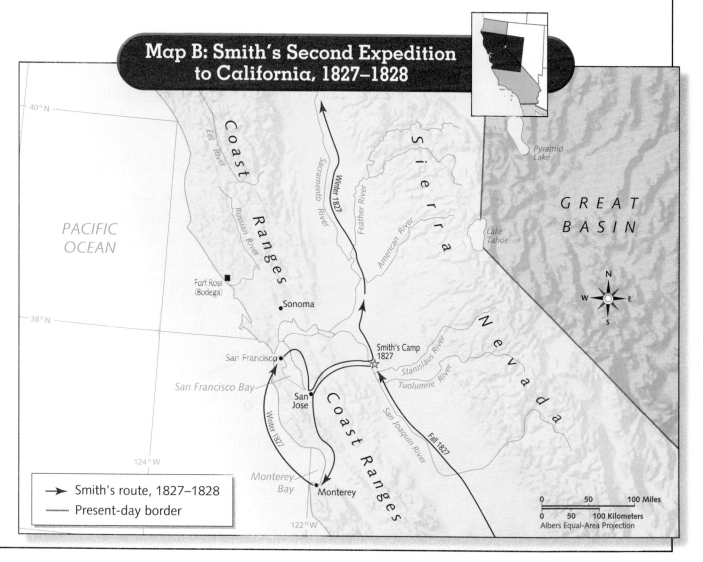

Map B: Smith's Second Expedition to California, 1827–1828

40°N

Eel River

Coast Ranges

Russian River

Sacramento River

Winter 1827

Feather River

American River

Sierra

Pyramid Lake

GREAT BASIN

PACIFIC OCEAN

Lake Tahoe

Fort Ross (Bodega)

•Sonoma

38°N

San Francisco•

San Francisco Bay

San Jose•

Smith's Camp 1827

Stanislaus River

Tuolumne River

Nevada

Coast Ranges

San Joaquin River

Fall 1827

124°W

Winter 1827

N W E S

Monterey Bay

Monterey

122°W

→ Smith's route, 1827–1828
— Present-day border

0   50   100 Miles
0   50   100 Kilometers
Albers Equal-Area Projection

FOCUS

How do people travel to California today?

Main Idea Read to find out how settlers from the United States traveled to California in the 1840s.

Vocabulary

immigrant
frontier
pioneer
wagon train

Trails to California

1840   1844   1848

F ur trappers were not the only people coming to California. Among the other newcomers were a small number of immigrants (IH•mih•gruhnts). An **immigrant** is a person who comes from another place to live in a country.

Most immigrants worked in the hide and tallow trade or in the fur trade. A few, like Abel Stearns, became Mexican citizens and started ranchos or businesses. Stearns came to California from the United States in 1828. He started a successful trading business in Los Angeles and became the richest person in southern California.

Sutter's Fort

Another immigrant who settled in California was John Augustus Sutter, from Switzerland. Sutter left Europe in 1834 after his business there failed. Sutter hoped to make his fortune in North America. He moved from New York City to St. Louis to Santa Fe and then to Oregon, Hawaii, and Alaska without making much money. In 1839 he reached California.

In California, Sutter's luck changed. In 1840, after he became a Mexican citizen, the governor gave him a huge land grant in the Sacramento Valley. The next year he bought Fort Ross from the Russians.

Sutter started a settlement called New Helvetia (hel•VEE•shuh), or

John Augustus Sutter received a huge land grant in the Sacramento Valley. A wheel from an early settler's wagon is shown above.

People traveling overland to California from the United States were welcomed at Sutter's Fort. Settlers who came to the fort during the 1840s used canteens (left) to carry water.

New Switzerland. At its center he built a fort with adobe walls about 15 feet (5 m) high and 3 feet (1 m) thick. Inside Sutter's Fort were several cannons that Sutter had moved there from Fort Ross.

Sutter ran a settlement of many workers. He hired mostly Native Americans and Californios, but he also brought some workers from Hawaii, where he had lived. The workers of New Helvetia raised cattle and sheep, grew wheat, wove cloth, and made leather from cattle hides. Sutter also built a mill to grind grain.

Sutter's Fort was located near the place where the American and Sacramento rivers join. This is where the city of Sacramento is located today.

Sutter's Fort also stood at the end of several trails crossing the Sierra Nevada. In the 1840s people from the United States who crossed these mountains found a warm welcome at Sutter's Fort. Sutter fed the hungry travelers and hired those who needed jobs to work on his land. He also sold land and supplies to the newcomers.

REVIEW Where was Sutter's Fort?

The Bidwell-Bartleson Expedition

Sutter built his fort just as more people from the United States were becoming interested in California. These people saw California as a new frontier, a place where

John Bidwell was a teacher before becoming one of the leaders of the first group of pioneers from the United States to reach California by land. He later became a Mexican citizen and received a land grant.

they could get plenty of land. A **frontier** is the land beyond the settled part of a country.

Americans who had already settled in California praised the region. "This is beyond all comparison the finest country and the finest climate," wrote rancho owner John Marsh in 1840. "What we want here is more people."

Such reports soon brought other pioneers from the United States. A **pioneer**

is one of the first settlers in a place. One of the earliest groups of pioneers to make the overland trip to California from the United States was the Bidwell-Bartleson expedition.

In May 1841 a group of about 30 men, women, and children met in Missouri. They chose John Bartleson to lead them. John Bidwell took over later.

The Mexican government had warned Americans not to come to California without its permission. However, the pioneers believed that the Mexican government was not strong enough to stop

A Covered Wagon

Cover

Feed trough

Seat

Footrest

Toolbox

Yoke

Brake lever

Water bucket

Brake shoe

Tar pot

them. So they drove their wagons west along the Oregon Trail and across the Rocky Mountains. The Oregon Trail was the main route pioneers took from Missouri to Oregon—the lands north of California.

When the group reached what is today southeastern Idaho, about half of the pioneers decided to go to Oregon. The others turned southwest toward California. The trail they followed was later called the California Trail. It became the main overland route to California.

Day after day the wagon train rolled on. A **wagon train** is a group of wagons, each pulled by horses or oxen. In present-day Nevada, the pioneers ran out of food and had to kill their oxen.

LEARNING FROM DIAGRAMS Pioneers packed as many household goods as they could into their covered wagons.
■ Why would a toolbox be important to pioneers?

With no animals to pull their wagons, they had to continue on foot.

Bidwell knew that his group needed to cross the Sierra Nevada before winter. Deep snow would make the mountains impossible to cross. Luckily, the first snowfall was late that year. In October the group struggled across the Sierra Nevada. "We ate the last of our beef [the oxen meat] this evening," Bidwell wrote in his journal.

Finally, after weeks of hardships, the tired travelers "beheld [saw] a wide valley." It was the Central Valley. The pioneers in Bidwell's group were the first settlers from the United States to cross overland into California. Bidwell later founded Chico, a city in the northern Sacramento Valley.

REVIEW Why did the pioneers need to cross the Sierra Nevada before winter?

John C. Frémont

Pioneers faced hunger, thirst, and sickness on the overland trails. Sometimes they were attacked by Indians who were afraid the settlers would take their lands. But all the hardships and dangers did not stop people from moving to California.

The pioneers who traveled to California often followed trails that were first used by trappers. Later pioneers were also helped by mapmakers and explorers such as John C. Frémont.

In 1841 Frémont married Jessie Benton, the daughter of United States Senator Thomas Hart Benton. Senator Benton wanted the United States to

John C. Frémont and his wife, Jessie Benton Frémont, shown here, became famous after *Reports*, their book about exploring California, was published.

expand westward, and so did his new son-in-law.

Frémont made several journeys to the West, where he drew maps of the land for the United States government. During the winter of 1843–1844, Frémont traveled across the Sierra Nevada to California. He used Carson Pass, named for his guide, Kit Carson.

Frémont arrived at Sutter's Fort in March 1844. From there he traveled south and explored the San Joaquin Valley. Frémont returned home by crossing through a pass in the Tehachapi (tih•HACH•uh•pee) Mountains. These mountains lie between the Sierra Nevada and the Coast Ranges at the southern end of the San Joaquin Valley.

Frémont's wife helped him write a book about his travels. It had much useful information about California. Even more pioneers decided to set out for California after reading this book and others like it.

REVIEW **How did John Frémont help settlers who wanted to come to California?**

BIOGRAPHY

Kit Carson
1809–1868

Kit Carson, whose real name was Christopher, was born in Kentucky but grew up in Missouri. As a child he learned how to ride and take care of horses. These skills later helped him become one of the West's best-known trail guides. After guiding John C. Frémont and others to California, Carson moved to New Mexico and later served in the Civil War. Carson City, Nevada, is named for him.

Kit Carson guided John C. Frémont across the Sierra Nevada during the winter of 1843–1844.

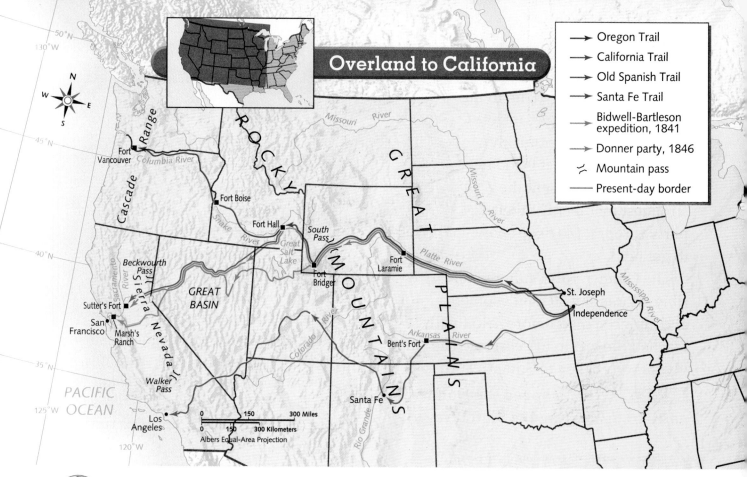

Overland to California

Map Legend:
- → Oregon Trail
- → California Trail
- → Old Spanish Trail
- → Santa Fe Trail
- → Bidwell-Bartleson expedition, 1841
- → Donner party, 1846
- ⤳ Mountain pass
- — Present-day border

Movement Pioneers could take several trails to the West in the 1840s.

■ Which trail starting from Independence did both the Bidwell-Bartleson expedition and the Donner party use? Where did they turn onto different routes?

The Donner Party

In May 1846 about 87 men, women, and children left Independence, a city in Missouri. Their leader was George Donner, and the group has come to be known as the Donner party.

Donner's daughter, Eliza, later wrote about the journey. She wrote that on the day they left, "our people [were] in the best of spirits." The children rode horses "with the breeze playing through our hair."

By summer, however, the journey had become difficult. The weather was hot, and water was hard to find. In July the Donner party decided to take a shortcut they had read about in a book, *Emigrant's Guide to Oregon and California*. This book had been written by Lansford Hastings, a guide who had never been on this shortcut. That shortcut turned out to be a terrible mistake. It led the group over ground so rough that it took nearly a month longer to go that way.

The Donner party did not reach the Sierra Nevada until November, and a heavy snowfall trapped them in the mountains. One member of the group, Patrick Breen, described the snow. He wrote in his journal, "Snowing fast, looks as likely to continue as when it commenced [started]; no living thing without wings can get about." The people quickly built huts near what is today Donner Lake and sent the strongest members of their party through the deep snow to get help.

The Donner party suffered terribly. More than 30 men, women, and children died before help finally reached the group in February. The survivors were taken to Sutter's Fort.

REVIEW What stopped the Donner party from crossing the Sierra Nevada?

LESSON 2 REVIEW

1840

1844

1848

1841
• The Bidwell-Bartleson expedition arrives in California

1846
• The Donner party sets out for California

1844
• John C. Frémont explores California

1840
• John Sutter founds New Helvetia

Check Understanding

1 **Remember the Facts** What was the name of John Sutter's settlement?

2 **Recall the Main Idea** How did settlers from the United States reach California in the 1840s?

Think Critically

3 **Think More About It** Why do you think hardships did not stop pioneers from coming to California?

4 **Personally Speaking** Imagine that you were in Missouri in 1841.

Would you have joined the Bidwell-Bartleson expedition? Explain.

Show What You Know

Writing Activity Write a guidebook for people who are thinking about going to California in the 1840s. Describe the land and climates they will pass through, and the hardships they will face. Draw a map to go with your guidebook. Then take the role of a guide and convince classmates that California is the place they should go.

Tell Fact from Opinion

1. Why Learn This Skill?

A good listener or reader can tell facts from opinions. A **fact** is a statement that can be checked and proved to be true. An **opinion** is a statement that tells what the person who makes it thinks or believes. Knowing how to tell a fact from an opinion can help you better understand what you hear or read.

2. Remember What You Have Read

Some of the statements you read in the last lesson gave facts about California's early pioneers, for example, *John Augustus Sutter reached California in 1839.* You could check whether that statement is true by looking in an encyclopedia or in books about California. Other statements in the lesson give opinions, for example, John Marsh's statement *This is beyond all comparison the finest country and the finest climate.* There is no way to prove which is the finest country or climate in the world.

John Marsh was a rancho owner in California.

3. Understand the Process

Facts often give dates, numbers, or other pieces of information. To tell whether a statement is a fact, ask yourself these questions.

- Do I know this idea to be true from my own experience?
- Can the idea be proved true by testing?
- Is the idea from a book or another source I can trust?

An opinion is what a speaker or writer believes. Looking for these clues can help you know when a statement is an opinion.

- Key words such as *I think, I believe, I doubt,* and *in my opinion* tell you that you are reading or hearing an opinion.
- Words such as *finest, wonderful, worst,* and *terrible* are often part of an opinion.

Even though opinions cannot be proved, they can still be helpful. Some opinions are based on facts or experience. Historians, for example, use facts to help them form opinions about the past. Thoughtful opinions can help people better understand the past or prepare for the future.

4. Think and Apply

A newspaper is a good place to find facts and opinions. Use a crayon or marker of one color to underline five statements of fact in a newspaper. Use another color to underline five statements of opinion. Explain to classmates how you were able to tell the facts from the opinions.

FOCUS
Why might people
want to change their
government?

Main Idea Read to
learn how settlers
from the United
States tried to
make California an
independent country.

Vocabulary
squatter
manifest destiny
rebel
republic

The Bear Flag Revolt

| 1845 | 1846 | 1847 |

In 1845 California had about 7,000 settlers. Most were Californios, but almost 700 were people from the United States. And more Americans were on their way.

Mexican leaders were worried about the newcomers. In order to own land, settlers had to become Mexican citizens. However, many Americans did not want to become citizens of Mexico. Instead, some became squatters on the land. A **squatter** is someone who lives in a place without permission.

There was another reason the Mexican government was worried about the newcomers from the United States. Many of them wanted to make California part of the United States.

Manifest Destiny

By the 1840s many Americans shared a belief that the United States should stretch from sea to sea—from the Atlantic Ocean to the Pacific Ocean. This belief was

James K. Polk became
the eleventh President
of the United States on
March 4, 1845.

called **manifest destiny**. *Manifest* means "easy to see," and *destiny* means "what is to be." One American wrote,

> We, the people of the United States, have spread, are spreading, and intend to spread, and should spread . . . and this our destiny has now become so manifest that it cannot fail.

Americans wanted ports on the Pacific, and they wanted more land, too. So they set out to make Texas, Oregon, and California part of the United States. Texas had already won its independence from Mexico in 1836. In 1845 it became part of the United States. Oregon was claimed by both Britain and the United States, and California was still part of Mexico.

In 1845 James K. Polk became President of the United States. Polk believed strongly in manifest destiny. He offered Mexico $40 million for Alta California and New Mexico. New Mexico included lands that are now part of the states of New Mexico and Arizona. Mexico, however, would not sell its lands.

REVIEW What was manifest destiny?

The Bear Flaggers

Many of the American settlers in California did not like living under the Mexican government. Many squatters were also afraid that Mexico might force

The Bear Flag Revolt, 1846

Location The Bear Flag Revolt took place in Sonoma.
■ In which direction is Sonoma from New Helvetia?

them to leave. Feelings against Mexican rule were so strong that some of the Americans began a revolt to win independence for California.

Many Californios were also unhappy with Mexico. They felt that the leaders of the Mexican government did not pay enough attention to the needs of California. Some Californios were willing to work with the Americans to win independence.

Mexico had its own troubles. Its government was weak, and its leaders often changed. Because of these problems, Mexico had little control over far-off California.

At dawn on June 14, 1846, about 35 American settlers marched into the small town of Sonoma, in northern

California. One member of the group later described what he saw.

> Almost the whole party was dressed in leather hunting-shirts, many of them very greasy; taking the whole party together, they were about as rough a looking set of men as one could well imagine.

The rebels quickly surrounded the home of General Mariano Vallejo (mar•ee•AHN•oh vah•YAY•hoh), a Californio and a commander of Mexican forces. A **rebel** is a person who fights against the government. The rebels then called on the general to surrender, or give up.

Vallejo had no reason to fight the Americans. In fact, he, too, wanted independence for California. Still, the rebels made Vallejo stay in his home to keep him from doing anything to stop the revolt. The rebels then took down the

While they kept the commander of Mexican forces, General Mariano Vallejo (right), in his home, American settlers raised the Bear Flag (below) and declared California an independent republic.

Mexican flag in the plaza and raised their own handmade flag. On it were a bear, a star, and the words "California Republic."

This was the beginning of the Bear Flag Revolt. The Bear Flaggers, as the Americans called themselves, declared that California was now an independent republic. A **republic** is a form of government in which people elect their leaders.

John C. Frémont, who had returned to California in 1845, became a leader of the Bear Flag Revolt. However, the California Republic lasted for less than three weeks. Soon other events would change California once again.

REVIEW What did the Bear Flaggers want for California?

LESSON 3 REVIEW

1845   1846   1847

1845
• James K. Polk becomes President of the United States

1846
• The Bear Flag Revolt takes place

Check Understanding

1 Remember the Facts What concerns did Americans living in California have about the Mexican government in the 1840s?

2 Recall the Main Idea How did settlers from the United States try to make California an independent country?

Think Critically

3 Think More About It Why would the Bear Flaggers want a republic?

4 Explore Viewpoints Why might some Californios have wanted independence? Why might others have been against it?

Show What You Know

Art Activity Imagine that you must create a new flag for California today. Draw a flag and create a motto, or saying, to go on it. Then present your flag and motto to your classmates. Explain why you chose your design and motto.

The Mexican-American War

| 1846 | 1847 | 1848 | 1849 |

FOCUS

Why do countries sometimes fight wars?

Main Idea   Read about how the Mexican-American War made California part of the United States.

Vocabulary

right

treaty

When the Bear Flag Revolt began in June 1846, the United States and Mexico were already at war. But no one in California knew that. News did not travel as fast in those days as it does today.

The war between the United States and Mexico had started in May 1846. The Mexican-American War had several causes. One was the American dream of manifest destiny. Another was the United States government's decision to make Texas a state. The Mexican government was very angry about this because Texas had once belonged to Mexico.

The War in California

Most of the fighting in the Mexican-American War took place outside California. United States General

Commodore John Sloat raised the United States flag over the Customs House at Monterey on July 7, 1846. The canteen shown above was carried by a soldier during the Mexican-American War.

Stephen Kearny (KAR•nee) led soldiers into New Mexico. Another group of American soldiers landed on the east coast of Mexico and captured Mexico City.

John Sloat, an officer in the United States Navy, first brought news of the war to California. He had sailed from Mexico and entered the port of Monterey on July 2, 1846. Five days later, Sloat's forces took over Monterey without firing a single shot.

Sloat raised the United States flag over Monterey and told the people,

66 I declare to the inhabitants of California that altho' I come in arms with a powerful force, I do not come among them as enemy to California: but on the contrary I come as their best friend; as henceforward California will be a portion of the United States. 99

Sloat also told Monterey's people that California would be helped by American rule. They would be free of Mexican rule and would have the same rights as citizens of the United States. A **right** is a freedom that belongs to a person.

In several small battles, some Californios resisted the United States forces. But most did not. American troops, led by Robert F. Stockton and John C. Frémont, quickly captured Los Angeles, San Francisco, and other towns on the coast. John Bidwell later wrote,

66 We simply marched all over California, from Sonoma to San Diego, and raised the American flag without protest. We tried to find an enemy, but could not. 99

In one town, however, the Californios rebelled against their new American rulers. In September 1846 the people of Los Angeles surrounded the American troops. The Americans were forced to leave Los Angeles and go to nearby San Pedro, where they could sail back to the United States.

In October 1846, United States Navy ships arrived at San Pedro with more troops. The Americans decided to march inland and try to take back Los Angeles. In the Battle of Domínguez Rancho, the Californios defeated the Americans and forced them back to their ships.

REVIEW Who first brought news of the Mexican-American War to California?

General Andrés Pico

General Kearny Arrives

While the Battle of Domínguez Rancho was being fought, General Kearny and his soldiers were marching west from New Mexico. They were guided by Kit Carson. In early December they met a group of Californios led by General Andrés Pico at San Pascual (pahs•KWAHL), northeast of San Diego.

The Californios were skilled horse-back riders, and they were able to drive back Kearny's soldiers. Kit Carson, however, was able to slip away and bring back help. With more soldiers, Kearny forced Pico and his troops to withdraw.

The Americans set out again to take back Los Angeles. On January 10, 1847, with supplies running low, the Californios

General Stephen Kearny

surrendered. The United States flag was again raised over the city.

General Pico agreed to meet with John C. Frémont near Cahuenga (cah•HWEN•gah) Pass. Pico feared that the Americans would punish the Californios for fighting against them. However, a California woman named Bernarda Ruiz (roo•EES) asked to meet with Frémont. She told him that he should

" win the Mexican Californians over to your side, rather than make enemies of them by inflicting [forcing on them] harsh peace terms. You will be governor . . . one day soon, and it would be better to have thousands of loyal supporters. "

Ruiz's advice made sense to Frémont. On January 13, 1847, he and Pico signed the Treaty of Cahuenga, which ended the fighting in California. A **treaty** is an agreement between groups or countries.

The Treaty of Cahuenga said that Pico and the other Californio leaders

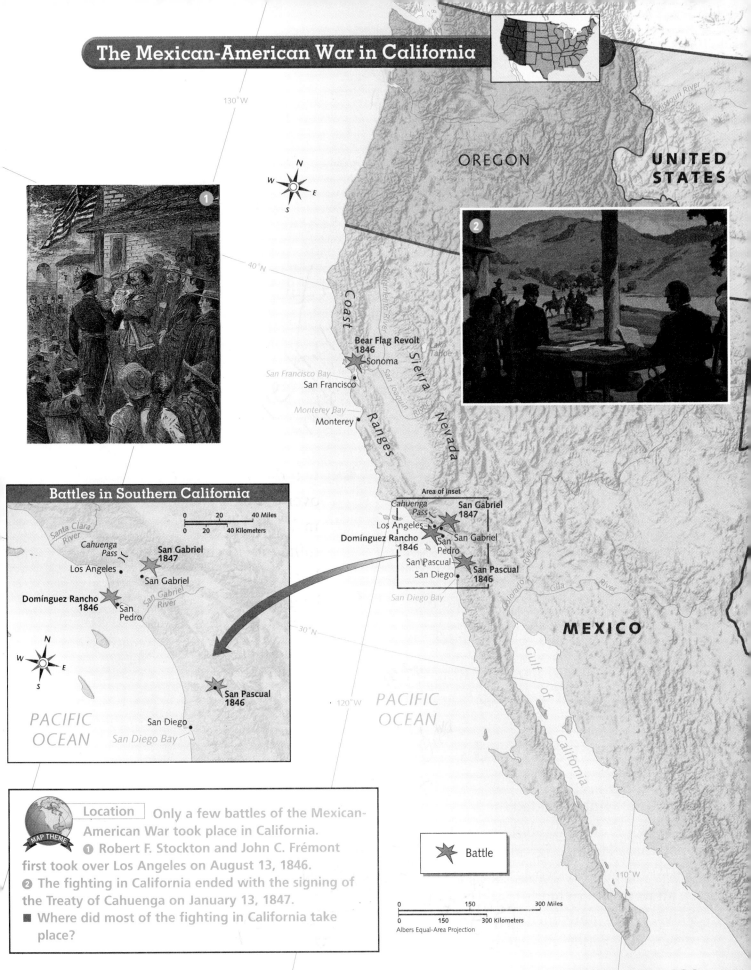

OREGON

UNITED STATES

Bear Flag Revolt
1846
Sonoma
San Francisco Bay
San Francisco

Monterey Bay
Monterey

Area of inset
Cahuenga
Pass
Los Angeles
Domínguez Rancho
1846
San Gabriel
1847
San Gabriel
San
Pedro
San Pascual
San Diego
San Pascual
1846
San Diego Bay

MEXICO

PACIFIC
OCEAN

Battles in Southern California

0   20   40 Miles
0   20   40 Kilometers

Santa Clara
River
Cahuenga
Pass
Los Angeles

San Gabriel
1847
San Gabriel

Domínguez Rancho
1846
San
Pedro

San Gabriel
River

N
W   E
S

San Pascual
1846

PACIFIC
OCEAN

San Diego
San Diego Bay

★ Battle

0   150   300 Miles
0   150   300 Kilometers
Albers Equal-Area Projection

Location   Only a few battles of the Mexican-American War took place in California.
❶ Robert F. Stockton and John C. Frémont first took over Los Angeles on August 13, 1846.
❷ The fighting in California ended with the signing of the Treaty of Cahuenga on January 13, 1847.
■ Where did most of the fighting in California take place?

Chapter 5 • **221**

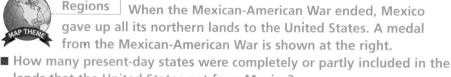

United States, 1848

0 200 400 Miles
0 200 400 Kilometers
Albers Equal-Area Projection

CANADA

Boston

New York City

Philadelphia

Chicago

UNITED STATES

St. Louis

PACIFIC OCEAN

Sonoma
San Francisco
Sutter's Fort
Monterey

Los Angeles
San Diego

Santa Fe
Albuquerque

Tucson

New Orleans

ATLANTIC OCEAN

MEXICO

Gulf of Mexico

Columbia River
Snake River
Missouri River
Lake Superior
Lake Michigan
Lake Huron
Lake Ontario
Lake Erie
Platte River
Colorado River
Arkansas River
Mississippi River
Ohio River
Tennessee R.
Rio Grande
Gila River

Land acquired by the U.S. from Mexico in 1848
Present-day border

130°W 120°W 90°W 80°W 70°W
40°N 30°N

Regions When the Mexican-American War ended, Mexico gave up all its northern lands to the United States. A medal from the Mexican-American War is shown at the right.

■ How many present-day states were completely or partly included in the lands that the United States got from Mexico?

MAP THEME

would not be punished. It also said that the rights of the defeated Californios would be respected.

REVIEW How did Bernarda Ruiz affect the Treaty of Cahuenga?

The War Ends

In February 1848 the United States and Mexico finally ended the Mexican-American War by signing the Treaty of Guadalupe Hidalgo (gwah•dah•LOO•pay ee•DAHL•goh). Mexico agreed to give up all its northern lands to the United States. These lands included all of present-day California, Utah, and

Nevada and parts of New Mexico, Arizona, Colorado, and Wyoming. In return, the United States agreed to pay Mexico $15 million.

Americans celebrated the treaty. Their dream of manifest destiny had come true. The United States now reached from Canada to Mexico, from the Atlantic Ocean to the Pacific Ocean. Mexico, however, was very upset about its losses. Under the treaty, it had given up almost half of its land.

The Treaty of Guadalupe Hidalgo also pleased many Californios. It made them citizens of the United States, and it allowed them to keep any land they had owned before the war. Some people said that the treaty was good to Californios because of the Treaty of Cahuenga that Frémont and Pico had signed.

Spanish-speaking people in California soon found out how United States rule would change their lives. In the next few years, it would bring many more Americans to California.

REVIEW What lands became part of the United States by the Treaty of Guadalupe Hidalgo?

The Treaty of Guadalupe Hidalgo ended the Mexican-American War. Mexico agreed to give up its northern lands, and, in return, the United States agreed to pay Mexico $15 million.

LESSON 4 REVIEW

1846	1847	1848	1849

1846
• The Mexican-American War begins

1847
• The Treaty of Cahuenga ends the fighting in California

1848
• The Treaty of Guadalupe Hidalgo ends the Mexican-American War

Check Understanding

1 **Remember the Facts** What happened at the Battle of San Pascual?

2 **Recall the Main Idea** How did the Mexican-American War make California part of the United States?

Think Critically

3 **Personally Speaking** If you had been John Frémont, would you have listened to Bernarda Ruiz's advice? Why or why not?

4 **Think More About It** Why might it be hard for people who were once enemies to become friends?

Show What You Know

Writing Activity Imagine that you are John Frémont, Andrés Pico, or Bernarda Ruiz. Write a journal entry that describes what you have seen happen in California and what you would like to see happen in the future. Compare your journal entry with that of a classmate.

	1825		1830

1826
• Jedediah Smith reaches California overland

1827
• Jedediah Smith crosses the Sierra Nevada

CONNECT MAIN IDEAS

Use this organizer to show that you understand how different events affected California's history. Complete it by writing an effect of each cause. A copy of the organizer may be found on page 48 of the Activity Book.

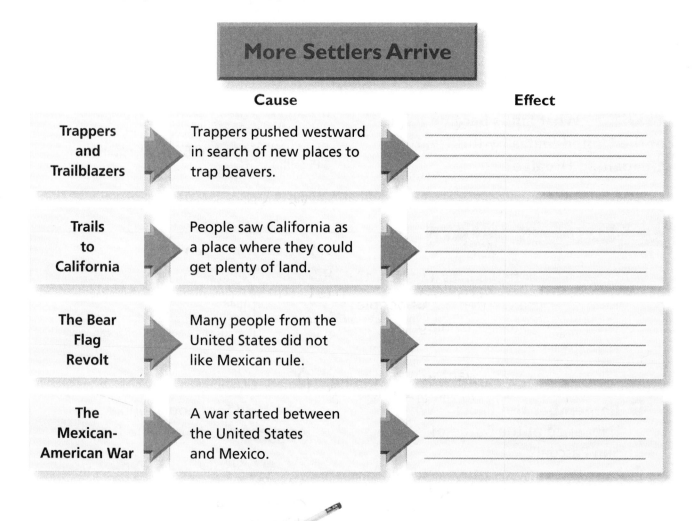

More Settlers Arrive

Cause — **Effect**

	Cause	Effect
Trappers and Trailblazers	Trappers pushed westward in search of new places to trap beavers.	
Trails to California	People saw California as a place where they could get plenty of land.	
The Bear Flag Revolt	Many people from the United States did not like Mexican rule.	
The Mexican-American War	A war started between the United States and Mexico.	

WRITE MORE ABOUT IT

Write Interview Questions Imagine that you are a reporter in the 1820s. Write a list of questions that you would like to ask a trapper who traveled to California from the United States.

Write a First-Person Story Suppose that you were a member of the Bidwell-Bartleson expedition to California. Write an "I Was There" story about your experience.

1835	1840	1845	1850

1834
• Joseph Reddeford Walker finds Walker Pass

1840
• John Sutter founds New Helvetia

1841
• The Bidwell-Bartleson expedition arrives in California

1844
• John C. Frémont explores California

1846
• The Bear Flag Revolt takes place
• The Mexican-American War begins

1848
• The Treaty of Guadalupe Hildago ends the Mexican-American War

USE VOCABULARY

Write a term from this list to complete each of the sentences that follow.

demand   right

republic   supply

1 A _____ is a desire for a good or service by people willing to pay for it.

2 A _____ is an amount of a good or service that is offered for sale.

3 A _____ is a form of government in which people elect their leaders.

4 A freedom that belongs to a person is a _____ .

CHECK UNDERSTANDING

5 Why were mountain passes important?

6 Why was Mexico worried about people from the United States coming to California?

7 Why did some people want to make California part of the United States?

8 What lands did Mexico give up after the Mexican-American War?

9 Why were many Californios pleased with the terms of the Treaty of Guadalupe Hidalgo?

THINK CRITICALLY

10 **Past to Present** Compare what it is like to move to a new place today with the way the pioneers of 150 years ago moved from the East to California.

11 **Personally Speaking** Imagine that you were living in California in 1846. Would you have joined the Bear Flag Revolt? Explain your answer.

APPLY SKILLS

Compare Distances on Maps
Use the maps on pages 204–205 to answer these questions.

12 What distance does 1 inch stand for on Map A? on Map B?

13 What does Map B show you about Smith's travels that Map A does not?

14 Why is Map B better able to show this information than Map A?

Tell Fact from Opinion News reports often give both facts and opinions. Listen to or watch a news report. Write down three facts and three opinions that you hear.

READ MORE ABOUT IT

Jim Beckwourth: Adventures of a Mountain Man by Louis Sabin. Troll. This short biography tells about Beckwourth's early life and his adventures as a mountain man.

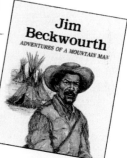

Visit the Internet at **http://www.hbschool.com** for additional resources.

STATEHOOD FOR CALIFORNIA

"I am going aboard the steamboat *Oregon* in the morning to go to California. . . . I shall pick up the lumps [of gold] and come home as quick as possible."

from a letter written by Mary Jane Megquier (meh•GWEER) to her daughter in 1849

Emma Johnson (right) was the daughter of a miner who came to California to seek gold.

The Gold Rush

| 1848 | 1849 | 1850 |

The Treaty of Guadalupe Hidalgo ended the Mexican-American War in February 1848. Older Californios could remember living first under Spanish rule and then under Mexican rule. Now they had become citizens of the United States.

The Treaty of Guadalupe Hidalgo made California a territory (TAIR•uh•tohr•ee) of the United States. A **territory** is a place owned and governed by a country. As a territory, California was owned and governed by the United States, but it was not yet a state.

Just weeks before this treaty was signed, an important discovery was made about 45 miles (72 km) from Sutter's Fort. That discovery changed California almost overnight.

Gold!

John Sutter had decided to build a sawmill at Coloma (kuh•LOH•muh), on the South Fork of the American River. The sawmill would cut logs into lumber to sell to new settlers coming to California. Sutter hired a carpenter named James Marshall and several other workers to build the sawmill.

On January 24, 1848, Marshall and some of the workers went rushing over to Jennie Wimmer, the cook and clothes washer at Sutter's Mill. One of them had found a small nugget, or lump, of something they thought might be gold. But was it? It was not nearly as bright as the shiny gold coin they compared it to.

Jennie Wimmer was making soap that day and had an idea. "I will throw it into my lye kettle," she said, ". . . and if it is gold, it will be gold when it comes out." Lye is a strong liquid used to make soap. The next morning she took out the soap. At the

FOCUS
How can the discovery of a valuable natural resource affect a place?

Main Idea Read to learn why people from all over the world came to California in 1849.

Vocabulary
territory   isthmus
gold rush   swamp
forty-niner   claim
cape
clipper ship

Using tools such as pickaxes and pans, miners hoped to uncover gold nuggets like the one at the top of the page.

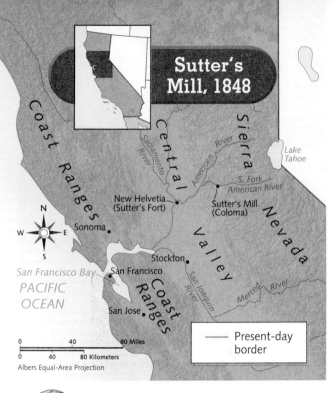

Sutter's Mill, 1848

Location Sutter's Mill was built about 45 miles (72 km) from Sutter's Fort.
■ In which direction was Sutter's Mill from Sutter's Fort?

James Marshall stands in front of Sutter's Mill, where the gold nuggets that brought thousands of people to California were found.

bottom of the kettle, there was the gold as bright as could be.

No one is sure who found the gold nugget, but Marshall said that he had. He took the gold to Sutter's Fort and showed it to John Sutter. When Sutter went to the mill, he learned that his workers had found more gold. Even Jennie Wimmer's children had found some!

Sutter wanted to keep the discovery a secret. He knew that if word about the gold got out, his workers would leave to search for more of it. However, news of the discovery soon spread.

By March the sawmill was built, but most of the workers had already left to hunt for gold. At Sutter's Fort, too, everyone "from the clerk to the cook" had gone off to hunt for gold.

REVIEW **Where and when was gold discovered in California?**

Gold Fever

In May a San Francisco merchant and newspaper owner named Sam Brannan visited Sutter's Mill. He wanted to see if all the stories he had been hearing about gold were true. He rushed back to San Francisco with a bottle of gold dust and went through the streets shouting "Gold! Gold! Gold from the American River!"

Soon many people in San Francisco, Monterey, and San Jose were leaving home to seek their fortunes. These people had caught "gold fever"—the dream of finding gold and getting rich. "A frenzy seized my soul," said one gold seeker, who imagined finding "piles of gold." He added, "I had a very violent attack of the gold fever."

In December 1848 President James Polk told Congress about the discovery of gold in California. Many newspapers across the country and around the world carried the story. This caused the gold fever to spread even faster and farther.

REVIEW What happened when people heard about the discovery of gold in California?

With his shovel, pickax, and pan, this gold miner is ready to head to the goldfields.

The Forty-Niners

Gold fever set off a **gold rush**, a huge movement of people trying to find gold. Almost 100,000 people headed for California. They were called **forty-niners** because the first of them arrived in 1849.

"I should like to go to California this Spring," wrote John Kelsey of Iowa, "as the best men we have in this part of the Country are going." Like thousands of other men, Kelsey soon headed west.

Women went west, too. Most traveled with their husbands, fathers, or brothers. Forty-niners Mary Jane and Thomas Megquier (meh•GWEER) left their home in Maine. Thomas Megquier, a doctor, was sure doctors would be needed in the goldfields. Mary Jane Megquier wrote to her daughter that "Women's help is so very scarce . . . that a woman that can work will make more money than a man."

As many as 1,000 Africans from the United States also joined the gold rush in 1849. Some were brought as slaves from the South, the states in the southern part

People from all over the United States and the world came to California during the gold rush.

of the United States, to help mine gold. Sometimes an owner would agree to give a slave freedom if that slave mined $2,000 worth of gold. Many of the slaves earned enough money to buy not only their own freedom but the freedom of their family members as well.

Many free Africans also came to California. One of them was Mifflin Gibbs. He set out for California from New York in 1849, telling himself to "go do some great thing!" Like many other free Africans in California, Gibbs used part of the

Mifflin Gibbs came to California from New York.

money he earned to help buy the freedom of enslaved Africans in the South.

Most forty-niners came from the United States. However, about one-fourth of the gold seekers were immigrants. They came to California from Mexico, South America, Europe, Asia, and Australia. By 1852 thousands of Chinese had also joined the gold rush. To them, California was *Gum Sam*, or "Gold Mountain." Like other gold seekers, they expected to get rich and return to their homes.

REVIEW Who were the forty-niners?

Routes to California

There were three main routes from the United States to California. The route that cost the least was the longest—the 18,000-mile (29,000-km) sea route around Cape Horn at the southern tip of South America. A **cape** is a point of land that reaches out into the ocean. The trip by this route took six to eight months. Because of dangerous storms and rough seas, the passengers were often seasick. Many also suffered from diseases. Still, more than 40,000 people arrived in California by ship in 1849.

Some forty-niners had the money to sail on the new **clipper ships**, which were the fastest ships of the time. Clipper ships could make the trip from New York to San Francisco in three to four months.

A second, faster route to California was by both sea and land. The forty-niners who chose this route sailed from the United States to the Isthmus (IS•muhs) of Panama in Central America. An **isthmus** is a narrow piece of land that connects two larger land areas. The Isthmus of Panama connects North and South America.

From Panama's east coast, the forty-niners set out across the isthmus by river boats, on mules, and on foot. They suffered in the region's hot, steamy climate and were often bitten by mosquitoes. Sometimes, as they waded through swamps, the forty-niners were even bitten by snakes! A **swamp** is a low, wet area, usually covered by shallow water.

Many forty-niners caught diseases and died while crossing Panama. Those who lived often had only bad food to eat. One forty-niner wrote that the "pork is rusty, the beef rotten, the duff [bread] half cooked and the beans contain two bugs to a bean." Once the forty-niners arrived on Panama's west coast, they boarded ships again and sailed north to San Francisco.

LEARNING FROM DOCUMENTS Traveling to California on a clipper ship was very expensive, but many people gladly paid the price, believing that they would find a fortune in gold when they reached California.

■ How many voyages has the ship in this advertisement made?

The third route to California was all by land. Most forty-niners joined wagon trains in Missouri. From there they followed the Oregon Trail to the Rocky Mountains and then the California Trail to Sutter's Fort. Others followed the Santa Fe and Old Spanish Trails, which lay farther south. By either way, the trip often took three months or longer.

More than 45,000 people reached the goldfields by traveling overland in 1849.

Like the pioneers before them, forty-niners faced dangers such as diseases and accidents. Sometimes they ran out of food or water. Sometimes Indians, worried about losing their lands, attacked the wagon trains. Along the trails, broken wagons, graves, and the bones of horses and oxen told sad stories of hardships.

REVIEW **What were the three main routes from the United States to California during the gold rush?**

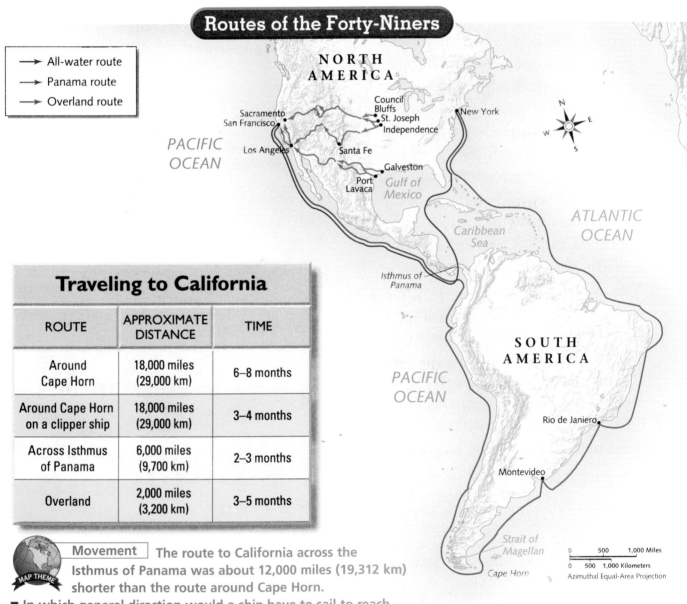

Routes of the Forty-Niners

- → All-water route
- → Panama route
- → Overland route

Traveling to California

ROUTE	APPROXIMATE DISTANCE	TIME
Around Cape Horn	18,000 miles (29,000 km)	6–8 months
Around Cape Horn on a clipper ship	18,000 miles (29,000 km)	3–4 months
Across Isthmus of Panama	6,000 miles (9,700 km)	2–3 months
Overland	2,000 miles (3,200 km)	3–5 months

Movement The route to California across the Isthmus of Panama was about 12,000 miles (19,312 km) shorter than the route around Cape Horn.
■ In which general direction would a ship have to sail to reach San Francisco from the Isthmus of Panama?

Life in the Mining Camps

To pass the time getting to California, the forty-niners often sang songs. This one was sung to the tune of "Oh, Susanna!"

66 Oh California, that's the place for me. I'm bound for San Francisco with my washbowl on my knee. 99

The "washbowl" was the pan miners used to "wash," or separate, gold from sand and gravel. A miner put some sand and gravel, along with some water, into a shallow pan. Then the miner swirled the pan around and around. The heavy bits of gold settled on the bottom of the pan as the miner carefully spilled out the water and dirt.

Miners set up camps where they lived while working their claims. A **claim** was the area a miner said belonged to him or her. Most claims were along streams that flowed from the Sierra Nevada into the Sacramento and San Joaquin rivers.

To keep other people away, miners often placed stakes, or posts, around their claims. This was called "staking a claim." Some claims were only a

Panning for gold

Some Leading Mining Towns, 1849–1859

Mining town
Other city or town
Gold-mining area
Present-day border

0   20   40 Miles
0   20   40 Kilometers
Albers Equal-Area Projection

Human-Environment Interactions

MAP THEME ■ On which river was Downieville located?

few feet wide, but others might cover hundreds of feet.

The first mining camps were little more than tent towns. Some miners even lived in covered wagons. Only later did they build wooden houses. Miners often called their camps by funny names like Bed Bug, Skunk Gulch, Rough and Ready, and Rich Dry Diggings.

Life in the mining camps was very hard. Food was often scarce, and there was little medicine. Many of the miners died from diseases. In fact, one-fifth of all the miners died less than six months after they arrived!

For those who lived, looking for gold was hard, tiring work. A miner named Prentice Mulford wrote, "It combines, within itself, the various arts of canal-digging, ditching, laying stone walls, ploughing, and hoeing potatoes." Another miner told of spending the day "under a hot sun, up to the knees in water and mud."

The miners entertained themselves as best they could. One miner wrote that after a day's work, "We . . . sit around the fireplace

A miner playing a tune on a banjo was a common sight in mining camps.

with our boots off . . . telling stories about what we heard and see, reading papers, re-reading old letters, reading books of whatever kind comes our way."

In nearly every camp, someone could play a musical instrument. As the musician played, miners sang or danced.

Sunday was most often a day of rest from mining. Preachers who traveled from one camp to another held religious services. Miners also spent the day washing, cleaning, or mending.

REVIEW **Where were most of the claims in California located?**

LESSON 1 REVIEW

1848	1849	1850

1848
• Gold is discovered at Sutter's Mill

1849
• Almost 100,000 forty-niners head to California

Check Understanding

1 **Remember the Facts** Why had John Sutter decided to build a sawmill?

2 **Recall the Main Idea** Why did people from all over the world come to California in 1849?

Think Critically

3 **Personally Speaking** Would you have rushed to the goldfields in California if you had been alive in 1849? Why or why not?

4 **Explore Viewpoints** How do you think most forty-niners felt when they first reached California?

Show What You Know

Map Activity On a large sheet of paper, draw a map that shows the three main routes forty-niners used to reach California from the United States. Then use your map to explain to classmates or family members the good and bad points of each route.

Good Times and Bad Times

FOCUS
How can an important event in history change the place where it happens?

Main Idea   As you read this lesson, look for some of the ways the gold rush changed California.

Vocabulary
industry
entrepreneur
free enterprise
consumer
population
vigilante
discrimination
technology

The gold rush brought people to California from all over the world. Among the newcomers were people of nearly every race, religion, and background. They brought with them to California their different customs, languages, and cultures. On the streets, people could be heard speaking Chinese, French, German, Italian, and Swedish as well as Spanish and English.

The gold rush also changed California's economy. It made both California and the United States rich. In fact, the United States became a leader in producing gold in the 1850s. In California, while many people mined gold, others started businesses. They provided goods and services to the miners.

Growing Cities

Almost overnight, the gold rush turned small towns near the goldfields into large cities. Before the gold rush began, San Francisco

During the gold rush, buildings were needed so badly in San Francisco that some ships were made into hotels, stores, and warehouses.

had only about 900 people. By 1849 it had 6,000 people. Just a year later, in 1850, more than 35,000 people filled its streets. Other towns, such as Sacramento, Stockton, and Marysville, were growing quickly, too.

Thousands of newcomers arrived by ship at San Francisco's port. Many dreamed of finding gold and getting rich. Others, like Lu Ng (LOO ING), came to California in search of a better life. Lu Ng, explaining why he left China to come to California, said, "Crops had failed and floods had ruined our field. There was no wood left to cut in the hills. What else could I do?"

San Francisco and the other cities and towns in California did not have enough houses or hotels for all the newcomers. In any case, few had the money for a hotel room. So people lived anywhere they could. Most lived in tents or in shacks they built. Mary Jane Megquier wrote,

66 There are six thousand people here that have no shelter, but some are going and coming from the mines, so we got a small room the size of my bedroom . . . for the five of us with our luggage. 99

Buildings were being put up as quickly as possible. In San Francisco the whole city woke each morning to the sounds of hammers and saws. "The city is humming with business and industry," wrote one newcomer. An **industry** is all the businesses that make one kind of product or provide one kind of service.

Most people arrived in California with only the things they could carry. They all needed to find a place to stay,

Ships that brought the forty-niners to California were often abandoned once they reached San Francisco. At one time, five hundred ships were left in the harbor.

and they all needed to buy food and other goods. That made California a good place for entrepreneurs (ahn•truh•pruh•NERZ). An **entrepreneur** is a person who sets up a new business.

Some entrepreneurs got rich by providing goods and services to miners. Mifflin Gibbs was one of them. He and a partner opened a shoe store in San Francisco that did very well. Gibbs later helped start the *Mirror of the Times,* the first newspaper owned by Africans in California.

Most of the women who came to California during the gold rush worked. Some searched for gold. Many others opened hotels, restaurants, and laundries. They worked long days buying and cooking food, changing beds, washing sheets, cleaning, and sewing. These women often made more

In Yuba City (above) and in other mining towns, women entrepreneurs started bakeries, hotels, and other businesses in the service industry.

money than the miners did searching for gold!

Having the right to start a new business is an important part of free enterprise. **Free enterprise** is a kind of economy in which people can own and run their own businesses. Business owners, not the government, decide

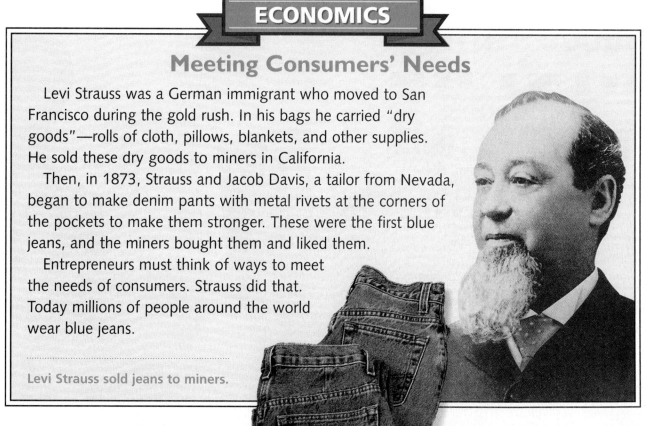

ECONOMICS

Meeting Consumers' Needs

Levi Strauss was a German immigrant who moved to San Francisco during the gold rush. In his bags he carried "dry goods"—rolls of cloth, pillows, blankets, and other supplies. He sold these dry goods to miners in California.

Then, in 1873, Strauss and Jacob Davis, a tailor from Nevada, began to make denim pants with metal rivets at the corners of the pockets to make them stronger. These were the first blue jeans, and the miners bought them and liked them.

Entrepreneurs must think of ways to meet the needs of consumers. Strauss did that. Today millions of people around the world wear blue jeans.

Levi Strauss sold jeans to miners.

what to make and sell and how much to charge. However, the owners must follow certain rules set by the government to protect **consumers**—the people who buy a product or a service.

Some people, however, claimed that store owners in California "mined the miners." That is, they often charged very high prices for scarce goods. Certainly, they took advantage of the difference between the supply of goods and the demand for them.

During the gold rush, stores often charged a dollar—more than a day's pay for many workers—for just one apple. A loaf of bread that cost just four or five cents in the East—the eastern part of the United States—cost fifty to seventy cents in San Francisco. A boiled egg in a restaurant could cost as much

as five dollars! Miners paid these high prices because they had no other way to get these goods.

REVIEW How does free enterprise make it possible for entrepreneurs to start businesses?

A Changing Society

The population of California grew very quickly during the gold rush. **Population** is the number of people who live in a place. California's non-Indian population grew from about 14,000 in 1848 to about 100,000 in 1850. By 1852 its population had grown to about 250,000 people.

The population of California during the gold rush was not made up the same way as the population of the eastern

LEARNING FROM DOCUMENTS This advertisement is for the Mormon Island Emporium. Such stores not only sold goods to miners but also served as mail and banking centers.
■ What are some items for sale at this store?

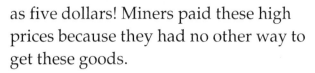

This San Francisco tinsmith offered his services to the forty-niners.

Even though many Chinese immigrants owned successful businesses, they still faced discrimination. At one time, California had a law against using baskets like these to carry loads. The law made it more expensive for the Chinese to do business.

United States. For one thing, at least nine out of ten gold seekers were men. Most were under the age of 30.

Only a few children lived in the mining camps, and most of them worked to help their families. There were not many schools, even in the growing cities.

In the early days of the gold rush, crime grew as the population grew. This rise in crime frightened many people and made them angry. Some became vigilantes (vih•juh•LAN•teez). A **vigilante** is a person who takes the law into his or her own hands. Instead of allowing law officers and judges to arrest and punish people who break the law, vigilantes make their own laws and punish the people who break them. Sometimes the vigilantes punished people who had done nothing wrong.

California had other problems, too. Native Californians, Californios, Mexicans,

Africans, and Chinese often faced discrimination (dis•krih•muh•NAY•shuhn). **Discrimination** is the unfair treatment of people because of such things as their religion, their race, or their birthplace.

Some people from the United States felt that California belonged to them. They sometimes forced the Africans, the Chinese, and the Spanish-speaking people to leave the mining camps. Lee Chew, a Chinese immigrant who owned a laundry in San Francisco, was often cheated by his customers. But at that time only white people could go to court against a white person, so he could do little about it.

California's Indians were also hurt by the gold rush. Many were forced off their lands when gold was found. Others died from diseases brought by the newcomers.

REVIEW What effect did the gold rush have on California's population?

The seal of the San Francisco Committee of Vigilance

New Kinds of Mining

In 1848 and 1849, miners could find gold using simple tools. With shovels and pickaxes, miners dug for gold in shallow streams and muddy ditches. They used pans to separate the gold from the sand, soil, and gravel they dug.

Sometimes two miners worked together to use a tool called a cradle. It was called a cradle because it was rocked back and forth like a baby's cradle. The cradle had two trays, one above the other. The miners filled the top tray with sand, soil, and gravel.

A cradle

Then, while one miner poured water over the dirt, the other miner rocked the cradle. Any large pieces of gravel were trapped in the top tray, and the rest of the dirt and the water flowed into the bottom one. The water washed the dirt out through an opening in the bottom tray, leaving the heavier gold behind.

By the mid-1850s, however, most of the gold lying at or near the top of the ground had been found. Miners could no longer find much gold with pans and cradles. So they started using a new technology (tek•NAH•luh•jee) called hydraulic (hy•DRAW•lik) mining to reach the gold that was deeper in the ground.

Hydraulic mining, another way to find gold, did a lot of damage to the environment.

To use a Long Tom, a long version of the cradle, several miners had to work together.

Technology is the way people use new ideas to make tools or machines.

Hydraulic mining used waterpower to separate dirt and rocks from the gold. Miners used huge hoses to spray water against riverbanks and hillsides. These streams of water were powerful enough to blast away whole hillsides and change the course of streams!

Hydraulic mining uncovered new sources of gold, but it caused big problems for the environment. It used up millions of gallons of water each day. It also washed tons of soil into streams and rivers in the Sacramento and San Joaquin valleys. This mud blocked the streams and rivers and caused them to flood when heavy rains fell. Sacramento, for example, had terrible floods in the late 1850s.

Farmers became angry about the flooded streams and ruined farmland. For years there was conflict between farmers and miners. Finally, in 1884, California made hydraulic mining against the law.

REVIEW **Why did miners start using hydraulic mining in the mid-1850s?**

LESSON 2 REVIEW

Check Understanding

1 **Remember the Facts** Why were prices in California high for some goods during the gold rush?

2 **Recall the Main Idea** What were some of the ways the gold rush changed California?

Think Critically

3 **Past to Present** Thousands of people came to California during the gold rush. Why do people come to California today? How are their reasons for coming like those of the forty-niners? How are they different?

4 **Cause and Effect** How did the gold rush lead to the growth of other businesses in California?

Show What You Know
Simulation Activity
Imagine that you are planning to go to California during the gold rush. With a partner, make a plan to "strike it rich." Decide whether you will become miners or start a business. Describe your goal and list the supplies you will take and some of the problems you might face. Share your plan with classmates, and explain why you made the decision that you did.

Use a Line Graph

1. Why Learn This Skill?

You read in the last lesson that California's population grew very quickly after gold was discovered in 1848. The numbers that show such changes are often large and may be hard to understand just by reading them. Putting these numbers on a line graph makes them easier to understand. A **line graph** is a graph that uses a line to show changes over time.

2. Understand the Process

The line graph on page 243 shows the changes in California's population from 1850 to 1890. The numbers along the left side of the graph show how many people lived in California. Across the bottom of the graph are years. As the red line moves across the graph from left to right, it shows how the population changed over each ten-year period.

1 Find the year 1850 at the bottom of the graph. Move your finger up from that date until you reach the red dot. Then move your finger left to the population numbers. Your finger will be a little below 100,000, so you will need to estimate the population. To *estimate* is to make a close guess. About how many people lived in California in 1850?

2 Now find 1860 at the bottom of the graph. Repeat the process. About how many people lived in California that year?

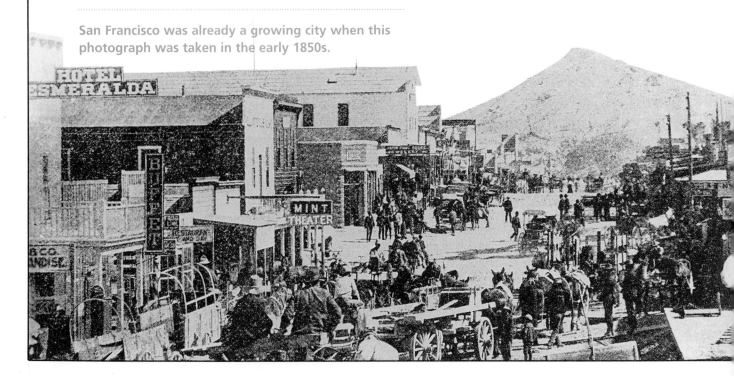

San Francisco was already a growing city when this photograph was taken in the early 1850s.

to See Change

3 About how many people lived in California in 1890?

4 Look at the red line on the graph. How did the population of California change between 1850 and 1890? About how many more people lived in California in 1890 than in 1850?

5 Did California's population grow more between 1850 and 1860 or between 1880 and 1890? How do you know this?

3. Think and Apply

Create a line graph that shows the changes in California's population between 1900 and 1950. Use these population numbers.

1,485,000 in 1900	5,677,000 in 1930
2,378,000 in 1910	6,950,000 in 1940
3,427,000 in 1920	10,643,000 in 1950

Use your graph to show your family how California's population grew in the first half of the twentieth century.

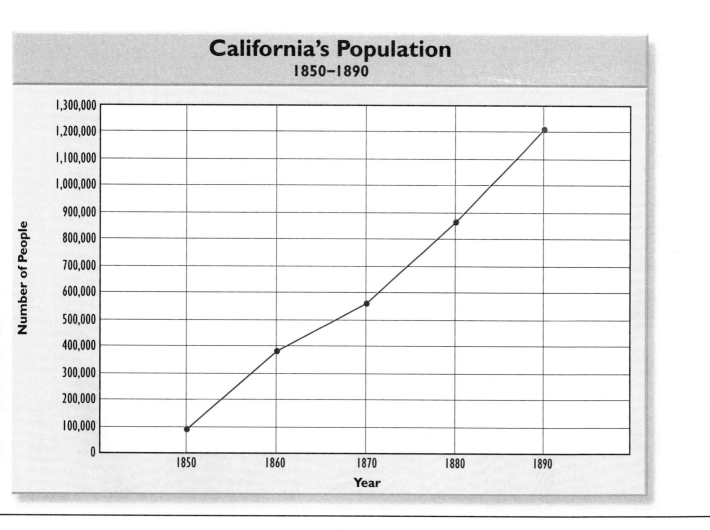

California's Population
1850–1890

FOCUS

How might people decide what to do when they disagree?

Main Idea Read to learn how California became the thirty-first state of the United States.

Vocabulary

convention
delegate
constitution
slavery
free state
slave state
compromise
commission

The Thirty-First State

1849	1850	1851

T he gold rush brought sudden wealth to California. It also brought large numbers of people from the United States. In fact, settlers from the United States quickly became the largest group of people in California. Many of them wanted California to become a state. So did many Californios.

The Monterey Convention

In 1849 the Americans and Californios chose 48 people to attend a **convention**, or important meeting, in Monterey. As **delegates** to this convention, these 48 people would represent, or speak and act for, all the Californians who had elected them. They would decide many things about California's future.

The delegates who gathered at Monterey's Colton Hall on September 3, 1849, came from all parts of

Many Californio families, such as the Lugo family, wondered how they would be affected if California became a state.

California. Most, like John Sutter and Abel Stearns, were Americans who had settled in California before the gold rush. Seven of the delegates were Californios. Among them was General Mariano Vallejo.

Delegates to the Monterey Convention met in this room in Colton Hall.

The delegates to the Monterey Convention quickly decided that California should become a state. They did not have to decide where three of California's borders should be. The Treaty of Guadalupe Hidalgo had set California's southern border with Mexico. The Pacific Ocean formed its western border. California's northern border was the Oregon Territory. However, the delegates had to decide where the new state's eastern border should be.

Under Spanish and Mexican rule, Alta California had reached almost to the Rocky Mountains. Since the Mexican-American War, all of this land had belonged to the United States. Some of the delegates at Monterey wanted California to stretch all the way to the Rockies. Others thought that such a large area would be too hard for one state to govern. Finally the delegates decided that two natural features—the Sierra Nevada and the Colorado River—should form California's eastern border.

The delegates also showed that they valued education. They voted to set up public schools in their new state.

REVIEW **What was the first thing the delegates to the Monterey Convention decided?**

A Constitution for California

The main job of the Monterey Convention was to write a **constitution**, or plan of government, for the new state of California. In just six weeks the delegates wrote the Constitution of 1849. It set up a government with a governor to head the state and a legislature (LEH•juhs•lay•cher), a group of people elected to make the laws.

California's constitution borrowed some ideas from Mexican law. Married women, for example, could own property. This was not allowed in other

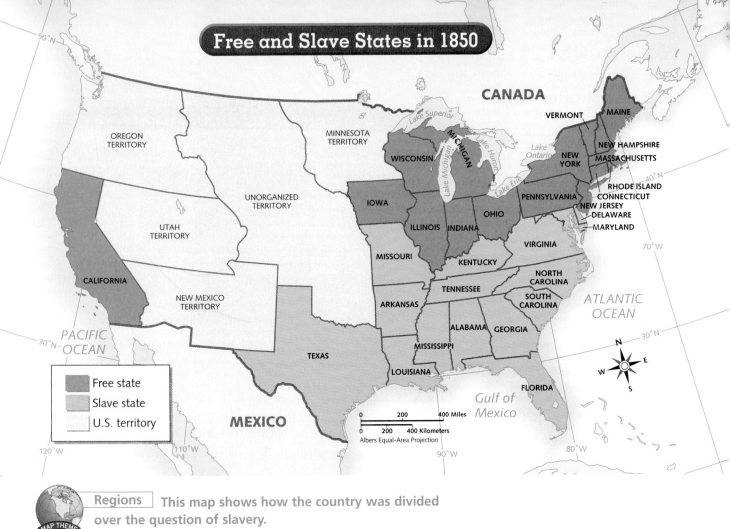

Free and Slave States in 1850

CANADA

OREGON TERRITORY

MINNESOTA TERRITORY

WISCONSIN

MICHIGAN

VERMONT

MAINE

NEW HAMPSHIRE

MASSACHUSETTS

NEW YORK

Lake Superior

Lake Huron

Lake Michigan

Lake Ontario

Lake Erie

UNORGANIZED TERRITORY

IOWA

RHODE ISLAND

CONNECTICUT

PENNSYLVANIA

NEW JERSEY

DELAWARE

MARYLAND

UTAH TERRITORY

ILLINOIS

INDIANA

OHIO

CALIFORNIA

MISSOURI

KENTUCKY

VIRGINIA

NEW MEXICO TERRITORY

TENNESSEE

NORTH CAROLINA

ARKANSAS

SOUTH CAROLINA

ATLANTIC OCEAN

PACIFIC OCEAN

ALABAMA

GEORGIA

MISSISSIPPI

Free state

Slave state

U.S. territory

MEXICO

TEXAS

LOUISIANA

FLORIDA

Gulf of Mexico

0   200   400 Miles

0   200   400 Kilometers

Albers Equal-Area Projection

Regions This map shows how the country was divided over the question of slavery.

■ Not counting California, how many free states were there in 1850? How many slave states?

states. Like the other states, however, California allowed only white men over the age of 21 to vote. Many years passed before all citizens over the age of 18 could vote.

In November 1849, California voters approved the new constitution. They elected state lawmakers and chose Peter H. Burnett to be California's first governor. The legislature chose two senators, John C. Frémont and William M. Gwin, to serve in Congress in Washington, D.C.

REVIEW What was the main job of the Monterey Convention?

California Becomes a State

Before California could become a state, the United States Congress had to vote to make it part of the United States. In 1849, however, the country was in conflict over the question of slavery. **Slavery** is the making of some people the property of other people. Enslaved Africans had no freedom and were forced to work without pay.

Most enslaved Africans worked on large farms in the southern states, where slavery was allowed. These farms, called plantations, grew mostly cotton and tobacco. Both crops could be sold for a lot of money, but many workers were needed to grow and harvest them.

Many people in the United States believed that slavery should be ended. Plantation owners, however, said they needed slaves as workers. Other people in the South also said they needed slaves. In addition to doing plantation work, enslaved Africans also worked as carpenters, blacksmiths, builders, painters, and house servants.

Slavery was against the law in the North, the states in the northern part of the United States. The new California constitution also did not allow slavery.

At the time, the United States had an equal number of **free states**, in which slavery was outlawed, and **slave states**, in which slavery was legal. If California joined the United States as a free state, the free states would have more votes in Congress. Many Southerners feared that the free states would then try to end slavery all

across the United States. The question of making California a state became part of the argument over slavery.

Finally, after almost a year, members of Congress worked out a compromise. In a **compromise**, each side in a conflict gives up some of what it wants in order to reach an agreement. Under the Compromise of 1850, Congress voted to admit California to the Union, or the United States, as a free state. As part of the Compromise, Congress also said that anyone who was caught helping enslaved people run away from their owners would be punished. California officially became the thirty-first state on September 9, 1850.

On October 18, 1850, the mail ship *Oregon* reached San Francisco. Its cannon boomed to let people know that it carried important news. Crowds gathered to hear that California was now a state. People cheered. "We're in the Union! California is a state!" they cried. They celebrated with parades, dances, and speeches. Some sewed a new star onto United States flags for

When people learned that California had become a state, they filled the streets of San Francisco to celebrate.

Sacramento, as seen in this painting by George Tirrell (above), was already a busy river port when it was chosen as California's state capital in 1854. The legislature began meeting in the California State Capitol building (right) in 1869.

the thirty-first state. The news soon spread all over California.

Now that California was a state, it needed a capital. Many people hoped their cities would be chosen. Monterey, San Jose, Vallejo, Benicia (buh•NEE•shuh), and San Francisco each served for a short time as the capital. Then, in 1854, state lawmakers moved the capital to Sacramento. Sacramento has remained the capital ever since.

REVIEW **When did California become a state?**

The End of the Ranchos

By the time California became a state, almost 14 million acres of land had been given as land grants to rancho owners. But the way of life on these ranchos

was changing forever. Many of the Americans who came to California during the gold rush did not find the wealth they had dreamed of. Instead of returning home, however, many of them stayed in California. Like the settlers before them, some became squatters and settled on the huge, unfenced lands of the ranchos.

The squatters wanted the right to stay on the land where they lived. Other Americans wanted to be allowed to settle on what seemed like empty land. So Congress passed the Land Act of 1851. This law set up a land commission (kuh•MIH•shuhn) to decide who the rancho lands belonged to. A **commission** is a group of people chosen to make a decision about a certain problem.

To keep their ranchos, the rancheros had to prove to the land commission that they were really the owners. For many of them this was hard to do. Most did not speak English, and few commission members spoke Spanish. Also, the old hand-drawn *diseños* often were not correct.

Many rancheros had to hire lawyers to represent them before the land commission. Often, their cases were not settled

for many years. By that time many rancheros had been forced to sell their lands in order to pay their bills.

In the end, most large ranchos were broken up and sold. Without their land, the rancheros' way of life came to an end.

REVIEW What did the Land Act of 1851 do?

LESSON 3 REVIEW

1849 — 1850 — 1851

1849
• California voters approve the Constitution of 1849

1850
• California becomes the thirty-first state

1851
• Congress passes the Land Act of 1851

Check Understanding

1 **Remember the Facts** Did California come into the Union as a free state or a slave state?

2 **Recall the Main Idea** How did California become the thirty-first state of the United States?

Think Critically

3 **Link To You** The delegates to the Monterey Convention set up public schools. Why would schools be important to a new state? How are schools important to you?

4 **Think More About It** Why is a compromise often the only way for people in conflict to reach an agreement?

Show What You Know

Writing Activity Imagine that you are a newspaper reporter covering the Monterey Convention. Write an article that tells about the important matters being decided by the delegates. Display your article where members of your class can read it.

Resolve Conflict

1. Why Learn This Skill?

Most people work well together when they agree. Sometimes, however, people have different ideas about how things should be done. That can lead to conflict.

There are many ways to resolve, or settle, conflict. You can walk away from a conflict and give strong feelings time to fade. You can explain your ideas and try to get others to change their minds and agree with you. Or you can work out a compromise.

As you know, a compromise is an agreement in which each side gives up some things it wants in order to get other things. By working out a compromise, people can resolve conflicts and settle disagreements peacefully.

Members of the United States Congress in Washington, D.C., discuss California statehood and the Compromise of 1850.

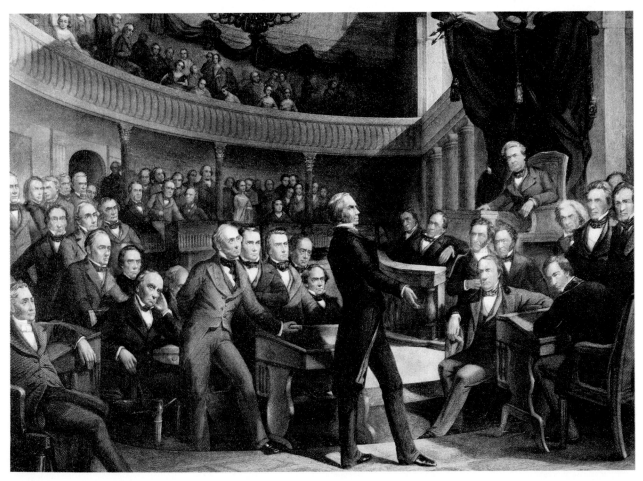

by Compromise

2. Remember What You Have Read

In the last lesson you read that members of the United States Congress did not agree about letting California become a state. Most members from the North wanted California to become a state. Then there would be more free states than slave states, and the free states would have more votes in Congress. For that reason, members from the South did not want California to become a state. They feared that the free states would try to end slavery all across the United States.

To resolve this conflict, the members of Congress had to work out a compromise. Think about how the Compromise of 1850 affected both sides.

1. What did each side have to do in order to make the compromise work?
2. What did the North get? What did the North give up?
3. What did the South get? What did the South give up?

3. Understand the Process

To resolve a conflict by compromise, you can follow steps like the ones listed on this page. The members of Congress from the North and from the South followed steps like these to work out the Compromise of 1850.

- Identify what is causing the conflict.
- Tell the people on the other side what you want. Then listen to what they want.
- Decide which things are the most important to you.
- Make a plan for a compromise. Explain your plan and listen to the other side's plan. Together, talk about the two plans.
- If you still do not agree, make a second plan for a compromise. This time, give up one of the things that is important to you. Ask the other side to do the same thing. Look for a way to let each side have most of what it wants.
- Keep talking until you agree on a compromise. If people on either side become angry, take a break to let them calm down.
- Plan your compromise so that it will work for a long time.

4. Think and Apply

Suppose the school board would like all the students to wear uniforms. Many of the students would like to wear what they want. Work with a classmate, each of you taking one of the sides. Using the steps in Understand the Process, work out a compromise that will resolve the conflict. Compare your compromise with those of other students. Which ones do you think would work best? Why?

Biddy Mason

FROM *Women of the Wild West*
BY **Ruth Pelz**
ILLUSTRATED BY **Nneka Bennet**

Even though California joined the Union as a free state, some slave owners still brought slaves with them to California. Biddy Mason was an enslaved African woman who was brought to California in 1852 by her owner, Robert Smith. When Smith decided to move from California to the slave state of Texas, Biddy Mason decided to fight for the right to stay in California and be free. Read now to find out what happened to Biddy Mason.

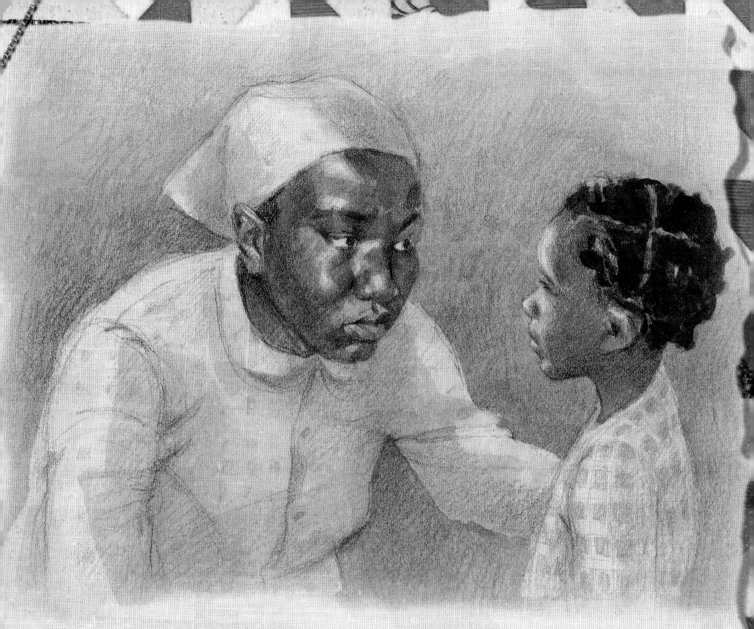

"Mama, I'm tired," said the little girl. "It's hot and I'm tired of walking. Why can't we stop now? Why can't we stay where we are?"

"Hush now," said Biddy, comforting her daughter. "I know you're tired. I've had more than enough of traveling myself. But it isn't my choice, child. It's Mr. Robert Smith says if we're walking or staying. And Mr. Smith is a traveling kind of man. You get up in the wagon with your sister for a while."

Sometimes it seemed they would never stop traveling. First there had been the long trip to Utah. All day Biddy had walked along behind the wagons, tending the cattle. For months they had walked, getting farther and farther from Mississippi. It was a hard trip, especially for the children. But what could Biddy do? She was born a slave. She was a slave today. Her master told her to walk across the plains and she did it.

They had been in Utah for only one year when word came of a new settlement in Southern California. The master, Robert Smith, decided to go. Again the wagons were packed. Again they began the long days of walking.

Biddy had plenty of time for thinking along the way. What she mostly thought about was freedom. As a child she had never known an African American person who wasn't a slave. Oh, she heard about them, about the ones who escaped to the North. But it was all so hard to imagine!

Then came the trip west. Things were different here. She had seen African American families, traveling west with their own wagons! Just think of it! They planned to find their own land, start their own farms, or find work in the towns. Biddy kept thinking about them.

Then there was Salt Lake City. Mormon families had come there from all over the country. Some came from the South and brought slaves with them. Many families came from the northern states, though, where slavery wasn't allowed. It was different, all right. It got you thinking.

Biddy looked down at her bare feet. They were tired and sore and covered with dust. These feet walked every mile from Mississippi, she thought. And they remember every step. They have

walked for Mr. Smith and his family. They have walked after his crops and his wagons and his cattle. But someday they are going to walk for me. Someday these feet will walk me to freedom! I'm sure of it.

A few days later, the tired travelers arrived at San Bernardino, California. It was a lovely place. It was their new home.

There were many reasons to enjoy living in California in 1852. The climate was pleasant. The land was good. The air was fresh and warm. Cities were booming. Everywhere there was a sense of promise and excitement.

The most important thing for Biddy was the promise of freedom. She had heard people talking. The new state of California did not permit slavery, they said. By law all people here were free. Biddy looked again at her dusty traveling feet. Soon, she said to herself, soon.

Three years passed. Life was pretty good, but Mr. Smith must have loved traveling. Even this beautiful settlement could not hold him. He decided to move again, this time to Texas. The wagons were loaded and made ready to go.

Biddy knew she had to act. As soon as the wagons left San Bernardino, she

began looking for an opportunity. She found one. Somehow she sent word to the sheriff in Los Angeles. He stopped the wagons before they left California.

"I hear you have slaves in your party," said the sheriff. "I suppose you know that's against the law. Is it true?"

Biddy came forward. In all her life this was the first time she had ever spoken to a white sheriff. Still her voice was strong. "It is true," she said. "Mr. Smith is taking us to Texas and we don't want to go."

That statement led to the most important slavery trial in Southern California. Biddy and another slave woman and their children were taken to court. Biddy spoke to the judge, and once again, her words were strong and clear: "I want to stay in California. I want to be free."

The judge sided with Biddy. He scolded Mr. Smith for breaking the law. He gave all the slaves their freedom.

Biddy gathered up her children and said, "We are moving once more, but it won't be very far. We are going to Los Angeles, and this time," she said, looking at her tired feet, "I am walking for me!"

She started her new life by taking Biddy Mason as her full name. She went to work as a nurse and housekeeper. Before long she saved enough money to buy a house. Soon she bought other property too. Biddy Mason was a good businesswoman. She became one of the wealthiest African Americans in Los Angeles.

She shared that wealth with others. She gave land to build schools and hospitals and nursing homes. She supported the education of African American children and helped people in need. Biddy Mason had come a long way from that slave's cabin in Mississippi. She still remembered the walking. And she made sure she helped others along their way.

For the first time in her life, Biddy Mason could work for herself. The land that she bought soon became the center of downtown Los Angeles. The land that she paid $200 for was worth $200,000 just five years later.

Biddy Mason used her money to help others. She paid the bills of her church and bought food and clothes for poor people. She also helped set up the first elementary school for African Americans in Los Angeles. When she died in 1891, the *Los Angeles Times* wrote that she would be remembered for "40 years of good works."

LITERATURE REVIEW

1 What important promise did California hold for Biddy Mason?

2 As Biddy Mason began her walk to Los Angeles, she said, "This time I am walking for me!" What do you think she meant by this?

3 In 1856 a California judge ruled that Biddy Mason and her children "are entitled to their freedom and are free forever." Write a paragraph describing how you think Biddy Mason felt when she heard these words.

CHAPTER 6
REVIEW

1848		1849

1848
• Gold is discovered at Sutter's Mill

1849
• Almost 100,000 forty-niners head to California
• Voters approve the Constitution of 1849

CONNECT MAIN IDEAS

Use this organizer to show that you understand how the chapter's main ideas are connected. Complete it by writing two details about each main idea. A copy of the organizer may be found on page 56 of the Activity Book.

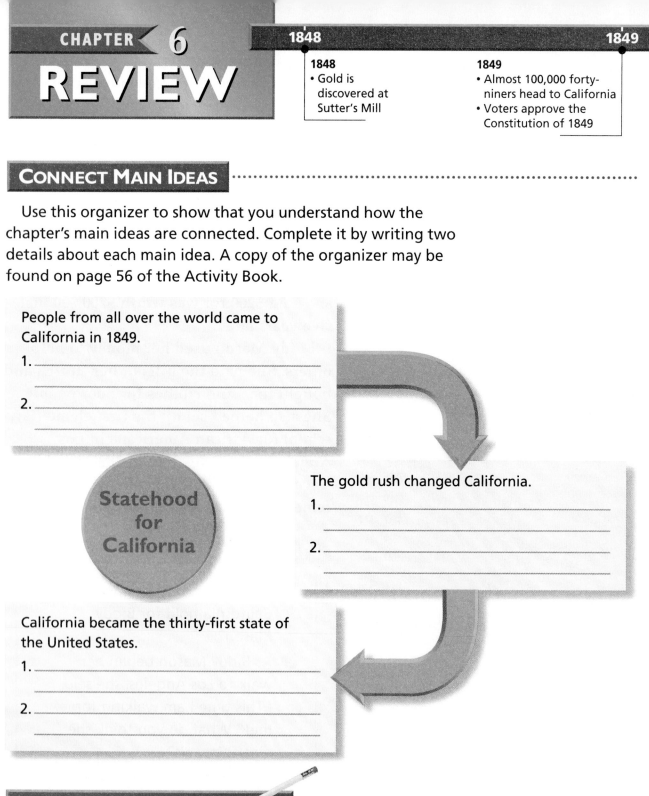

People from all over the world came to California in 1849.

1. _____
   _____
2. _____
   _____

Statehood for California

The gold rush changed California.

1. _____
   _____
2. _____
   _____

California became the thirty-first state of the United States.

1. _____
   _____
2. _____
   _____

WRITE MORE ABOUT IT

Write a Speech Imagine that you are the owner of a clipper ship. You want to get a group of gold seekers to sail on your ship. Write a speech that tells them why traveling on your ship is the best way for them to get to California.

Create a Banner In 1850 the United States Congress had to decide whether California should become a state. Make up a saying that calls for statehood for California. Then write your saying on a long strip of paper to make a banner.

1850   1851

1850
• California becomes
  the thirty-first state

1851
• Congress passes the
  Land Act of 1851

USE VOCABULARY

For each pair of terms, write a sentence or two explaining how the terms are related.

1. gold rush, forty-niner
2. entrepreneur, free enterprise
3. convention, delegate
4. free state, slave state

CHECK UNDERSTANDING

5. Where was gold first discovered in California?

6. What were the three main routes from the United States to California in 1849?

7. Why was California a good place for entrepreneurs?

8. How was the population of California different from the population of the eastern United States?

9. Which two geographic features did the delegates to the Monterey Convention choose to form California's eastern border?

10. Why were most large ranchos broken up and sold after California became a state?

THINK CRITICALLY

11. **Personally Speaking** Why does a free enterprise economy give you many choices about what to buy and where to buy it?

12. **Cause and Effect** Why did miners start using hydraulic mining by the mid-1850s? What effect did this technology have on California's environment?

APPLY SKILLS

Use a Line Graph to See Change Look in newspapers or old magazines for a line graph. Cut out the graph and tape it to a sheet of paper. Below the graph, describe the change it shows.

Resolve Conflict by Compromise Think about a conflict you have or have had with a friend or a family member. Then list steps you might follow to resolve the conflict by compromise.

READ MORE ABOUT IT

By the Great Horn Spoon! by Sid Fleischman. Little, Brown and Company. Young Jack and his aunt's butler, Praiseworthy, have many adventures as they set out to make their fortune in California in 1849.

HARCOURT BRACE

Visit the Internet at **http://www.hbschool.com** for additional resources.

Digging For GOLD TODAY

The gold rush that began at Sutter's Mill in 1848 was over by the 1860s. However, along the rivers and streams of California's gold country, you might still see people looking for gold.

Some of today's gold seekers have been searching for many years, while others are first-timers. Many come with their families just for weekend fun. "It's not about having the gold," explains a miner named Scott Dawson. "It's about getting the gold, the adventure of it."

John Evans might agree. For more than 20 years he has spent many of his weekends digging for gold. "As soon as you go out and look for gold and you actually find it, you feel it — you get gold fever," he said.

Scientists think that there is still a lot of gold in California, but it lies deep underground. Most of today's gold seekers will not find more than a few small flakes.

Of course, all the gold seekers would like to become rich, but they know the chances of that are very small. However, that does not keep them from trying. Many of them are looking for more than just gold. They are also looking for a connection to the past.

Coyote Creek is one place in California where people still look for gold.

The tools these modern day gold miners are using are not very different from the ones the forty-niners used.

Think and Apply

Think about the forty-niners and about the people who search for gold today. How are they alike? How are they different? Make a chart comparing the gold seekers of the past with those of the present.

HARCOURT BRACE

Visit the Internet at **http://www.hbschool.com** for additional resources.

Turner Le@rning

Check your media center or classroom video library for the Making Social Studies Relevant videotape of this feature.

VISUAL SUMMARY

Summarize the Main Ideas
Study the pictures and captions to help you review what you read about in Unit 3.

Write a Diary Entry
Imagine that you are taking part in one of the events shown in the visual summary. Write a diary entry that explains what you are doing and what is taking place around you.

1 To reach California, fur trappers opened up new overland routes through the West.

4 The Mexican-American War reached California in July 1846, when the United States navy captured Monterey.

5 The discovery of gold brought thousands of newcomers to California.

During the Bear Flag Revolt in June 1846, the Bear Flaggers declared California an independent republic.

Pioneers from the United States traveled to California in wagon trains, often following the trails first used by trappers.

 Entrepreneurs started businesses to supply miners with goods. Towns such as San Francisco grew into cities.

 California became the thirty-first state on September 9, 1850.

USE VOCABULARY

Use each term in a sentence that helps explain its meaning.

1. pass
2. immigrant
3. frontier
4. pioneer
5. wagon train
6. right
7. territory
8. isthmus
9. industry
10. technology

CHECK UNDERSTANDING

11. Who was the first American to travel overland from the United States to California?

12. How did the location of Sutter's Fort make it important to newcomers?

13. What was manifest destiny?

14. What happened because of the Bear Flag Revolt?

15. How did the Treaty of Guadalupe Hidalgo affect California?

16. Which of the three main routes forty-niners took to California was the longest?

17. What new technology did many gold miners start using in the mid-1850s? Why?

18. What was the main job of the Monterey Convention?

THINK CRITICALLY

19. **Cause and Effect** How did supply and demand affect the prices charged for goods during the gold rush?

20. **Think More About It** People who want to become entrepreneurs are often advised, "Find a need and fill it." How did entrepreneurs during the gold rush follow this advice? Explain.

APPLY SKILLS

Compare Distances on Maps
Use the map and the inset map below to answer these questions.

21. How far is Oxnard from Long Beach? Which map did you use to find this?

22. Which map would you use to find the distance from Pasadena to Compton?

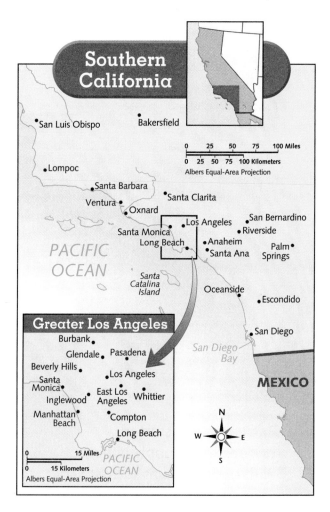

REMEMBER

- Share your ideas.
- Cooperate with others to plan your work.
- Take responsibility for your work.
- Help one another.
- Show your group's work to the class.
- Discuss what you learned by working together.

ACTIVITY

Design Postage Stamps

Work with a group of classmates to design postage stamps that honor some of the people or events that you read about in Unit 3. Draw a design for each person or event on a sheet of paper. Then write a paragraph explaining why you chose to honor that person or event. Display your stamps on a bulletin board for everyone to see.

Unit Project Wrap-Up

Make a 3-D Time Line Work with a group of classmates to finish the Unit Project described on page 191. As a group, decide which five events you will show on the time line. Then create a time line by writing the dates and captions for the events on large pieces of paper. Tape the time line to the floor, and use art materials to build three-dimensional models to illustrate the events. As your group presents its time line to the class, explain why the events shown are important to California's history.

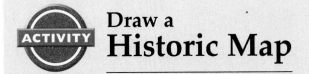

ACTIVITY

Draw a Historic Map

Work with your group to draw a large map showing the overland route that the Bidwell-Bartleson expedition or the Donner Party used to reach California. Maps in your textbook and in atlases and books in the school library can help you. Label major bodies of water and large landforms along the route. Then point out places on the map as your group takes the rest of your class on a "journey" to California.

A CHANGING STATE

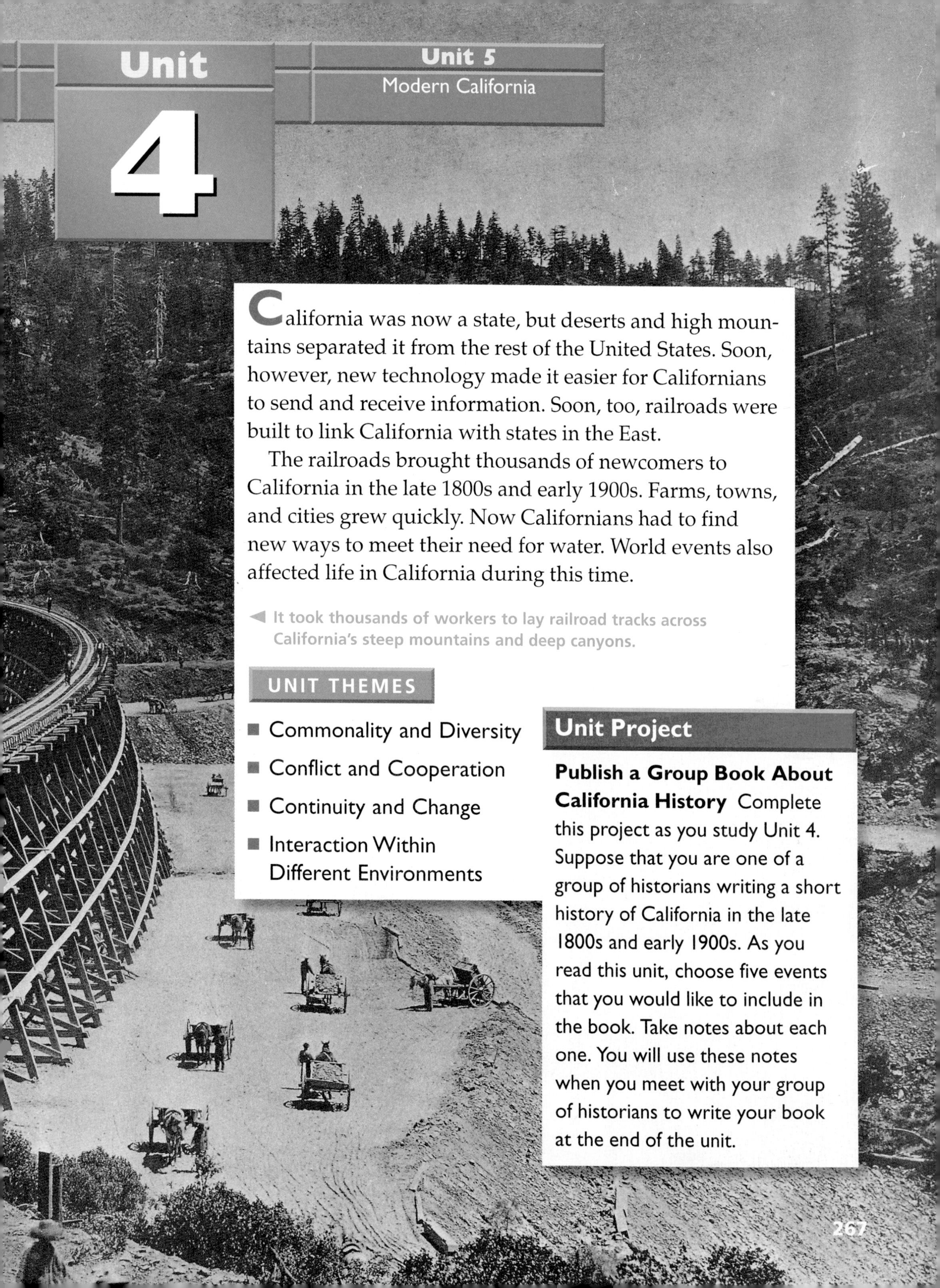

California was now a state, but deserts and high mountains separated it from the rest of the United States. Soon, however, new technology made it easier for Californians to send and receive information. Soon, too, railroads were built to link California with states in the East.

The railroads brought thousands of newcomers to California in the late 1800s and early 1900s. Farms, towns, and cities grew quickly. Now Californians had to find new ways to meet their need for water. World events also affected life in California during this time.

◀ It took thousands of workers to lay railroad tracks across California's steep mountains and deep canyons.

UNIT THEMES

- Commonality and Diversity
- Conflict and Cooperation
- Continuity and Change
- Interaction Within Different Environments

Unit Project

Publish a Group Book About California History Complete this project as you study Unit 4. Suppose that you are one of a group of historians writing a short history of California in the late 1800s and early 1900s. As you read this unit, choose five events that you would like to include in the book. Take notes about each one. You will use these notes when you meet with your group of historians to write your book at the end of the unit.

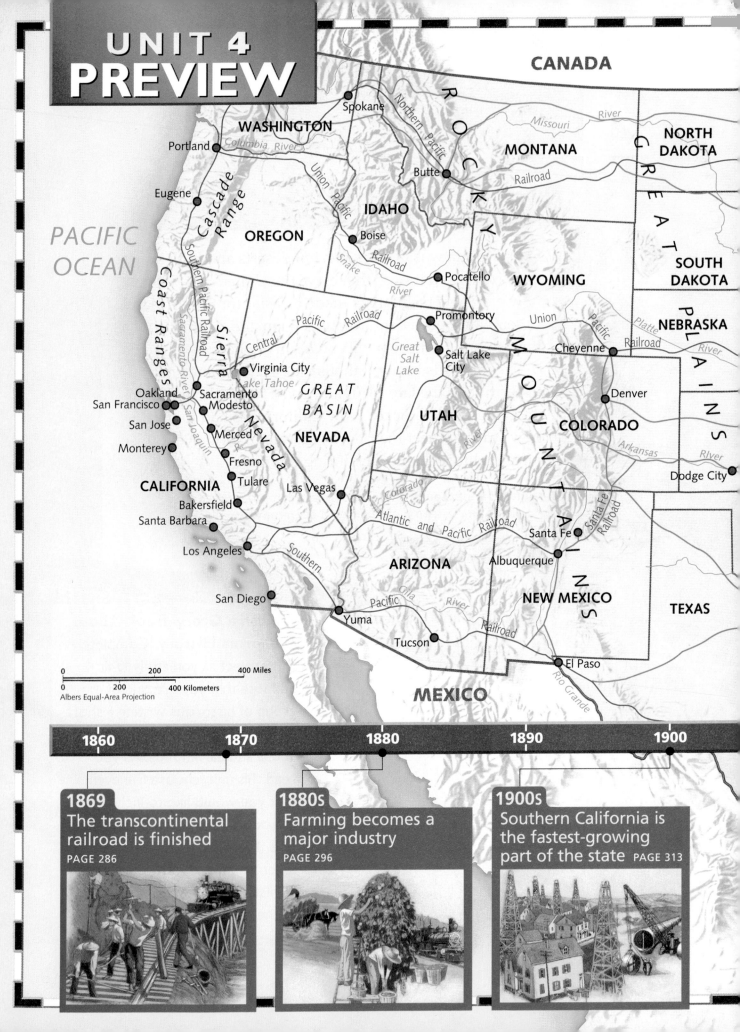

CANADA

PACIFIC OCEAN

WASHINGTON

Spokane

Portland

Columbia River

Eugene

Cascade Range

OREGON

Union Pacific Railroad

IDAHO

Boise

Snake River

Northern Pacific Railroad

MONTANA

Missouri River

Butte

R O C K Y

Railroad

NORTH DAKOTA

SOUTH DAKOTA

Pocatello

WYOMING

G R E A T

Southern Pacific Railroad

Central Pacific Railroad

Promontory

Great Salt Lake

Salt Lake City

Union Pacific Railroad

Cheyenne

Platte River

NEBRASKA

P L A I N S

Coast Ranges

Sacramento River

Sierra Nevada

Lake Tahoe

Virginia City

GREAT BASIN

UTAH

M O U N T A I N S

Denver

COLORADO

Oakland

San Francisco

Sacramento

Modesto

San Jose

Merced

San Joaquin R.

NEVADA

Fresno

Monterey

Tulare

CALIFORNIA

Bakersfield

Santa Barbara

Los Angeles

Las Vegas

Colorado River

Atlantic and Pacific Railroad

Arkansas River

Dodge City

Santa Fe

Santa Fe Railroad

Albuquerque

San Diego

Yuma

Southern Pacific Railroad

Gila River

ARIZONA

Tucson

El Paso

Rio Grande

NEW MEXICO

TEXAS

MEXICO

0   200   400 Miles
0   200   400 Kilometers
Albers Equal-Area Projection

1860   1870   1880   1890   1900

1869
The transcontinental railroad is finished
PAGE 286

1880s
Farming becomes a major industry
PAGE 296

1900s
Southern California is the fastest-growing part of the state PAGE 313

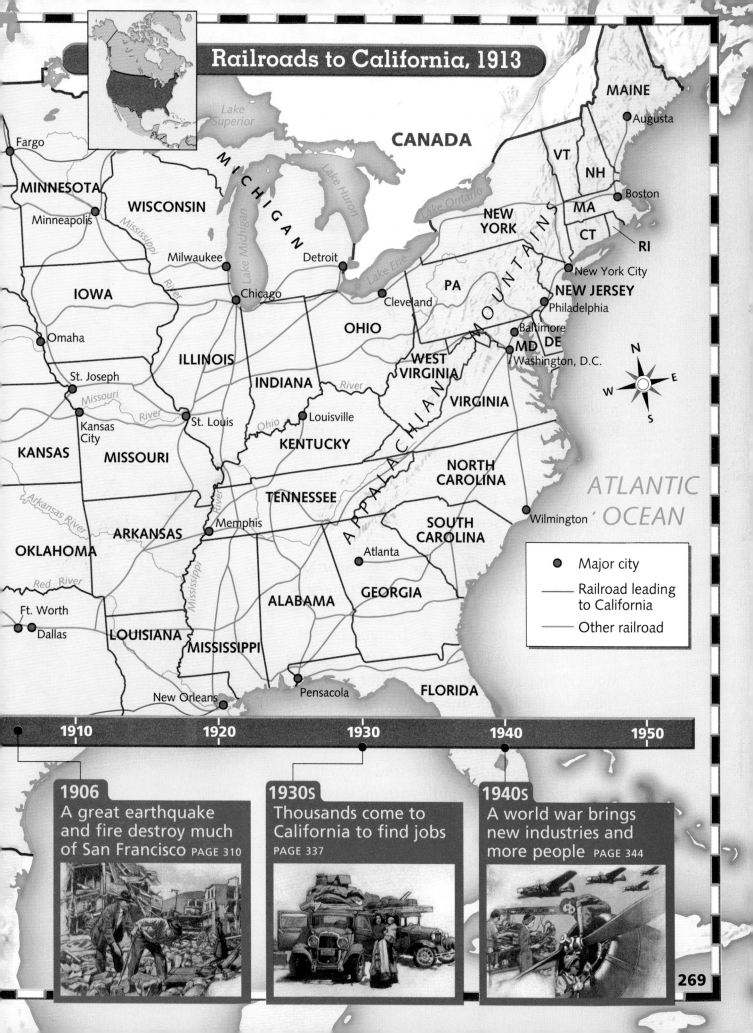

Railroads to California, 1913

CANADA

Lake Superior

MINNESOTA
Fargo

Minneapolis

WISCONSIN

MICHIGAN

Lake Huron

Lake Michigan

Milwaukee

Detroit

Chicago

Lake Ontario

Lake Erie

Cleveland

NEW YORK

New York City

MAINE

Augusta

VT

NH

Boston

MA

CT

RI

IOWA

ILLINOIS

Mississippi River

Omaha

St. Joseph

INDIANA

OHIO

PA

NEW JERSEY

Philadelphia

Baltimore

MD **DE**

Washington, D.C.

WEST VIRGINIA

River

MISSOURI

St. Louis

Missouri River

Kansas City

KANSAS

KENTUCKY

Louisville

Ohio River

VIRGINIA

ATLANTIC OCEAN

Arkansas River

ARKANSAS

Memphis

TENNESSEE

NORTH CAROLINA

SOUTH CAROLINA

Wilmington

OKLAHOMA

Red River

APPALACHIAN MOUNTAINS

Atlanta

Ft. Worth

Dallas

LOUISIANA

MISSISSIPPI

Mississippi River

ALABAMA

GEORGIA

FLORIDA

New Orleans

Pensacola

N
W E
S

Legend	
●	Major city
—	Railroad leading to California
—	Other railroad

1910   **1920**   **1930**   **1940**   **1950**

1906
A great earthquake and fire destroy much of San Francisco PAGE 310

1930s
Thousands come to California to find jobs PAGE 337

1940s
A world war brings new industries and more people PAGE 344

269

PONY EXPRESS!

by Steven Kroll • illustrated by Dan Andreasen

Californians wanted to be able to get news from the rest of the country quickly, but the great distance was a problem. In 1860 William H. Russell came up with an idea called the Pony Express. By his plan, a team of riders on horses would rush the mail from St. Joseph, Missouri, to Sacramento, California, in 10 days. From there the mail could be taken downriver to San Francisco by steamship.

The Pony Express riders changed horses at stations every 10 to 15 miles (16 to 24 km) along their part of the route. After about 100 miles (160 km), one rider would hand the mail, which was carried in leather boxes called *cantinas* (kan•TEE•nuhz), to a fresh rider. The tired rider then rested before riding back over his route with mail coming from the other direction. Read now how the Pony Express riders rushed the first mail from California to the East in April 1860.

Just before 4:00 P.M., James Randall mounted up. In his excitement, he mounted from the wrong side (the right). Then, with the crowd cheering, he headed for the water-front and the stern-wheeler *Antelope*.

That was as far as he would ride. For opening day, San Francisco wanted a show. From then on, there would be no fanfare as mail was delivered to a steamship and taken upriver to Sacramento. There the eastbound Pony Express really began.

The *Antelope* didn't reach Sacramento until after two in the morning. By then it was raining hard.

Billy Hamilton was at the dock. The express agent grabbed the *mochila*, inserted the local mail, and flung it on the pony's back. Hamilton was off into the soggy night with no one to wish him well. He rode hard, knowing that rain in the valley meant snow in the mountains for the next rider. He wanted to give that rider extra time.

He passed Fort Sutter and went up the American River. At Five Mile House, he got a fresh horse and sped on to do the same at Fifteen Mile House, Mormon Tavern, Mud Springs, and Placerville. When he pulled into Sportsman's Hall, he'd beaten the schedule by half an hour.

Warren Upson, son of the editor of the *Sacramento Union*, was next. A great rider, great shot, and "weatherproof," he chose a stocky, trail-wise pony for the difficult trail ahead, the most grueling stint on the entire route. As he started for Strawberry Station, it was

stern-wheeler
a steamship that had a paddle wheel at the back

mochila
(moh•CHEE•lah) a leather covering that fit over a saddle and held four cantinas

snowing. The wind blew the snow into his face. More often than not, he had to dismount and lead his pony.

Blinded by snow and wind, he kept heading upward, winding up the slopes of the Sierra Nevadas. Only when he felt himself going down did he know he'd crossed the summit of a pass.

Strawberry was snowed in, but Upson changed horses and slogged on through to Lake Valley House and Woodfords. From there to Genoa, his home station, conditions got better. He handed the *mochila* to his relief rider, "Pony Bob" Haslam.

slogged moved slowly and with difficulty

Between Carson City and Salt Lake City was a wasteland thick with alkali dust. There were forty-seven lonely stations, each one little more than a place to change horses. But Pony Bob had courage and spirit. He galloped on to Buckland's Station.

alkali (AL•kuh•ly) a kind of salt found in the soil of some dry regions

And on they went—to Ruby Valley and Egan Canyon, to Deep Creek, Utah, and Camp Floyd. East of Salt Lake City, sometime on April 8, the east and westbound riders crossed. No one knows if they even waved their hats.

Heading east through the Rocky Mountains, the Wyoming wilderness loomed, followed by the Continental Divide, Devil's Gate, and the foaming Sweetwater River. The rider made a stop at Fort Laramie, then went on to Chimney Rock, Nebraska.

Outside Julesburg, the Platte River was flooded. Horse and rider plunged in, but the horse lost its footing and was hurled downstream. The rider saved the *mochila* and reached the opposite bank. A spectator gave him another horse. Someone else went after the one in the river.

After Fort Kearney, there were grassy plains. When Bill Richardson rode back off the ferry in St. Joseph, Missouri, and delivered the eastbound mail to the Pony Express office at the Patee House, it was 3:55 P.M. on April 13.

Crowds cheered. There were fireworks and bonfires. The cannon boomed again. Ten days across the continent! The Pony Express had done it.

spectator
(SPEK•tay•ter)
a person who watches an event

CALIFORNIA TAKES SHAPE

"It will be built, and I'm going to have something to do with it."

Theodore D. Judah to his wife, Anna, in the 1850s about building a railroad across the country

New Links
to the East

California became a state in 1850, but many Californians still felt cut off from the rest of the United States. Deserts, high mountains, and nearly 2,000 miles (3,219 km) separated them from people in the other states. Travel to and from California remained slow and dangerous. News traveled slowly, too. In fact, it took six weeks for Californians to learn that the Congress in Washington, D.C., had admitted their state to the Union!

Californians wanted better forms of communication (kuh•myoo•nuh•KAY•shuhn) with people in the East. **Communication** is the sending and receiving of information. United States Senator John B. Weller spoke for many Californians in 1856 when he said, "The state of California, when she speaks, desires to be heard."

Californians also wanted better transportation (trans•per•TAY•shuhn). **Transportation** is the moving of people and goods from place to place. Californians had to pay high prices for goods from the East because getting those goods to California was very expensive. But communication and transportation were about to be greatly improved.

Overland Mail Service

At 4:00 P.M. on October 10, 1858, a large crowd gathered outside a post office in San Francisco. The people cheered loudly as a

FOCUS

How are people in different places linked?

Main Idea Read to find out how travel and ways of sending information improved after California became a state.

Vocabulary

communication
transportation
stagecoach
telegraph

With a stamp like the one above on it, a piece of mail could be sent overland on a stagecoach (right).

As they pass Mount Shasta, these stagecoach travelers are near the end of their overland journey to California.

dusty **stagecoach**—an enclosed wagon pulled by a team of horses—came to a stop. This stagecoach was carrying mail from back East.

In less than 25 days, it had traveled more than 2,800 miles (4,506 km) from Tipton, a town in Missouri, to San Francisco. It had started its journey in Missouri because that was where the railroad lines from the East ended. The trains carried mail to that point.

While this stagecoach was racing west to California, another stagecoach was traveling east from California to Missouri. Both stagecoaches were part of John Butterfield's new Overland Mail Company. It started the first regular mail service between California and the East.

Twice a week the Overland Mail Company carried mail between California and Missouri. On flat land the stagecoaches were able to travel about 10 miles (16 km) an hour. In the mountains, however, they could cover no more than 2 or 3 miles (3 to 5 km) in an hour. Still, with no stops except to change horses and drivers, they were able to complete their journeys in about 25 days.

The main purpose of the Overland Mail Company was to deliver mail, but its stagecoaches also carried passengers. The trip, however, was not a pleasant one. Passengers were bounced along bumpy, dusty roads, and they suffered from the cold in winter and the heat in summer. Even worse, the trip cost as much as $200. This was more than most workers made in three months!

Before the Overland Mail Company was started, stagecoach lines had carried mail and passengers within California. Stagecoaches connected the northern and southern parts of the state. They also ran between growing cities like San Francisco and Sacramento and the nearby mining communities.

REVIEW **Why was the Overland Mail Company set up?**

The Pony Express

In 1860, just two years after the Overland Mail Company first began, an advertisement appeared in California newspapers. It read,

> 66 WANTED—YOUNG SKINNY WIRY FELLOWS not over eighteen. Must be expert riders willing to risk death daily. Orphans preferred. WAGES $25 per week. 99

At that time, $25 a week was very good pay. However, the job would be hard and dangerous. The young men would work for a new mail service called the Pony Express. It promised to carry mail by horseback from Missouri to California in just 10 days—less than half the time it took the stagecoaches.

HISTORY

Camels in California

Camels can carry heavy loads over long distances without needing water. So in the 1850s the United States government decided to use camels to carry goods from Texas to California.

The first group of camels left Texas in June 1857. The 1,200-mile (1,931-km) trip through New Mexico and Arizona to Los Angeles took about seven months. The camels, however, did not work out well over time. They were hard to handle, they smelled bad, and the cactus plants that grew along the trails hurt their feet.

By 1864 the government had sold its camels. Some went to zoos, while others were sold to businesses. Some probably escaped or were turned loose in the desert. For many years amazed travelers told tales of seeing camels in the desert!

After the government stopped using camels, some of them were sold to miners in Nevada.

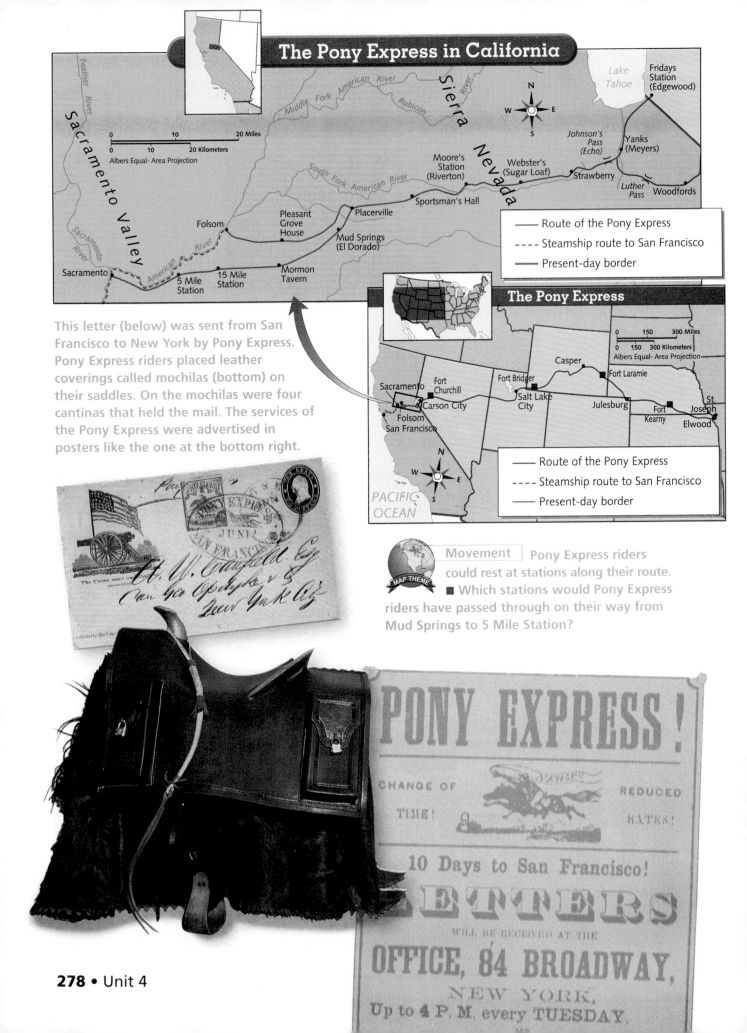

The Pony Express in California

Feather River

Sacramento Valley

Sacramento River

American River

Middle Fork American River

Rubicon River

South Fork American River

Sierra Nevada

Lake Tahoe

Fridays Station (Edgewood)

Johnson's Pass (Echo)

Yanks (Meyers)

Webster's (Sugar Loaf)

Strawberry

Luther Pass

Woodfords

Moore's Station (Riverton)

Sportsman's Hall

Placerville

Mud Springs (El Dorado)

Pleasant Grove House

Folsom

Mormon Tavern

15 Mile Station

5 Mile Station

Sacramento

0 — 10 — 20 Miles
0 — 10 — 20 Kilometers
Albers Equal-Area Projection

— Route of the Pony Express
---- Steamship route to San Francisco
— Present-day border

The Pony Express

Sacramento

Fort Churchill

Carson City

Folsom

San Francisco

Fort Bridger

Salt Lake City

Casper

Fort Laramie

Julesburg

Fort Kearny

Elwood

St Joseph

PACIFIC OCEAN

0 — 150 — 300 Miles
0 — 150 — 300 Kilometers
Albers Equal-Area Projection

— Route of the Pony Express
---- Steamship route to San Francisco
— Present-day border

This letter (below) was sent from San Francisco to New York by Pony Express. Pony Express riders placed leather coverings called mochilas (bottom) on their saddles. On the mochilas were four cantinas that held the mail. The services of the Pony Express were advertised in posters like the one at the bottom right.

Movement Pony Express riders could rest at stations along their route.
■ Which stations would Pony Express riders have passed through on their way from Mud Springs to 5 Mile Station?

PONY EXPRESS!

CHANGE OF

TIME!

REDUCED

RATES!

10 Days to San Francisco!

LETTERS

WILL BE RECEIVED AT THE

OFFICE, 84 BROADWAY,

NEW YORK,

Up to 4 P.M. every TUESDAY,

The Pony Express kept its promise. On April 13, 1860, the first Pony Express rider galloped into Sacramento. "Hip, hip, Hurrah for the Pony Carrier!" read a Sacramento newspaper. Pony Express riders had carried the mail more than 1,900 miles (3,058 km) in just 9 days and 23 hours!

The young Pony Express riders rode day and night. They had to cross grassy plains, dry and empty deserts, and steep mountain passes. They rode through the scorching heat and wild thunderstorms of summer and the freezing temperatures and blinding snowstorms of winter. Their motto was "The mail must go through."

REVIEW **How was the Pony Express different from the Overland Mail Company?**

LEARNING FROM CHARTS In Morse code each letter of the alphabet was represented by dots, dashes, or a combination of both.

■ How would you write your name in Morse code?

The Original Morse Code

a	•—	h	••••	o	••	v	•••—
b	—•••	i	••	p	•••••	w	•——
c	•••	j	—•—•	q	••—•	x	•—••
d	—••	k	—•—	r	••••	y	•• ••
e	•	l	—	s	•••	z	••• •
f	•—•	m	——	t	—		
g	——•	n	—•	u	••—		

Samuel F. B. Morse developed a telegraph with a sounder to click out messages as they came in.

The Telegraph

The Pony Express lasted less than 18 months. Soon the horses were sold, and the young riders had to find new jobs. When the Pony Express riders made their last trip in 1861, a California newspaper wrote sadly, "Goodbye, Pony! . . . You have served us well."

Why did the Pony Express end so soon? In 1861 it was replaced by an even faster form of communication—the telegraph. A **telegraph** was a machine that used electricity to send messages over wires. With the telegraph, messages could be sent across the country in just minutes!

Samuel F. B. Morse, one of the inventors of the telegraph, created a special code for sending the messages over the wires. The Morse code was a kind of alphabet. It used "dots and dashes"— short and long signals—to stand for letters and numbers. Operators on one end tapped out the signals. Operators on the other end heard signals and translated them into letters and words. For the first time, news could travel faster than people.

By the 1850s telegraph lines had been strung across most of the East.

By 1860 they had also been strung across California, linking Los Angeles and San Francisco. However, telegraph lines did not link California with states in the East until the fall of 1861.

On October 24, 1861, a telegraph operator in San Francisco sent the first message from California to the East. It was addressed to President Abraham Lincoln in Washington, D.C. It read, "The Pacific to the Atlantic sends greetings." Soon messages were being sent back and forth across the country.

Workers strung telegraph wires on poles.

With the telegraph linking California and the East, the Pony Express was no longer needed. However, the telegraph could send and receive only short messages. People, goods, and most mail still traveled the way the forty-niners had—overland by wagon, by sea around Cape Horn, or by the land-and-sea route across the Isthmus of Panama.

REVIEW How did the telegraph improve communications between California and the East?

LESSON 1 REVIEW

1855 — 1860 — 1865

1858
• The Overland Mail Company begins service

1860
• The Pony Express begins

1861
• The telegraph links California with the East
• The Pony Express ends

Check Understanding

1 Remember the Facts What company started the first regular mail service between California and the states in the East?

2 Recall the Main Idea How did transportation and communication improve after California became a state?

Think Critically

3 Past to Present Compare the ways people get information today with the ways Californians got news in the 1850s and 1860s. How are they alike? How are they different?

4 Think More About It Many young men wanted to be Pony Express riders even though the job was very dangerous. Why do you think they wanted to be riders?

Show What You Know

Writing Activity Imagine that you are a newspaper reporter. You have been asked to write an article about the sending of the first telegraph message from California to the East. Explain to your readers how the telegraph will help link California with the rest of the country. Share your article with classmates.

Linking East and West

1860	1865	1870

For many years people in the United States had talked about the need to build a transcontinental (trans•kahn•tuhn•EN•tuhl) railroad. A **transcontinental railroad** would cross the North American continent, linking the Atlantic and Pacific coasts. It would make it possible for people and goods to travel from coast to coast in just days instead of weeks or months.

Planning the Railroad

Many Americans wanted a transcontinental railroad to be built, but they could not agree on a route for it or on how to pay for it. Other Americans believed that such a railroad would never be built. They said that it would be impossible to lay tracks through the steep Sierra Nevada. One young man, however, was determined to see the railroad built. His name was Theodore D. Judah.

Judah was an engineer who had come to California from Connecticut in 1854. An **engineer** is a person who plans and builds roads, bridges, and railroads. Judah believed he could solve the problems of building a transcontinental railroad. But he first had to find a route through the Sierra Nevada. He made 23 trips into the mountains before he finally chose a route.

FOCUS

Why is good transportation important to people?

Main Idea Read to learn how a railroad was built to link the Pacific and Atlantic coasts of the United States.

Vocabulary

transcontinental railroad
engineer
invest
civil war
laborer

The Central Pacific's Locomotive No. 1, the *Governor Stanford*, once chugged its way across California.

Judah had a route for the railroad, but he needed something else. His dream of building a transcontinental railroad would take money—a lot of money! To raise the money, Judah had to find people to invest in a company to build his railroad. To **invest** is to buy something, such as a share in a company, in the hope that it will make money in the future.

Among those who agreed to invest in the company were Leland Stanford, Collis P. Huntington, Mark Hopkins, and Charles Crocker. All four had come to California during the gold rush years and had grown rich selling goods to miners. In later years these men became so rich and powerful that they were called the Big Four.

In June 1861 the Central Pacific Railroad Company was founded.

Stanford became its president, and Huntington became its vice president. Judah became its chief engineer.

REVIEW Why did some people think that building a transcontinental railroad was impossible?

The Civil War

Two months earlier, on April 12, 1861, the guns had roared at Fort Sumter, in South Carolina. These were the opening shots of the Civil War. A **civil war** is a war between groups of people in the same country or in what had been the same country. For years the Northern and Southern states had disagreed about slavery and other issues. Now the Southern states had left the Union—the United States of America—and formed

The Big Four, (left to right) Leland Stanford, Charles Crocker, Mark Hopkins, and Collis P. Huntington, met with Theodore Judah in a room above a hardware store in Sacramento.

Union and Confederate States

CANADA

WASHINGTON TERRITORY

OREGON

NEVADA TERRITORY

CALIFORNIA

UTAH TERRITORY

DAKOTA TERRITORY

NEBRASKA TERRITORY

COLORADO TERRITORY

NEW MEXICO TERRITORY

INDIAN TERRITORY

TEXAS

MEXICO

MINNESOTA

WISCONSIN

MICHIGAN

IOWA

ILLINOIS   INDIANA

MISSOURI

KANSAS

ARKANSAS

MISSISSIPPI

LOUISIANA

OHIO

KENTUCKY

TENNESSEE

ALABAMA

GEORGIA

WEST VIRGINIA (1863)   VIRGINIA

NORTH CAROLINA

SOUTH CAROLINA

FLORIDA

MAINE

VT   NH

NEW YORK   MA

CT   RI

PENNSYLVANIA   NJ

MD   DE

Lake Superior

Lake Michigan

Lake Huron

Lake Ontario

Lake Erie

PACIFIC OCEAN

ATLANTIC OCEAN

Gulf of Mexico

0   200   400 Miles
0   200   400 Kilometers
Albers Equal-Area Projection

40°N   120°W   30°N   90°W   80°W   70°W   40°N   30°N

- Union state
- Confederate state
- Territory

Regions During the Civil War, 11 states left the Union and formed the Confederate States of America.
■ Which Union state bordered California?

a new country called the Confederate States of America, or the Confederacy.

Congress wanted to link California with the rest of the states in the Union, so it decided that the time had come to build a transcontinental railroad. In 1862, with the support of Theodore Judah, Congress passed the Pacific Railroad Act. This act gave the Central Pacific Railroad money to build a railroad east from Sacramento. It gave another railroad company, the Union Pacific, money to build a railroad west from Omaha, Nebraska. Railroad lines from the East ended in Omaha at that time.

The Civil War lasted four years, from 1861 to 1865. Californians were divided by the war, but most of them remained loyal to the Union. About 16,000 Californians joined the Union army.

Only a few Californians fought in battles, but California's gold helped the Union pay for the supplies used by its armies. The war finally ended on April 9, 1865, when the Union won. After the war, slavery was against the law in all parts of the United States.

REVIEW Which two companies received money from Congress to build a transcontinental railroad?

Building the Railroad

Work on the transcontinental railroad began early in 1863, while the Civil War was still being fought. Theodore Judah, however, did not live to see his dream come true. He and the Big Four had argued about how the railroad should be built. So Judah decided to travel to New York to find new people to invest in the company. While crossing the Isthmus of Panama, he caught a fever and became very sick. Judah died soon after he reached New York.

The Central Pacific Railroad built eastward from Sacramento, and the Union Pacific Railroad built westward from Omaha. To help them pay for building the railroad, the government promised to give each company thousands of acres of land and millions of dollars in loans. The amount each company got,

Movement

The first transcontinental railroad linked Omaha, Nebraska, and Sacramento, California.

■ Which states and territories did the Central Pacific Railroad pass through?

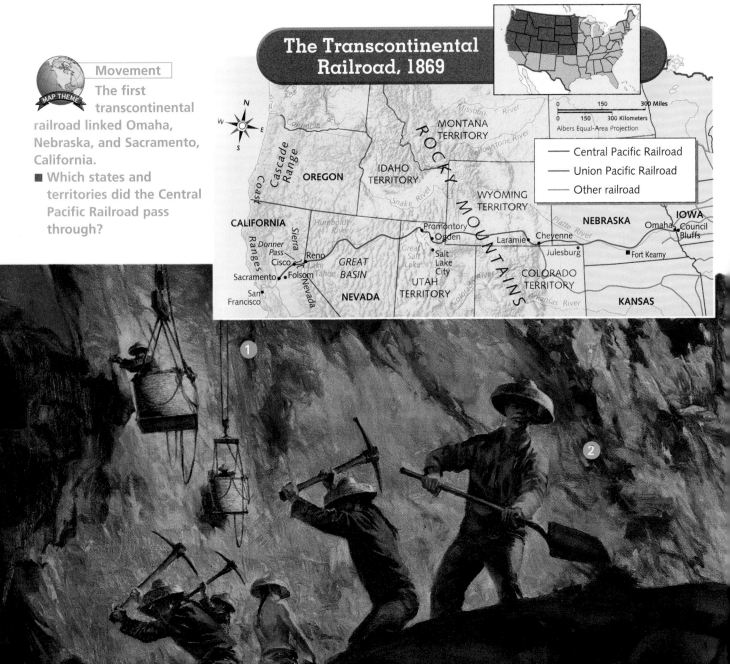

The Transcontinental Railroad, 1869

Central Pacific Railroad
Union Pacific Railroad
Other railroad

however, depended on how many miles of track it laid. So each one raced to lay the most track.

From Sacramento the work was fairly easy until the workers reached the Sierra Nevada. There they had to carve a path for the tracks on rugged mountainsides. They had to blast tunnels through solid rock and build bridges across deep canyons. To keep snow off the tracks, the workers had to build wooden roofs over the tracks in some places.

Once the tracks had crossed the Sierra Nevada, workers faced the dry lands of the Great Basin. For miles on end there were few trees and very little water.

Both companies had a hard time finding enough **laborers** (LAY•ber•erz), or workers. The Union Pacific hired thousands of immigrants, mainly from Ireland. Most of the Central Pacific's workers were from China. The Chinese proved to be such good workers that the Central Pacific tried to hire every Chinese man in California. It even hired workers in China and brought them to California.

The Chinese workers did many difficult and dangerous jobs. They were often lowered in baskets down the sides of mountains to set explosives. Sometimes the explosives went off too soon, and the workers were killed before the baskets could be raised. Yet, because of discrimination against them, the Chinese were paid less than other workers.

REVIEW **Why was building a railroad through the Sierra Nevada so difficult?**

Building the Railroad

LEARNING FROM DIAGRAMS
❶ Workers were lowered in baskets down the sides of the mountains to set off explosives. ❷ Workers used simple tools such as pickaxes and shovels to dig through the mountains. ❸ Sheds were built over the tracks to keep snow off them.

■ Besides laying tracks, what other kinds of jobs did the railroad workers have to do?

Railroads Change California

Finally it was agreed that the two railroad lines would meet at Promontory, Utah. On May 10, 1869, leaders of the two companies gathered in the desert. There were speeches and prayers, and a band played. Chinese and Irish workers carefully laid the last two rails so that they connected. Then the last spike, a solid gold one, was driven in place to complete the great Pacific Railroad. A telegram was sent to President Ulysses S. Grant. It said,

> 66 The last rail is laid, the last spike is driven. The Pacific Railroad is completed. 99

Poet Bret Harte wrote a poem to celebrate the event. It began,

> 66 What was it the Engines said,
> Pilots touching—head to head
> Facing on the single track,
> Half a world behind
> each back? 99

People celebrated all over the country. In San Francisco and Sacramento, the celebrations lasted for days.

People knew that California—and the United States—would never be the same. People could now reach California in

When the Central Pacific and Union Pacific railroads met at Promontory, Utah, on May 10, 1869, North America became the first continent to have a rail line from coast to coast.

On the golden spike that completed the first transcontinental railroad was written a prayer and the names of Central Pacific officers and directors.

10 to 12 days by train. For $100, wealthy travelers sat on red plush seats in fancy train cars. For $40, others rode west on hard benches.

The transcontinental railroad also made it easier for Californians to send products to markets in the East. Goods from the East could be sent by railroad to California, too. As a result, those goods cost less than ever before. Goods brought from the East could also be shipped from California to Asia, so trade increased sharply. This helped San Francisco and other port cities to grow.

REVIEW How did the transcontinental railroad change California?

LESSON 2 REVIEW

1860		1865		1870

1861
• The Civil War begins

1863
• Work on the transcontinental railroad begins

1865
• The Civil War ends

1869
• The transcontinental railroad is completed

Check Understanding

1 Remember the Facts What name was later given to the group of four Sacramento business people who invested in Theodore Judah's railroad?

2 Recall the Main Idea Why did the United States Congress finally vote to build a transcontinental railroad?

Think Critically

3 Past to Present Do you think railroads are as important today as they were in the late 1800s? Why or why not?

4 Link to You Many people told Theodore Judah that it was impossible to build a railroad through the Sierra Nevada. Have you ever had an idea that others thought was impossible? Explain.

Show What You Know

Writing Activity Imagine that you have been asked to give a speech at Promontory on May 10, 1869. Write a speech telling why the transcontinental railroad is important and describing the hardships faced by the workers who built it. Then give your speech to your class.

TEN MILE DAY

AND THE BUILDING OF THE TRANSCONTINENTAL RAILROAD

WRITTEN AND ILLUSTRATED BY MARY ANN FRASER

Each of the two railroad companies building the transcontinental railroad tried to lay more track than the other. On October 26, 1868, workers for the Union Pacific Railroad laid a record seven miles of track in just one day. When Charles Crocker, the construction boss for the Central Pacific Railroad heard about this, he bragged that his workers could lay ten miles of track in a single day! But Dr. Thomas C. Durant, vice president of the Union Pacific Railroad, did not believe it could be done. Read now to find out what happened on April 28, 1869, when Crocker and his assistant, James Strobridge, decided to prove Durant wrong.

From the first pioneer to the last tamper ran a line of men nearly two miles long. Like a mammoth machine with hundreds of well-oiled parts, Crocker's men moved rhythmically forward. The ribbon of track rose across the plain at the pace of a walking man. Tired workers were pulled from the line and replaced. But many, including the eight ironmen, showed no signs of quitting.

Alongside the grade the telegraph construction party worked frantically to keep pace with the track layers. They set the poles; hammered on the crossbars; and hauled out, hung, and insulated the wire.

pioneer a worker who straightens the wooden ties under the rails

tamper a worker who packs down the gravel and rocks used to hold the ties in place

ironmen railroad workers who lay the rails on the ties

The track boss stalked up and down the line, barking out commands and encouragement. The steady hammering of spikes, the rhythmic thud of iron rails, and even the men's labored breathing beat like a drum across the barren plain.

barren empty

A reporter pulled out his pocket watch and counted the rails as they were laid down. To everyone's amazement 240 feet of iron were placed in one minute and twenty seconds.

By 9 A.M. almost two miles of track had been spiked and tamped. Even the Union Pacific men, who had laughed at the Central Pacific crews, had to admit it was quality work.

Water, food, and tool wagons creaked up and down the line as the heat rose with the morning sun. Chinese workers wove in and out of the men, delivering water and tea to quench their thirst.

At the front Crocker and Strobridge oversaw every detail. Now and then when something amusing happened, Crocker's merry laugh echoed from his carriage.

With the completion of another two miles of track, the second supply train pulled back to the siding and the third train steamed forward, belching thick clouds of black smoke. Next in line, ready to serve the midday meal, was the so-called Pioneer Train—the boarding house for some of the workers, and the office and living quarters of James and Hannah Strobridge.

siding a set of tracks running alongside the main tracks

At 1:30 the whistle sounded, calling a halt for lunch. Whirlwind No. 62, the Pioneer Train locomotive, pushed the kitchen cars up, and the boarding boss served hot boiled beef.

A quick measurement showed that six miles of track had already been laid, spiked, and bolted that morning. Whoops and hollers went up as the news spread among the men. They were now confident they could reach their goal of ten miles in one day, and they named their rest stop Camp Victory.

At 2:30 work began again, but a special crew had to be called in. The tracks were now climbing the west slope of the Promontory Mountains. The climb was steep and full of curves, and the rails had to be bent.

Lacking measuring instruments, this new crew judged the curves by sight. They jammed the rails between blocks and then slowly and carefully hammered them into the right shapes. Every rail now took extra time to mold and fit.

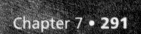

As the afternoon wore on, the foreman continued to ride the line, encouraging the men. Although the horses pulling the iron cars were changed every two hours, they could no longer run up the grade. Now they had to walk slowly up the steep hillside. The rail gang was dripping with sweat, and their muscles must have burned from overuse, but not one man stopped to rest. With each hour another mile of track reached toward Promontory Summit.

By 7 P.M. the sun was dipping behind Monument Point. Strobridge signaled for the final blast from the train whistle. The exhausted men cast down their tools, and the day's work came to an abrupt end.

fishplate a flat piece of iron used to connect two rails

How much rail had the men of the Central Pacific laid? Two Union Pacific engineers took out their surveying chains and began to measure. Everyone waited for the final count. Then it came. The railhead was ten miles, fifty-six feet farther east than it had been the previous evening.

The crews flung their hats into the air, cheering and shaking hands all around. They had done the impossible again. The Union Pacific's record was destroyed, and Thomas Durant lost the bet. A total of 3,520 rails, twice that number of fishplates, 28,160 spikes, and 14,080 nuts and bolts had been placed to complete the job.

The eight track layers were declared heroes and were featured in later histories. Each had lifted over 125 tons of iron. No single crew has ever beaten their record. The Chinese workers had once again proven themselves to their biased rivals. Each team had something to celebrate.

April 28, 1869, became known as Ten Mile Day. Crocker and Strobridge had chosen 1,400 of their best workers to lay the tracks, and promised them four times their usual pay for that day.

LITERATURE REVIEW

1. What caused the work to slow down in the afternoon?
2. What do you think would have happened if the railroad workers had not cooperated?
3. Historical markers often show where important events took place. Design a historical marker for the Ten Mile Day. Describe on your marker what took place on April 28, 1869.

Use a Time

1. Why Learn This Skill?

The coming of the transcontinental railroad made it necessary to create a single way of keeping time. Before then, each town across the United States set its own time, using the sun as a guide. Clocks were set at noon when the sun was highest in the sky. As the Earth turns, however, it is noon in different places at different times.

Because of this, the towns along train routes all had their own times. It was impossible for the railroads to make and keep schedules!

A group of people was asked to study the problem. They decided to divide the Earth into 24 time zones—one for each hour of the day. A **time zone** is a region in which people use the same time. To figure out the time anywhere in the United States, you can use a time zone map like the one on page 295.

All the people in a time zone use the same time.

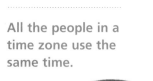

2. Understand the Process

The United States has six time zones—the eastern time zone, the central time zone, the mountain time zone, the Pacific time zone, the Alaska time zone, and the Hawaii-Aleutian time zone. The Earth rotates from west to east, so time zones to the east of you always have a later time than your time zone has. El Paso, Texas, is in a time zone east of San Diego, so the time in El Paso is later than the time in San Diego. Time zones west of you have an earlier time than your time zone has. Anchorage, Alaska, is in a time zone west of San Diego, so the time in Anchorage is earlier than the time in San Diego.

1 Find Los Angeles on the time zone map. In which time zone is Los Angeles?

2 Find the clock face near the Pacific time zone. What time does the clock show?

3 Now find Denver. It is in the mountain time zone. What time does the clock above this time zone show? When it is 7:00 A.M. in the Pacific time zone, it is 8:00 A.M. in the mountain time zone. Moving east, you must add one hour when you enter each time zone. What time is it in the central time zone? in the eastern time zone?

4 Now find Salt Lake City. In which time zone is it? When it is 8:00 A.M. in the mountain time zone, it is 7:00 A.M. in the Pacific time zone. Moving west, you

Zone Map

must subtract one hour when you enter each time zone. What time is it in the Alaska time zone? the Hawaii-Aleutian time zone?

5 Imagine that you are in San Francisco. Is the time earlier, later, or the same as the time in Chicago?

6 If it is 4:00 P.M. in Dallas, what time is it in Atlanta? in San Diego?

3. Think and Apply

Look at a watch or a classroom clock. What time is it in your time zone? Now figure out the time for each of these cities.

Anchorage	Honolulu
Boise	Minneapolis
Boston	Seattle

United States Time Zones

FOCUS

How is farming important to Californians?

Main Idea Read to learn what helped farming to become a major industry in California in the late 1800s.

Vocabulary

levee
advertising
tenant farmer

Farming Becomes a Major Industry

1870	1880	1890

During the gold rush, and in the years that followed, thousands of newcomers arrived in California. Many of them started farms. Between 1850 and 1860 the number of farms in California grew from fewer than 900 to more than 18,700.

When the transcontinental railroad was finished, even more people came to California. Many of them were farmers, too.

By the late 1800s farming had become a major industry in California. Soon the state's farmers were able to feed the people of California and help feed the rest of the country and the world.

Wheat Farming in the Central Valley

The San Joaquin and Sacramento valleys were among the first areas of the state to be farmed. The land there was fertile, and because it was flat and had few trees, it was easy to plow. One California official said, "Riches, other than gold, have been found in the soil."

Many kinds of crops, including barley and oats, were raised in the Central Valley, but wheat was the main crop. The Central Valley's climate, with its hot, dry summers and mild, wet winters, was perfect for growing wheat.

Oranges (above) and wheat (below) were California's largest crops in the late 1800s.

This detail from the painting *Harvest Time* by William Hahn shows how farmers in the Central Valley harvested wheat in the late 1800s.

New kinds of machines allowed farmers to plant and harvest large amounts of wheat. Within a few years wheat farms covered thousands of acres in the Central Valley. Charles Nordhoff described the valley in his 1874 book *California for Travelers and Settlers*. He wrote,

66 Wheat, wheat, wheat, and nothing but wheat is what you see on your journey as far as the eye can reach over the plain in every direction. Fields of two, three, and four thousand acres make but small farms. 99

By 1890 California grew more wheat than any other state except Minnesota. California wheat was sold around the world. In Europe the British and the French used it to make flour for bread. The Italians used it to make pasta.

REVIEW What was the main crop grown in the Central Valley in the late 1800s?

Too Much Water, Too Little Water

Farmers in the Central Valley faced the same kinds of hardships as farmers everywhere. Along the Sacramento River, for example, they sometimes lost their crops to spring floods. Starting in the 1850s they built levees (LEH•veez) along the river to help control the flooding. A **levee** is a high wall made of earth. Many of the Chinese workers who had helped build the transcontinental railroad also helped build these levees.

In later years Californians began to reclaim, or make usable, more of the land in the Central Valley. One area that was reclaimed was the delta where the Sacramento and San Joaquin rivers join. Californians reclaimed this wet, low-lying land by draining away the water and building dams to help prevent floods.

In other parts of the state, especially in the southern San Joaquin Valley, the land was too dry to farm. Before farmers could plant crops there, they had to build irrigation systems to bring water to their fields. These irrigation systems opened up thousands of acres of new land to farming.

In 1881 George Chaffey and his brother built an irrigation system in southern California on 2,500 acres of land they called Etiwanda. Then they sold pieces of the land to farmers. Soon, other people were building farming communities like Chaffey's.

REVIEW **Why did farmers build levees along the Sacramento River?**

New Crops, New Markets

The first oranges in California had been planted on the missions. Those oranges were sour and had thick skins and many seeds. By the late 1800s, however, a new kind of orange was being grown in California.

Eliza and Luther Calvin Tibbets were farmers who had moved to Riverside, in southern California. In 1873 they received two small orange trees from the Department of Agriculture in Washington, D.C. The trees had been grown in Brazil, a country in South America, and sent to the United States by a missionary who worked there.

The Tibbetses planted the trees near their home and tended them carefully. In time the trees produced a seedless orange called the Washington navel orange. Soon other growers were also planting navel oranges. They planted other new kinds of delicious oranges, too. By 1900 California had more than five million orange trees.

Wheat and oranges were the main crops grown in California in the late 1800s, but the state's farmers also grew cotton and many kinds of fruits and vegetables. They planted lemon and

LEARNING FROM ILLUSTRATIONS Growers used colorful advertisements to get people to buy their crops.

■ What is the name of the brand of oranges advertised in this poster?

The work of Eliza Tibbets and her husband, Luther, changed the orange industry in California forever.

A Refrigerated Railroad Car, Late 1800s

Air vent

Ice tank

Roof hatch

Air pipes

ORANGES LEMONS

U.S.A.

REFRIGERATED CAR
COMMERCIAL
EXPRESS

Door

Water tank

Sawdust

LEARNING FROM DIAGRAMS In this refrigerated railroad car, ice was poured into the ice tank through the roof hatches. Air passed through the air vents and through air pipes under the ice.
■ Why do you think sawdust was put in the space under the floor?

peach trees. They also grew olives, dates, sugar beets, walnuts, almonds, grapes, avocados, rice, potatoes, lettuce, melons, and artichokes.

Railroads were able to carry some of the state's farm products across the country to markets in the East, but they could not carry most fresh fruits and vegetables. These products spoiled during the long trip. In the late 1800s, however, a way was found to use ice to chill, or refrigerate, railroad cars. Refrigerated railroad cars made it possible for farmers to send

Fruits and vegetables were shipped from California to markets all over the United States.

oranges and other fresh fruits and vegetables to the East.

The growers used advertising to spread the word about their crops. **Advertising** is information that a business provides about its product or service to make people want to buy it.

Each navel orange, for example, was wrapped in a piece of paper with the message, "I am a Riverside Washington navel orange. I have no seeds to choke the young or worry the old."

REVIEW Why were refrigerated railroad cars important to farmers?

Improving Farm Crops

During the late 1800s plant scientists worked to create new and better kinds of plants for farmers to grow. One of these scientists, Luther Burbank, came to Santa Rosa, California, from Massachusetts in 1875. He fell in love with the Sonoma Valley, which he called "the chosen spot of all this earth as far as nature is concerned."

Burbank studied plants from all over the world. Then he crossed, or mixed the seeds from, different plants to grow new and better kinds of plants.

Another Californian who worked to improve crops was Harriet Russell Strong. She grew walnuts on her farm in the dry San Gabriel Valley, east of Los Angeles. She used irrigation to water her crops and found new ways to store water for irrigation.

REVIEW How did Luther Burbank help farming in California?

The Farmers and the Railroads

After the transcontinental railroad was finished, the Big Four started building another railroad. This railroad, called the Southern Pacific, ran south through the Central Valley. In return for building the railroad, the Southern Pacific was given more than 11 million acres of land.

The Southern Pacific saw that it could make money by selling some of its land to farmers. The railroad advertised this land to people in the East and in other countries, offering to sell it at low prices. Many of the people who bought the land, however, had a hard time. Drought was always a problem, and many people could not afford irrigation systems to bring water to their crops.

In 1879 Californians approved a new state constitution. One of its purposes was to try to limit the power of the Southern Pacific Railroad. But even after the new constitution was approved, the railroad remained very powerful.

At Mussel Slough (MUH•suhl SLOO), in the San Joaquin Valley, disagreements between farmers and the railroad ended in bloodshed. The Southern Pacific said the farmers could buy the land for as little as $2.50 an acre. It invited settlers to begin farming the land before the sale was final.

Thinking that they owned the land, the farmers joined together to build irrigation systems. They plowed the land and planted crops. Then the railroad decided that it could sell the land for much more money. It now

Luther Burbank grew new fruits and vegetables that tasted better and stayed fresh longer.

wanted as much as $80 an acre for some land.

The farmers refused to pay the higher prices. They also refused to leave the land. A battle broke out in May 1880 when people from the railroad tried to force the farmers to leave. Seven people were killed, and the railroad took over the land.

Farmers had problems in other parts of the state as well. Many could not earn enough to pay their bills and pay the high prices that the railroads charged to ship their

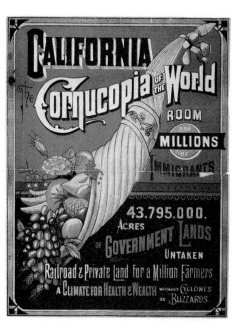

Railroads in California advertised the riches of the state all across the United States and even in Europe.

crops. Many had to sell their land. Some then became **tenant farmers**, who paid rent to use the land. Most paid the rent by giving the landowner part of their crop. Many tenant farmers felt trapped. Because they owed the landowner money, they could not move away.

REVIEW **What problems did farmers face?**

LESSON 4 REVIEW

1870		1880		1890
1873 • The Tibbetses plant California's first navel orange trees	**1879** • Californians approve a new state constitution	**1880** • Disagreements lead to bloodshed at Mussel Slough	**1890** • California grows more wheat than any other state except Minnesota	

Check Understanding

1 Remember the Facts What did farmers in the Central Valley do, starting in the 1850s, to help control flooding?

2 Recall the Main Idea What helped farming to become a major industry in California in the late 1800s?

Think Critically

3 Think More About It How did the railroad both help and hurt farmers?

4 Explore Viewpoints How do you think the events at Mussel Slough made California farmers feel about the railroad?

Show What You Know

Art Activity Write and illustrate an advertisement for a farm product that California farmers raised in the late 1800s. In your ad, tell where the crop is grown and why people will like it. Then add your advertisement to a classroom display titled *California Farm Products*.

Read a Pictograph

1. Why Learn This Skill?

Have you ever tried to compare two things? How did you do it? As you know, a graph is a drawing that helps you compare numbers. The graph below compares the amount of wheat grown in California in 1860, 1870, 1880, and 1890. Instead of using numbers, however, this graph uses symbols.

A graph that uses symbols to stand for numbers is called a **pictograph**. A pictograph always has a key that tells how much each symbol stands for. To read the pictograph, you must use both the key and the symbols.

2. Understand the Process

Follow these steps to understand the symbols used on this pictograph.

① Look at the key. How much does each symbol 🌾 stand for?

② Find the year 1870. How many whole symbols are next to it?

③ Figure out how much wheat three whole symbols stand for. If one symbol stands for 5 million bushels of wheat, how much do the three whole symbols stand for?

④ Find 1870 again. There is about one-fifth of another symbol shown there. One-fifth of 5 million equals 1 million. So this part of a symbol stands for about 1 million bushels. Add the two amounts. About how many bushels of wheat did California produce in 1870?

3. Think and Apply

Find the year 1890 on the graph. About how much wheat was raised in that year? Think about the changes that took place in California in the late 1800s. Why do you think so much more wheat was raised in California in 1890 than in 1860?

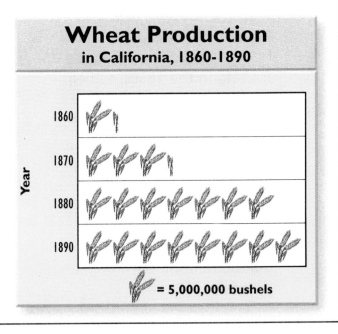

Wheat Production
in California, 1860-1890

Year	
1860	
1870	
1880	
1890	

🌾 = 5,000,000 bushels

Newcomers from Near and Far

1870	1890	1910

In the late 1800s and early 1900s the population of the United States—and of California—exploded. Millions of immigrants from all over the world arrived at ports on both the Atlantic and Pacific coasts of the United States. Trains from the East carried many immigrants west to California. Many people from other parts of the United States also traveled by train to California.

A Land of Hope and Promise

Why did so many people choose to come to California? For farmers from the Middle West, California promised a better life in a milder climate. Many African Americans, freed from slavery after the Civil War, came hoping to find jobs and a better life, too.

Many newcomers came to California from countries in Europe, such as Denmark, Germany, Ireland, Italy, Finland, Portugal, and Sweden. Others came from Asia, mainly from China. Later immigrants came from other Asian countries such as Japan and the Philippines. People from Mexico continued coming north to California, as they had for hundreds of years. For all these people, California was a land of hope and promise.

FOCUS
What problems might newcomers face in a community or a state?

Main Idea Read to learn about some of the problems different groups of people faced in California in the late 1800s.

Vocabulary
prejudice
reservation

Immigrants from all over the world came to California. One family brought along the baby carriage shown above.

This Chinese butcher was one of the thousands of immigrants who came to California in the late 1800s and early 1900s.

Immigrants had many reasons for coming to California and to the rest of the United States. Some were escaping from governments that did not treat them fairly. Others were seeking freedom to follow their own religion. Many were poor and wanted only a good job and a chance for a better life.

Land was what many immigrants wanted. At age 17, Paul Mariani (mah•ree•AH•nee) left his home in southern Europe and sailed for the United States. "There was hardly enough dirt [in their homeland] for a family to survive on," his son later wrote.

Mariani was amazed by the rich soil he found in California's Santa Clara Valley. He worked hard and saved money to buy land of his own. "Whenever he had fifty cents," said his son, "he put it down on a piece of land."

California's rich soil brought many other immigrants to the state. In 1857 a group from Germany settled on land about 30 miles (48 km) southeast of Los Angeles. They called their land Anaheim. The name came from its location in the Santa Ana Valley and *heim*, the German word for *home*. These settlers planted more than 400,000 grape vines on their land.

Most immigrant families worked long and hard to save money to buy land. As a boy, Khatchik Minasian (khat•CHEEK mih•NAH•see•ahn) spent his summers "picking grapes, turning grapes, making boxes, doing all kinds of . . . labor [for] long hours in the heat." Minasian was an Armenian immigrant from western Asia.

REVIEW **Why did immigrants leave their homelands for California?**

Problems of Discrimination

Many immigrants, especially people from China, faced discrimination in their new country. They were often treated unfairly because they were different from other Californians. They looked different, dressed differently, spoke a different language, and had different customs and religions. Before 1943 the Chinese were not even allowed to become citizens.

Chinese immigrants could not get certain jobs, and they usually were forced to live in separate communities. Their settlements in San Francisco and in other cities became known as Chinatowns. Today San Francisco's Chinatown is the largest one in the United States.

Chinese workers had been needed to help mine gold and build the transcontinental railroad and the levees. During the 1870s, however, California and the rest of the United States faced hard economic times. Many businesses closed, and many workers lost their jobs. Across the country, some people began to blame their problems on immigrants. They thought the immigrants had been taking their jobs. In California, many workers shouted, "The Chinese must go!"

Discrimination against the Chinese and other immigrants grew out of prejudice. **Prejudice** is an unfair feeling of hate or dislike for members of a certain group because of their background, race, or religion.

Chinese homes and businesses were often attacked. In 1882, and again in 1892, Congress passed laws that stopped most Chinese immigrants from entering the United States unless they had family members living in the country. This was the first time that people from a certain country were not allowed to enter the United States.

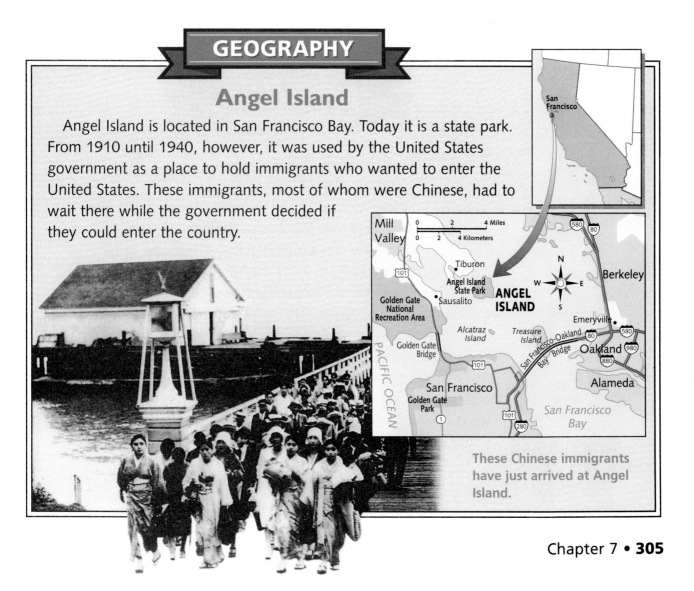

GEOGRAPHY

Angel Island

Angel Island is located in San Francisco Bay. Today it is a state park. From 1910 until 1940, however, it was used by the United States government as a place to hold immigrants who wanted to enter the United States. These immigrants, most of whom were Chinese, had to wait there while the government decided if they could enter the country.

These Chinese immigrants have just arrived at Angel Island.

One of the people who worked for the rights of the Chinese was Ng Poon Chew (N POON CHEE•oh). He had come to San Francisco from China in 1881, when he was 15 years old. In 1899 he started a weekly newspaper for Chinese readers. He called it the *Hua Mei Hsin Pao*, or Chinese American Weekly. He used the paper to fight for the rights of the Chinese.

The paper was such a success that the following year Ng started to publish the paper every day. He changed the paper's name to the *Chung Sai Yat Po*, or Chinese Western Daily. It was the first Chinese daily newspaper published in the United States.

REVIEW What problems did Chinese immigrants face?

Defeat of the Native Americans

The gold rush and the arrival of thousands of newcomers led to terrible problems for California's Indians. The miners and settlers often did not understand the Indians' ways of life. They moved onto lands where the Indians hunted or gathered food. Many Indians were killed. Others, forced off their lands, died from hunger and disease.

The United States government tried to move the Indians onto reservations. A **reservation** is land set aside by the government for use by Indians. Often, however, the land on the reservations was poor and the Indians could not find or grow enough food.

BIOGRAPHY

Ishi

1861?–1916

In 1911 a man stumbled into the mining town of Oroville. He spoke a language that the townspeople did not understand. They learned that he was a Yahi Indian.

During the gold rush, most of the Yahis had been killed or forced from their homes. Ishi and a few others survived. They hid far from towns and farms. One by one, however, Ishi's people died, leaving him alone.

Two scientists became friends with the man, but he would not tell them his name. That was something he would share only with another Yahi. So the scientists named him Ishi, the Yahi word for *man*. Ishi taught the scientists about Yahi customs and traditions. Ishi, the last of the Yahis, died in 1916.

Why do you think scientists wanted to learn about Yahi customs from Ishi?

Many Native Californians did not want to live on reservations, and some fought to keep their native lands. In 1864 the Modoc Indians were sent to live on a reservation in Oregon. Twice they left the reservation and returned to their land in northern California. The United States Army was sent to force the Modocs back onto the reservation.

In 1873 about 200 Modocs held off nearly 1,000 United States soldiers for more than three months. The Modocs were led by Chief Kientepoos, who was known to Californians as Captain Jack. The Modocs fought bravely, but they were finally defeated. Captain Jack was captured and killed. This was the last battle between Indians and the United States Army in California.

REVIEW Where did the United States government want the Indians to live?

Contributions from All Californians

In 1900 California celebrated its fiftieth year as a state. By then it was home to almost a million and a half people. They came from different backgrounds—from many cultures and many countries. All of these people helped California to grow.

The newcomers brought to California new ideas and ways of doing things. They brought different holidays and different kinds of music, dance, and food. They used their talents and skills as farmers, fishers, entrepreneurs, laborers, artists, writers, teachers, and community leaders. Across the state, they built new towns and, like the Chinese, created their own neighborhoods within cities.

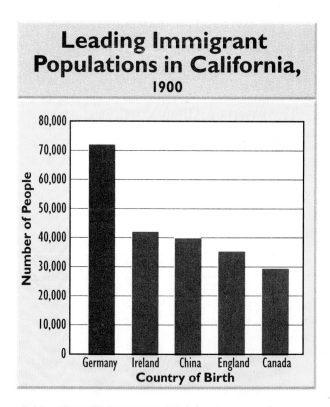

Leading Immigrant Populations in California, 1900

LEARNING FROM GRAPHS This bar graph shows the five largest groups of immigrants living in California in 1900.
■ About how many more Germans lived in California than Irish?

Africans had first come to California with the Spanish. By 1900 there were about 11,000 African Americans living in California. Like the Chinese, they often faced prejudice and had trouble getting good jobs. In some places African American children could not go to public schools.

In 1908 a group of African Americans in the San Joaquin Valley decided that the best way to solve these problems was to build their own town. They called their new town Allensworth. It was named for Colonel Allen Allensworth, one of the town's founders.

Colonel Allensworth had been a slave in Kentucky, but he escaped and later served in the Union army during the Civil War. He stayed in the army until he retired as a lieutenant colonel in 1906. At the time he was the highest-ranking African American in the military.

The town of Allensworth had its own government and its own school, library, post office, and church. Entrepreneurs opened stores and other businesses, but most of the town's citizens earned their living by farming.

Allensworth grew quickly at first. However, the town's wells began to dry up, and farmers could not get enough water for irrigation. By the 1920s people began to leave the town. Today Allensworth is a state historic park, and visitors can see the town's school and some of the other buildings there.

Japanese immigrants began coming to California in the late 1800s. Many soon became successful farmers. They grew fruits such as grapes and strawberries.

The town that Colonel Allen Allensworth (right) founded is now a state historic park (below).

The Japanese also showed that rice could be grown in California. They brought seeds from Japan for pearl rice, one of the main kinds of rice grown today in the state.

Potatoes were also grown by many Japanese farmers. In the early 1900s a Japanese immigrant named George Shima grew most of the state's potato crop. He was known as the Potato King.

Armenians also began arriving in California in the late 1800s. Like the

George Shima

Japanese and many other immigrants, they were mainly farmers at first. Immigrant farmers often raised crops they knew from their old countries. The Armenians grew figs and other crops they had raised in their homeland, such as grapes, melons, and pistachio nuts.

REVIEW Why did a group of African Americans decide to build Allensworth?

LESSON 5 REVIEW

1870		1890		1910

1873
• The last battle in California between Indians and the United States Army takes place

1882
• Congress passes a law to stop most new Chinese immigration

1900
• California celebrates its 50th year as a state

Check Understanding

1 Remember the Facts   What was the name of the town founded in 1908 by a group of African Americans living in the San Joaquin Valley?

2 Recall the Main Idea   What were some of the problems different groups of people faced in California in the late 1800s?

Think Critically

3 Think More About It   Why might immigrants want to come to California today?

4 Link to You   What might your life be like today if so many different groups of people had not come to live in California?

Show What You Know
Research Activity
Research the history of your community. Find out when it was founded and who or what it was named for. Also find out which groups of people first settled there and why. Share with classmates and family members what you learn.

FOCUS

Why do so many
people choose to live
in cities?

Main Idea Read
to learn why San
Francisco and Los
Angeles grew quickly
in the late 1800s and
early 1900s.

Vocabulary

urban growth
competition
boom
derrick

Cities North and South

| 1885 | 1900 | 1915 |

During the late 1800s and early 1900s cities were
growing quickly all across the United States. This
urban growth, or growth of cities, took place in
California, too.

At first, many of the newcomers to California settled
in towns and cities in the northern part of the state.
They worked in factories or opened small family businesses. San Francisco, just a small town before the gold
rush, had quickly become the largest and most important city in California. By 1900 it had a population of
about 350,000. At that time, only six cities in the whole
United States were larger.

Earthquake and Fire

Just after 5 A.M. on April 18, 1906, most people in San
Francisco were asleep. Charles Dobie later remembered
that he woke up from a deep sleep "with the confused
notion [idea] that I was on a bucking horse. The plunging continued, followed by a deafening roar."

News of the earthquake and fire
in San Francisco in 1906 shocked
the world.

In his painting *San Francisco Fire, 1906,* William A. Coulter shows how many San Franciscans fled to boats in the harbor to escape the fire.

Another citizen of San Francisco, Mary Exa Atkins Campbell, later wrote,

66 The moment I felt the house tremble and the plaster and bric-a-brac begin to fall, I leaped out of bed and rushed out to the front door, which I had a time unbolting on account of [the] shifting of [the] house, and while trying to get it opened I was bumped back and forth against it until I was sure the house would fall before I got out. It rocked like a ship on rough seas. 99

The heat of the fire that followed the San Francisco earthquake was so great that it melted silverware onto this china.

Out in the streets, lamps swung wildly. Sidewalks cracked and broke into pieces. Buildings collapsed, and glass windows crashed to the street. This violent shaking was an earthquake. People in San Francisco had felt earthquakes before, but not one as bad as this one.

In most places the earthquake lasted less than a minute. But when the ground stopped shaking, there was a new danger. Fires broke out as gas escaped from broken pipes. Firefighters rushed into action only to discover that they had no water. The earthquake had also broken most of the city's water pipes! For three days and two nights, fires burned across the city.

Jack London, a famous writer who lived near San Francisco at the time, rushed to the city. He wrote, "Before the flames, throughout the night, fled tens of

Cable Cars

Traveling up and down San Francisco's hills was very difficult. Andrew Hallidie (HAL•uh•dee), an immigrant from Scotland, came up with an idea for solving this problem. He decided to use underground wire cables to pull cable cars up the city's steep hills. By the 1870s, cable cars were taking passengers up and down the city's steepest hills.

When the people of San Francisco rebuilt their city after the earthquake of 1906, they also rebuilt the city's cable-car system. Today, San Franciscans and visitors from all over the world enjoy riding the cable cars.

Many people today ride the cable cars to see the sights of San Francisco.

thousands of homeless [people]. Some were wrapped in blankets. Others carried bundles of bedding and dear household treasures. . . . Baby buggies, toy wagons, and go-carts [hand carts] were used as trucks, while every other person was dragging a trunk."

People all over San Francisco left their homes to escape the flames. Charles Dobie and his family watched the fire from a friend's garden. By morning their home was gone. "The suspense was over," wrote Dobie, "—for us at least."

No one knows exactly how many people were killed in the earthquake and fire, but the number may have been as high as 3,000. About 300,000 people were left homeless. Nearly 30,000 buildings—more than half of all those in the city—were in ruins. Most of the city's businesses had also been destroyed.

REVIEW How did the 1906 earthquake and fire affect San Francisco?

San Francisco Rebuilds

Even before the smoke cleared, the people of San Francisco decided that they wanted to rebuild their city. Money, food, and supplies poured in from all over the country to help them. Signs soon appeared saying "DON'T TALK EARTHQUAKE, TALK BUSINESS."

Business and government leaders, as well as ordinary citizens, pitched in to help one another. One of the first to help was an Italian American banker named Amadeo Pietro Giannini (ah•mah•DAY•oh PYEH•troh jee•uh•NEE•nee). During the fire, he had rescued cash and bank records from his tiny Bank of Italy building. At a safe distance from the flames, Giannini set up a table and began to make loans so that people would have money to rebuild their homes. In less than 10 years, a beautiful new city rose from the ashes.

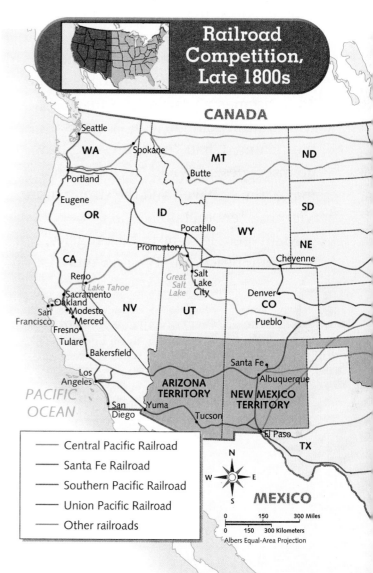

Amadeo Pietro Giannini's tiny bank in San Francisco later grew into one of the world's largest—the Bank of America.

REVIEW **What did the people of San Francisco do after the earthquake and fire?**

Southern California Grows

While San Francisco was rebuilding, many cities and towns in central and southern California were growing larger. Much of that growth was due to the Big Four's Southern Pacific Railroad. All along its path, towns grew quickly. Among them were Modesto, Merced, Fresno, Tulare, and Bakersfield.

In 1876 the Southern Pacific Railroad finally reached Los Angeles. For the first time a railroad linked Los Angeles with cities in the northern part of the state. By 1882 the railroad reached from Los Angeles to Texas. There it linked with other railroads coming from the East. The Southern Pacific Railroad reached San Diego in 1885.

In 1887 another railroad, the Santa Fe, reached Los Angeles from the east. Both the Southern Pacific and the Santa Fe

Railroad Competition, Late 1800s

- —— Central Pacific Railroad
- —— Santa Fe Railroad
- —— Southern Pacific Railroad
- —— Union Pacific Railroad
- —— Other railroads

Movement The Southern Pacific and the Sante Fe railroads were the first to connect Los Angeles with the rest of the country.
■ On which railroad would a person have traveled to get from Merced to Los Angeles?

wanted people to use their lines. The two railroads were in competition (kahm•puh•TIH•shuhn) with each other. In business, **competition** is the contest among companies to get the most customers or sell the most products.

Each railroad kept lowering its fares to get more business. The cost of a ticket from Kansas City, Missouri, to Los Angeles fell to $3 and then to $2. For a short time the price even went down to $1. The same trip had once cost $125!

These cheap fares brought thousands of people to Los Angeles and other parts of southern California. The railroads, of course, hoped to sell some of their extra land to the newcomers.

To get even more people to come to southern California, the railroads wrote advertisements praising the area's warm, sunny climate. Los Angeles, they claimed, had "no depressing heat, no insect pests." It had "a climate that makes the sick well and the strong more vigorous [energetic]."

Many people came to Los Angeles, Long Beach, San Diego, Santa Barbara, San Bernardino, and other places in southern California because they believed the climate would help make them healthier. Others came to grow and sell navel oranges.

Thousands of people came to southern California and bought land, setting off a boom in land sales. A **boom** is a time of fast economic growth. Prices for land doubled and doubled again. The population of Los Angeles grew from 11,000 in 1880 to more than 100,000 in 1900. By 1910 the population had grown to more than 300,000 people.

Unlike San Diego and San Francisco, Los Angeles had no natural harbor. Workers had to dig a harbor in San Pedro Bay, south of the city. They protected the harbor by piling up huge stone blocks to form an ocean wall. Inside this wall, ships could dock in calm waters. The harbor, completed in 1914, helped Los Angeles become one of the busiest ports on the Pacific Coast of the United States.

REVIEW What changes helped Los Angeles grow?

The discovery of large amounts of oil in Los Angeles started an oil boom there.

Oil in Southern California

By the late 1800s petroleum was being discovered all along the California coast. One of the largest discoveries was made by Edward Doheny (duh•HEE•nee) in Los Angeles in 1893. This started an oil boom there.

People quickly began drilling for oil in all parts of the city. Soon they had built more than 1,000 oil rigs. A strange new skyline of tall wooden derricks sprang up. A **derrick** is a tower built over an oil well to hold the machines used for drilling. Some people had derricks in both the front and back yards of their homes!

At first there was little demand for oil. Then the railroads switched from coal to oil as a fuel. When locomotives burned coal, the smoke left a trail of black dust. Oil burned cleaner than coal. At that time, it was also cheaper than coal.

The demand for oil grew quickly once people began driving automobiles. The gasoline that automobiles use is made from petroleum. Oil became so valuable that it was known as "black gold."

The demand for gasoline set off a new oil boom. This boom brought even more people to Los Angeles and southern California. The oil industry soon became a major part of California's economy.

REVIEW **What made the demand for oil grow?**

LESSON 6 REVIEW

1885		1900		1915

1893
• Edward Doheny discovers oil in Los Angeles

1906
• An earthquake and fire destroy much of San Francisco

1914
• Los Angeles completes its harbor

Check Understanding

❶ **Remember the Facts** Why did firefighters have trouble fighting the fire that followed the San Francisco earthquake?

❷ **Recall the Main Idea** Why did San Francisco and Los Angeles grow quickly in the late 1800s and early 1900s?

Think Critically

❸ **Explore Viewpoints** What did San Franciscans mean when they put up the signs saying "DON'T TALK EARTHQUAKE, TALK BUSINESS"?

❹ **Think More About It** Why do you think more people settled in northern California at first than in southern California?

Show What You Know

Art Activity Posters are often used to get people to take action. Draw a poster that might have been used to get people to move to southern California in the late 1800s, or draw one that might have called on people to help rebuild San Francisco. Display your poster where others can see it.

Read a Cross-

1. Why Learn This Skill?

Have you ever looked closely at the trunk of a tree after the tree has been cut down? If you have, you probably saw circles, or rings, on the end that was cut. The rings were layers of wood. The layers of wood looked like rings because you were looking at a cross section of the tree. A **cross section** is a slice or piece cut straight across something.

The drawing on page 317 is a cross-section diagram of an oil rig and the ground below it. A **cross-section diagram** is a drawing that shows what you would see if you could slice through something. The cross-section diagram on the next page helps you see the layers of soil, rock, natural gas, and oil under the ground.

Reading a cross-section diagram can help you understand what you cannot see. It can also help you understand how something works.

Most trees grow a layer of wood each year. Each ring in a trunk represents one year in a tree's life.

2. Understand the Process

Millions of years ago, oceans covered most of the Earth's surface. As tiny sea organisms (AWR•guh•nih•zuhmz) died, their remains sank to the bottoms of the oceans. Mud and sand washed into the oceans and covered the organisms. Over time, layers of mud and sand hardened into rock. The layers of rock pressed down on the organisms' remains, turning them into oil.

Oil is often found in layers of porous (PAWR•uhs) rock hundreds of feet below the Earth's surface. Porous rock has tiny holes in it. These holes hold oil the way a sponge holds water. Above and below the porous rock are layers of nonporous rock that the oil cannot soak through.

1 Find the derrick in the cross-section diagram. The derrick supports the tools needed to drill for oil. On what does the derrick stand?

2 Several layers of rock lie beneath the soil. Find the oil that lies trapped in the rock. What natural resource is found on top of the oil?

3 To reach the oil, a large drill bit, called a rotary bit, digs a hole through the layers of rock. As the workers push the rotary bit farther into the ground, they need to keep adding more and more drill pipe to it. At the top of the drill pipe is another piece of pipe called the kelly. What does the kelly rest on?

Section Diagram

4 Find the rotary table motor. When it turns, it spins the rotary table. This causes the kelly to turn. What other parts of the drill also turn?

5 When workers reach the oil, they replace the drill pipe and rotary bit with other pipes that bring up the oil. Where do you suppose the oil is taken after it is brought up?

3. Think and Apply

Find a cross-section diagram in an encyclopedia or a library book or on the Internet, or draw your own. Use the diagram to tell classmates about the object shown. Explain what the object looks like on the inside or how it works.

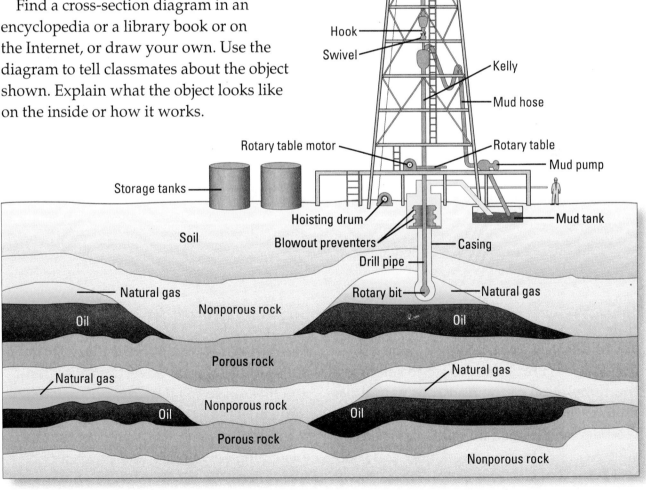

Safety platform

Derrick

Safety platform

Hook
Swivel

Kelly
Mud hose

Rotary table motor
Rotary table
Mud pump

Storage tanks
Hoisting drum
Mud tank

Soil
Blowout preventers
Casing

Drill pipe

Natural gas
Rotary bit
Natural gas

Nonporous rock

Oil
Oil

Porous rock

Natural gas
Natural gas

Oil
Nonporous rock
Oil

Porous rock

Nonporous rock

1855		1865		1875

1861
• The telegraph links California with the East
• The Civil War begins

1863
• Work on the trans-continental railroad begins

1869
• The trans-continental railroad is completed

CONNECT MAIN IDEAS

Use this organizer to show that you understand some important events that took place in California in the late 1800s and early 1900s. Complete it by writing the main idea of each lesson. A copy of the organizer may be found on page 70 of the Activity Book.

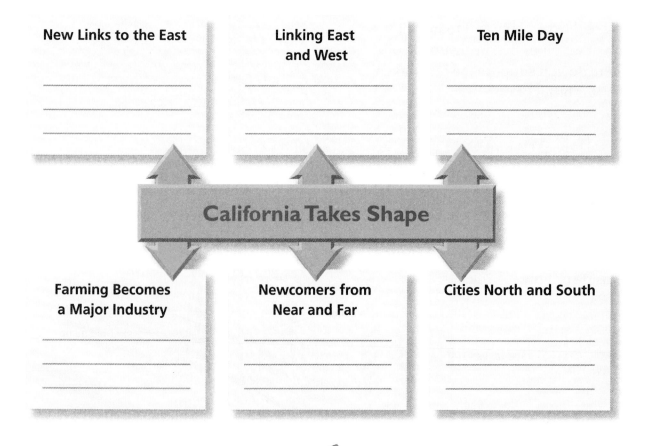

New Links to the East

Linking East and West

Ten Mile Day

California Takes Shape

Farming Becomes a Major Industry

Newcomers from Near and Far

Cities North and South

WRITE MORE ABOUT IT

Write a Poem Look again on page 286 at the poem Bret Harte wrote to celebrate the completion of the transcontinental railroad. Imagine that you are one of the laborers who helped build this railroad. Write a poem that describes how you feel about the railroad and the work you did.

Explain What You Would Have Done Railroad companies advertised their land and offered to sell it at low prices. Imagine that you lived in the East and read one of those advertisements. Write a paragraph explaining why you would or would not have agreed to buy the land.

1879
• Californians approve a new state constitution

1906
• An earthquake and fire destroy much of San Francisco

1914
• Los Angeles completes its harbor

USE VOCABULARY

Use each vocabulary term in a sentence that helps explain its meaning.

1 communication
2 transportation
3 levee

4 prejudice
5 reservation
6 competition

CHECK UNDERSTANDING

7 What two companies built the first transcontinental railroad? From which city and in which direction did each one build?

8 What new crop did Eliza and Luther Calvin Tibbets start to grow?

9 Why were farmers at Mussel Slough angry with the Southern Pacific Railroad?

10 Why was Allensworth founded?

11 How did the discovery of oil affect Los Angeles?

THINK CRITICALLY

12 **Think More About It** Immigrants often faced discrimination, but thousands of them still chose to come to California. Why do you think that was so? Would you have come? Explain.

13 **Link to You** Think about why cities grew so quickly in California during the late 1800s and early 1900s. Is the community where you live growing quickly today? Why or why not?

APPLY SKILLS

Use a Time Zone Map Use the time zone map on page 295 to answer these questions.

14 In what time zone is Detroit? In what time zone is Omaha?

15 Is mountain time one hour earlier or one hour later than Pacific time?

16 If it is noon in Atlanta, what time is it in San Diego?

Read a Pictograph Look again at the pictograph on page 302. About how much more wheat was grown in California in 1880 than in 1870?

Read a Cross-Section Diagram Study the cross-section diagram on page 317. What turns the rotary table? What does the rotary table turn?

READ MORE ABOUT IT

If You Lived at the Time of the Great San Francisco Earthquake by Ellen Levine. Scholastic. This book answers questions about how the 1906 earthquake and fire affected the people of San Francisco.

Visit the Internet at **http://www.hbschool.com** for additional resources.

PROGRESS
AS A
STATE

"I compared it with the journeys the pioneers made when they traveled West in covered wagons, accepting discomfort and danger in order to try to establish a new life for themselves."

baseball player Jackie Robinson, recalling his family's decision to move to California in the 1940s

Water for a Thirsty Land

1900	1910	1920

California's farms, factories, and growing cities needed lots of water. As more and more people moved to the state, the need for water grew even greater.

Most people lived near the San Francisco Bay, in the Central Valley, or along the coast of southern California. Most of California's water, however, was hundreds of miles away, in the mountains and the Colorado River. So huge water projects were built to bring water from places that had plenty of it to the places that needed it. A **water project** is made up of dams, reservoirs, and water pipes that store water, carry it, and control its flow. Sometimes, these water projects caused serious problems.

The Imperial Valley

In 1901 George Chaffey, the person who had developed Etiwanda, built a canal to bring water from the Colorado River to the Colorado Desert. A **canal** is a waterway dug across land. The irrigated land, which was named the Imperial Valley, became one of the richest farming regions in the United States.

Once this huge water project was finished, more people moved to the Imperial Valley. They built towns,

FOCUS
Why is water so important to California?

Main Idea Read to learn how California met its growing need for water in the early 1900s.

Vocabulary
water project
canal
aqueduct

Irrigation has made farming possible in the Imperial Valley.

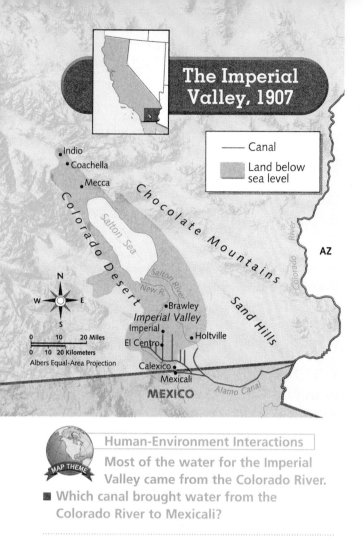

The Imperial Valley, 1907

Legend:
— Canal
Land below sea level

Indio
Coachella
Mecca
Colorado Desert
Salton Sea
Chocolate Mountains
Colorado River
AZ
New R.
Salton River
Brawley
Imperial Valley
Imperial
Holtville
El Centro
Sand Hills
Calexico
Mexicali
MEXICO
Alamo Canal

N
W E
S

0 10 20 Miles
0 10 20 Kilometers
Albers Equal-Area Projection

MAP THEME

Human-Environment Interactions
Most of the water for the Imperial Valley came from the Colorado River.
■ Which canal brought water from the Colorado River to Mexicali?

including Brawley, El Centro, and Holtville. Farmers began to raise many kinds of crops in the Imperial Valley's fertile soil. Some grew barley, alfalfa, and cotton. Others grew tomatoes, grapes, lettuce, and melons. The Imperial Valley soon became known as the Winter Garden of the World because farmers could grow crops there all year round.

In 1905, however, the changes that had been made to the land caused a terrible flood. Much of the Imperial Valley lies below sea level. When heavy rains filled the Colorado River, the river overflowed the canal. For almost two years water from the river flooded the Imperial Valley. It covered farms, towns, and railroad tracks. It even created a

new lake—the Salton Sea. Over time, however, the flood damage was repaired, and more land was irrigated.

REVIEW How was farming made possible in the Imperial Valley?

Water for Los Angeles

The fastest growing part of California in the early 1900s was Los Angeles. Agriculture, oil, and other new industries brought more and more people to the area. At first, Angelenos—the people of Los Angeles—had gotten most of their water from the Los Angeles River and nearby reservoirs. By the early 1900s, however, the river could no longer supply all the water that Los Angeles needed.

The head of the city's water department, William Mulholland (muhl•HAH•luhnd), had an idea. He wanted the city to get its water from the Owens River. This river flowed through the Owens Valley on the eastern side of the Sierra Nevada. The Owens River, however, was more than 200 miles (322 km) from Los Angeles!

Mulholland decided to build an aqueduct (A•kwuh•duhkt) to carry water from the Owens River to Los Angeles.

William Mulholland was the chief engineer of the Los Angeles Aqueduct.

An **aqueduct** is a large pipe or canal that carries water from one place to another.

Work on the Los Angeles Aqueduct began in 1908, but building it proved to be a very difficult job. Workers had to blast tunnels through the Sierra Nevada. Then they had to build the aqueduct across the very hot Mojave Desert. They also had to build reservoirs near Los Angeles to store the water.

On November 5, 1913, the Los Angeles Aqueduct was finally opened. Thousands of Angelenos cheered as water raced through the aqueduct to their city. Mulholland made a very short speech. "There it is! Take it," he said.

The aqueduct supplied enough water for about two million people. The water was also used to irrigate farms and ranches in the San Fernando Valley. Just as important, there was now enough waterpower to create hydroelectric power. This electricity was used by the many new homes and businesses being built in the Los Angeles area.

REVIEW Why was the Los Angeles Aqueduct built?

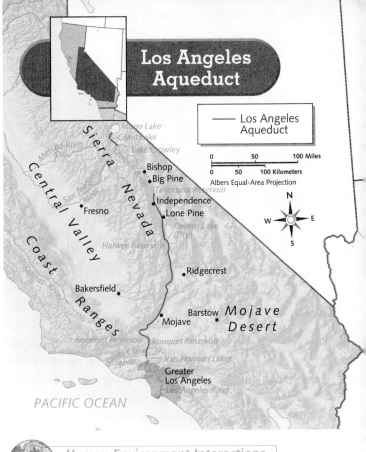

Los Angeles Aqueduct

Los Angeles Aqueduct

0   50   100 Miles
0   50   100 Kilometers
Albers Equal-Area Projection

Human-Environment Interactions

In 1913 the Los Angeles Aqueduct was 233 miles (375 km) long. By 1940 its length had grown to 338 miles (544 km).

■ Which reservoir is between Big Pine and Independence?

Problems for the Owens Valley

The Los Angeles Aqueduct helped Angelenos, but it hurt many people living in the Owens Valley. To get the water it needed, Los Angeles bought much of the land on both sides of the Owens River. With the land came the right to use the water in the river. Los Angeles took so much water,

An excited crowd watches the first rush of water from the Owens River come down the spillway near Los Angeles.

Nearly 12 billion gallons (45 billion L) of water rushed through the Santa Clara Valley when the St. Francis Dam broke on March 12, 1928.

holes in the aqueduct. Their efforts failed, however, and the aqueduct was repaired.

In 1928 a terrible accident happened along another part of the water project. On March 12, just before midnight, St. Francis Dam, one of the dams built near Los Angeles, broke. A huge wall of water swept down the Santa Clara Valley. It destroyed almost 1,300 homes and ruined thousands of acres of farmland. Nearly 450 people were killed.

REVIEW How did the Los Angeles Aqueduct affect people living in the Owens Valley?

Water for San Francisco

San Francisco gets more rainfall than Los Angeles, but it, too, needed more water for its growing population. City leaders asked the United States government for permission to build a dam on the Tuolumne (too•AH•luh•mee) River. This dam would create a large reservoir that could hold a lot of water for San Francisco. An aqueduct would be built

however, that the valley's farmers and ranchers did not have enough for their crops and farm animals.

Several years after the aqueduct was built, some ranchers near Big Pine tried to stop the flow of water out of their valley. A few, armed with rifles, took over a pumping station along the aqueduct. Others used dynamite to blow

The Hetch Hetchy Reservoir lies behind the Tuolumne Dam.

to carry the water to the city. However, the dam would flood the Hetch Hetchy Valley, a part of Yosemite National Park.

Plans for the water project set off a bitter struggle. People in favor of the dam believed it was the only way for San Francisco to get the water it needed. People against the dam did not want any part of Yosemite National Park to be flooded.

In 1913 San Francisco won the right to build the dam and the Hetch Hetchy Aqueduct. But many Californians continued to speak out against this water project for many years. The dam and the aqueduct were not finished until 1931.

REVIEW Why did San Francisco want to build a dam on the Tuolumne River?

Hetch Hetchy Aqueduct

NV

- ⟋ Dam
- —— Hetch Hetchy Aqueduct

Berkeley • Oakland • San Francisco • Stockton • Fremont • San Jose • Modesto • Tuolumne • Coast Ranges • Central Valley • Sierra Nevada • San Joaquin River • Merced River • Stanislaus River • Mokelumne River • Hetch Hetchy Reservoir • Hetch Hetchy Valley • Mono Lake • Yosemite National Park

N W E S

0   25   50 Miles
0   25   50 Kilometers
Albers Equal-Area Projection

Human-Environment Interactions

MAP THEME

The Hetch Hetchy Aqueduct carried the first water from the Hetch Hetchy Valley to San Francisco.

■ Which rivers on this map does the Hetch Hetchy Aqueduct cross?

LESSON I REVIEW

1900   1910   1920

1901
• A canal is built to bring water to the Imperial Valley

1905
• Flooding in the Imperial Valley creates the Salton Sea

1913
• The Los Angeles Aqueduct opens
• San Francisco wins the right to build the Hetch Hetchy Aqueduct

Check Understanding

1 Remember the Facts Why is the Imperial Valley known as the Winter Garden of the World?

2 Recall the Main Idea How did California meet its growing need for water in the early 1900s?

Think Critically

3 Personally Speaking Do you think it is important for you and other Californians to save water? Explain.

4 Explore Viewpoints Why do you think people had such different opinions about building a dam on the Tuolumne River?

Show What You Know

Research Activity Find out where your community's water comes from. Then draw a map or diagram that shows how the water gets to you. Use your drawing as you explain to classmates what you learned.

What Should Be Done

O n many maps, Owens Lake is shown in the color gray or brown rather than blue. That is because the lake has no water. It is dry. Water that once flowed into the lake from the Owens River now flows into the Los Angeles Aqueduct instead.

For many years windstorms have blown large clouds of dust from the dry lake bed through the Owens Valley. The dust in the air causes breathing problems for many people in the valley.

A Plan to Control the Dust

To control the dust, leaders in the Owens Valley now want Los Angeles to return some of the water it gets from the Owens River. The water would be pumped onto 35,000 square miles (90,643 square km) of the lake bed. However, this would take millions of gallons of water each year—enough to meet the water needs of 250,000 people in Los Angeles.

Ted Schade works for the Great Basin Unified Air Pollution Control District, the group that developed the plan. He says,

66 What we'd like to see is [Los Angeles] saying 'Let's get going on this now and maybe down the road we'll find a way to use less water.' [Los Angeles] has to fix the problem. There is no way around that. 99

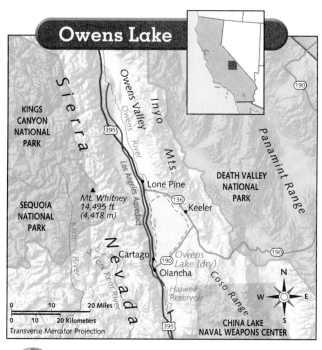

Owens Lake

Place Owens Lake was once about 18 miles (29 km) long and 10 miles (16 km) wide.

■ From what river did Owens Lake get its water?

At Owens Lake, large clouds of dust often form over the dry lake bed. A worker for the Great Basin Unified Air Pollution Control District checks the quality of the air near the lake bed (right).

About Owens Lake?

Will the Plan Work?

Los Angeles has said that it will help solve the dust problem. But the city's leaders think that the Owens Valley plan would cost too much money and use too much water. They also say that it is impossible to know if the plan would solve the dust problem.

Gerald Gewe works for the Los Angeles Department of Water and Power. He says,

> 66 There is too much money and too much water involved. It's a problem we all would like to solve, but I cannot recommend to our customers they spend $300 million on [a solution] that is unproven. 99

Ruth Galenter is a member of the Los Angeles City Council. She believes that the people of Los Angeles and the people of the Owens Valley need to work together to solve the dust problem. She says,

> 66 The question is: Can we work out a solution that is economically good for the citizens of Los Angeles and the citizens of Owens Valley? It's an answer that will have to be worked out jointly. 99

Compare Viewpoints

1. What is the viewpoint of each person about solving the dust problem in Owens Valley?

2. How is Ruth Galenter's point of view different from those of Ted Schade and Gerald Gewe?

3. Why do you think each person holds the viewpoint that he or she does?

Think and Apply

People often hold different views about issues because of their jobs, their backgrounds, or where they live. Think of a problem that people in your community disagree about. Talk with someone about his or her views. Find out why that person thinks the way he or she does. Then share with your classmates what you have learned.

Main Idea   Read to learn about some important changes that took place in California in the early 1900s.

Vocabulary

bribe
reform
amendment
suffrage
consumer good
aviation

After Hiram Johnson was California's governor, he was a United States senator from 1917 to 1945.

Changing Times

1900	1915	1930

ailroads, oil companies, and other big businesses helped make California's economy strong, but they also caused problems. In California and in many other places at that time, business people sometimes gave government leaders bribes to get what they wanted. A **bribe** is something promised to a person—money, a gift, or a favor—to get him or her to do something. In exchange for these bribes, government leaders let the companies charge high prices and run their businesses as they pleased.

To limit the power of the Southern Pacific Railroad and other big businesses, Californians had approved a new state constitution in 1879. But even after the new constitution was approved, these companies remained very powerful.

Reforming the Government

Many Californians saw the need to reform their state government. To **reform** is to change for the better. They wanted to make the government more honest and to control the power of big businesses.

Many reformers—the people who favored reform—wanted Hiram (HY•ruhm) Johnson for governor in 1910. One of Johnson's promises was to "kick the Southern Pacific . . . out of California politics." Johnson won the election and was reelected governor in 1914.

As governor, Johnson worked to reform California's government. He stopped most government officials from taking bribes, and he helped pass new laws to control railroad prices. In 1911 California added more than 20 **amendments**, or changes, to the state constitution. These amendments gave Californians more control over their government.

REVIEW How did reformers work to improve government?

Women Demand Their Right to Vote

In the early 1900s women could not be elected to office. In fact, they were not even allowed to vote! However, many women in California still worked to reform the government.

Years earlier, some women in California and across the country had begun to demand **suffrage** (SUH•frij), or the right to vote. Laura de Force Gordon, a Fresno newspaper editor, had tried but failed to get women's suffrage into the Constitution of 1879.

Many California women continued to work for suffrage. They also worked for better living and working conditions for women and their families. Across the United States many men, women, and children worked long hours for little pay. Some of the places where they worked were unsafe.

Charlotte Perkins Gilman wrote poems and books asking people to

Women from California and Wyoming—two of the first states to recognize women's right to vote—joined a parade calling for women's suffrage.

support reforms. She called for women's suffrage and for equal pay for women doing the same work as men. She believed that women would finally get equal rights in the 1900s. "This is the woman's century," she wrote.

Caroline Severance (SE•vuh•ruhns) set up women's clubs in Los Angeles to work for reform. Her home became a gathering place for reformers.

One of the amendments added to the state constitution in 1911 allowed California women to vote in state elections. Severance was given the honor of being the first woman to sign up to vote. She was 91 years old at the time.

California women could now vote in state elections, but they still were not allowed to vote in national elections. It was not until the Nineteenth Amendment to the United States Constitution was passed in 1920 that women were allowed to vote in all elections.

REVIEW **How were California women finally able to vote in state elections?**

World Events Affect California

While many changes were taking place in California, events in far-off places were also affecting the state. One of these was the opening of the Panama Canal in 1914. The United States built the Panama Canal across the Isthmus of Panama.

Once the Panama Canal opened, ships no longer had to sail around South America to get from the Pacific Ocean to

GEOGRAPHY

The Panama Canal

People had long dreamed of building a canal across the Isthmus of Panama. In 1903 the United States paid the country of Panama for the right to build a canal there, and work began the next year. It took workers about 10 years to complete the 51-mile (82-km) canal.

The Panama Canal changed shipping routes around the world and made travel between the Pacific and Atlantic oceans faster. The voyage from San Francisco to New York City was shortened by more than 7,000 miles (11,265 km).

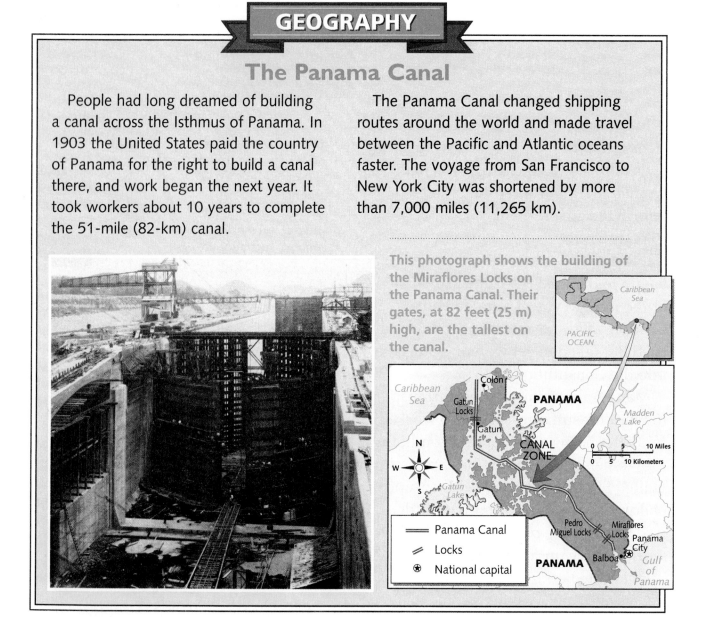

This photograph shows the building of the Miraflores Locks on the Panama Canal. Their gates, at 82 feet (25 m) high, are the tallest on the canal.

the Atlantic Ocean. Goods could now be shipped between ports in California and ports in the East in about one month. Just as the transcontinental railroad had done earlier, the Panama Canal helped trade grow between California and the rest of the world.

Most Californians were excited about the opening of the Panama Canal. They were sure that it would help the state's economy grow even faster. Many people in Los Angeles were happy because the Panama Canal would bring more ships to their city's new harbor.

Another event that affected California in the early 1900s was World War I. The United States entered the war in 1917 and sent soldiers to fight in Europe. The war lasted until November of the following year.

California was far from the fighting, but many Californians served in the

armed forces. Californians helped fight the war in other ways, too. The state's farms and industries supplied food, cotton for uniforms, ships, and oil for fuel.

As the demand for goods grew during the war, so did California's economy. Farmers raised more crops, and factories produced more goods. Many women took jobs left by men who had gone to fight, but still more workers were needed. The state's economy boomed as thousands of people moved to California to find jobs.

REVIEW How did the Panama Canal and World War I affect California's economy?

These soldiers received their training near Monterey. Posters like the one to the far right encouraged people to buy war bonds during World War I. A war bond is a paper that shows that the buyer has loaned money to a government to help pay the costs of a war.

On the Move in Cars and Planes

The years after World War I brought many other changes to the way people in California lived. New industries in the United States began making consumer goods that ran by electricity. A **consumer good** is a product made for personal use. Vacuum cleaners, radios, washing machines, and other electrical products for the home were sold for the first time in the 1920s.

Changes in transportation were taking place, too. The first automobiles were seen on California roads in the early 1900s. Before long it seemed as if everyone wanted a car. By 1920 there were about 600,000 cars in California. "The paramount ambition [main goal] of the average man a few years ago," said a banker in 1925, "was to own a home and have a bank account. The ambition of the same man today is to own a car."

In the early 1920s huge new sources of oil were found at Huntington Beach, Santa Fe Springs, and Signal Hill. By 1924 California was producing more oil than any other state. Because the oil industry was producing so much oil, the price of gasoline was very low.

The automobile was beginning to change the way people lived. People began driving to work and taking car trips for family vacations. People liked their cars so much that one woman even said, "I'll go without food before I'll see us give up our car."

The invention of the airplane also brought changes to California in the early 1900s. Southern California became an important center for the aviation (ay•vee•AY•shuhn) industry. **Aviation** is the making and flying of airplanes.

Many leaders in the aviation industry liked southern California. The region's mild climate made it possible for them to test-fly their planes during most of the year. In 1909 Glenn Martin built California's first airplane factory in Santa Ana.

Donald Douglas worked for Martin, but in 1920 he began his own aviation company in Los Angeles. Soon his factory was building a plane a week. Two of Douglas's planes made the first round-the-world flight in 1924. Another early aviation company in California was founded by brothers Allan and Malcolm Lockheed and John Northrop.

One of the most famous planes in history, the *Spirit of St. Louis*, was built in San Diego by T. Claude Ryan. Flying in this plane in 1927, Charles Lindbergh became the first person to fly alone across the Atlantic Ocean.

REVIEW **Why did southern California become a center for the aviation industry?**

Making Movies

The new century brought another industry to California—moviemaking. Moviemakers, too, liked southern California. Its sunny skies and mild climate allowed them to make movies outdoors all year round. California also had nearly every kind of landscape needed for the movies—mountains, valleys, deserts, and beaches. Hollywood, an area of Los Angeles, soon became the center of the movie industry.

The first movies had no sound, but people paid a nickel to see a silent picture. Going to the movie theater, called a nickelodeon, became a weekly event for many people. Nickelodeons hired someone to play music on a piano or an organ to match the movie's actions.

Charles Lindbergh named his plane the *Spirit of St. Louis* to honor that city's citizens who had paid for it.

By the late 1920s the silent pictures had become "talkies"—they had sound. Movie-making became one of the country's ten largest industries. Movie stars like Mary Pickford and Charlie Chaplin were recognized everywhere they went.

REVIEW Why did moviemakers like southern California?

Charlie Chaplin wrote and directed nearly all his films. In the photograph at the right, he talks with actors Douglas Fairbanks and Mary Pickford about a scene he is filming.

This is the great picture upon which the famous comedian has worked a whole year.

6 reels of Joy.

Charles Chaplin in "THE KID"

Written and directed by Charles Chaplin

A First National Attraction

LESSON 2 REVIEW

1900   1915   1930

1911
• Women in California win the right to vote in state elections

1914
• The Panama Canal opens

1917
• The United States enters World War I

1927
• Charles A. Lindbergh flies across the Atlantic Ocean

Check Understanding

1 **Remember the Facts** What reforms did Hiram Johnson help make as governor of California?

2 **Recall the Main Idea** What were some important changes that took place in California in the early 1900s?

Think Critically

3 **Explore Viewpoints** Many people in California worked for government reform in the early 1900s. How do you think most leaders of big businesses felt about them?

4 **Past to Present** Going to a nickelodeon became a weekly event for many people in the 1920s. What kinds of things do people today do for fun?

Show What You Know

Writing Activity Write a speech that might have been given at the opening of the Panama Canal. Be sure it explains how the canal will help California's economy. Practice your speech, and then present it to classmates.

The Great Depression

| 1925 | 1930 | 1935 | 1940 |

FOCUS
How can hard economic times hurt the people in a state or country?

Main Idea Read to learn why many people in California and in the other states could not find jobs in the 1930s.

Vocabulary
depression
unemployment
labor union
strike
migrant worker

The 1920s were a boom time for many people in California. Advertisements invited people to "live and get rich in happy, healthy California." But the good times soon came to an end.

In 1929 California and the rest of the country faced an economic depression (dih•PRE•shuhn). A **depression** is a time when there are few jobs and people have little money. This depression, which continued through the 1930s, was so bad that it became known as the Great Depression.

Hard Times

The Great Depression started because many people had made poor business decisions. Banks that had lent too much money had to close. When the banks closed, people lost their savings. Many people were left without money to pay their bills or feed their families.

Because people had less money, they bought fewer goods. This caused many businesses to fail. Workers in those businesses then lost their jobs. The prices for most crops dropped, too. Many farmers lost their land because they could not pay back the money they had borrowed to buy it.

For much of the decade of the 1930s, **unemployment**, or the number of people without jobs, was high in California and the rest

Unemployed people are given soup and sandwiches at the Los Angeles Plaza Church during the Great Depression. What other kinds of help would people have needed?

of the country. By 1934 one in every five workers in California did not have a job. Even people who had jobs faced hard times.

Low pay and difficult working conditions caused many workers to join labor unions. A **labor union** is a group of workers who try to get better working conditions. During the Great Depression the number of labor unions grew quickly.

Members of labor unions sometimes go on **strike**, or stop work, to get business owners to listen to them. In 1934, dock workers at San Francisco's port went on strike. This strike soon spread along the Pacific Coast. Ports from San Diego north to Seattle, Washington, were forced to close. The workers finally went back to work after gaining better working conditions, including higher pay.

REVIEW **What was the Great Depression?**

The worst dust storms came in the spring, when the snow that protected the soil had melted, the winds were strong, and the new plants were not big enough to hold the soil.

The Dust Bowl

Times were bad in California, but they were even worse in other states. In the 1930s there was a terrible drought in parts of several states, including Kansas, Oklahoma, New Mexico, and Texas. The drought left the soil so dry in some places that it turned into dust. Strong winds caused huge dust storms that blew away the dry soil. These dust storms filled homes with choking dust, killed cattle, and destroyed many farms.

The area where those storms took place became known as the Dust Bowl.

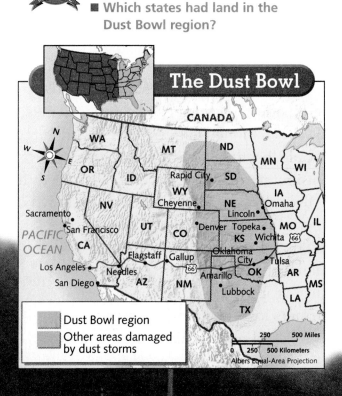

Regions The Dust Bowl covered about 50 million acres of land.
■ Which states had land in the Dust Bowl region?

In his book *Children of the Dust Bowl*, Jerry Stanley wrote about what people had to do when the dust storms came.

66 Cracks around windows and doors were taped or stuffed with wet towels, but it was impossible to escape the dust. At night families slept with wet washcloths or sponges over their faces to filter out the dust, but in the morning they would find their pillows and blankets caked with dirt, their tongues and teeth coated with grit [sand]. 99

REVIEW What was the Dust Bowl?

Job-Seekers Come to California

Many people in the Dust Bowl lost their farms and their homes. They had no work and no hope of finding any.

Many people just wanted to get away from their troubles and start a new life somewhere else. California seemed like a good place to do that.

The movies showed California as a place with fertile, green fields and warm, sunny beaches. California, people heard, also had many jobs that paid well. So thousands of Dust Bowl families piled everything they could fit into their cars and trucks and headed west. Most traveled on Route 66, the main highway to California at that time. In all, about 350,000 people left the Dust Bowl for California.

Woody Guthrie was a famous singer who wrote many songs about the Great Depression. In one of them he described the hopes of people leaving the Dust Bowl.

66 Lots of folks back east, they say,
leavin' home ev'ry day,
Beatin' the hot old dusty way
to the California line. 99

This photograph by Dorothea Lange shows a Missouri family on its way to California to find a better life.

This family from Texas stayed at a migrant worker camp near Exeter, California. Many camps were crowded and were unhealthful places for people to live in.

BIOGRAPHY

John Steinbeck
1902–1968

John Steinbeck, who grew up in Salinas, was one of California's most famous writers. Steinbeck was angry about the way some Californians treated people from the Dust Bowl. In his novel *The Grapes of Wrath* he told the story of the Joad family. Steinbeck's book describes the hardships the Joads faced as they traveled west from Oklahoma and after they reached California.

The people who came to California from the Dust Bowl were not always welcomed. Many Californians were afraid that the newcomers would take jobs from them. Some Californians even tried to pass a law to keep new people from entering the state.

Most of the newcomers went to the Central Valley. They were farmers, and they hoped to find steady work on the farms there. But there were very few jobs to be found. Many men, women, and children became migrant workers. A **migrant worker** is someone who moves from place to place with the seasons, harvesting crops.

Migrant workers were often paid less than a dollar a day. Many could not afford to pay rent, so they lived in camps that they set up along rivers. They slept in tents or in their cars and trucks. They had little food and no running water.

REVIEW Why did people from the Dust Bowl come to California?

New Water Projects for California

In 1932 Franklin D. Roosevelt was elected President of the United States. He promised a "New Deal" for Americans. The New Deal was the name given to the programs set up by the United States government to help end the Great Depression. These programs gave people jobs building post offices, schools, and other public buildings. They also paid for new roads, parks, and water projects.

Since the 1905 flood in the Imperial Valley, people had talked about building a dam on the Colorado River. Supporters pointed out that a dam would control flooding and provide more water and hydroelectric power for nearby states.

Work finally began on Hoover Dam in 1931, and it was completed in 1936. The dam formed Lake Mead, one of the world's largest reservoirs.

Other dams and reservoirs were also built on the river. Among them was Parker Dam, which formed Lake Havasu. Over time, aqueducts were built to carry water from Lake Havasu to Los Angeles, San Diego, and many other cities in southern California. New canals were also built to carry more

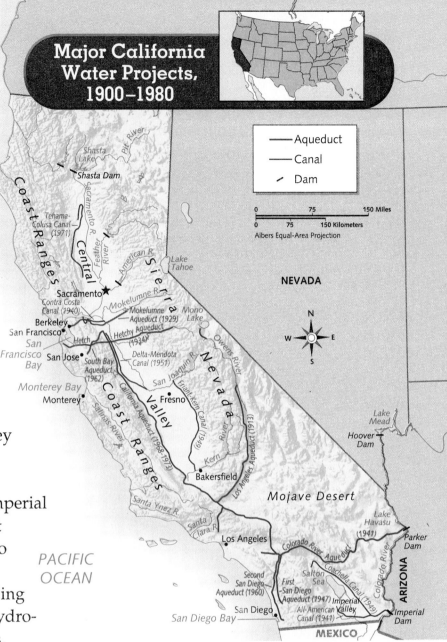

Major California Water Projects, 1900–1980

Legend:
— Aqueduct
— Canal
⌐ Dam

0   75   150 Miles
0   75   150 Kilometers
Albers Equal-Area Projection

Human-Environment Interactions

MAP THEME

Water projects have been built to bring water to all parts of the state.

■ Which canal connects the San Joaquin River and the Kern River?

water from the Colorado River to the Imperial Valley.

Another important water project was also started in the 1930s. The Central Valley Project, or CVP, was built to move water from the wetter Sacramento

Valley to the drier San Joaquin Valley. Like other water projects, the CVP also produced electricity for California.

As part of the CVP, dams such as Shasta Dam were built on rivers in the Central Valley. Water stored in the reservoirs formed by these dams could be released when it was needed during the dry summer months. Canals carried the water to different parts of the San Joaquin Valley.

The CVP increased the amount of irrigated land in the San Joaquin Valley by thousands of acres. The system was later made larger so that even more farmland was irrigated.

REVIEW Which water project moved water from the Sacramento Valley to the San Joaquin Valley?

The Golden Gate Bridge

During the Great Depression thousands of people in California found jobs building the Golden Gate Bridge. This huge bridge was built high over San Francisco Bay. For years ferryboats had carried people and goods across the bay to Marin County. Now many people wanted a bridge to link San Francisco with the growing cities on the north side of the bay.

Building the bridge was dangerous work. A safety net was placed under the floor of the bridge to catch any workers who fell. The net saved the lives of 19 people, but 11 workers lost their lives building the bridge.

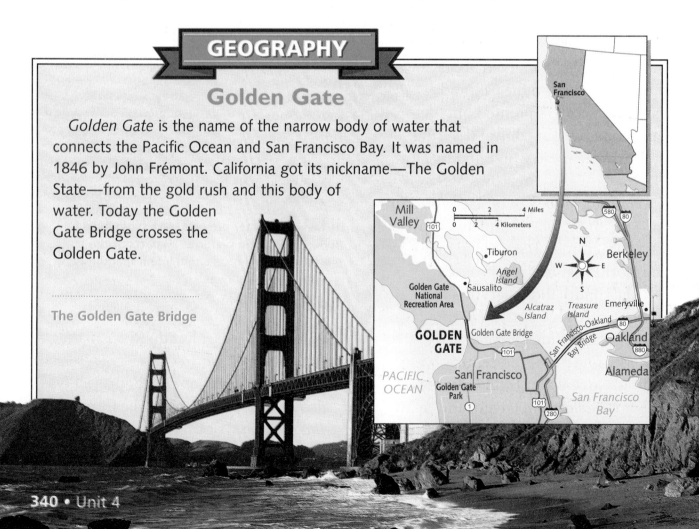

GEOGRAPHY

Golden Gate

Golden Gate is the name of the narrow body of water that connects the Pacific Ocean and San Francisco Bay. It was named in 1846 by John Frémont. California got its nickname—The Golden State—from the gold rush and this body of water. Today the Golden Gate Bridge crosses the Golden Gate.

The Golden Gate Bridge

These workers had the dangerous job of hanging the cables on the Golden Gate Bridge.

Fog often covered San Francisco, so Irving Morrow, who helped design the bridge, wanted it to be painted a bright color. He chose a reddish-orange for the bridge and gold for its towers.

The Golden Gate Bridge opened in 1937. Almost two miles (3 km) long, it was the longest bridge in the world at that time. It quickly became one of the most famous as well.

REVIEW How did building the Golden Gate Bridge help people during the Great Depression?

LESSON 3 REVIEW

1925	1930	1935	1940

1929
• The Great Depression begins

1934
• One in every five workers in California does not have a job

1936
• The Hoover Dam is completed

1937
• The Golden Gate Bridge opens

Check Understanding

1 **Remember the Facts** Why did many workers join labor unions during the Great Depression?

2 **Recall the Main Idea** Why were many people in California and in the other states unable to find jobs during the Great Depression?

Think Critically

3 **Cause and Effect** How did the Dust Bowl affect the population of California?

4 **Think More About It** How did the 1930s compare with the 1920s?

Show What You Know

Writing Activity Imagine that you and your family are among the thousands of people from the Dust Bowl traveling to California. Write a diary entry describing how you felt when you left home and what you are looking forward to in California. Compare your diary entry with those written by your classmates.

Tell Primary from

1. Why Learn This Skill?

People who study history learn about the past from many sources. Some of the best sources of information are primary sources. A **primary source** gives the real words and views of people who were there when an event took place. Their words may be found in letters or diaries or records of interviews. Their drawings or photographs may show people, places, or events as they saw them.

Sometimes the only way to learn about the past is from a secondary source. A **secondary source** gives information written at a later time by someone who was not there to see what happened. Your social studies book is a secondary source. Encyclopedias and other reference books are also secondary sources.

2. Understand the Process

Sometimes the words used in a source can help you tell whether the source is a primary one or a secondary one. Words like *I, we, my,* and *our* are often found in primary sources. Primary sources let a reader "hear the voices" of people telling about their own experiences.

Each kind of source can be helpful. A primary source can make you feel that you were there when an event happened. A secondary source may give more facts about a happening, such as names and dates.

There can also be problems with each kind of source. A primary source might give just one person's view of what happened. The writer of a secondary source might not understand what really happened, since he or she was not there at the time. In both kinds of sources, the writer might state his or her own opinion as a fact.

During the Great Depression, people from all over the country wrote letters to the President of the United States. They told him their troubles in the hope that he could help them. On page 343 you can read a letter from a woman who was living in Lawndale, California, in 1934. Compare it with what you read in Lesson 3 about how the Great Depression affected people. Which is a primary source, and which is a secondary source? How do you know?

3. Think and Apply

Write a short journal entry telling what you thought and did during one afternoon. Then trade journal entries with a classmate. Write a paragraph that tells what your classmate thought and did. Together, compare the primary sources with the secondary sources. How closely do your reports match each other's experiences?

Secondary Sources

Lawndale, California,
Feb. 1 — 34.

Most Honorable President:

I am writing you this morning in all faiths, that if I can get word to you of our horrible plight [hard time] you will not pass it by unnoticed.

I am a mother of seven children, and utterly heart broken, in that they are hungry [and we] have only 65 cents in money. The father is in L.A. trying to find something to do,—provisions all gone—at this writing—no meat, milk—sugar—in fact, [we have only] about enough flour for bread [for] two meals—and that's all. I have two children in High School—and our pride isn't all gone, our story is this—and if we have a chance we can care for ourselves and be happy.

We have a boy 17 yrs. old who is capable of holding a good position as a musician. . . . O, President, my heart is breaking, as I see him go from home with half enough to eat, and go all day without a bite of lunch, to be sure he could beg his lunch but he's [too] proud to beg as long as he can help it, and I have spent the day yesterday praying God to help me bear this. . . . O, what a burden and how helpless I am, how proud I am of my children, and how dark a future [we face] under this condition.

Their father is 62 yrs. old—a preacher [and] a good carpenter . . . but Industry won't hire a man This age, scarcely, even if they are strong in body, and he has no church to preach in. . . .

I humbly pray God's Divine blessing on you, for you have tried every way to help the people.

Very sincerely,
Mrs. I. H.

California in World War II

1940   1945

Since 1939 many countries around the world had been fighting in another world war, called World War II. The United States, however, had been able to stay out of this war. That changed on Sunday, December 7, 1941, when Americans heard shocking news on their radios. Planes from Japan had just attacked a United States military base at Pearl Harbor, Hawaii. In less than two hours, nearly 2,500 people had been killed. More than 140 planes and 8 battleships had been destroyed or damaged.

The next day President Franklin D. Roosevelt asked Congress to declare war on Japan. The United States would fight on the side of the Allies. The Allies included Great Britain, France, and the Soviet Union. The Allies fought against the Axis Powers, which included Germany, Japan, and Italy.

FOCUS

How do events that happen outside California affect you and your family?

Main Idea
Read to learn how World War II affected California and its people.

Vocabulary

human resource
capital resource
Great Migration
relocation camp

Californians and the War Effort

The United States needed people and resources to fight the war, and California helped provide them. About 750,000 Californians joined the armed forces

The *USS West Virginia* and the *USS Tennessee* were among the ships that were destroyed in the attack on Pearl Harbor.

California's factories and shipyards amazed the world with the number of airplanes and ships they produced for the war.

during the war, and the United States set up many military bases in California. Soldiers, sailors, and flyers from all over the country came to those bases for training. Fort Ord, located between Monterey and Salinas, was the largest training center in the country.

The aviation industry in southern California quickly prepared for war. To manufacture airplanes or any other product, businesses need three kinds of resources. They must have natural resources, such as land, water, fuels, and minerals. They also must have **human resources**, or workers, and capital resources. **Capital resources** are the money, buildings, machines, and tools needed to run a business.

To meet the demand for warplanes, aviation companies hired more than 200,000 new workers. They made their old factories larger, and they built new

ones in Burbank, Santa Monica, Long Beach, San Diego, and several other cities. All these factories worked around the clock building airplanes. They built almost 100,000 planes in 1944 alone.

The United States also needed ships to fight in battles and to carry soldiers and supplies. With Henry Kaiser as a leader, California quickly became the center of the shipbuilding industry. Kaiser, who had helped build the Hoover and Shasta dams, owned four shipyards at Richmond. He developed new ways to build cargo ships more quickly than in the past.

Shipyards in California produced one of every four ships built during the war. At shipyards from Eureka to Richmond to San Pedro, people worked night and day building ships. By 1943, shipyards in California had more than 280,000 workers.

The "flying nurses" shown above were among the thousands of women who joined the armed forces during the war. Posters, like the one to the right, urged people to work together to help the United States win the war.

TOGETHER FOR VICTORY

MORE PRODUCTION EVERY HOUR— GIVES OUR FORCES GREATER POWER

Thousands of men and women worked in other California factories. They made machines, weapons, uniforms, and other war goods. Many other people worked on farms. They grew food not just for the United States but also for the other Allies. Fuel made from California oil helped run the country's warplanes, ships, and tanks.

World War II provided many new jobs for women. Some joined the armed forces. They served as nurses, drivers, and even pilots.

Because workers were badly needed, government posters called on women to take jobs. Many did so for the first time. Some went to work in factories, making airplane parts, ships, and steel. Others became office workers and bus conductors. Women also delivered the mail and ran family businesses. On farms, they planted and harvested crops.

REVIEW How did California take part in the war effort?

In steel mills, shipyards, and aircraft factories, women did the work of the men who had left to fight the war.

More People for California

The population of California grew by more than two and a half million people during the war years. Some came to work on the military bases. Others came to plant and harvest crops on farms. Many of these workers came from Mexico to help fill the farm jobs that were left when American farmworkers went off to war. Most newcomers, however, came to work in the state's growing number of factories.

Many newcomers settled in cities near their jobs. Vallejo, for example, grew from 20,000 people in 1941 to more than 100,000 in 1943. Little new housing was built during the war, so many cities, such as Los Angeles and San Diego, grew very crowded.

Many of the newcomers were African Americans. Large numbers of African Americans had come to California in the boom years after World War I. Now, during World War II, the number of African Americans grew by more than 300,000.

Most African Americans had migrated, or moved, to California from states in the South. This movement of African Americans from the South to California and to states in the North became known as the **Great Migration**.

World War II created a need for thousands of new workers in California. And African Americans, like other newcomers, were eager to find jobs and to help the war effort.

REVIEW How did World War II affect California's population?

The Japanese Americans

At the time of the attack on Pearl Harbor, about 125,000 Japanese Americans lived in the United States, most of them in California. Most Japanese Americans had been born in the United States and were citizens. The attack on Pearl Harbor shocked them as much as anyone.

There had been prejudice against people from Asia since the time of the gold rush. After Pearl Harbor, anger against Japanese Americans grew. Some people claimed that the Japanese Americans might help Japan invade California.

Many Californians wanted the United States government to move all Japanese Americans out of the state.

Large numbers of African Americans came to California to work at factory jobs during the war.

Relocation camps were usually built in bare and isolated areas (above). The photograph to the left shows a mealtime scene at a relocation camp.

In February 1942 about 110,000 Japanese Americans in California, Oregon, Washington, and Arizona were ordered to go to **relocation camps**. These camps were like prisons.

There were ten relocation camps. Two were in California, at Tule Lake in the northeastern part of the state and at Manzanar in the Owens Valley. The rest were located in other western states.

Life in the relocation camps was difficult. The camps had been built very quickly and were cold indoors in winter and hot in summer. Each person received just a mattress and a blanket.

There was no running water in the rooms where people lived.

One man described what his family found when they arrived. "There were seven beds in the room and no [other] furniture. . . . I just sat on the bed staring at the bare walls."

Slowly families created homes in their small, crowded spaces. They made furniture out of scraps of wood and metal. They planted gardens and grew vegetables for the war effort. They even started schools and baseball teams. Still, they remained prisoners in a place where they did not want to be.

Most Japanese Americans spent the rest of the war in the relocation camps. Young Japanese American men, however, were allowed to join the army. Most who joined became members of

The United Nations

In April 1945 delegates from more than 50 countries gathered in San Francisco. On June 26 they signed an agreement to set up the United Nations to work for world peace and cooperation. Today more than 180 countries are members of the United Nations.

President Harry S. Truman (far left) watches as Secretary of State Edward R. Stettinius, Jr., signs the Charter of the United Nations for the United States.

the 442nd Regimental Combat Team, which fought in Italy and Germany. This group won more medals for bravery than any other group.

Much later, in 1988, the United States government finally apologized for its mistreatment of Japanese Americans during the war. The government also paid $20,000 to every person who had been sent to a relocation camp.

REVIEW Why were Japanese Americans forced to go to relocation camps during World War II?

442nd Regimental Combat Team

Results of the War

Some of the war's best-known leaders were Californians. General George Patton, who was born in San Gabriel, led United States troops across Europe and into Germany. General James Doolittle of Alameda led the first planes that dropped bombs on Japan.

Doolittle was one of 13 Californians to win the Congressional Medal of Honor, the country's highest award for bravery in war. Eight of the 13 medal winners, including David M. Gonzales (guhn•ZAH•luhs), gave their lives to save other soldiers.

World War II was long and terrible. By the time the Allies won in 1945, millions of people around the world had been killed. About 400,000 people from the United States had died. More than 17,000 Californians had died while fighting in the war.

In San Francisco, crowds filled Market Street to celebrate the end of the war.

All over the state of California and the rest of the United States, people celebrated the end of the war. Americans were also looking forward to better times at home. World War II had ended the Great Depression and created millions of new jobs for Californians and other Americans.

REVIEW How did World War II bring an end to the Great Depression?

LESSON 4 REVIEW

1940 ● ● **1945**

1941
• Japan attacks Pearl Harbor

1942
• Japanese Americans are sent to relocation camps

1945
• World War II ends

Check Understanding

❶ **Remember the Facts** How did Californians help the war effort?

❷ **Recall the Main Idea** How did World War II affect Californians?

Think Critically

❸ **Think More About It** Why was California a good place for military bases?

❹ **Personally Speaking** How do you think you might feel, as a citizen of the United States, if you were forced to live in a relocation camp?

Show What You Know

Interviewing Activity Interview an older person who lived during World War II. Ask him or her questions to find out what life was like during the war. Write down what you learn, and give a report to the class.

Understand Point of View

1. Why Learn This Skill?

Looking for a writer's feelings and beliefs —or point of view—about his or her subject can help you better understand what you are reading. Artists and photographers also express their feelings and beliefs in their works. If you know how to look for an artist's or a photographer's point of view, you will have a better idea of why he or she made the drawing or painting or took the photograph. Then you may learn more about the picture's meaning.

2. Understand the Process

Look again at the picture on page 350. It shows Californians celebrating the end of World War II.

Now look at the photograph on this page. What does it show? Like the photograph on page 350, it tells something about people's feelings at the time of World War II.

Follow these steps to look for the two photographers' points of view.

1. Think about how each picture makes you feel. Your own feelings can help you understand the photographer's point of view. Look at the people's faces in both pictures. How do they make you feel?

2. Study the details of the pictures for any information they can give you. What details tell you at what time during the war each photograph might have been taken?

3. Ask yourself what each photographer wants to show you about how people felt about the war. Think about what feelings of their own about the war the photographers were sharing with you. How are their points of view different?

3. Think and Apply

Look in books, magazines, or newspapers for a photograph, a painting, or a drawing that gives you a strong feeling. Describe how the picture makes you feel. What did the photographer or the artist show to make you feel as you do? What is his or her point of view?

A young soldier says good-bye as he leaves to fight in the war.

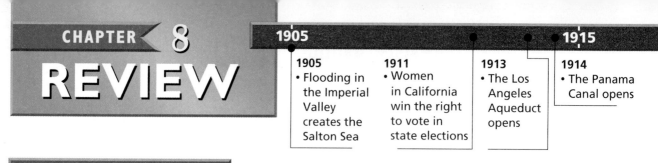

1905

1905
• Flooding in the Imperial Valley creates the Salton Sea

1911
• Women in California win the right to vote in state elections

1913
• The Los Angeles Aqueduct opens

1914
• The Panama Canal opens

1915

CONNECT MAIN IDEAS

Use this organizer to show that you understand how the chapter's main ideas are connected. Complete it by writing two details about each main idea. A copy of the organizer may be found on page 78 of the Activity Book.

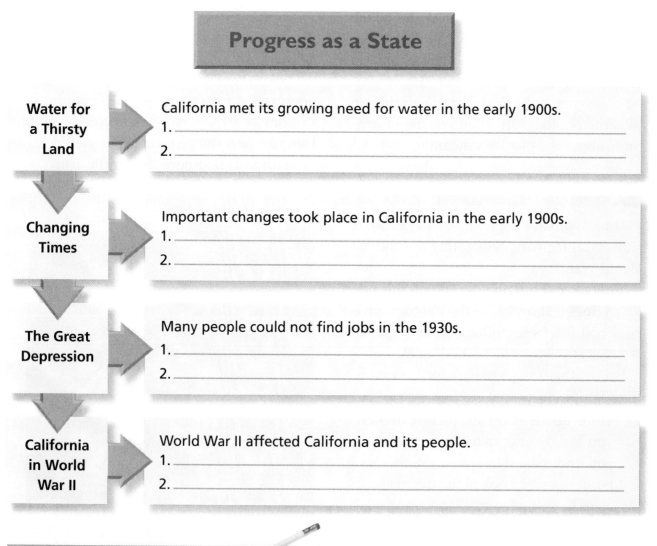

Progress as a State

Water for a Thirsty Land
California met its growing need for water in the early 1900s.
1. _____
2. _____

Changing Times
Important changes took place in California in the early 1900s.
1. _____
2. _____

The Great Depression
Many people could not find jobs in the 1930s.
1. _____
2. _____

California in World War II
World War II affected California and its people.
1. _____
2. _____

WRITE MORE ABOUT IT

Write Your Opinion Think about one of the water projects discussed in this chapter. Then write a paragraph telling why you would or would not have voted for it.

Write Headlines Write three newspaper headlines, one about each of the following: the Panama Canal, the Great Depression, and World War II.

1929
• The Great Depression begins

1937
• The Golden Gate Bridge opens

1941
• Japan attacks Pearl Harbor, and the United States enters World War II

1945
• World War II ends

USE VOCABULARY

Write the term that correctly matches each definition.

canal   human resource

capital resource   suffrage

depression

1 a waterway dug across land

2 the right to vote

3 a time when there are few jobs and people have little money

4 a worker

5 the money, buildings, machines, and tools needed to run a business

CHECK UNDERSTANDING

6 From which valley did the Los Angeles Aqueduct get its water?

7 Why was the Panama Canal important to California?

8 Why did southern California become the center of the aviation and movie industries?

9 What happened to places in the Dust Bowl? How did this affect California?

10 How were factories in California important to the war effort during World War II?

11 What was the Great Migration?

12 What happened to the Japanese Americans who lived in California during World War II?

THINK CRITICALLY

13 **Think More About It** How might California be different today if water projects had not been built?

14 **Personally Speaking** Which event in this chapter do you think had the greatest effect on California? Explain.

APPLY SKILLS

Tell Primary from Secondary Sources
Answer these questions.

15 Is a description of an event in a history book a primary or a secondary source?

16 Is a diary entry by someone who saw an event a primary or a secondary source?

Understand Point of View
Find a painting or a photograph that you like. Tell what it shows, and describe the artist's or photographer's point of view.

READ MORE ABOUT IT

Baseball Saved Us by Ken Mochizuki. Lee & Low Books. This book describes life in a relocation camp for one Japanese American boy and his family.

Visit the Internet at **http://www.hbschool.com** for additional resources.

MAKING Social Studies RELEVANT

Responding to EARTHQUAKES

Many earthquakes have struck California since the one that nearly destroyed San Francisco in 1906. There still is no way to know when an earthquake will happen. However, Californians have learned a lot about how to prepare for them and what to do after one strikes.

Northridge was one of the Los Angeles neighborhoods struck by an earthquake in 1994. People there rushed to help their neighbors escape from damaged homes and get medical help. They also shared food and shelter.

Later, an interesting fact was noticed. In neighborhoods that had "Neighborhood Watch" groups, people were better able to help each other. Neighborhood Watch is a program for groups of neighbors who meet often and work with the police to prevent crime. People in these groups knew who lived in their neighborhoods, so they could quickly tell if anyone was missing and might need help.

Police and city leaders liked the way members of the Neighborhood Watch groups worked together. They decided to turn the groups into disaster teams. Members took classes in first aid, and they received lists of things to check for in emergencies.

Such disaster teams have now been started in other neighborhoods. Los Angeles City Councilwoman Laura Chick was one of the people who came up with the idea of training the Neighborhood Watch groups. "We can turn a disaster into an opportunity to do things better," she said.

This boy walks past one of the 24,000 buildings that were destroyed in the earthquake that struck Los Angeles on January 17, 1994.

Think and Apply

BUILDING CITIZENSHIP

Earthquakes cannot be prevented, but there are things people can do to prepare for one. Storing items that would be needed in the emergency is one example. Work in a small group to list at least ten items that would be important to have in an earthquake emergency. Share your group's ideas, explaining why you chose to include each item on your list.

HARCOURT BRACE

Visit the Internet at **http://www.hbschool.com** for additional resources.

CNN Turner Le@rning

Check your media center or classroom video library for the Making Social Studies Relevant videotape of this feature.

Members of Neighborhood Watch groups distributed drinking water to earthquake victims. Part of their Neighborhood Watch training now includes classes in first aid.

WARNING

THIS IS A
NEIGHBORHOOD WATCH
COMMUNITY

WE IMMEDIATELY REPORT
ALL SUSPICIOUS ACTIVITIES
TO OUR POLICE DEPARTMENT

CALL 911

VISUAL SUMMARY

Summarize the Main Ideas
Study the pictures and captions to help you review what you read about in Unit 4.

Write More of the Story
Choose one of the events in the visual summary. Write a paragraph that describes what happened and how it affected California's history.

1 The transcontinental railroad was finished in 1869. It linked California with the rest of the country.

4 Much of San Francisco was destroyed by a great earthquake and fire in 1906.

5 Railroads and the discovery of oil caused booms in southern California. Water projects were built to bring water and electricity to growing cities.

6 New industries, such as moviemaking and aviation, provided thousands of jobs for Californians.

Thousands of immigrants came to California in the late 1800s and early 1900s. Many of them faced prejudice. The Chinese often lived in separate communities.

2 Farming became a major industry in the late 1800s. Railroads carried farm products across the country to markets in the East.

7 During the Great Depression, people from other states came to California looking for jobs.

 World War II brought new industries and new people to California.

UNIT 4 REVIEW

USE VOCABULARY

Write a term from this list to complete each of the sentences that follow.

amendment	migrant worker
boom	urban growth
invest	

1 If you _____ in a company, you are hoping to make money from it in the future.

2 Many newcomers settled in cities, which added to _____ in California.

3 A time of fast economic growth is called a _____.

4 A change made to a government's constitution is called an _____.

5 A person who moves from place to place with the seasons to harvest crops is a _____.

CHECK UNDERSTANDING

6 What linked California to the East before the transcontinental railroad?

7 What made it possible for railroads to carry fresh fruits and vegetables from California to the East?

8 At first most people settled in northern California. What later caused southern California to grow quickly?

9 What area of California is known as the Winter Garden of the World? Why?

10 Why did many people come to California during World War II?

THINK CRITICALLY

11 **Past to Present** Why is it still important for people to have good communication and transportation today?

12 **Link to You** Find out where your community's water comes from. Does it come from any of the water projects you read about in this unit? Explain.

APPLY SKILLS

Use a Time Zone Map Use the time zone map below to answer these questions.

13 Which two states use both Pacific and mountain times?

14 If it is 3:00 P.M. in El Paso, Texas, what time is it in Boise, Idaho? in Portland, Oregon?

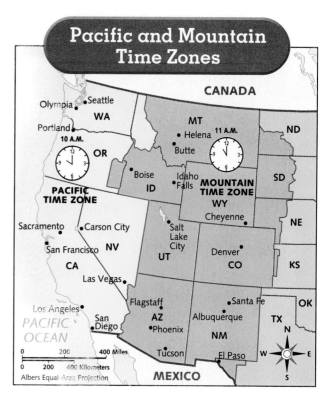

Pacific and Mountain Time Zones

REMEMBER

- Share your ideas.
- Cooperate with others to plan your work.
- Take responsibility for your work.
- Help one another.
- Show your group's work to the class.
- Discuss what you learned by working together.

ACTIVITY

Make a Set of
Historic Postcards

Work in a group of five. Each member should draw a picture on one side of an index card, showing a person or an event from this unit. Stack all the drawings from the class upside down, and have your teacher shuffle them. Have someone in your group take five cards from the top of the stack. Work together to write descriptions of the people or events shown.

Unit Project Wrap-Up

Publish a Group Book About California History Work with a group of historians from your class to finish the Unit Project described on page 267. As a group, decide which events you will include in your book. Then use the events to create a table of contents. Work together to write a story about each event, and draw pictures and maps to go with each one. Once all the stories have been put together, give your book a title. Ask permission to display your book in the school library.

ACTIVITY

Make a
Time Line

Work in a group to make a large time line to display on a classroom wall. The time line should show some of the important events that took place in California between 1855 and 1945. Find the events for the time line by using your textbook, encyclopedias, and library books. Be sure to show the date of each event on the time line. Also, remember to give your time line a title.

MODERN CALIFORNIA

Unit 5

Since World War II many people have come to California to find jobs and a better way of life. This growth has made California a more exciting place to live. It has also given the people of California many problems to solve. They must deal with much greater needs for food, water, shelter, and transportation. At the same time they must protect their environment and their resources. Californians, however, are ready to solve any problems that come their way.

◀ Los Angeles

UNIT THEMES

- Conflict and Cooperation
- Continuity and Change
- Individualism and Interdependence
- Interaction Within Different Environments

Unit Project

Hold a Class Fair Com
this project as you study
Choose a topic from this
for a display at a class fair.
fair will celebrate Califorr
its culture, people, histor
economy, and governmen
your textbook, books fro
library, and the Internet t
out more about your top
Then think about how yo
might work with other st
to share what you have le

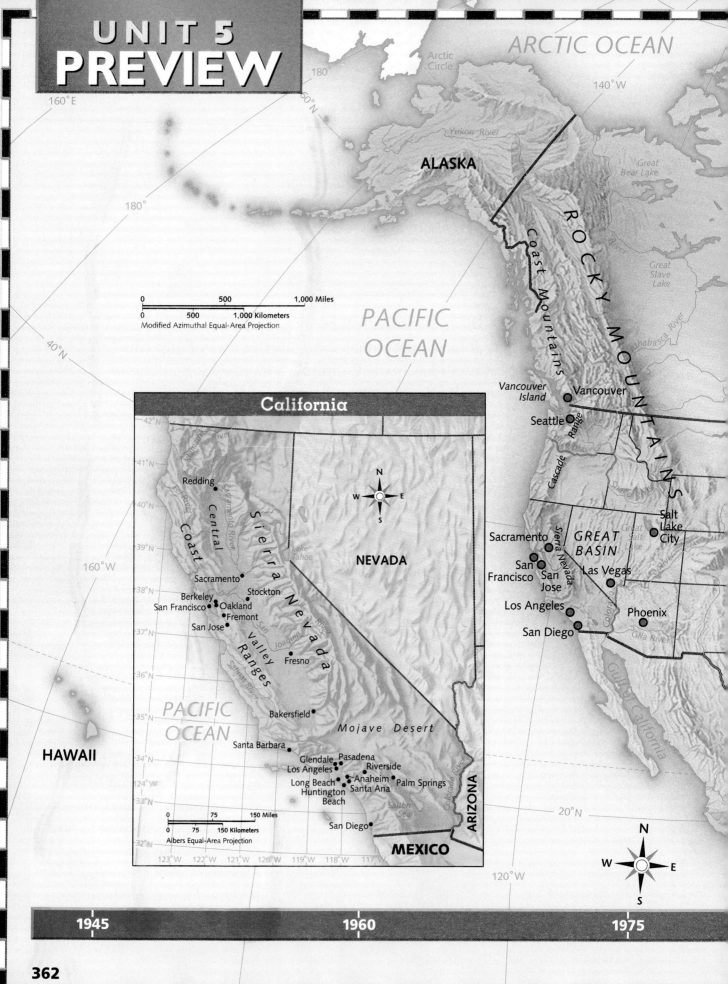

ARCTIC OCEAN

180°

160°E

140°W

60°N

ALASKA

Yukon River

Arctic Circle

Great Bear Lake

180°

ROCKY MOUNTAINS

Great Slave Lake

40°N

0   500   1,000 Miles

0   500   1,000 Kilometers

Modified Azimuthal Equal-Area Projection

PACIFIC OCEAN

Coast Mountains

160°W

Vancouver Island

Vancouver

Seattle

Range

Cascade

Salt Lake City

Sacramento

Sierra Nevada

GREAT BASIN

Great Salt Lake

San Francisco

San Jose

Las Vegas

HAWAII

Los Angeles

San Diego

Phoenix

Gila River

Gulf of California

California

42°N

Klamath River

Redding

Central

41°N

Coast

40°N

Sierra Nevada

N
W   E
S

NEVADA

39°N

Lake Tahoe

Sacramento

Feather River

Stockton

38°N

Berkeley

Oakland

San Francisco

Fremont

San Joaquin River

San Jose

37°N

Valley Ranges

Salinas River

Fresno

36°N

PACIFIC OCEAN

35°N

Bakersfield

Mojave Desert

Santa Barbara

34°N

Glendale

Pasadena

Los Angeles

Riverside

Long Beach

Anaheim

Palm Springs

Huntington Beach

Santa Ana

Colorado River

ARIZONA

33°N

Salton Sea

0   75   150 Miles

0   75   150 Kilometers

Albers Equal-Area Projection

San Diego

32°N

MEXICO

20°N

123°W 122°W 121°W 120°W 119°W 118°W 117°W

120°W

N
W   E
S

160°E

180°

40°N

160°W

124°W

1945

1960

1975

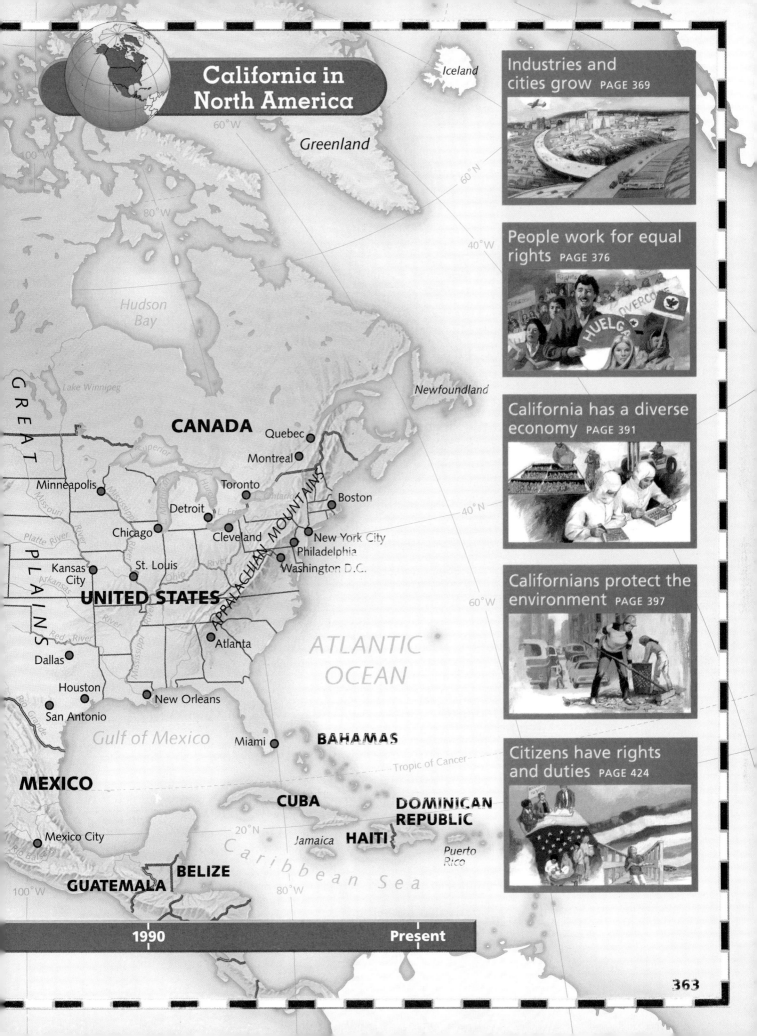

Iceland

Greenland

60°W

60°N

40°W

Hudson
Bay

Lake Winnipeg

Newfoundland

G
R
E
A
T

CANADA

Quebec

Montreal

Toronto

Boston

Minneapolis

Detroit

L. Erie

New York City

Chicago

Cleveland

Philadelphia

Washington D.C.

40°N

St. Louis

Kansas
City

Platte River

Missouri

Red River

P
L
A
I
N
S

UNITED STATES

Ohio River

APPALACHIAN MOUNTAINS

Arkansas

60°W

Dallas

Atlanta

ATLANTIC
OCEAN

Houston

Rio Grande

New Orleans

San Antonio

Gulf of Mexico

Miami

BAHAMAS

MEXICO

Tropic of Cancer

CUBA

DOMINICAN
REPUBLIC

20°N

Mexico City

Jamaica

HAITI

Puerto
Rico

Rio Balsas

C a r i b b e a n   S e a

GUATEMALA

BELIZE

100°W

80°W

1990   Present

I Love You, California

CALIFORNIA REPUBLIC

words by F. B. Silverwood
illustrated by Doug Henry

"I Love You, California" became California's official state song in 1988. The song was played aboard the first ship that passed through the Panama Canal in 1914.

I love you, California, you're the greatest state of all.
I love you in the winter, summer, spring and in the fall.
I love your fertile valleys; your dear mountains I adore.
I love your grand old ocean and I love her rugged shore.

Chorus:

Where the snow crowned Golden Sierras
Keep their watch o'er the valleys bloom,
It is there I would be in our land by the sea,
Ev'ry breeze bearing rich perfume,
It is here nature gives of her rarest. It is Home Sweet
    Home to Me,
And I know when I die I shall breathe my last sigh
For my sunny California.

KEY TO STATE SYMBOLS

1. Grizzly bear, state animal
2. California valley quail, state bird
3. Golden poppy, state flower
4. California dogface butterfly, state insect
5. Desert tortoise, state reptile
6. Golden trout, state fish
7. California gray whale, state marine mammal
8. California redwood, state tree

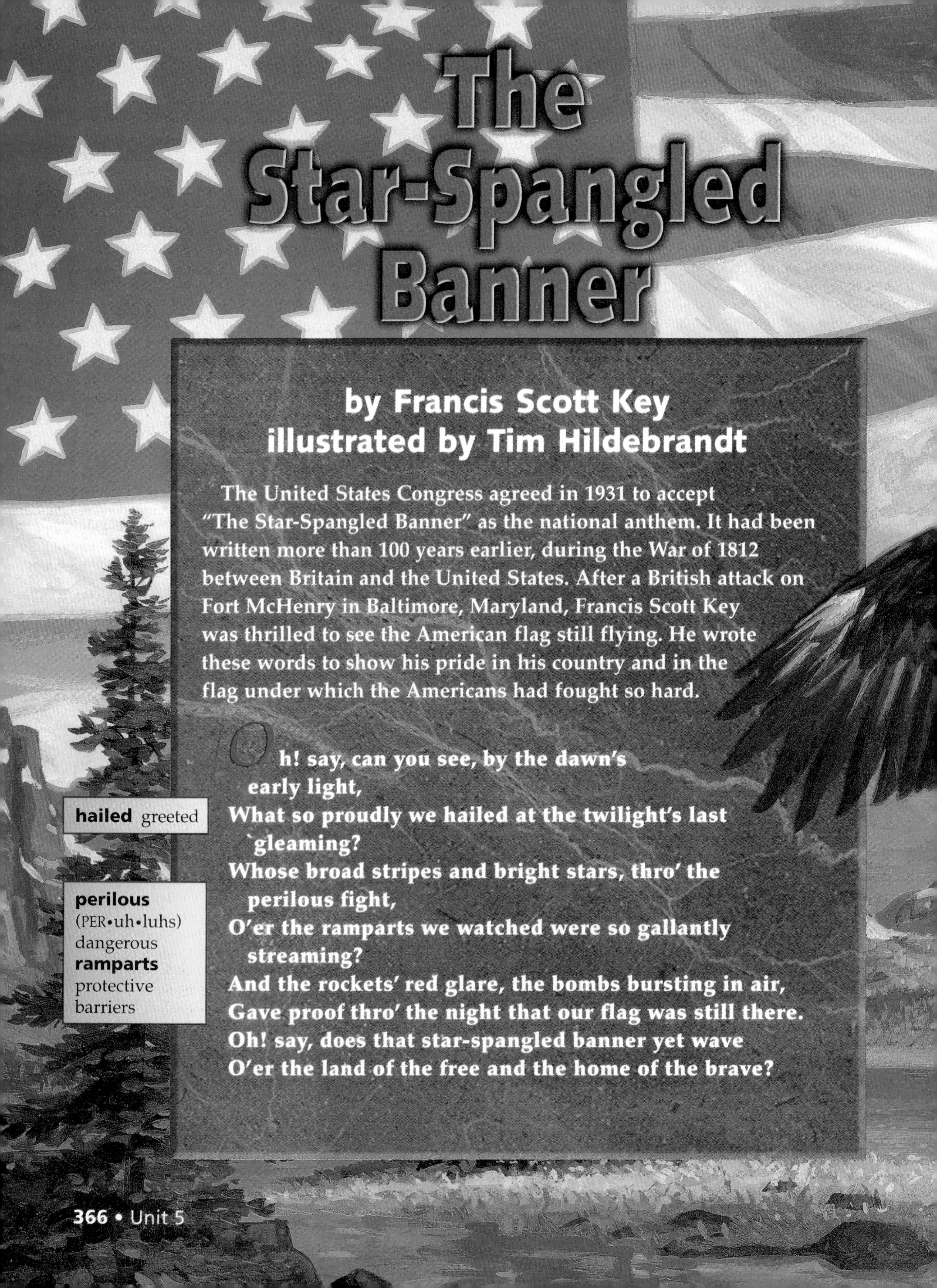

The Star-Spangled Banner

by Francis Scott Key
illustrated by Tim Hildebrandt

The United States Congress agreed in 1931 to accept "The Star-Spangled Banner" as the national anthem. It had been written more than 100 years earlier, during the War of 1812 between Britain and the United States. After a British attack on Fort McHenry in Baltimore, Maryland, Francis Scott Key was thrilled to see the American flag still flying. He wrote these words to show his pride in his country and in the flag under which the Americans had fought so hard.

hailed greeted

perilous
(PER•uh•luhs)
dangerous
ramparts
protective
barriers

Oh! say, can you see, by the dawn's
    early light,
What so proudly we hailed at the twilight's last
    `gleaming?
Whose broad stripes and bright stars, thro' the
    perilous fight,
O'er the ramparts we watched were so gallantly
    streaming?
And the rockets' red glare, the bombs bursting in air,
Gave proof thro' the night that our flag was still there.
Oh! say, does that star-spangled banner yet wave
O'er the land of the free and the home of the brave?

CHALLENGES FOR CALIFORNIA

"All of us must understand our own past in order to move ahead into the future."

Yoshiko Uchida (yoh•shee•koh oo•chee•dah) was born in Alameda in 1921. She wrote many popular books for children.

Lisa (right) is one of the more than 32 million people who live in California today.

California Grows and Changes

1945	1950	1955	1960

Once again a boom was bringing people to California. This time, however, the boom was not in gold or railroads or farming. It was in manufacturing. During World War II and in the years that followed, millions of newcomers arrived from other parts of the United States and other parts of the world. Many of these people were looking for jobs in California's new factories.

The Growth of Manufacturing

Before the war, California's economy had centered around agriculture and a few other important industries—oil, moviemaking, aviation, and shipbuilding. All of these industries grew after the war ended. But many new kinds of industries also grew, especially new manufacturing industries.

In the years following World War II, California's economy became more diverse. A **diverse economy** is one that is based on many kinds of industries. New factories were making all kinds of products. Some made clothing, shoes, cosmetics, and sports equipment. Others made chemicals, electronic and refrigeration equipment, tires, and automobiles. In fact, Los Angeles was second only to Detroit, Michigan, in the number of cars made.

REVIEW How did California's economy change after World War II?

FOCUS
Why might people want to move to a place that has a growing economy?

Main Idea Read to find out what caused California's economy to grow after World War II.

Vocabulary
diverse economy
silicon chip
aerospace
suburb
urban sprawl
freeway
metropolitan area

These cars were built in a factory in Los Angeles in 1949.

In this Bell X-1 test plane, Chuck Yeager flew 45,000 feet (13,716 m) above the Earth—higher than any pilot before him.

GLAMOROUS GLENNIS

New Industries

During World War II scientists and engineers had come to California to help in the war effort. When the war ended, many of them stayed. Some found work teaching at California's universities. Others worked at developing new kinds of products and technologies. One of the most important of these was jet airplanes.

The United States government had chosen Edwards Air Force Base in the Mojave Desert as a testing place for its new fighter jets. Scientists and engineers were building airplanes that could go faster and faster. But could they build one that could fly at supersonic (soo•per•SAH•nik) speed—faster than the speed of sound? They were about to find out.

On the morning of October 14, 1947, Chuck Yeager (YAY•ger) climbed aboard

a Bell X-1 test plane and prepared for takeoff. Yeager had flown fighter planes during World War II. Now he worked as a test pilot at Edwards Air Force Base.

Yeager was both excited and nervous as the test plane took off. Would it break apart when it reached supersonic speed? No one knew, but Yeager kept going faster and faster until he reached a speed of about 700 miles (1,127 km) per hour. Yeager had done what no pilot had done before. He had flown faster than the speed of sound!

By the 1950s, airplane factories in California were building fighter jets for the United States military and jet airplanes for the airlines. Other factories made engine parts and electrical equipment for the planes.

In 1959 something happened that led to an even bigger advance in technology. Scientists in California invented the

silicon chip, a tiny device that can store millions of bits of computer information. Silicon chips allowed businesses to make smaller, faster, and cheaper computers.

As computers were improved and planes became bigger and faster, scientists thought about the next step—traveling into outer space. Scientists in California helped start the aerospace (AIR•oh•spays) industry. The **aerospace** industry builds and tests equipment for air and space travel.

Factories in California helped build many of the rockets that were used to send American astronauts into space. In 1966, scientists at the Jet Propulsion Laboratory in Pasadena guided a spacecraft to land on the moon. No people were on that spacecraft, but three years later two American astronauts—Neil Armstrong and Edwin Aldrin—became the first people to walk on the moon.

Several Californians have been astronauts. Among them are Sally Ride, Ellen Ochoa (oh•CHOH•uh), and Kevin Chilton. Ride, who was born in Los Angeles, became the first American woman to travel in space. She made her first flight into space on the space shuttle *Challenger* in 1983. Ochoa, who was also born in Los Angeles, first flew into space on the space shuttle *Discovery* in 1993. Chilton has made three trips into space.

REVIEW What is the aerospace industry?

Ellen Ochoa, Sally Ride, and Kevin Chilton are all astronauts from California who have flown on space shuttles.

The Construction Boom

New industries needed new factories and office buildings. The people who were moving to California to work in those factories and offices needed places to live, to go to school, and to shop. All these needs led to a boom in construction following World War II. Thousands of engineers, architects, and construction workers came to California to build houses, apartments, schools, offices, factories, and government buildings.

In the past, houses had been built one at a time, with each house having a different plan. After the war, however, builders started to build planned communities called subdivisions. Each subdivision had hundreds of houses. All the houses looked very much alike.

There was such a demand for these houses that on one day in 1946, salespeople at a planned community near Los Angeles sold 107 of them in one hour!

REVIEW **What was the new way of building houses after World War II?**

Cities Grow Larger

As more houses were built, cities stretched out farther and farther into the countryside. The suburbs around them grew larger, too, as more land was used for buildings. A **suburb** is a town or small city near a large city.

Automobiles helped create this **urban sprawl**, the spread of urban areas. With automobiles, people could live in one place and work in another. They could drive from their homes to banks, stores, and shopping centers.

In subdivisions built after World War II (left), houses that looked very much alike filled block after block. Many drive-in restaurants (below) opened in California in the years after World War II.

In 1940 the state's first freeway, the Pasadena Freeway, opened. A **freeway** is a wide, divided highway with no cross streets or stoplights. Special lanes direct traffic on and off. These features allow traffic to move quickly. The Pasadena Freeway links downtown Los Angeles with Pasadena.

During World War II, no more freeways were built but traffic increased. By the time the war ended, California had about 3 million cars on its highways. In 1947 the state government voted to create a 12,500-mile (20,116-km) freeway system to link the state's largest cities and metropolitan (meh•truh•PAH•luh•tuhn)

Freeways in Los Angeles today

areas. A **metropolitan area** is a large city together with its suburbs.

Today, California's largest metropolitan area is the Los Angeles–Long Beach area. Almost one-third of all Californians live there. This metropolitan area includes Los Angeles, California's largest city both in area and in population. It also includes Long Beach, Anaheim, Santa Ana, and several other cities. In all of the United States, only New York City's metropolitan area has more people.

REVIEW How did automobiles help create urban sprawl?

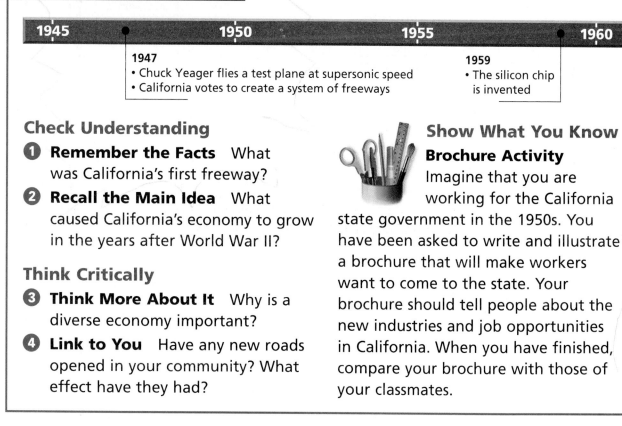

LESSON 1 REVIEW

1945	1950	1955	1960

1947
• Chuck Yeager flies a test plane at supersonic speed
• California votes to create a system of freeways

1959
• The silicon chip is invented

Check Understanding

1 Remember the Facts What was California's first freeway?

2 Recall the Main Idea What caused California's economy to grow in the years after World War II?

Think Critically

3 Think More About It Why is a diverse economy important?

4 Link to You Have any new roads opened in your community? What effect have they had?

Show What You Know

Brochure Activity Imagine that you are working for the California state government in the 1950s. You have been asked to write and illustrate a brochure that will make workers want to come to the state. Your brochure should tell people about the new industries and job opportunities in California. When you have finished, compare your brochure with those of your classmates.

Use a Road Map

1. Why Learn This Skill?

Imagine that this is the first day of your family's vacation. You pack the car, buckle your seat belts, and are on your way. About an hour later your little brother asks, "How much farther do we have to go?"

To answer his question, you can use a road map like the one below. As you know, a road map shows the routes between places. A road map, however, can also tell you the distances between places. Knowing distances helps people choose the best and fastest routes.

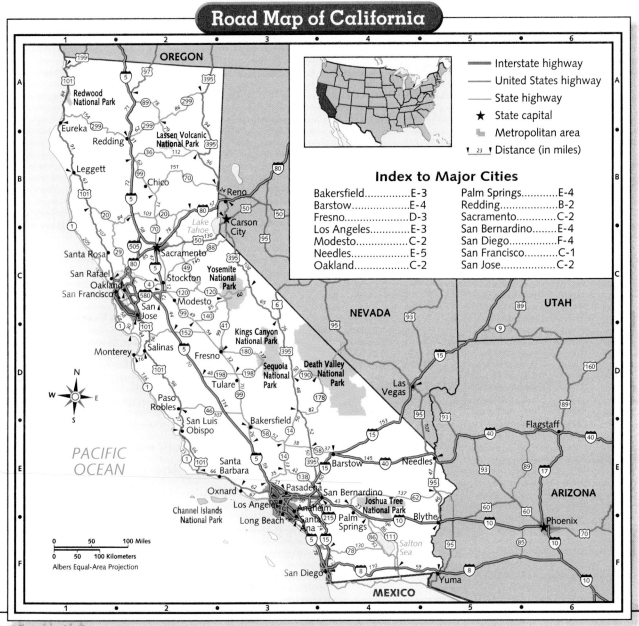

Road Map of California

Interstate highway
United States highway
State highway
★ State capital
Metropolitan area
Distance (in miles)

Index to Major Cities

Bakersfield	E-3	Palm Springs	E-4
Barstow	E-4	Redding	B-2
Fresno	D-3	Sacramento	C-2
Los Angeles	E-3	San Bernardino	E-4
Modesto	C-2	San Diego	F-4
Needles	E-5	San Francisco	C-1
Oakland	C-2	San Jose	C-2

0   50   100 Miles
0   50   100 Kilometers
Albers Equal-Area Projection

and a Mileage Table

2. Understand the Process

Suppose that you want to drive from San Diego to Needles. What route should you take? First, use the map index to find San Diego and Needles. Next, use the map to find out which routes connect the two cities.

1 Which highways would you use to drive from San Diego to Needles? In which direction would you travel on each one?

Suppose that you want to drive from Fresno to Needles. How far would you have to drive? You can find the driving distance, or mileage, between places by using special features of road maps.

On many road maps, highways are marked with small numbers that show the mileage between places. Each place has a small wedge called a distance marker.

2 Find the distance markers near Fresno and the place where Highway 198 crosses Highway 99, southeast of Fresno. Then find the number between those two markers. What is the distance?

Using distance markers to find the mileage between cities that are far apart—such as Fresno and Needles—would take a lot of time. You would have to find the mileage between many places and then add all the numbers together.

A much easier way to find the mileage between cities is to use a mileage table like the one shown. A **mileage table** gives the number of miles between the listed cities.

3 Find the column labeled Fresno in the row at the top of the table. Go down the column until you come to the row labeled Needles. What number is in that box? That is the number of miles between the two cities.

4 Find Palm Springs in the first column of the table. Go across the row until you come to the column labeled San Diego. What is the mileage between Palm Springs and San Diego?

3. Think and Apply

Work with a partner to plan a trip to three different cities in California. Begin your trip in Sacramento. Use the road map to decide which routes you will follow. Use the road map and the mileage table to find out the number of miles you will travel between those cities.

California Mileage Table

	Fresno	Los Angeles	Sacramento	San Diego	San Francisco
Fresno		219	178	342	190
Los Angeles	219		388	124	385
Needles	393	263	571	326	568
Palm Springs	324	110	493	143	490
Sacramento	178	388		511	87
San Diego	342	124	511		508
San Francisco	190	385	87	508	
San Jose	153	342	115	465	43

FOCUS

What are some ways people can change things that they think are unfair?

Main Idea Read this lesson to learn what some groups in California did to work for equal rights.

Vocabulary

ethnic group
segregation
civil rights
protest
boycott

Dr. Martin Luther King, Jr., spoke at the University of California at Berkeley several times.

Movements for Equal Rights

| 1960 | 1965 | 1970 | 1975 |

Many people came to California during the 1950s and 1960s in search of a better way of life. Some spoke of the California Dream—the idea that life was better in California than anywhere else. With its booming economy and mild climate, California was a wonderful place to live. But not everyone enjoyed the same opportunities.

The Civil Rights Movement

The people who came to California were from other parts of the United States and other countries. The state became home to many ethnic groups. An **ethnic group** is a group of people from the same country, of the same race, or with a shared culture.

Some ethnic groups, such as Latinos, African Americans, and Asian Americans, faced discrimination. They often were paid low wages and were kept out of higher-paying jobs. Sometimes they were not allowed to live in certain neighborhoods. Because of this segregation, their children often went to poor schools. **Segregation** is keeping people of one race or culture separate from other people.

In the 1950s many people joined the civil rights movement, which worked to end discrimination. **Civil rights** are the rights of citizens to equal treatment. One of the movement's leaders was Dr. Martin Luther King, Jr., an African American minister from Georgia. He and millions of other Americans made speeches and took part in other actions

to show their support of civil rights. In 1957 Dr. King spoke at the University of California at Berkeley. He said, "We have a great opportunity in America to build here a great nation, a nation where all men live together as brothers. . . . We must keep moving toward that goal."

In spite of the calls for civil rights, discrimination continued. In 1963 a lawyer named Odis Jackson tried to buy a house in a new Los Angeles suburb. The builder, however, would not sell a house to Jackson because he was an African American. When African Americans and other people in the community heard about this, they decided to protest. To **protest** is to act against something. They marched in front of the building site, carrying signs telling how they felt. The builder sold Jackson the house.

Protests of this kind were held all over the country. Over time, new laws were passed to protect people's civil rights. Change came slowly, however. Many ethnic workers were still paid less than other workers to do the same jobs. Many could not find jobs at all.

People continued to protest against discrimination. Mostly these protests were peaceful, but sometimes fighting broke out. In 1965 there was a riot in Watts, a neighborhood of Los Angeles. Thirty-four people were killed and thousands were hurt or arrested. During the next year, there were more riots across the United States.

Most people, however, continued to work peacefully to end discrimination. They elected civil rights leaders to serve in government. By the early 1970s, more than 30 California cities had Latino, African American, or Asian mayors.

REVIEW What are civil rights?

BIOGRAPHY

Thomas Bradley
1917–1998

Thomas Bradley and his family moved to Los Angeles when he was a boy. Bradley worked hard in school and got a job as a police officer. He later served on the Los Angeles City Council. In 1973 he became the city's first African American mayor. He was reelected four times—more often than any other mayor in the city's history.

Thomas Bradley

The Farmworkers

In places outside the cities, another group of people also faced discrimination. Much of the work on California's farms was done by migrant workers, most of them Latinos. These workers and their families were often treated badly by farm owners. They were charged high rents to live in unsafe shelters, and they were paid very little for their work—an average of 90 cents per hour. Laws at that time said that most other workers were to be paid at least $1.25 per hour.

To help improve the lives of migrant workers, César Chávez (SAY•zar CHAH•vez), Dolores Huerta (HWAIR•tah), and others decided to form a labor union. In 1962 they formed the United Farm Workers Association, which later became known as the United Farm Workers (UFW). The UFW worked to get more pay and better working conditions for farmworkers. "Together," Chávez said of the farmworkers' union, "all things are possible."

In 1965 Chávez led grape pickers on a strike. He also called for a boycott against grapes. A **boycott** is a decision

BIOGRAPHY

César Chávez
1927–1993

César Chávez was born on a farm in Arizona. When he was ten years old, his family moved to California, where they became migrant workers. When Chávez was 15, he had to quit school to work in the fields. While harvesting vegetables, he had to bend over a hoe with a very short handle. Years later the United Farm Workers union helped end the use of these hoes. For his work to improve the lives of farmworkers, Chávez was awarded the Presidential Medal of Freedom in 1993.

Dolores Huerta
1930–

Dolores Huerta was born in New Mexico but grew up in Stockton, California. Her mother worked in a canning factory there. Huerta became a teacher, but she stopped teaching, she said, because "I couldn't stand seeing kids come to class hungry and needing shoes. I thought I could do more by organizing farmworkers than by trying to teach their hungry children."

César Chávez and Dolores Huerta

Boycott button

California Women in Government

ACHIEVEMENT	NAME	ELECTED
First women in the State Assembly	Esto Broughton, Grace S. Dorris, Elizabeth Hughes, and Anna L. Sayor	1918
First woman from California in the U.S. House of Representatives	Mae Ella Nolan	1922
First African American woman in the State Assembly	Yvonne W. Braithwaite-Burke	1966
First Asian American woman in the State Assembly	March Fong Eu	1966
First African American woman from California in the U.S. House of Representatives	Yvonne W. Braithwaite-Burke	1972
First woman in the State Senate	Rose Ann Vuich	1976
First African American woman in the State Senate	Diane E. Watson	1978
First Hispanic woman in the State Assembly	Gloria Molina	1982
First women from California in the U.S. Senate	Dianne Feinstein and Barbara Boxer	1992
First Hispanic woman from California in the U.S. House of Representatives	Lucille Roybal-Allard	1992

LEARNING FROM TABLES This table lists some important California women in government.
■ Who was the first woman in the State Senate? In what year was she elected?

by a group of people not to buy something, as a protest. As more people across the country joined the boycott, the grape growers began to lose money. Finally, in 1970, they agreed to give the workers more pay and better working conditions. That ended the strike.

REVIEW How did farmworkers change their working conditions?

Civil Rights for Other Groups

During the 1960s other groups across the state and country began to work for equal rights. Many women now had jobs outside the home, but they often earned less than men did for the same jobs. Like other groups, women began to work together for equal rights.

California soon became a center of the women's rights movement. In fact, the first women's studies department at a university in this country was started at San Diego State University in 1971. Partly as a result of the women's rights movement, more

Yvonne W. Braithwaite-Burke

women were elected to serve in government.

American Indians worked together for equal rights, too. In November 1969, a group of 89 Indians took over Alcatraz (AL•kuh•traz) Island in San Francisco Bay. The island, which was once a prison, was a symbol to them of all the land once held by the American Indians. The protesters remained on the island for nearly two years. This protest brought attention to the Indian civil rights movement.

REVIEW Why did women begin to demand equal rights in the 1960s?

A Changing Population

California's population has grown with amazing speed in the last 50 years.

The group of Indians that took over Alcatraz Island in 1969 called itself "Indians of All Tribes." Its members wanted to build a center there for the study of Indian culture.

Today, more than 32 million people live in California—more than in any other state.

At least part of this growth is because of the arrival of people from other countries. Large numbers of immigrants have come from Mexico, Central America, South America, and Asia. Many of those from Asia are from Laos, Cambodia, and Vietnam. These countries are in Southeast Asia, a region damaged by many years of war. Many other Asian immigrants have come from the Philippines, China, South Korea, India, and Japan.

About 200,000 immigrants arrive in California each year. Instead of arriving on ships, as immigrants often did in the past, most immigrants today arrive by plane at one of California's international airports. These immigrants belong to many ethnic groups, each with its own culture. Cultural differences can be seen in the languages people speak, their religious beliefs, the kinds of music they listen to, and the foods they eat. The different cultures have made California a more diverse place and have given all Californians a richer life.

Many of the new people who come to live in California each year are legal immigrants. That means they have permission from the government to live in the United States. Some people, however, find ways to enter the country illegally. The government has passed laws making it harder for these illegal immigrants to stay in the United States.

REVIEW How has California's population changed in the last 50 years?

California's Growing
Population, 1950–1990

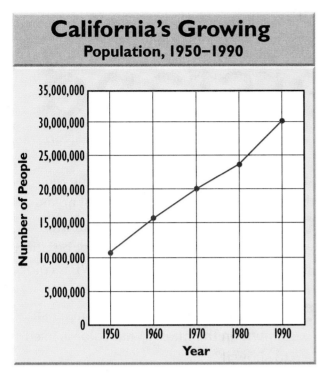

LEARNING FROM GRAPHS By 1964 California had more people than any other state.
- What was the population of California in 1970?

Leading Birthplaces
of Recent Immigrants to California

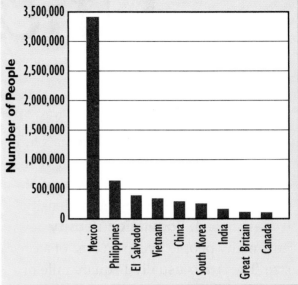

LEARNING FROM GRAPHS Immigrants have come to California from all over the world.
- From which country have the greatest numbers of recent immigrants come?

LESSON 2 REVIEW

1960	1965	1970	1975

1964
- California for first time has more people than any other state

1965
- César Chávez leads a grape boycott

1971
- The first women's studies department at a university in this country is started, at San Diego State University

Check Understanding

1 Remember the Facts Why did the civil rights movement begin?

2 Recall the Main Idea What have groups in California done to work for equal rights?

Think Critically

3 Personally Speaking People in the 1950s spoke of the California Dream. Do you think there is still a California Dream today? Explain.

4 Link to You Have you ever felt that you were being treated unfairly? What did you do about it?

Show What You Know

Writing Activity Think about some cultural differences that you have noticed in your community or in a place you have visited. Then write a paragraph describing how cultures have affected your community.

Understand a

1. Why Learn This Skill?

You may live in one of California's large cities or in a suburb. Perhaps you live in a small town or a rural area. Each kind of place has a different population density (DEN•suh•tee). **Population density** tells how many people live in an area of a certain size. The size is usually 1 square mile or 1 square kilometer. A square mile is a square piece of land. Each of its four sides is 1 mile long. A square kilometer is a square piece of land with sides that are each 1 kilometer long.

The population density of your area may affect the way you live. Suppose that three people live on each square mile of land where you live. With only three people per square mile, there would be lots of space around you. Now suppose that 10,000 people live on each square mile. The area would be very crowded.

Like resources, people are not spread evenly across the Earth. More people live in some areas than in others. Would you expect to find the highest population density in cities, in small towns, or in rural areas? In which kind of area would you expect to find the lowest population density?

2. Understand the Process

The map on page 383 is a population map of California. A population map

shows where people live. It also shows the population density of different areas.

① The map key shows four population densities. What is the lowest population density shown on the map? What color is used to show it?

② What is the highest population density shown on the map? What color is used to show it?

③ Find the city of Long Beach on the map. What is the population density of the area in which it is located?

④ Which city has the higher population density, Redding or Red Bluff?

⑤ Some of California's cities have very high population densities. The population density of San Francisco, for example, is more than 15,000 people per square mile. How do you think such a high population density affects the lives of people living in San Francisco?

⑥ Which parts of California have very large areas of land with low population density? Why do you think so few people live in those places?

3. Think and Apply

Study the information on the map on page 383. Then show the same information in a chart, graph, or table. For example, you might make a bar graph comparing the population densities of several California cities.

Population Map

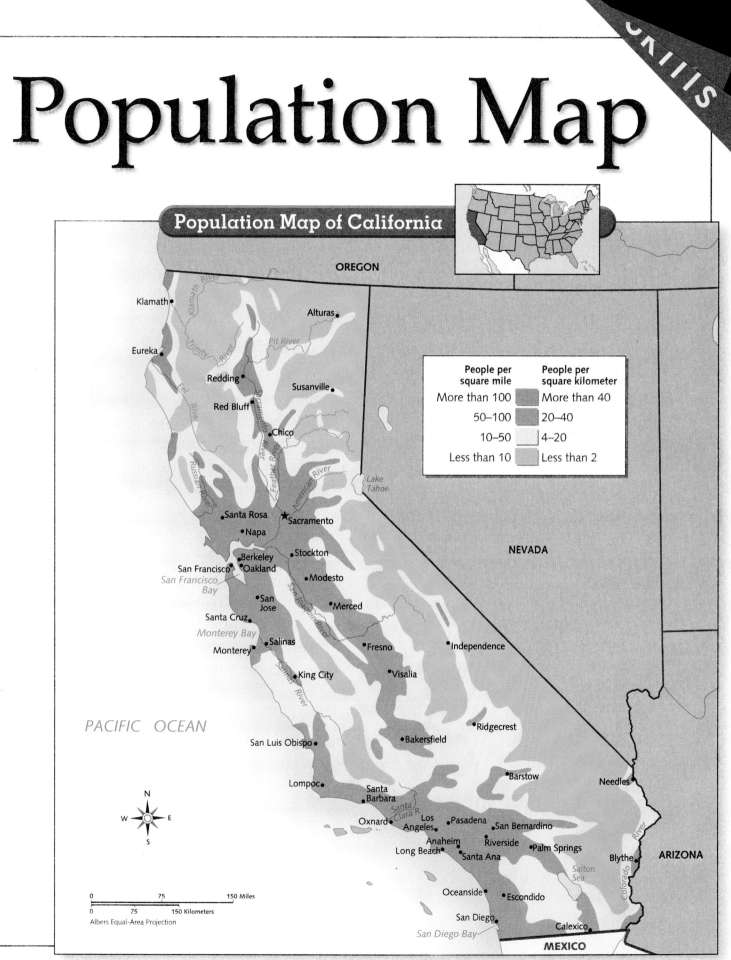

Population Map of California

OREGON

Klamath

Alturas

Eureka

Pit River

Redding

Susanville

Red Bluff

Chico

People per square mile	People per square kilometer
More than 100	More than 40
50–100	20–40
10–50	4–20
Less than 10	Less than 2

Lake Tahoe

Santa Rosa

Sacramento

Napa

Berkeley • Stockton

San Francisco • Oakland

San Francisco Bay

Modesto

NEVADA

San Jose

Merced

Santa Cruz

Monterey Bay

Salinas

Fresno

Independence

Monterey

King City

Visalia

PACIFIC OCEAN

Ridgecrest

San Luis Obispo

Bakersfield

Barstow

Lompoc

Needles

Santa Barbara

Oxnard

Los Angeles • Pasadena • San Bernardino

Anaheim • Riverside

Long Beach • Santa Ana

Palm Springs

Blythe

ARIZONA

Salton Sea

Oceanside

Escondido

San Diego

Calexico

San Diego Bay

MEXICO

N
W E
S

0   75   150 Miles
0   75   150 Kilometers
Albers Equal-Area Projection

Education and Culture

FOCUS
Why is education important to people?

Main Idea Read this lesson to find out about some of the things that all Californians share.

Vocabulary
tax
heritage
festival
recreation
professional team

How is the education you are receiving in California preparing you for the future?

Many groups of people now live in California, and each group has added some of its way of life to California's culture. No matter where they or their ancestors came from, Californians share many things.

California Schools

At this very moment you and your classmates are sharing an important part of life in California—education. By going to school and learning, you are becoming an important part of California's future. People who get a good education do better in what they choose to do, and this helps their state as well.

Education has a long history in California. The state's first constitution provided for public schools. It was not until 1852, however, that the state government passed a tax law to pay for them. A **tax** is money that a government collects from its citizens, usually to pay for services.

At the local level, the first public school paid for by taxes opened in San Francisco in 1850. It was paid for by the city. At that time, public schools did not include high schools. The first public high school, also located in San Francisco, did not open until 1856.

Today there are about 8,000 public schools in California, and more than 5 million students go to them. In fact, more students attend public schools in California than in any other state.

California also has about 600,000 students in private schools. Private schools generally do not get money from taxes. Instead, parents, churches, and other groups pay for these schools.

Private schools have an even longer history in California than public schools. Church groups have been teaching religion and other subjects ever since the missions first set up schools more than 200 years ago.

California's first constitution also set up a state university. Today California has the largest system of higher education in the country. Public universities receive money from the government, but students still have to pay to attend. However, the state often provides some money to help those students who cannot afford to pay the whole cost themselves.

California's university system includes two large state universities—the University of California and California State University. Together they offer courses to about 500,000 students at many places across the state. There are also many community colleges, which offer two-year programs.

REVIEW How are public schools paid for?

Important scientific research is done at California's universities.

BIOGRAPHY

Phoebe Apperson Hearst
1842–1919

Phoebe Apperson Hearst was one of the founders of the National PTA. This group works to improve schools in California and across the United States.

Hearst was born in Missouri and taught school there before coming to live in San Francisco in 1862. Her husband, George Hearst, had come to California during the gold rush. Over time, the Hearsts became one of California's wealthiest families. Mrs. Hearst used some of the family's money to open free kindergartens in San Francisco. She also gave money to the University of California.

The Great Wall of Los Angeles is painted on the concrete walls of the Tujunga Wash flood control channel.

Sharing Cultures

Good education has been one of the main reasons for California's growth and success. It has provided industries with the skilled workers they need. It has also helped the state's people learn how to express themselves in many ways. That is one reason why California is such an interesting place. Many kinds of artists—painters, writers, musicians, and others—live in the state. They often share their cultures in their work.

Judith Baca (BAH•kah), for example, is an artist who tells stories through her paintings. Baca's art shows that she values her Mexican heritage. A **heritage** is a way of life, a custom, or a belief that has come from the past and continues today.

While Baca was in college, she studied murals from Mexico's past. In the 1970s the leaders of Los Angeles gave Baca money to create murals for their city. One of these murals, *The Great Wall of Los Angeles*, tells the history of Los Angeles. This huge mural in the San Fernando Valley is about half a mile (almost 1 km) long! More than 200 teenagers helped paint it.

There are many ways for people to share the heritage and history of the different groups of people who live in California. One way is to go to one of the state's many museums, such as the Oakland Museum of California, in Oakland. At the California African American Museum in Los Angeles, visitors can see exhibits about African American culture and history. At the Japanese American National Museum, also in Los Angeles, visitors can learn about Japanese American culture and history.

The Old Spanish Days Fiesta in Santa Barbara features the largest parade of horses in the country.

Many groups in California have worked to keep their cultures alive and to share them with others. In many California cities, there are festivals that celebrate the heritage of different groups. A **festival** is a celebration that takes place every year, usually at the same time of the year. These festivals share cultures in a way that all Californians can enjoy.

Some of the earliest California festivals were the fiestas that took place on the ranchos. Santa Barbara keeps alive this tradition with the Old Spanish Days

CULTURE

The Watts Towers

In the 1920s Simon Rodia (roh•DEE•uh) began an unusual work of art in the Los Angeles neighborhood of Watts. First he built several towers out of building scraps and other unwanted materials such as pipes and bed frames. Then he covered the towers with bits of glass, plates, tiles, and more than 70,000 seashells. The towers took Rodia 33 years to complete. Today they are part of an art center, at which people can take classes and enjoy many kinds of art.

Simon Rodia called his sculpture *Nuestro Pueblo*, which means "Our Town" in Spanish. The highest tower is 99 feet (30 m) high.

In San Francisco and in cities all over California, people watch fireworks displays on Independence Day.

These dancers are performing a traditional Danish dance at the Danish Days festival in Solvang.

Fiesta every summer. Thousands of people take part in the events, which include the largest parade of horses in the country. Other events include dancing, a special parade for children, and, of course, a rodeo.

There are hundreds of other festivals that are held throughout the year. You might sample dishes like souvlaki (soov•LAH•kee)—grilled meat—at the Greek Food Festival in Sacramento. Or you might want to choose your favorite Danish food at Danish Days in Solvang. In San Jose you can enjoy Mexican foods, music, and dancing at the Mexican Independence Day celebrations.

Many celebrations are linked to holidays. One of the most important holidays Californians and other Americans share is Independence Day, or the Fourth of

July. On that date in 1776, the United States declared its independence from Britain. Each July 4, millions of Californians get together to enjoy this holiday.

Every winter, people from Asian countries celebrate their New Year. Chinese Americans greet each other with the words *Gung Hay Fat Choy*, or *Happy New Year*. Parades through San Francisco's Chinatown feature colorful costumes and floats. In Korean American neighborhoods, families get together to enjoy holiday foods like sweet bean cakes and sticky rice. At the Hmong National New Year Celebration in Fresno, people enjoy traditional Hmong dancing and music.

REVIEW What are some ways Californians can share the heritage and history of different groups of people?

California's hills and valleys are great places to bike.

Sports and Recreation

Californians can also take part in sports and other kinds of recreation (reh•kree•AY•shuhn). **Recreation** is an activity that people do for fun. California's sunny climate, variety of landforms, and long coastline are great for many kinds of activities. Because of this, California has become known for outdoor recreation.

Californians also have plenty of chances to watch professional (pruh•FEH•shuh•nuhl) sports teams in action. A **professional team** is made up of players who are paid for playing. California has more professional sports teams than any other state. Fans can watch professional baseball, football, basketball, and hockey teams.

Parades with colorful floats like this one are part of Chinese New Year festivals in California.

On New Year's Day, millions of people across the country watch on television the Tournament of Roses parade in Pasadena. They enjoy the marching bands and the beautiful floats covered with flowers. After the parade ends, it is time for the Rose Bowl game, in which top college football teams in the nation compete.

REVIEW Why is California known for outdoor recreation?

Every float in the Tournament of Roses parade must be completely covered with flowers or other natural materials such as leaves and bark.

LESSON 3 REVIEW

Check Understanding

❶ **Remember the Facts** What is the difference between public and private education?

❷ **Recall the Main Idea** What are some of the things that all Californians share?

Think Critically

❸ **Think More About It** Why is it important for Californians to learn about the heritage of the different groups of people in their state?

❹ **Link to You** What kinds of things might you learn by going to one of California's many festivals?

Show What You Know

Art Activity Imagine that you have been asked to help plan a festival to celebrate some part of your community's history. First decide what the festival will celebrate and what it will be called. Then design a poster for it. Be sure to include the name and dates of the festival. Add drawings or pictures cut out of magazines to show what the festival celebrates. Place your poster where other students can see it.

A Modern Economy

| 1970 | 1980 | 1990 | Present |

LESSON
4

FOCUS

What kinds of jobs are important to California's economy today?

Main Idea   Read to learn how California's location and new technologies have affected the state's economy.

Vocabulary

international trade
export
import
high-tech
Internet
food processing
tourism

Hundreds of years ago Native Californians traded clay pots and strings of shell beads for things they could not grow or make in their own lands. In Mexican California, people traded cattle hides and tallow for manufactured goods. During the gold rush, trade helped build the cities of Sacramento and San Francisco. Trade is still an important part of California's economy. But California's economy has changed in ways that people could not have imagined in the past.

Business can now take place instantly by telephone and with computers, and jet planes can rush goods to places around the world in just a few hours. Yet some things are still the same. People still trade goods they have for goods they need or want. And Californians are still making the most of the state's rich natural resources.

A Strong Economy

Today, California leads all other states in **international trade**, or trade with other countries. One reason is the state's location. Most of California's international trade takes place with countries of the Pacific Rim. About one-third of this trade is with Japan.

California also leads the United States in exports. An **export** is a product shipped

Workers in California have jobs in more than 120 different industries.

from one country to be sold in another. California's leading exports are electronic equipment and computers, machinery, scientific tools, and food products.

Many goods that are shipped from other countries to be sold in the United States arrive at California ports. Many products from Japan come to the Port of Los Angeles. These imports include cars, cameras, and clothing made of silk. An **import** is a product brought into one country from another country to be sold. Other imports arrive at San Diego and Long Beach and at ports in the "Bay Area," such as San Francisco, Oakland, Vallejo, and Alameda.

International trade is an important reason that California's economy is strong and growing. If California were a country, it would have the seventh-largest economy in the world!

California's economy is one of the most diverse in the world. Workers have jobs in more than 120 different industries. California leads all the other states in food products, aerospace products, machinery, electronic equipment such as computers, and many other products. In fact, California leads all other states in manufacturing.

California's diverse economy includes both manufacturing industries and service industries. Together these industries help keep the state's economy strong. When one kind of industry is not doing well, other industries often remain strong.

REVIEW What are some reasons for California's strong economy?

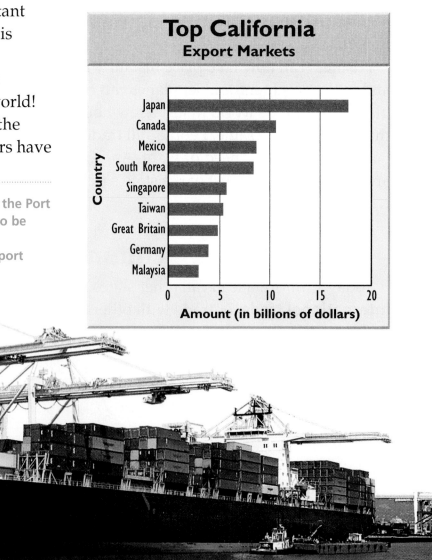

Top California
Export Markets

Country vs. Amount (in billions of dollars)

Country	Amount
Japan	~17.5
Canada	~10.5
Mexico	~8.5
South Korea	~8
Singapore	~5.5
Taiwan	~5
Great Britain	~4.5
Germany	~4
Malaysia	~3

LEARNING FROM GRAPHS This ship at the Port of Oakland is being loaded with goods to be exported.
■ What country is California's largest export market?

PRESIDENT POLK

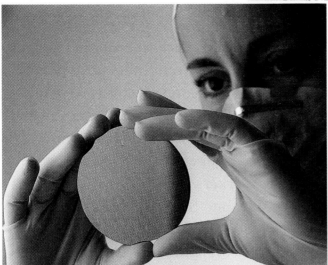

The making of computer chips is an important high-tech business in California.

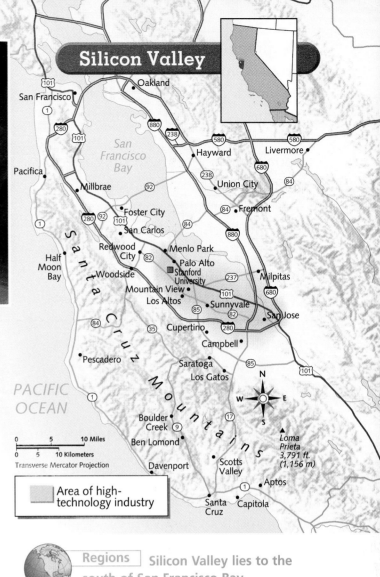

Silicon Valley

Area of high-technology industry

Loma Prieta 3,791 ft. (1,156 m)

0 5 10 Miles
0 5 10 Kilometers
Transverse Mercator Projection

PACIFIC OCEAN

Regions Silicon Valley lies to the south of San Francisco Bay.
■ What mountain range lies to the west of Silicon Valley?

Changing Technologies

High-technology, or "high-tech," businesses now make up one of California's most important industries. **High-tech** businesses are those that invent, build, or use computers or other electronic equipment.

By the 1970s several computer companies had been started in the area between San Jose and Palo Alto. Soon, so many computer companies had joined them that the area was nicknamed Silicon Valley, for the silicon chips computers use.

Stanford University, in Palo Alto, and other, nearby universities trained many of the scientists who made the computer industry possible. These scientists, and others, found ways to make silicon chips smaller and smaller. This allowed computers to be built smaller, faster, and cheaper.

In 1976 a computer company in Los Altos built one of the first personal computers. At first, very few people could afford to own a personal computer. Over time, however, the prices went down and more people bought them. Today nearly four of every ten homes in the United States have a personal computer. Most schools, offices, and libraries also have them.

With computers, people can now connect to the **Internet**, a network that links computers. Through the Internet, people can find information on just about any topic, and they can use electronic mail, or E-mail, to communicate with each other.

Today another center for high-tech businesses is located in southern California. This area, sometimes nicknamed the Tech Coast, includes parts of Orange, San Bernardino, Riverside, Los Angeles, and San Diego counties. It now has more high-tech businesses than Silicon Valley.

High-tech businesses have created hundreds of thousands of jobs in California. They have also helped other industries grow. Silicon chips are now used in everything from stuffed toys to calculators to car engines.

Using computers, moviemakers are able to create amazing special effects in movies and television shows. When Walt Disney first made animated movies, or cartoons, in the 1920s, hundreds of pictures were painted by hand just to make a character take a step. Now most animation is done by computers.

REVIEW How is the Internet useful to people?

Changes in Agriculture

Technology has also brought changes to agriculture. Computers have helped scientists develop new kinds of plants and new ways of farming. Using modern machines, farmers can now harvest larger crops on less land with fewer workers.

Nearly one-third of California's land is used for agriculture, and California produces more farm products than any other state. It also leads all other states in the amount of food exported.

Most farms in California now specialize. That means they grow only one or two crops. For example, most farms in the Napa Valley grow only grapes. Many farms in the Santa Clara Valley grow plums for prunes, while Sylmar is a leading olive-growing region.

Some of California's most important agricultural products are dairy products, grapes, garden plants and other nursery products, beef cattle, cotton, almonds, hay, and lettuce. California is the number one dairy state. It also grows more than half of the nation's fruits, nuts, and vegetables. California produces almost all of the avocados and almonds sold in the United States.

Agriculture creates jobs for many people who do not work on farms. In fact, it creates about 1 of every 10 jobs in the state. **Food processing**, which includes cooking, canning, drying, and freezing foods and preparing them for

Your favorite animated movies and television shows are most likely created on computers.

market, is a big business in California. Taking the food products to markets and selling them are other businesses that provide many jobs.

REVIEW How has technology affected agriculture?

California and the World

Somewhere in Japan a company is putting together a computer. A worker puts in a silicon chip made in California. The computer is then shipped to France, where it is sold to a hospital.

This example shows how international trade links California to the world. California is also connected to the rest of the world in many other ways. For example, movies and television shows made in California are watched by people all over the world.

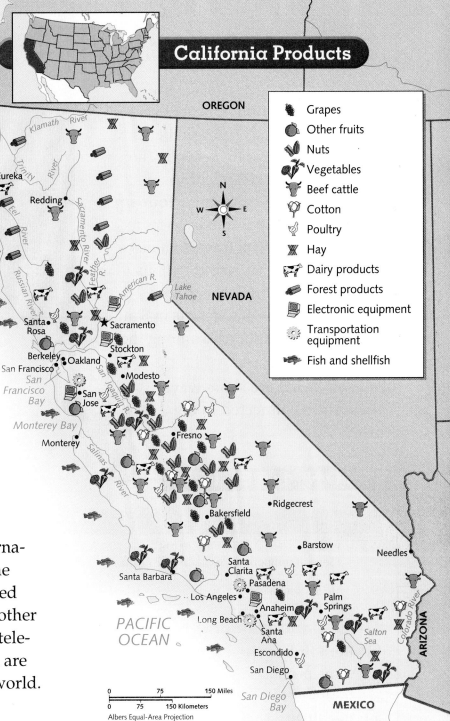

California Products

Legend:
- Grapes
- Other fruits
- Nuts
- Vegetables
- Beef cattle
- Cotton
- Poultry
- Hay
- Dairy products
- Forest products
- Electronic equipment
- Transportation equipment
- Fish and shellfish

0 75 150 Miles
0 75 150 Kilometers
Albers Equal-Area Projection

Human-Environment Interactions
This map shows some of the products of California.

■ What are the main products produced along the Feather River?

The workers in this food processing plant are sorting avocados.

Many tourists visit the San Diego Zoo. The zoo cares for 3,800 animals of 800 different species.

More than 100 million people visit California each year. This number is higher than for any other state in the country. About 600,000 Californians work in the tourism industry. **Tourism** is the selling of goods and services to tourists—people who travel to a place for pleasure. Tourists spend billions of dollars in California every year. They help to make the airports in San Francisco and Los Angeles among the world's busiest.

REVIEW What are some ways California is connected to the world?

LESSON 4 REVIEW

1970	1980	1990	Present

1970s
• Several computer companies are started in Silicon Valley

1976
• One of the first personal computers is built

Present
• California has become the leading state for international trade, manufacturing, agriculture, and tourism

Check Understanding

1 Remember the Facts What are some products made by high-tech businesses?

2 Recall the Main Idea How have California's location and new technologies affected the state's economy?

Think Critically

3 Think More About It How might a diverse economy be important to a state and its workers? to a country and its workers?

4 Link to You How do computers and other high-tech products affect your life or the lives of your family members?

Show What You Know

Research Activity
Choose an industry in California. Find out how that industry is important to California's economy. If your school or library has a computer, use it to gather the information you need. Then share with classmates what you learned.

The Challenge of the Environment

People use natural resources for almost everything they need. At work they use natural resources to make or grow products. By using those resources, however, people cause changes in their environment.

People and the Environment

As more people have moved to California and as industries have grown, more land has been cleared for communities and businesses. More highways, water projects, and power plants have been built. In some places people have filled in wetlands. **Wetlands** are low-lying areas in which the water level is always near or above the surface of the land. Many kinds of wildlife need wetlands to live.

Sometimes people's activities hurt the environment. Most cars, trucks, machines, and factories put some pollution into the air. **Pollution** is anything that makes a natural resource dirty or unsafe to use. Polluted air is unsafe for people to breathe. Polluted water in rivers, lakes, and oceans can kill fish and other animals.

Californians have been working for a long time to protect their environment. John Muir was one of the

FOCUS
What are some things you can do to protect the environment?

Main Idea Read to learn about what some Californians have done to help protect the state's environment.

Vocabulary
wetlands
pollution
conservation
smog
emissions
watershed
recycle

Oil spills in the ocean can harm wildlife and spoil beaches.

John Muir took many of the country's leaders, including President Theodore Roosevelt, on tours of the Yosemite Valley.

early leaders of conservation in the state. **Conservation** is the protection and wise use of natural resources. Muir's advice led the United States Congress to create California's first two national parks, Yosemite and Sequoia, in 1890.

California now has 8 national parks, 18 national forests, and 1 national seashore. It also has almost 100 state parks. Laws protect the land and resources in state and national parks. Because they are protected, these places can remain unspoiled for everyone to enjoy.

REVIEW How was John Muir a leader of conservation in California?

Working for Clean Air

California has more cars and trucks than any other state. They burn gasoline

The National Park System in California

Place | There are eight national parks in California.
■ Which national park is nearest to Palm Springs?

and diesel fuel and send harmful pollution into the air. **Smog**, a layer of dirty, yellow-brown air, sometimes hangs over many California cities.

As early as 1960, California began passing laws to help clean up this air

People in the San Francisco Bay area created BART to help solve their transportation problems.

pollution. Cars must now burn fuel more cleanly. Today, California leads the country in limiting car emissions (ee•MIH•shuhnz). **Emissions** are the chemicals put into the air by cars and factories. Since these laws were passed, the air has slowly become cleaner in some places. But at times smog still hangs over many cities.

The state has also passed a law saying that by the year 2003, one out of every 10 cars sold in California must have "zero emissions." In order to be ready for that time, automobile manufacturers have started to make electric cars. Electric cars do not put any emissions into the air. This new technology will do much to make California's air cleaner.

To help people get around town in fewer cars, many California cities have improved their public transportation systems. San Francisco is part of a system of trains and buses called the Bay Area Rapid Transit, or BART. Many other cities, including Los Angeles, are setting up similar systems to lower the number of cars on their streets.

REVIEW What has California done to help make its air cleaner?

Water Conservation

Think about the many times you use water in a single day. Now imagine the more than 32 million people in California all using water as you do.

Offices, factories, and farms need water, too. California's farms use a lot of water, because nearly all of their crops are grown with irrigation. In fact, California's farms use about four times as much water as homes and industries.

Taking too much water from Mono Lake caused the water levels to drop too low. No more water can be taken until the level rises to a certain point. This is expected to take about 20 years.

To keep up with the growing demand for water, more water projects have been built since World War II. However, these projects continue to create problems for the state's rivers and watersheds. A **watershed** is the region from which a river drains water. When a water project takes water away from a watershed, it leaves the land there drier.

Many kinds of wildlife live in and around lakes and rivers. Dams and aqueducts can harm wildlife by changing the water level in those bodies of water. When a lake's water level drops too low, animals in the lake may die. Dams also stop rivers from flowing freely, and they can prevent fish, such as salmon, from swimming to where they must lay their eggs.

In the future, California will need to balance two goals—growth and conservation. To grow, it will need to provide water and electricity for its people, factories, and farms. At the same time, it will need to find new ways to protect its natural resources.

The energy saved by recycling one aluminum can could run a television set for three hours. Imagine how much energy can be saved from recycling all these cans!

You and other Californians can help conserve water, or use it wisely, by not wasting it or using too much of it. There are many other ways people can help conserve resources and protect the environment. They can **recycle**, or reuse, materials. They can volunteer to clean up rivers and parks. Everyone can help make California a cleaner, more healthful, and more beautiful place to live.

REVIEW How do dams and aqueducts affect lakes and rivers?

LESSON 5 REVIEW

Check Understanding

1 Remember the Facts Why do California's farms use so much water?

2 Recall the Main Idea What have Californians done to help protect the state's environment?

Think Critically

3 Explore Viewpoints What might John Muir think about California's environment today?

4 Link to You What are some things you do in your daily life that affect the environment?

Show What You Know

Art Activity Design a button or a bumper sticker showing a way to conserve a natural resource. Use your button or bumper sticker to explain to classmates how your idea will help conserve that natural resource.

Solve a Problem

1. Why Learn This Skill?

Think about some problems you have faced in the past few weeks. Perhaps you had trouble making good grades in one of your classes at school. Perhaps you had trouble learning how to do something. Or perhaps you had trouble getting along with a brother or sister at home.

People everywhere have problems at some time. Learning how to solve problems is an important skill that you can use now and in the future.

2. Remember What You Have Read

In the last lesson, you read about some of the things Californians have done to help protect the state's environment. Think again about the air pollution the large number of cars and trucks has caused in California and how Californians have worked to solve this problem.

1 California passed laws to help solve this problem. What do these laws do?

2 How are automobile manufacturers helping to solve the problem?

3. Understand the Process

You can follow these steps to help you solve most problems.

- Identify the problem. If it is a big problem, divide it into smaller parts.
- Think of ideas for solving the problem or each part of the problem.
- Compare your ideas. Ask yourself what is good and bad about each. Then choose the best idea.
- Plan how to carry out your idea. Can you do it yourself, or do you need help?
- Follow your plan, and then think about how well it worked. Did it solve the problem? If not, try other ideas until the problem is solved.

4. Think and Apply

Look around your school or your neighborhood. What problems do you see? Which one seems the most important to you? Use the steps listed above to think of ways to solve that problem. Share your ideas with your classmates, and ask them for their ideas.

Scientists are working to develop clean-running cars. This experimental car runs on batteries powered by solar energy.

What Should Be Done

About one hundred years ago, John Muir called Yosemite National Park a shelter from "the roar and dust . . . of the lowlands." Of course, that was before there were cars in the park! Today more than four million visitors a year come to enjoy Yosemite's beauty. Most of them come by car, and their cars, some people say, bring "roar and dust" into the park. There are so many cars in Yosemite Valley in the summer that a drive that should take five minutes can take almost an hour.

The National Park Service has a plan to lower the number of cars in the park. By their plan, visitors would park their cars and travel in the park on shuttle buses, on bicycles, or on foot.

Most people agree that there is a traffic problem in the park, but not everyone agrees on what to do about it. Some people think that no cars at all should be allowed in Yosemite. Other people think that this would mean fewer visitors. People who work in the park and in nearby communities worry that they would lose money if fewer visitors came.

Brian Huse

Brian Huse is the Director of the Pacific Region National Park Trust and Conservation Association. This group of citizens works to protect the country's national parks. He says,

    66 We are approaching [coming to] a time when the private automobile is not the best way to travel within a national park. . . . The private automobile will go the way of the dinosaur at some point. Yosemite should be thinking ahead. 99

About Yosemite?

Jerry Mitchell

Jerry Mitchell works for Yosemite National Park. It is his job to make needed changes in the park. He says,

66 With . . . visitors coming in increasing numbers, the auto now dominates [controls] the experience for many people. [The experience] should be dominated by meadows, rivers, waterfalls, valleys, and the Sierras. 99

Bromwyn Hogan

Bromwyn Hogan works for the Automobile Association of America in San Francisco. This company provides services to car owners. She says,

66 Before actually banning or limiting cars in Yosemite, we would encourage that other alternatives [ways] be sought out [tried]. We would like to see the best alternative for drivers while also keeping the best possible environment for them. 99

Each year, millions of people come to Yosemite National Park to enjoy its beauty. Many of them come by car.

Compare Viewpoints

1. How are the viewpoints of Brian Huse and Jerry Mitchell alike? How are their viewpoints different from that of Bromwyn Hogan?
2. What might all three people agree on?
3. What is your viewpoint on this issue? Give reasons for your answer.

Think and Apply

Suppose it was your job to come up with a plan that Brian Huse, Jerry Mitchell, and Bromwyn Hogan would all agree on. What ideas would you suggest? Who else's viewpoints would be good to know? Why? Share your plan with your class. How is it different from your classmates' plans? How is it the same?

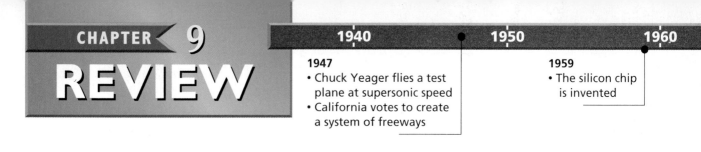

1940   **1950**   **1960**

1947
• Chuck Yeager flies a test plane at supersonic speed
• California votes to create a system of freeways

1959
• The silicon chip is invented

CONNECT MAIN IDEAS

Use this organizer to show that you understand how the chapter's main ideas are connected. Complete it by writing the main idea of each lesson. A copy of the organizer may be found on page 92 of the Activity Book.

California Grows and Changes

Challenges for California

Movements for Equal Rights

Education and Culture

A Modern Economy

The Challenge of the Environment

WRITE MORE ABOUT IT

Write a Want Ad Imagine that you run a company in one of California's industries. You want to hire a person to fill a job. Write a classified advertisement telling what your company does and describing the job.

Write a Persuasive Letter Imagine that you are a member of an equal rights organization. Write a letter to the editor of a newspaper or magazine, giving three reasons people in the community should support your movement.

1970	1980	1990	Present

1965
• César Chávez leads a grape boycott

1970s
• Several computer companies are started in Silicon Valley

Present
• California has become the leading state for international trade, manufacturing, agriculture, and tourism

USE VOCABULARY

For each pair of vocabulary terms, write one or two sentences explaining how the words are related.

1 suburb, metropolitan area

2 segregation, civil rights

3 heritage, festival

4 import, export

5 pollution, emissions

CHECK UNDERSTANDING

6 How did California's economy become more diverse after World War II?

7 What contributed to the growth of suburbs in California?

8 What are some problems that migrant workers in California have faced?

9 Why is it important for California to have educated and informed citizens?

10 How does California's geography give it an advantage in international trade?

11 What are two ways that technology has helped California's economy?

THINK CRITICALLY

12 **Think More About It** Has rapid population growth made life in California better or worse? Explain your answer.

13 **Personally Speaking** What do you think is the greatest challenge California faces today?

APPLY SKILLS

Use a Road Map and a Mileage Table Using a road map of California, describe the route you would take to get from your city or town to the state capital. About how many miles is it to the state capital? If you live in the state capital, describe a route from your city to another city in California, and figure out the mileage.

Understand a Population Map Look at the population map of California on page 383. Imagine that you are advising a restaurant company that is about to open some new branches in California. In which three cities would you tell the company to open its new branches? Why?

Solve a Problem Develop a plan you could follow at home in case of an earthquake. Share your plan with a family member.

READ MORE ABOUT IT

Dia's Story Cloth: The Hmong People's Journey of Freedom by Dia Cha. Lee and Low Books. Told through a Hmong story cloth, this is the story of the author's family.

HARCOURT BRACE

Visit the Internet at
http://www.hbschool.com
for additional resources.

GOVERNMENT IN CALIFORNIA

"With all the profound [important] wording of the Constitution, probably the most meaningful words are the first three: 'We, the People.'"

Ronald Reagan, governor of Calfornia from 1967 to 1975 and President of the United States from 1981 to 1989

State Government

LESSON

1

FOCUS
Why is the work of government often shared by different groups?

Main Idea Read to find out how the work of California's state government is shared.

Vocabulary
legislative branch
budget
executive branch
bill
veto
judicial branch
recall
initiative
petition
referendum

The governor of California, in taking the oath of office, promises "to support the Constitution of the United States and the Constitution of California." Both constitutions list the rights of citizens and describe how the governments should work.

The California Constitution

"All people are by nature free. . . ." These are the first words of the Declaration of Rights, which is found near the beginning of the California Constitution. The Declaration of Rights lists the rights and freedoms of California's citizens. Many are the same as those listed in a part of the United States Constitution called the Bill of Rights. Some of these rights are freedom of speech, freedom of the press, and freedom of religion.

Like the United States Constitution, the California Constitution sets up a government with three branches, or parts. Each of these branches has its own work. One branch makes the laws. Another sees that the laws are obeyed. The third branch judges people accused of breaking the law. It also decides if the laws themselves are fair.

REVIEW What are some freedoms that the California Declaration of Rights lists?

LEARNING FROM SYMBOLS The Great Seal of the State of California shows Minerva, the Roman goddess of wisdom. The wheat and grapes at her feet stand for California's many agricultural products. In the sky is the state's motto, *Eureka*, which means "I have found it."

■ Why do you think a grizzly bear, a gold miner, ships, and 31 stars are also shown on the seal?

The Legislative Branch

The California State Legislature is the legislative (LEH•juhs•lay•tiv) branch of California's state government. The **legislative branch** makes state laws.

The Legislature has two houses, or parts. They are the Senate and the Assembly. The California Senate has 40 members. They are elected to four-year terms and may serve no more than two terms. The California Assembly has 80 members. They are elected to two-year terms and may serve no more than three terms.

The members of the Senate and the Assembly meet at California's State Capitol building in Sacramento. There they pass, or make, new laws to protect the lives, freedoms, and property of the people of California. They also pass tax laws and vote on plans for spending the money the state gets from taxes people pay. A written plan for spending money is called a **budget**.

The money from state taxes is used to pay the costs of running the state government and providing state services. It pays for building and repairing state roads, highways, and ports and for keeping state parks clean and safe. State tax money is spent on public schools and on state colleges and universities. It also helps people who do not earn enough money to pay for their food, shelter, and health care.

REVIEW **What are the two houses of the California State Legislature?**

The Legislature (right) meets in the California State Capitol (below) in Sacramento. The small dome on top of the capitol is covered with California gold.

The Executive Branch

Another branch of the state government is the executive (ig•ZEH•kyuh•tiv) branch. The **executive branch** prepares the state budget. It also makes sure that laws passed by the legislative branch are carried out.

The governor of California is the leader of the state's executive branch. The governor is elected by the state's voters and serves a term of four years. No governor may serve more than two terms.

The governor can suggest **bills**, or plans for new laws, to the Legislature but cannot vote on them. However, all bills passed by the Senate and the Assembly are given to the governor. If the governor agrees to a bill and signs it, the bill becomes a law. If the governor does not sign the bill but does not try to stop it, it will become a law after 12 days.

If the governor does not think a bill is a good one, he or she can veto (VEE•toh) it. To **veto** a bill is to reject it and to

This house in Sacramento was the home of 13 governors. Today it is a state historic park.

try to stop it from becoming law. The Legislature can still pass a bill that has been vetoed by the governor if two-thirds of the members of both the Senate and the Assembly vote to do so.

The governor shares the work of the executive branch with other leaders. Some of them are chosen by the governor. Other leaders, such as the lieutenant (loo•TEN•uhnt) governor, are elected by California voters. The

LEARNING FROM DIAGRAMS No branch of the California state government is more powerful than the others.
■ Why do you think the California state government has three branches?

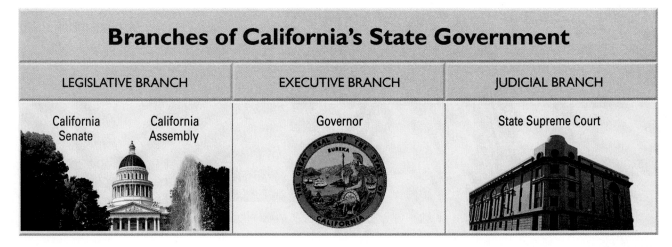

Branches of California's State Government

LEGISLATIVE BRANCH	EXECUTIVE BRANCH	JUDICIAL BRANCH
California Senate California Assembly	Governor	State Supreme Court

lieutenant governor acts as governor if the governor is traveling out of the state or is unable to work.

REVIEW Who is the leader of the executive branch of California's state government?

The Judicial Branch

The third branch of state government is the judicial (juh•DIH•shuhl) branch. The **judicial branch** is made up of courts and judges that hear and decide law cases. The judges make sure that California laws are used fairly and that they agree with the state constitution.

The highest court in California is the state Supreme Court. It decides cases about the California Constitution and the rights and freedoms of California's citizens. Seven judges, called justices, make up the Supreme Court. One of the justices is chosen to be the chief justice, or head judge. New Supreme Court justices are chosen by the governor.

Citizens then vote for or against the governor's choices in an election.

Below the Supreme Court are the state courts of appeal. These courts hear cases asking for changes in decisions made in California's lower courts. Judges study the decisions and decide whether or not they follow the law and are fair.

REVIEW What is the highest court in the state of California?

The Power of the Voters

The legislative, executive, and judicial branches all have important powers. However, there is one more group that has the most power of all—California's voters. California's voters even have some special powers that the voters in most other states do not have.

Voters in all 50 states elect their governors and the members of their state legislatures. But in California and just a few other states, voters can also

Justices of the Supreme Court of California serve 12-year terms.

a new law. A **petition** is a signed request for action. If enough Californians sign the petition, the initiative is voted on in the next election. If more than half of the voters are in favor of the initiative, it becomes a law. Californians can also make changes to the state constitution in this way.

If voters do not like a law that already has been passed by the state government, they can take action against it. They can sign a petition asking that a referendum (reh•fuh•REN•duhm) be held. A **referendum** is an election in which voters can vote to keep or get rid of a law that already exists.

vote to **recall** their officials, or remove them from their jobs.

California voters can also pass initiatives (ih•NIH•shuh•tivz). An **initiative** is a law made directly by voters instead of by a legislature.

The first step in passing a state initiative is for voters to sign a petition (puh•TIH•shuhn) saying that they want

REVIEW What special powers do California voters have?

LESSON I REVIEW

Check Understanding

1 Remember the Facts What are the three branches of the California state government?

2 Recall the Main Idea How is the work of California's state government shared among its three different branches?

Think Critically

3 Link to You Describe three ways in which state tax money is spent in your community. How might the lives of Californians be different without those services?

4 Think More About It Why is it important for California voters to be able to make changes to the laws of their state?

Show What You Know

Simulation Activity With two classmates, role-play a conversation between the governor of California, a member of the California Senate, and the chief justice of the California Supreme Court. Each of you should describe the work you do in the government and explain why your work is important.

Follow a

1. Why Learn This Skill?

Some information is easier to understand when it is explained in a drawing. The drawing on page 413 is a flow chart. A **flow chart** is a drawing that shows the order in which things happen. The arrows on a flow chart help you read the steps in the correct order.

2. Understand the Process

The flow chart on page 413 shows you how the California state government makes new laws. The top box of the flow chart shows the first step in passing a law. In this step a member of the Assembly or the Senate writes a bill. A bill may begin in either house of California's legislative branch.

In the second step the bill is sent to a special committee. The committee is a small group of members of the Assembly or the Senate. The committee members study the bill and tell the rest of the Assembly or the Senate whether they think the bill would make a good law. If the committee likes the bill, what happens next? To find out, read the next step in the flow chart.

Antonio Villaraigosa, Speaker of the California Assembly, discusses a bill with Assembly members Joe Baca and Carl Washington.

Read the remaining steps. What happens after both the Assembly and the Senate approve the bill? How can the bill become a law if the governor vetoes it?

3. Think and Apply

Work with a partner to make a flow chart that explains to younger students how something works. Write each step on a strip of paper. Then paste the strips in order onto a sheet of posterboard, and connect the steps with arrows. Give your flow chart a title, and use it with a group of younger students.

Flow Chart

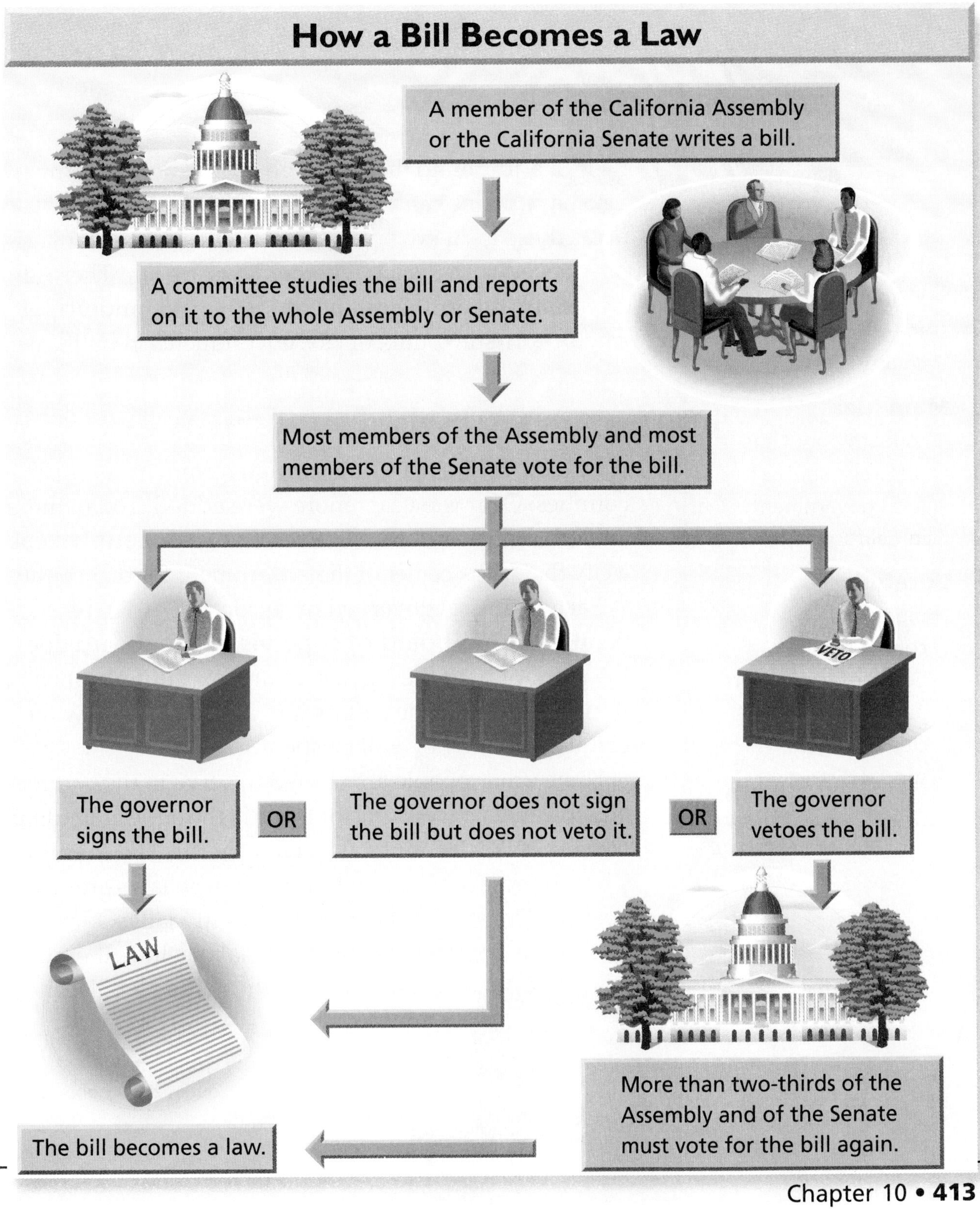

How a Bill Becomes a Law

A member of the California Assembly or the California Senate writes a bill.

A committee studies the bill and reports on it to the whole Assembly or Senate.

Most members of the Assembly and most members of the Senate vote for the bill.

The governor signs the bill.

OR

The governor does not sign the bill but does not veto it.

OR

The governor vetoes the bill.

LAW

The bill becomes a law.

More than two-thirds of the Assembly and of the Senate must vote for the bill again.

FOCUS
Who makes the laws for your city and county?

Main Idea Read to learn about the different kinds of local government in California.

Vocabulary
municipal
county seat
board of supervisors
jury trial
city manager
special district

Local Government in California

In addition to their state government, Californians also have county and city governments. In their own areas these local governments make laws, see that laws are obeyed, and decide whether laws are fair. There are 58 county governments and more than 450 **municipal** (myuh•NIH•suh•puhl), or city, governments in California.

County Governments

In 1850 California's first state government set up 27 counties. Over the years more were added. Today there are 58 counties in the state. Each one has a **county seat**, a city that is the center of the government for that county.

Each county is governed by an elected group of people called a **board of supervisors**. The board does the work of both the legislative and executive branches. It makes laws for the county and also decides how the county's tax money will be spent.

Some other people are elected to serve in the county government as well. One of these is the superintendent of schools. Each county also has a sheriff. The sheriff's job is to protect people and to make sure laws are obeyed. The sheriff also runs the county jails. Other elected county officials include the treasurer, who pays the county's bills, and

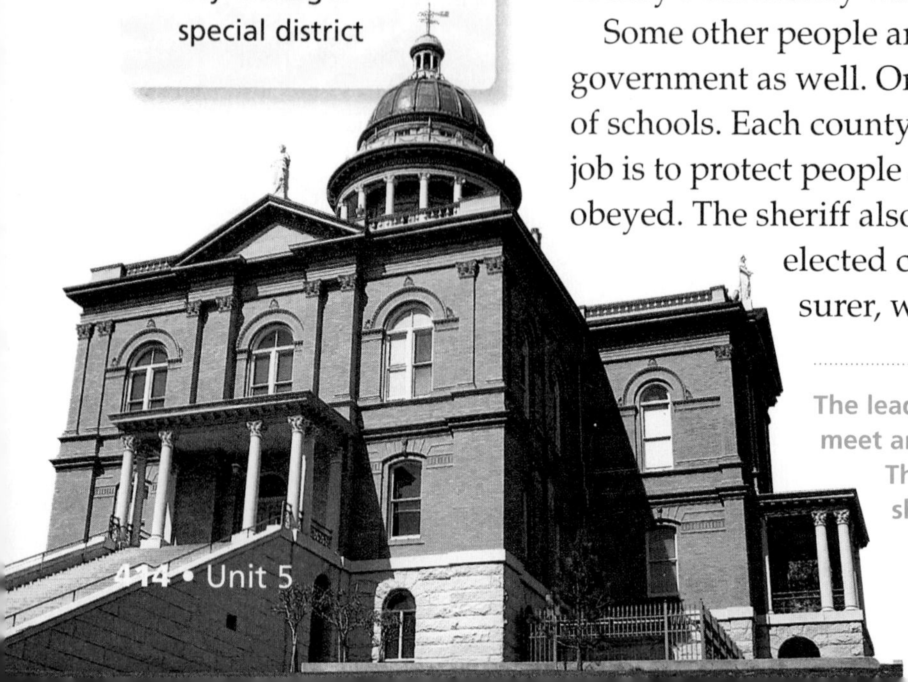

The leaders of a county government usually meet and work at the county courthouse. The Placer County courthouse is shown here.

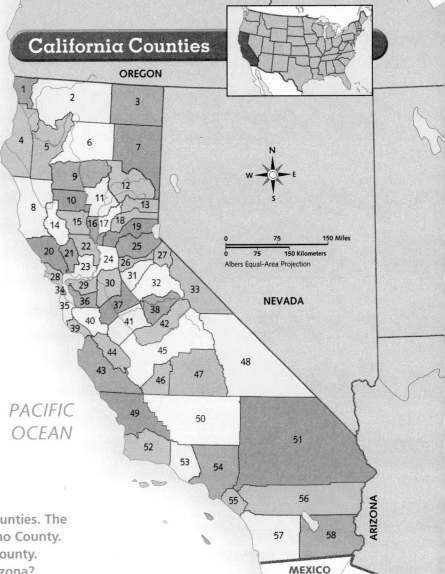

California Counties

Alameda	36	Orange	55
Alpine	27	Placer	19
Amador	26	Plumas	12
Butte	11	Riverside	56
Calaveras	31	Sacramento	24
Colusa	15	San Benito	44
Contra Costa	29	San Bernardino	51
Del Norte	1	San Diego	57
El Dorado	25	San Francisco	34
Fresno	45	San Joaquin	30
Glenn	10	San Luis Obispo	49
Humboldt	4	San Mateo	35
Imperial	58	Santa Barbara	52
Inyo	48	Santa Clara	40
Kern	50	Santa Cruz	39
Kings	46	Shasta	6
Lake	14	Sierra	13
Lassen	7	Siskiyou	2
Los Angeles	54	Solano	23
Madera	42	Sonoma	20
Marin	28	Stanislaus	37
Mariposa	38	Sutter	16
Mendocino	8	Tehama	9
Merced	41	Trinity	5
Modoc	3	Tulare	47
Mono	33	Tuolumne	32
Monterey	43	Ventura	53
Napa	21	Yolo	22
Nevada	18	Yuba	17

Regions California has 58 counties. The largest in area is San Bernardino County. The smallest is San Francisco County.
■ Which counties border the state of Arizona?

the district attorney. The district attorney is a lawyer who speaks for the county in court.

Counties also have a judicial branch of government. Each county in California has a superior court. Its judges are elected by the county's voters.

Jury trials are often held in superior courts. In a **jury trial** a group of citizens decides whether a person accused of a crime or other wrongdoing should be found guilty or not guilty.

REVIEW What group is elected to run the county government?

Municipal Governments

About nine out of every ten people in California live in cities. Each city has a municipal government that passes laws, makes sure the laws are obeyed, and decides some law cases. Municipal governments also provide people who live in cities with services such as fire and police protection, libraries, and parks.

Different cities have different forms of municipal government. Most of the state's largest cities have a mayor-council

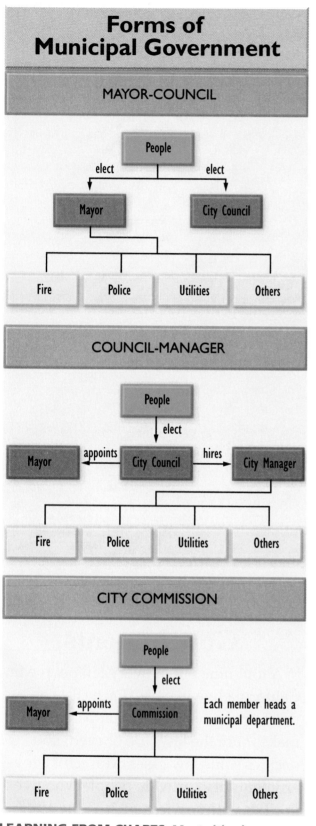

Forms of Municipal Government

MAYOR-COUNCIL

People

elect → Mayor
elect → City Council

Mayor → Fire | Police | Utilities | Others

COUNCIL-MANAGER

People

elect → City Council

Mayor ← appoints — City Council — hires → City Manager

City Manager → Fire | Police | Utilities | Others

CITY COMMISSION

People

elect → Commission

Mayor ← appoints — Commission

Each member heads a municipal department.

Commission → Fire | Police | Utilities | Others

LEARNING FROM CHARTS Most cities in California use one of three forms of municipal government.

■ In which form of municipal government do the people elect both a mayor and a city council?

form. Voters in these cities elect both a mayor and a city council. The city council is the legislative branch. It makes laws for the city and collects taxes. The mayor is the leader of the executive branch. It is the mayor's job to make sure that city laws are carried out. The mayor often hires people to run the different departments of the municipal government, such as the police department and the fire department.

Other cities have a council-manager form of municipal government. In these cities voters elect a city council to make the laws, but they do not elect a mayor to run the city. Instead, the city council

Municipal governments provide services such as police and fire protection for citizens.

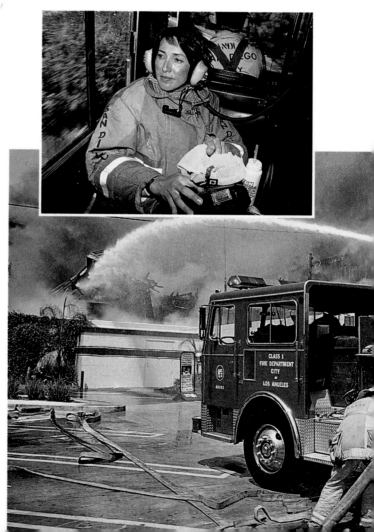

hires a **city manager**, who runs the city the way the city council wants. The city manager then hires workers for the different departments of the municipal government. The city council also appoints one of its members to be mayor. The mayor represents the city on special occasions.

A third form of municipal government that some California cities have is the commission. In these cities voters elect a city commission to run the city. Each commissioner, or member of the city commission, is in charge of a different department of the municipal government.

The judicial branch of most cities is the municipal court. In smaller cities it is the justice court. These courts decide the cases of people who are accused of breaking traffic laws and other city laws.

REVIEW What are the three forms of municipal government used in California cities?

The mayor listens to speakers at this city council meeting in Laguna Niguel (luh•GOO•nuh nee•GEL).

Special Districts

California also has special districts. A **special district** is an area in which a certain problem, such as flooding, needs to be solved, or a certain service, such as libraries, needs to be provided.

A special district may be smaller than a city, or it may be made up of a number of cities or even counties. Sometimes different governments work together to run a special district.

California has special districts to work on many different problems. There are water districts, irrigation districts, and flood-control districts. There are also districts for fire prevention and for air pollution control.

One kind of special district that most students know about is a school district. Voters in a school district elect a school board to make decisions about running the district's schools. There are more than 1,000 school districts in California.

California's county governments, municipal governments, and special districts make sure the needs of every community are met. From providing books for the school library to keeping the streets safe and clean, local governments work for all the citizens of California.

REVIEW What is a special district?

School districts are just one type of special district in California. In which school district do you live? What other special districts do you live in?

LESSON 2 REVIEW

Check Understanding

1 Remember the Facts How is a city manager different from a mayor? How are their jobs alike?

2 Recall the Main Idea What are the different kinds of local government in California?

Think Critically

3 Link to You How do decisions made by local governments affect you and your family? your school? your neighborhood?

4 Think More About It What are some problems in California that might be solved by forming special districts?

Show What You Know

Art Activity Draw a chart that shows the form of municipal government used in your city or in the city closest to where you live. Explain the main job of each group or official, and find out the names of the present officials. Share your chart with classmates.

Make Economic Choices

1. Why Learn This Skill?

Whenever you buy a new T-shirt or decide what to order at a restaurant, you are making an economic choice. Some economic choices are hard to make. To buy one thing, you may have to give up the chance to buy something else. Giving up one thing to get another is called a **trade-off**. What you give up is called the **opportunity cost** of what you get. Knowing about trade-offs and opportunity costs can help you make thoughtful economic choices.

2. Remember What You Have Read

Like people, governments have to make many economic choices. It costs money for state and local governments to provide services such as fire protection, libraries, and parks. They pay for these services with tax money they get from citizens. Often, however, governments do not get enough money to pay for everything that people would like to have done.

3. Understand the Process

Imagine that you are the mayor of a city in California. You have to make an economic choice. Should the municipal government pay to build a bike path, or should it use the money for a basketball court in the park?

1 **Think about the trade-offs.** Building a bike path would make it safer for people to ride their bicycles away from traffic. The trade-off is that it would not leave enough money to build a basketball court. Building a basketball court would give people a place to play. What would be the trade-off of this choice?

2 **Think about the opportunity costs.** Your town government does not have enough money to pay for both projects, so you will have to give up one. Which choice should you make? What is the opportunity cost of your choice?

Because you usually cannot have everything you want, you will often face opportunity costs as you trade off one product or service for another. This does not mean that the product or service you give up has no value. It means that at the time, another product or service has more value to you.

4. Think and Apply

Imagine that you have $5 to spend. You want to buy a book. But you also want to rent a movie. You do not have enough money for both. Explain to a partner the trade-offs and the opportunity costs of your choices.

FOCUS

Why is it important to have good leaders in government?

Main Idea Read to learn about some national leaders from California.

Vocabulary

federal government

Three Californians have lived in the White House as President of the United States.

Californians and the National Government

Threaking the national government, also called the **federal government**, is divided into three branches. Like the California state government, it has an executive branch, a legislative branch, and a judicial branch. The executive branch is led by the President and the Vice President. The legislative branch is made up of the two houses of Congress—the Senate and the House of Representatives. The judicial branch is made up of the United States Supreme Court and the federal court system. Californians have served, and still serve, in all three branches of the federal government.

Presidents from California

Three Californians have served as President of the United States. They are Herbert Hoover, Richard Nixon, and Ronald Reagan. Of the three, only Richard Nixon was born in California. The other two were living in California when they became President.

Herbert Hoover founded the Hoover Institution on War, Revolution and Peace in 1919 as a place where people could study the causes and effects of World War I.

Herbert Hoover was born in Iowa in 1874 but came to California as a young man to study engineering at Stanford University, in Palo Alto. He worked in the federal government for several years before being elected President in 1928.

The Great Depression began while Hoover was President. Many people blamed him for not doing more to stop it, and he was not elected to a second term.

Hoover spent much of his life trying to find ways to improve the lives of people around the world. The Hoover Institution on War, Revolution and Peace, which Hoover founded at Stanford University, is a place where people today can go to study free enterprise. It is also a place where people talk about ways countries can work together for peace.

Richard Nixon was born in Yorba Linda in 1913 and went to California's Whittier College. After serving in the navy during World War II, he returned to Whittier to practice law. In 1946 Nixon was elected to the United States Congress. He was elected Vice President in 1952. Then, in 1968, he was elected President of the United States. He was elected to a second term in 1972.

As President, Nixon worked to improve the United States' relations with Russia and China. He visited both countries to work for peace.

At home Nixon faced protests against the Vietnam War, a war that the United States was fighting in southeast Asia. During his second term, Nixon agreed to a plan to end the fighting and to bring American soldiers home from Vietnam.

Richard Nixon was born in this house in Yorba Linda. Today it is part of the Richard Nixon Library and Birthplace.

421

Ronald Reagan and his wife, Nancy, returned to California after his presidency. Today people visit the Ronald Reagan Presidential Library in Simi Valley.

California, where he became a movie actor.

Reagan later became active in politics. In 1966 he was elected as California's governor and served two terms. In 1980 he was elected President of the United States. Four years later he was elected to a second term.

Reagan believed that the federal government was too large and had too much power. As President he worked with Congress to lower the amount of taxes Americans had to pay. At the same time, however, the government spent more money.

REVIEW Which three Californians have served as President of the United States?

Nixon's second term ended after he was accused of trying to cover up, or hide, crimes done by people who worked for him. In 1974 Nixon resigned, becoming the only President to leave office before his term was over.

Ronald Reagan was born in Illinois in 1911. After graduating from college in Illinois, Reagan became a radio sports announcer in Iowa. He later moved to

Other California Leaders

California has also sent leaders to the legislative and judicial branches of the federal government. Each state sends two people to serve in the United States Senate.

Senators Barbara Boxer (far left) and Dianne Feinstein (left) were elected in 1992. Earl Warren (below) served as California's governor from 1943 to 1953 before he became chief justice of the United States Supreme Court.

The number of people a state sends to the United States House of Representatives depends on the state's population. California sends 52, the largest number of any state, because it has the largest population.

In 1992 the voters of California elected Barbara Boxer and Dianne Feinstein to the United States Senate. That was the first time any state had elected two women as senators.

Californians have also been chosen to serve on the United States Supreme Court. Perhaps the best known of these was Earl Warren. Warren was the chief justice of the Supreme Court from 1953 to 1969. As chief justice, Warren wrote an important decision that ended the segregation of African American children in public schools. Today, another Californian, Anthony Kennedy, serves on the Supreme Court.

REVIEW Which Californian served as a chief justice of the United States Supreme Court?

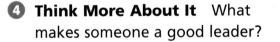

LESSON 3 REVIEW

Check Understanding

1 **Remember the Facts** Which President of the United States was born in California?

2 **Recall the Main Idea** Who are some national leaders from California?

Think Critically

3 **Link to You** Who represents your community in the United States House of Representatives?

4 **Think More About It** What makes someone a good leader?

Show What You Know

Writing Activity Imagine that you are running for election to Congress. Write a short speech to tell voters why they should vote for you. Be sure to describe the things you will do to help California's people. Read your speech to your classmates.

FOCUS

What does it mean
to be a citizen?

Main Idea Read
to find out about
the rights and
responsibilities
of citizens of the
United States and
of California.

Vocabulary

responsibility
naturalized citizen
register
democracy
volunteer

Californians are citizens
both of the United States
and of California.

California Citizenship

Since 1850, when California became a state, Californians have been citizens of both the United States and the state of California. Citizens have certain rights that people who are not citizens of their state or country do not have. At the same time, citizens also have responsibilities. A **responsibility** is a duty—something that a person should do.

Becoming a Citizen

The United States Constitution says that "all persons born or naturalized in the United States . . . are citizens of the United States and of the State wherein they reside [live]."

People who are born in this country are citizens of the United States. A **naturalized citizen** is an immigrant who has become a citizen by taking the steps described in the law. When adults become naturalized citizens of the United States, their children under 18 years of age become citizens as well.

When an immigrant has lived in the United States for at least five years (or three years if he or she is married to a United States citizen), that person can follow three steps to become a naturalized citizen. First, he or she must ask a judge in writing to become a citizen. Second, the person must pass a test to show that he or she understands United States history and how the United States government works. Third, the person must take part in a ceremony in which he or she promises to be loyal to the United States.

REVIEW **How can immigrants become citizens of the United States?**

Citizenship Day

In 1940 the United States Congress decided that a day should be set aside to honor the country's new citizens. At first, this day was called I Am an American Day. Then, in 1952, that name was changed to Citizenship Day. September 17 was chosen as Citizenship Day because it was the date on which the United States Constitution was signed in 1787. Citizenship Day honors all citizens—those born in the United States and those who have become naturalized citizens.

These people are about to become citizens of the United States. Why do you think they want to become citizens?

The Rights of Citizens

Citizens of California have the rights listed in the constitutions of both the United States and California. Citizens have the right to vote and the right to hold public office. They have the right to travel through their home state and all of the United States. Citizens have freedom of speech, freedom of the press, freedom of religion, and freedom to gather in groups.

Governments cannot take away a citizen's constitutional rights unless that person has been found guilty of serious crimes. However, governments can place certain limits on a citizen's rights.

For example, a citizen must be at least 18 years old to vote. State governments can say that a citizen must **register**, or sign up, before he or she can vote.

REGISTER HERE

★ ★ ★ ★

VOTER REGISTRAR

California has about 14 million registered voters.

People who are not citizens have many of the same rights as citizens. However, they cannot vote, hold public office, or be members of trial juries.

REVIEW Where are the rights of California citizens listed?

The Responsibilities of Citizens

With rights come responsibilities. With the right to vote, for example, comes the responsibility to vote. The United States is a democracy (dih•MAH•kruh•see). A **democracy** is a form of government in which the people rule by making decisions themselves or by electing leaders to make decisions for them. In a democracy every person's opinion is important, so voting is an important responsibility of citizenship. With freedom of speech and freedom of the press comes the responsibility to be an informed citizen—someone who understands the problems California and the United States are facing.

Some responsibilities are stated in laws. The laws of the United States and of California state that it is a citizen's responsibility to pay taxes, obey laws, and be loyal.

Some people also take on responsibilities that help make their communities better places to live. **Volunteers** (vah•luhn•TIRZ), or people who work without pay, help out in places such as hospitals and schools. A group called San Francisco School Volunteers provides about 2,700 volunteers to the city's schools. Volunteers help students with their studies or take students on tours of their workplaces. They read to younger students and help out in the library. One of the volunteers says that "every child has the right to a good education. And every member of our community has a role to play in the schools."

There are many other ways to volunteer in the community. Cleaning up a park or beach or helping an elderly neighbor are only two of the many ways to show responsibility as a citizen.

Freedom of the press is one of the most important rights of citizens of the United States and of California. Why do you think this right is important in a democracy?

Sharing responsibilities can help bring people together. Californians often help one another in time of need. They also work together to solve problems. By sharing their ideas they find the best ways to solve the challenges our state faces.

REVIEW What are some responsibilities that citizens have?

These volunteers are painting a neighborhood wall and helping to build a low-cost home for people who need it.

LESSON 4 REVIEW

Check Understanding

1 **Remember the Facts** At what age can citizens vote in the United States?

2 **Recall the Main Idea** What are some of the rights and responsibilities of citizens of the United States and of California?

Think Critically

3 **Think More About It** Why do you think people need to be responsible citizens?

4 **Link to You** What are some ways in which you could volunteer in your community?

Show What You Know

Poster Activity Make a poster showing ways Californians can act as responsible citizens today. You might find or draw pictures of people who are showing responsibility as citizens. Explain your poster to classmates, and display it in the classroom.

Make a Thoughtful

1. Why Learn This Skill?

Think of a time when you made a bad decision. Perhaps you said or did something and later wished you had not. Maybe you hurt someone's feelings.

The decisions you make can have good or bad consequences (KAHN•suh•kwen•suhz). A **consequence** is what happens because of an action. If you decide to go swimming in a safe place, you will get some good exercise and have fun. However, if you swim in an unsafe place, you could get hurt or become ill. To make thoughtful decisions, you need to think about the consequences before you act.

2. Remember What You Have Read

In this chapter you read about the San Francisco School Volunteers. Their goal is to see that every child in their community gets a good education. To help reach that goal, about 2,700 people decided to volunteer their time to help students. Think about their decision to volunteer and the consequences they must have thought about.

1 If they did not volunteer, what would the consequences be?

2 What would the consequences be if they did volunteer?

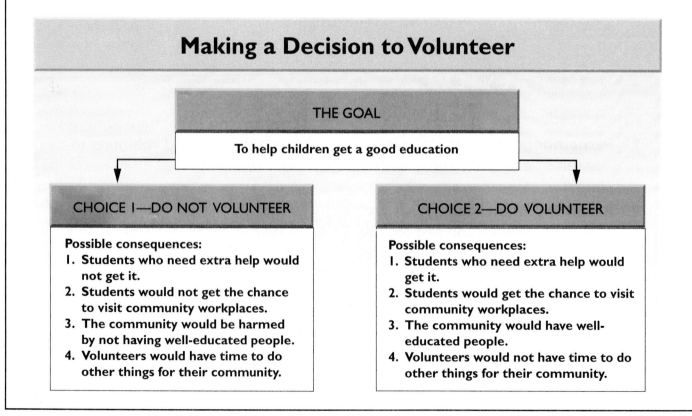

Making a Decision to Volunteer

THE GOAL

To help children get a good education

CHOICE 1—DO NOT VOLUNTEER

Possible consequences:
1. **Students who need extra help would not get it.**
2. **Students would not get the chance to visit community workplaces.**
3. **The community would be harmed by not having well-educated people.**
4. **Volunteers would have time to do other things for their community.**

CHOICE 2—DO VOLUNTEER

Possible consequences:
1. **Students who need extra help would get it.**
2. **Students would get the chance to visit community workplaces.**
3. **The community would have well-educated people.**
4. **Volunteers would not have time to do other things for their community.**

Decision

3. Understand the Process

Here are some steps you can use to help you make wise decisions.

- Identify a goal.
- Make a list of choices that might help you reach your goal.
- Think about the possible good and bad consequences of each choice.
- Decide which choice you think will have the best consequences.

- Think about your choice. Could it have bad consequences you have not thought of? If so, you may need to make a different choice.
- Make the best choice and follow it.

4. Think and Apply

What were the consequences of a decision that you made recently? Do you think your decision was a thoughtful one? Explain.

These adults have made the decision to volunteer their time to help students.

CONNECT MAIN IDEAS

Use this organizer to show that you understand government in California. Complete it by listing the parts of each level of government and by describing the special powers of California's voters. A copy of the organizer may be found on page 100 of the Activity Book.

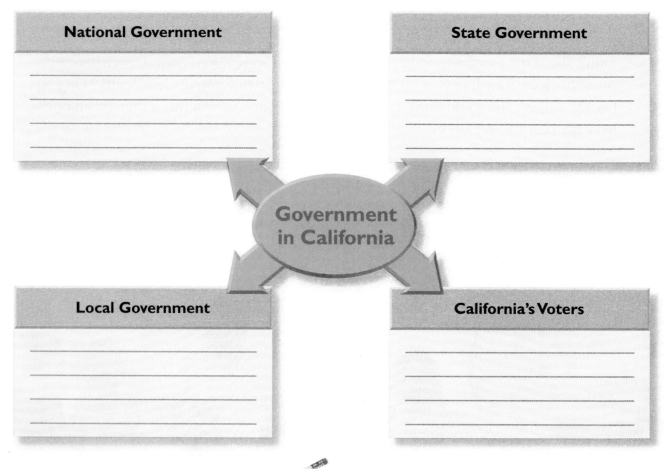

National Government

State Government

Government in California

Local Government

California's Voters

WRITE MORE ABOUT IT

Write a Comparison Choose two current leaders at different levels of government. Write a paragraph about each person that describes what he or she does. Then write a third paragraph that compares the responsibilities of the two leaders.

Write a Journal Entry Imagine that you have just become a naturalized citizen. Write a journal entry that describes the steps you went through and how you feel about being a citizen. Share your entry with a classmate.

USE VOCABULARY

Write the word or phrase that completes each of the sentences that follow.

democracy   legislative branch

executive branch   referendum

1 The _____ of California's state government makes laws.

2 The governor is the head of the _____ of state government.

3 An election in which voters can vote to keep or get rid of a law that already exists is a _____.

4 In a _____, the people elect leaders to make decisions for them.

CHECK UNDERSTANDING

5 How does California's Declaration of Rights help protect the rights of the state's citizens?

6 Which branch of the California state government prepares the state budget?

7 What are three special powers that California's voters have that voters in most other states do not have?

8 How are the jobs of mayor, governor, and United States President alike?

9 What are three rights that citizens of California have?

THINK CRITICALLY

10 **Think More About It** How is the California Constitution similar to the United States Constitution?

11 **Think More About It** Why do you think it is important for citizens to have both rights and responsibilities?

APPLY SKILLS

Follow a Flow Chart Think about something you do often. List the steps you follow when performing the task. Then make a flow chart, placing the steps in order.

Make Economic Choices Imagine that you must choose between buying a video game or buying a new pair of soccer shoes. How would you go about making this economic choice? What would be the trade-offs and the opportunity costs?

Make a Thoughtful Decision Imagine that you have been asked to play in an important ball game that will take place at the same time as a going-away party for a friend. What steps would you follow to make a thoughtful decision about what to do?

READ MORE ABOUT IT

Our Constitution by Linda Carlson Johnson. Millbrook. This book tells about the United States Constitution and the ideas it contains.

HARCOURT BRACE

Visit the Internet at **http://www.hbschool.com** for additional resources.

California Citizens in Action

Every Tuesday after lunch about 25 students from Millikan Middle School in Sherman Oaks walk one block to Riverside Drive Elementary School. For four hours they take part in a special program called Project Success. As trained volunteers, they help the students and teachers of Riverside Drive Elementary.

To become volunteers, the middle schoolers first fill out a form telling why they want to join the program. If they are chosen, they complete a six-week training period. During this time the volunteers learn how to help students and their teachers in the classroom. They also learn computer and office skills.

The Millikan volunteers tutor, or help teach, the Riverside Drive students in reading and math. They also help them with library research and art projects. Some volunteers even help teachers grade papers.

Bryanna is one of the volunteers. "I like to help other kids at the school I went to in fifth grade," she says. "I think it's very important that kids can be whatever they [want] to be."

Project Success was started by Linda McManus, co-president of the Millikan Parent Teacher Association and director of the kindergarten program at Riverside. "When the kids learn to volunteer, it's so magical," she says. "They will find out about education, about living, about life."

Project Success volunteers are really making a difference in the lives of the children and teachers they help each week. Ivy Sher, a third-grade teacher, says, "I look forward to when the helpers come to the room. My experience of the teens is that they have pride in their work and a great sense of responsibility."

Think and Apply

What groups work to help people in your community? In a small group, discuss why it is important for people to volunteer their time to help with community projects. Then list some volunteer activities you think could help make your school or community a better place. Share your group's ideas with your classmates.

HARCOURT BRACE

Visit the Internet at **http://www.hbschool.com** for additional resources.

CNN
Turner
Le@rning

Check your media center or classroom video library for the Making Social Studies Relevant videotape of this feature.

After receiving instructions from a teacher, these student volunteers help younger students at Riverside Drive Elementary School with a science project.

UNIT 5 REVIEW

Summarize the Main Ideas
Study the pictures and captions to help you review the events you read about in Unit 5.

Write About an Event
Choose the event from the visual summary that you think has had the greatest effect on your life today. Write a paragraph to explain your choice.

1 During and after World War II, manufacturing industries in California grew. As more people came for jobs, cities grew and freeways were built.

4 California has one of the most diverse economies in the world. International trade, manufacturing, high-tech businesses, agriculture, and tourism keep the state's economy strong.

5 Californians are working to conserve resources and protect the environment.

3 Many groups of people live in California, and all add to California's culture. Though their cultures may be different, Californians share many things.

2 In the 1960s and 1970s many groups of Californians worked for equal rights.

6 The state government of California has three branches—the executive, the legislative, and the judicial.

 7 Citizens of the United States and of California have both rights and responsibilities.

USE VOCABULARY

Write the term that correctly matches each definition.

boycott	recycle	segregation
heritage	register	veto

1. the keeping of people of one race or culture separate from other people

2. a form of protest in which a group decides not to buy a certain thing

3. a way of life, custom, or belief from the past that continues today

4. to reuse materials

5. to try to stop a bill from becoming law

6. to sign up to vote

CHECK UNDERSTANDING

7. Why did California become a leader in the aerospace industry?

8. What are high-tech businesses, and how have they affected California's economy?

9. What are the three branches of California's state government?

10. What does it mean to be a "naturalized citizen"?

THINK CRITICALLY

11. **Cause and Effect** California's population has grown greatly since World War II. How has this affected the state?

12. **Link to You** What can you do to make California a better place in which to live?

APPLY SKILLS

Use a Road Map and a Mileage Table Use the map and the mileage table to answer these questions.

13. Describe the route you would follow to travel from Oakland to Sacramento.

14. How many miles is it from Sacramento to San Jose? Did you use the map or the mileage table to find the answer?

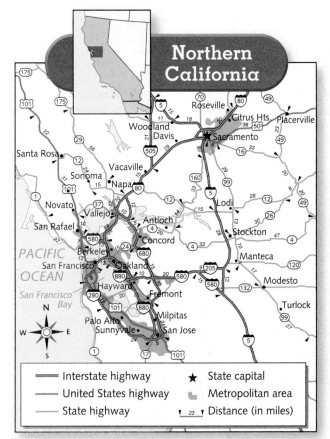

Northern California

Legend:
— Interstate highway
— United States highway
— State highway
★ State capital
■ Metropolitan area
▼ 23 ▼ Distance (in miles)

California Mileage Table

	Sacramento	San Francisco	San Jose
Sacramento		87	115
San Francisco	87		43
San Jose	115	43	

REMEMBER

- Share your ideas.
- Cooperate with others to plan your work.
- Take responsibility for your work.
- Help one another.
- Show your group's work to the class.
- Discuss what you learned by working together.

ACTIVITY

Make a Conservation Book

To show people how they can help the environment, make a conservation book. Explain how people change or pollute the environment, and give ideas for ways they can conserve natural resources. To illustrate your book, draw pictures or cut photographs from magazines and newspapers. Give your book a title, and display it where others in your school can read it.

ACTIVITY

Perform a Simulation

Work with classmates to plan a skit in which the characters are members of the California state government. There should be at least one character from each branch—for example, a state senator, the governor, and a justice of the state Supreme Court. Write a scene in which the characters talk about their jobs in state government and discuss their views of a bill that is about to become a law. Make name tags that list the government branch and job title for each character.

Unit Project Wrap-Up

Hold a Class Fair Working with a partner or a small group, choose a topic to highlight in a display at a class fair that celebrates California. Use your textbook, books from the library, and the Internet to find out more about your topic. Make your display, and decide with your classmates how the displays will be presented. You may want to invite another class to your fair.

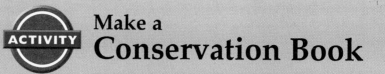

For Your Reference

Contents

The Japanese Tea Garden (above left) is part of Golden Gate Park in San Francisco. Hearst Castle (far left), the estate of millionaire newspaper publisher William Randolph Hearst, is now a state historical monument. Much of California's coastline (left) has a rocky, rugged look.

How to Gather and Report Information

To write a report, make a poster, or do many other projects in your social studies class, you may need information that is not in your textbook. You can gather this information from reference books, electronic references, or community resources.

HOW TO USE REFERENCE TOOLS

Reference works are collections of facts. They include books and electronic resources, such as almanacs, atlases, dictionaries, and encyclopedias. Books in libraries are organized through a system of numbers. Every book in a library has its own number, called a call number. The call number on the book tells where in the library the book can

All libraries have a reference section.

be found. In a library a reference book has *R* or *REF*—for *reference*—on its spine along with the call number. Most reference books are for use only in the library. Many libraries also have electronic reference materials on CD-ROM and on the Internet.

▶ WHEN TO USE AN ENCYCLOPEDIA

An encyclopedia is a good place to begin to look for information. An encyclopedia has articles on nearly every subject. The articles are arranged in alphabetical order by subject. Each article gives basic facts about people, places, and events. Some electronic encyclopedias allow you to hear music and speeches and to see short movies about the subject.

▶ WHEN TO USE A DICTIONARY

A dictionary gives information about words. Dictionaries explain the meanings of words and show how the words are pronounced. Some dictionaries also include the origins of words, and lists of foreign words, abbreviations, well-known people, and place names.

▶ WHEN TO USE AN ATLAS

You can find information about places in an atlas. An atlas is a book of maps. Some atlases have road maps. Others have maps of countries around the world. Some atlas maps show where certain crops are grown and where certain products are made. Others show the populations of different places. Ask a librarian to help you find the kind of atlas you need.

You can learn many things about the place where you live by looking at an atlas.

▶ WHEN TO USE AN ALMANAC

An almanac is a book or an electronic resource containing facts and figures. It often shows information in tables and charts.

The subjects in an almanac are grouped in broad categories, not in alphabetical order. To find a certain subject, you need to use the index, which lists the subjects in alphabetical order. Most almanacs are brought up to date every year. So an almanac can give you the latest information on a subject.

► HOW TO FIND NONFICTION BOOKS

Unlike fiction books, which tell stories that are made up, nonfiction books give facts about real people, places, and events. In a library all nonfiction books are placed in order on the shelves according to their call numbers.

You can find a book's call number by using a card file or a computer catalog. To find this number, you need to know the book's title, author, or subject. Below and on the next page are some entries for a book about the gold rush.

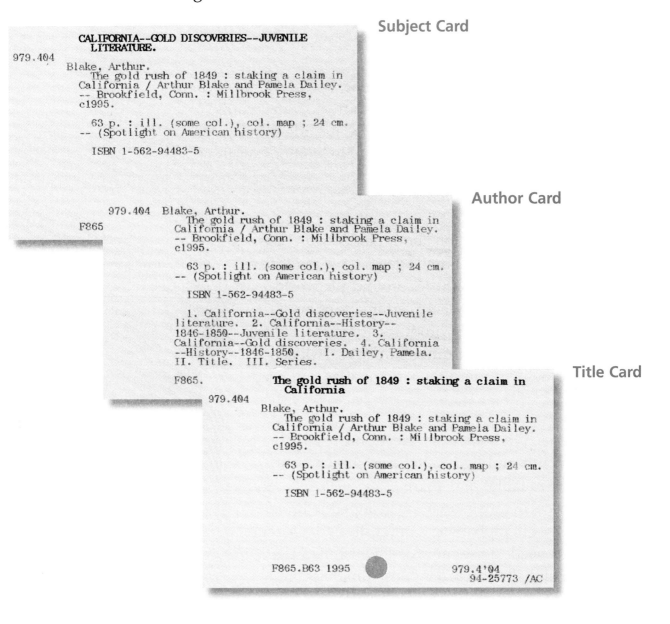

Subject Card

979.404

CALIFORNIA--GOLD DISCOVERIES--JUVENILE
LITERATURE.

Blake, Arthur.
The gold rush of 1849 : staking a claim in
California / Arthur Blake and Pamela Dailey.
-- Brookfield, Conn. : Millbrook Press,
c1995.

63 p. : ill. (some col.), col. map ; 24 cm.
-- (Spotlight on American history)

ISBN 1-562-94483-5

Author Card

979.404   Blake, Arthur.
The gold rush of 1849 : staking a claim in
F865   California / Arthur Blake and Pamela Dailey.
-- Brookfield, Conn. : Millbrook Press,
c1995.

63 p. : ill. (some col.), col. map ; 24 cm.
-- (Spotlight on American history)

ISBN 1-562-94483-5

1. California--Gold discoveries--Juvenile
literature. 2. California--History--
1846-1850--Juvenile literature. 3.
California--Gold discoveries. 4. California
--History--1846-1850. I. Dailey, Pamela.
II. Title. III. Series.

Title Card

F865.   **The gold rush of 1849 : staking a claim in
California**
979.404
Blake, Arthur.
The gold rush of 1849 : staking a claim in
California / Arthur Blake and Pamela Dailey.
-- Brookfield, Conn. : Millbrook Press,
c1995.

63 p. : ill. (some col.), col. map ; 24 cm.
-- (Spotlight on American history)

ISBN 1-562-94483-5

F865.B63 1995   979.4'04
94-25773 /AC

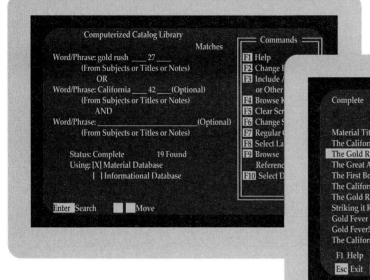

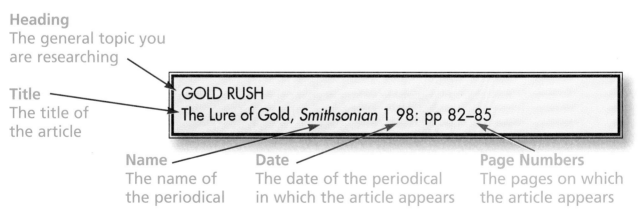

▶ HOW TO FIND PERIODICALS

Libraries have special sections for periodicals—newspapers and magazines. A periodical, which is usually published every day, week, or month, is a good source for the most up-to-date information and for topics not yet covered in books.

Most libraries have an index that lists magazine articles by subject. The most widely used indexes are the *Children's Magazine Guide* and the *Readers' Guide to Periodical Literature*. The entries in these guides are in alphabetical order by subject and author, and sometimes by title. Abbreviations may be used for many parts of an entry, such as the name of the magazine and the date of the issue. Here is a sample entry for an article about the gold rush.

Heading
The general topic you are researching

Title
The title of the article

GOLD RUSH
The Lure of Gold, *Smithsonian* 1 98: pp 82–85

Name
The name of the periodical

Date
The date of the periodical in which the article appears

Page Numbers
The pages on which the article appears

HOW TO FIND INTERNET RESOURCES

The World Wide Web, part of the Internet, is a rich resource for information. You can use the World Wide Web to read documents, see photographs and artworks, and examine other primary sources. You can also use it to listen to music, read electronic books, take a "tour" of a museum, or get the latest news.

Information on the World Wide Web changes all the time. What you find today may not be there tomorrow, and new information is always being added. Much of the information you find may be useful, but remember that some of it may not be accurate.

▶ PLAN YOUR SEARCH

1. Make a list of your research questions.
2. Think about possible sources for finding your answers.
3. Identify key words to describe your research topic.
4. Consider synonyms and variations of those terms.
5. Decide exactly how you will go about finding what you need.

▶ SEARCH BY SUBJECT

To search for topics, or subjects, choose a search engine. You can get a list of available search engines by clicking the SEARCH or NET SEARCH button at the top of your screen.

If you want to find all the Web sites for baseball, for example, enter "baseball" in the search engine field. Then click SEARCH or GO on the screen. You will see a list of sites all over the World Wide Web having to do with baseball. Because not all search engines list the same sites, you may need to use more than one search engine.

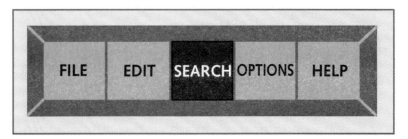

► SEARCH BY USING ADDRESSES

Each site on the World Wide Web has an address called a Uniform Resource Locator, or URL for short. A typical URL is shown in the box below.

To find URL listings, look in manuals, books, newspapers, magazines, and television and radio credits. To use a URL to go to a Web site, type the URL in the LOCATION/GO TO or NETSITE box in the upper left corner of the screen.

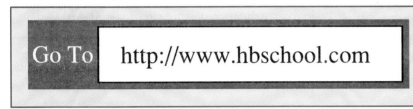

Go To   http://www.hbschool.com

► BOOKMARK YOUR RESOURCES

Once you have found a site that you think will be helpful, you can bookmark it. Bookmarking makes a copy of a URL and stores it so you can easily go back to the site later.

While you are at the site you want to bookmark, click BOOKMARKS at the top of your screen and choose ADD BOOKMARK. Your list of bookmarks might look like this:

You can find information on any subject on the World Wide Web.

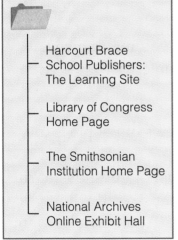

Harcourt Brace School Publishers: The Learning Site

Library of Congress Home Page

The Smithsonian Institution Home Page

National Archives Online Exhibit Hall

Conducting interviews is a good way to get primary source information.

HOW TO CONDUCT AN INTERVIEW

Conducting interviews, or asking people questions, is a good way to get facts and points of view on a topic.

▶ PLANNING AN INTERVIEW

1. Make a list of people to interview.
2. Ask each person for an interview. Identify yourself, and let the person know what you want to talk about.
3. Ask the person you will interview to set a time and place to meet.

▶ BEFORE THE INTERVIEW

1. Read more about your topic. That way you will be better able to talk to the person.
2. Make a list of questions to ask.

▶ DURING THE INTERVIEW

1. Listen carefully. Do not interrupt the person.
2. Take notes as you talk with the person, and write down the person's exact words.
3. If you want to use a tape recorder, first ask the person if you may do so.

▶ AFTER THE INTERVIEW

1. Before you leave, thank the person you interviewed.
2. Follow up by writing a thank-you note.

HOW TO CONDUCT A SURVEY

A good way to learn about the views of people is to conduct a survey.

1. Identify your topic, and make a list of questions. Write the questions so that they can be answered with "yes" or "no" or with "for" or "against." You may also want to give a "no opinion" or "not sure" choice.
2. Make a tally sheet for recording the responses.
3. Decide how many people you will ask and where you will conduct your survey.
4. During the survey, carefully record each person's responses on the tally sheet.
5. Count the responses and write a summary statement.

This survey has information about computer use.

Computer Survey		
Questions	Yes	No
1. Do you know how to use a computer?	III	II
2. Do you enjoy working on the computer?	III	II
3. Do you have a computer at home?	II	III
4. Do you use the computer when you do your homework?	I	IIII
5. Do you think that the computer is a helpful tool?	HHt	

HOW TO WRITE FOR INFORMATION

You can write to ask for information about a certain topic. When you write, be sure to do these things:

- Write neatly or use a computer.
- Say who you are and why you are writing.
- Make your request specific and reasonable.
- Provide a self-addressed, stamped envelope for the answer.

HOW TO WRITE A REPORT

You may be asked to write a report on the information you have gathered. Knowing how to write a report will help you make good use of the information. Follow these steps when writing a report.

▶ GATHER AND ORGANIZE YOUR INFORMATION

- Gather information about your topic from reference books, electronic references, or community resources.
- Take notes as you find information for your report.
- Review your notes to make sure you have all the information you need.
- Organize your information in an outline.
- Make sure the information is in the right order.

▶ DRAFT YOUR REPORT

- Review your information. Decide if you need more.
- Write a draft of your report. On paper, present your ideas in a clear and interesting way.

▶ REVISE

- Check to make sure that you have followed the order of your outline. Move sentences that seem out of place.
- Add any information that you feel is needed.
- Add quotations to show people's exact words.
- Reword sentences if too many follow the same pattern.

▶ PROOFREAD AND PUBLISH

- Check for errors.
- Make sure nothing has been left out.
- Make a clean copy of your report.

Knowing how to write a report is an important skill you will need to know in school.

Almanac
FACTS ABOUT CALIFORNIA

Did You Know?

The world's tallest tree currently standing is located in California's Mendocino County. The 367-foot (113-m) redwood is about as tall as a 37-story building, and the tree is still growing!

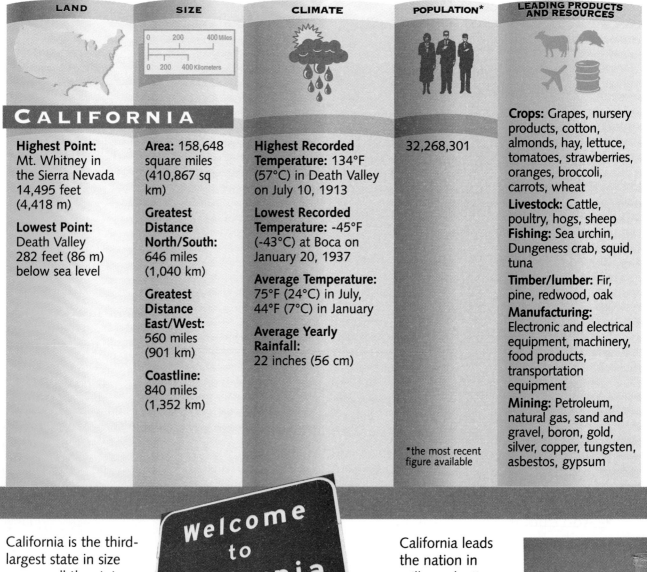

LAND	SIZE	CLIMATE	POPULATION*	LEADING PRODUCTS AND RESOURCES

CALIFORNIA

Highest Point: Mt. Whitney in the Sierra Nevada 14,495 feet (4,418 m)	**Area:** 158,648 square miles (410,867 sq km)	**Highest Recorded Temperature:** 134°F (57°C) in Death Valley on July 10, 1913	32,268,301	**Crops:** Grapes, nursery products, cotton, almonds, hay, lettuce, tomatoes, strawberries, oranges, broccoli, carrots, wheat
Lowest Point: Death Valley 282 feet (86 m) below sea level	**Greatest Distance North/South:** 646 miles (1,040 km)	**Lowest Recorded Temperature:** -45°F (-43°C) at Boca on January 20, 1937		**Livestock:** Cattle, poultry, hogs, sheep **Fishing:** Sea urchin, Dungeness crab, squid, tuna
	Greatest Distance East/West: 560 miles (901 km)	**Average Temperature:** 75°F (24°C) in July, 44°F (7°C) in January		**Timber/lumber:** Fir, pine, redwood, oak **Manufacturing:** Electronic and electrical equipment, machinery, food products, transportation equipment
	Coastline: 840 miles (1,352 km)	**Average Yearly Rainfall:** 22 inches (56 cm)	*the most recent figure available	**Mining:** Petroleum, natural gas, sand and gravel, boron, gold, silver, copper, tungsten, asbestos, gypsum

California is the third-largest state in size among all the states. Only Alaska and Texas are larger.

California has more people than any other state. In fact, one of every eight people in the United States live in California.

California leads the nation in milk production, producing more than one-sixth of the nation's milk.

The United States

Legend:
- ⊛ National capital
- ★ State capital
- National border
- State border

RUSSIA
ARCTIC OCEAN
ALASKA
CANADA
Juneau ★
0 200 400 Miles
0 400 Kilometers
PACIFIC OCEAN

CANADA

Olympia ★
WA
★ Salem
OR
★ Helena
MT
ID
★ Boise
ND
★ Bismarck
MN
St. Paul ★
Lake Superior
Lake Michigan
Lake Huron
WI
Madison ★
MI
Lansing ★
Lake Ontario
Lake Erie
NH   ME
★ Augusta
Montpelier ★   Concord
NY   VT   ★ Boston
Albany ★   MA
Hartford ★   Providence
RI
CT

WY
Cheyenne ★
SD
★ Pierre
IA
Des Moines ★

Carson City ★
Sacramento ★
NV
Salt Lake City ★
UT
Denver ★
CO
NE
Lincoln ★
IL
Springfield ★
IN
Indianapolis ★
Columbus ★
OH
Harrisburg ★
PA
NJ
Trenton ★
MD
★ Dover
DE
Annapolis ★
Washington, D.C. ⊛
WV
Charleston ★

CA
AZ
Phoenix ★
Santa Fe ★
NM
Topeka ★
KS
MO
Jefferson City ★
KY
Frankfort ★
VA
Richmond ★
Raleigh ★
NC

Oklahoma City ★
OK
AR
Little Rock ★
TN
Nashville ★
Columbia ★
SC

TX
Austin ★
MS
Jackson ★
AL
Montgomery ★
GA
Atlanta ★
LA
Baton Rouge ★
Tallahassee ★

PACIFIC OCEAN

HAWAII
Honolulu ★
0 100 Miles
0 100 Kilometers
PACIFIC OCEAN

MEXICO

FL

Gulf of Mexico

ATLANTIC OCEAN

N E S W

0 200 400 Miles
0 200 400 Kilometers
Albers Equal-Area Projection

CUBA

Los Angeles, with a population of more than 3,500,000, is the largest city in California and the second-largest city in the United States, after New York City. It is a leading financial, cultural, and distribution center. It ranks as the largest manufacturing center in the country and is the center of the country's movie industry.

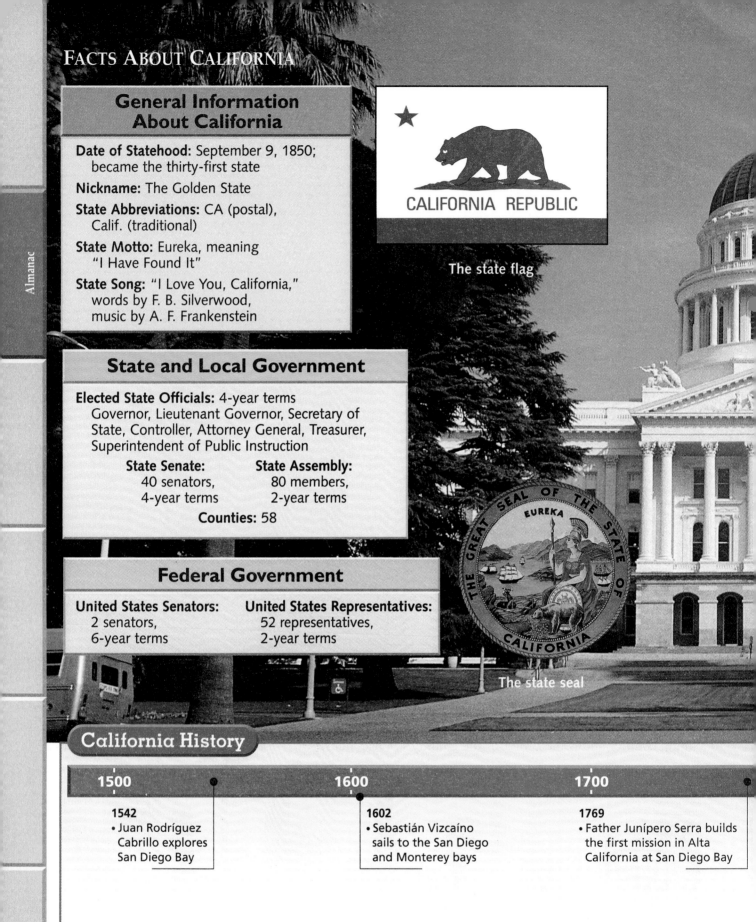

General Information About California

Date of Statehood: September 9, 1850; became the thirty-first state

Nickname: The Golden State

State Abbreviations: CA (postal), Calif. (traditional)

State Motto: Eureka, meaning "I Have Found It"

State Song: "I Love You, California," words by F. B. Silverwood, music by A. F. Frankenstein

CALIFORNIA REPUBLIC

The state flag

State and Local Government

Elected State Officials: 4-year terms
Governor, Lieutenant Governor, Secretary of State, Controller, Attorney General, Treasurer, Superintendent of Public Instruction

State Senate:	State Assembly:
40 senators, 4-year terms	80 members, 2-year terms

Counties: 58

Federal Government

United States Senators:	United States Representatives:
2 senators, 6-year terms	52 representatives, 2-year terms

The state seal

California History

1500	1600	1700
1542 • Juan Rodríguez Cabrillo explores San Diego Bay	**1602** • Sebastián Vizcaíno sails to the San Diego and Monterey bays	**1769** • Father Junípero Serra builds the first mission in Alta California at San Diego Bay

Almanac

Sacramento has been the state capital since 1854. The capitol building was completed in 1874 and is topped by a dome that reaches 237 feet (72 m) above the ground.

A Growing Population

Line graph: Number of People (in millions) on vertical axis (0, 7, 14, 21, 28, 35); Year on horizontal axis (1850, 1880, 1910, 1940, 1970, 2000).

California's Population

Population Density:
198 people per square mile

Population Distribution:
93 percent urban, 7 percent rural

Some State Symbols

State Animal ....Grizzly bear
State Bird......................................California valley quail
State Colors..Blue and gold
State Dance ....West Coast Swing Dancing
State Fish ....Golden trout
State Flower...Golden poppy
State Folk Dance ....Square dance
State Fossil ....Saber-tooth cat
State Gemstone...Benitoite
State Insect.....................California dogface butterfly
State Marine Fish ....Golden orange fish
State Marine Mammal................California gray whale
State Mineral..Gold
State Reptile...Desert tortoise
State Rock ....Serpentine
State Soil...San Joaquin soil
State Tree ....California redwood

The Ten Largest Cities in California

CITY	POPULATION*
Los Angeles	3,681,700
San Diego	1,197,100
San Jose	873,300
San Francisco	778,100
Long Beach	441,700
Fresno	406,900
Sacramento	388,700
Oakland	388,100
Santa Ana	307,000
Anaheim	295,500

*the most recent figures available

1800 — **1900** — **Present**

1821
• California becomes part of the new country of Mexico

1848
• Gold is discovered in California
• California becomes a territory of the United States

1850
• California becomes a state

1906
• An earthquake and fire destroy much of San Francisco

1964
• California has more people than any other state

FACTS ABOUT CALIFORNIA COUNTIES

County Name	County Seat	Population*	Year Organized	Named For
Alameda	Oakland	1,398,500	1853	"grove of trees" in Spanish
Alpine	Markleeville	1,200	1864	the mountainous Sierra Nevada
Amador	Jackson	33,450	1854	José María Amador, settler
Butte	Oroville	198,500	1850	Sutter Buttes or the Butte River
Calaveras	San Andreas	37,950	1850	"skulls" in Spanish
Colusa	Colusa	18,600	1850	a village of the Patwin Indians
Contra Costa	Martinez	896,200	1850	"opposite coast" in Spanish
Del Norte	Crescent City	28,400	1857	"of the north" in Spanish
El Dorado	Placerville	147,400	1850	"the gilded" or "the golden" in Spanish
Fresno	Fresno	778,700	1856	"ash tree" in Spanish
Glenn	Willows	26,900	1891	Hugh J. Glenn, physician and wheat grower
Humboldt	Eureka	126,100	1853	Friedrich Heinrich Alexander von Humboldt, German naturalist
Imperial	El Centro	142,700	1907	Imperial Land Company
Inyo	Independence	18,300	1866	Indian word for "where the great spirit dwells"
Kern	Bakersfield	634,400	1866	Edward M. Kern, topographer and artist
Kings	Hanford	117,700	1893	Kings River
Lake	Lakeport	55,100	1861	Clear Lake
Lassen	Susanville	33,850	1864	Peter Lassen, pioneer
Los Angeles	Los Angeles	9,524,600	1850	"the angels" in Spanish
Madera	Madera	113,500	1893	"lumber" in Spanish

The population figures are the most recent estimates.

Almanac

County Name	County Seat	Population*	Year Organized	Named For
Marin	San Rafael	243,300	1850	Marin, a mythical Indian leader, or "mariner" in Spanish
Mariposa	Mariposa	19,950	1850	"butterfly" in Spanish
Mendocino	Ukiah	86,000	1850	Antonio de Mendoza or Lorenzo Suarez de Mendoza, viceroys of New Spain
Merced	Merced	202,000	1855	Merced River, merced meaning "mercy" in Spanish
Modoc	Alturas	10,150	1874	Modoc Indian tribe
Mono	Bridgeport	10,500	1861	tribe of the Shoshone Indians
Monterey	Salinas	377,800	1850	Count of Monterey, a viceroy of New Spain, or Monterey Bay
Napa	Napa	121,200	1850	Wappo or Pomo Indian word, possibly meaning "village" or "fish"
Nevada	Nevada City	88,400	1851	Sierra Nevada, nevada meaning "snow-covered" in Spanish
Orange	Santa Ana	2,705,300	1889	the fruit
Placer	Auburn	215,600	1851	surface gold deposits
Plumas	Quincy	20,450	1854	"feathers" in Spanish, for the Feather River
Riverside	Riverside	1,423,700	1893	location near river
Sacramento	Sacramento	1,146,800	1850	Holy Sacrament
San Benito	Hollister	46,150	1874	St. Benedict
San Bernardino	San Bernardino	1,617,300	1853	St. Bernard of Siena
San Diego	San Diego	2,763,400	1850	St. Didacus
San Francisco	San Francisco	777,400	1850	St. Francis of Assisi
San Joaquin	Stockton	542,200	1850	St. Joachim

*The population figures are the most recent estimates.

County Name	County Seat	Population*	Year Organized	Named For
San Luis Obispo	San Luis Obispo	234,700	1850	St. Louis of Toulouse
San Mateo	Redwood City	711,700	1856	St. Matthew
Santa Barbara	Santa Barbara	400,800	1850	St. Barbara
Santa Clara	San Jose	1,671,400	1850	St. Clare of Assisi
Santa Cruz	Santa Cruz	247,200	1850	"holy cross" in Spanish
Shasta	Redding	163,300	1850	Shasta Indian tribe
Sierra	Downieville	3,370	1852	Sierra Nevada, *sierra* meaning "mountain range" in Spanish
Siskiyou	Yreka	44,300	1852	"bobtailed horse" in Cree or "six boulders" in French
Solano	Fairfield	378,600	1850	Chief Solano or St. Francis Solano
Sonoma	Santa Rosa	432,800	1850	Chief Tsonoma or Wintu Indian word, possibly meaning "nose"
Stanislaus	Modesto	425,400	1854	Chief Estanislao
Sutter	Yuba City	76,100	1850	John Augustus Sutter
Tehama	Red Bluff	54,700	1856	Indian word, possibly for "lowlands" or "shallow"
Trinity	Weaverville	13,250	1850	Trinity River
Tulare	Visalia	358,300	1852	"rush" or "reed" in Spanish, possibly from "cattail" in Aztec
Tuolumne	Sonora	52,200	1850	Indian word for "cluster of stone wigwams"
Ventura	Ventura	727,200	1873	St. Bonaventure
Yolo	Woodland	154,900	1850	Yolo Indian tribe, possibly meaning "place abounding in rushes"
Yuba	Marysville	61,200	1850	Maidu Indian village or tribal name

The population figures are the most recent estimates.

FACTS ABOUT THE GOVERNORS OF THE STATE OF CALIFORNIA

Governor	Birth/Death	Place of Birth	Political Party	Term
Peter H. Burnett	(1807–1895)	Nashville, Tennessee	Independent Democratic	1849–1851
John McDougal	(1818–1866)	Ohio	Democratic	1851–1852
John Bigler	(1804–1871)	Carlisle, Pennsylvania	Democratic	1852–1856
John Neely Johnson	(1828?–1872)	Indiana	American (Know-Nothing)	1856–1858
John B. Weller	(1812–1875)	Montgomery, Ohio	Democratic	1858–1860
Milton S. Latham	(1827–1882)	Columbus, Ohio	Democratic	1860
John G. Downey	(1826–1894)	Ireland	Democratic	1860–1862
Leland Stanford	(1824–1893)	Watervliet, New York	Republican	1862–1863
Frederick F. Low	(1820–1894)	Frankfort, Maine	Union	1863–1867
Henry H. Haight	(1825–1878)	Rochester, New York	Democratic	1867–1871
Newton Booth	(1825–1892)	Salem, Indiana	Republican	1871–1875
Romualdo Pacheco	(1831–1899)	Santa Barbara, California	Republican	1875
William Irwin	(1827–1886)	Butler County, Ohio	Democratic	1875–1880
George C. Perkins	(1839–1923)	Kennebunkport, Maine	Republican	1880–1883
George Stoneman	(1822–1894)	Busti, New York	Democratic	1883–1887
Washington Bartlett	(1824–1887)	Savannah, Georgia	Democratic	1887
Robert W. Waterman	(1826–1891)	Fairfield, New York	Republican	1887–1891
Henry H. Markham	(1841–1923)	Wilmington, New York	Republican	1891–1895
James H. Budd	(1853–1908)	Janesville, Wisconsin	Democratic	1895–1899
Henry T. Gage	(1852–1924)	Geneva, New York	Republican	1899–1903
George C. Pardee	(1857–1941)	San Francisco, California	Republican	1903–1907
James N. Gillett	(1860–1937)	Viroqua, Wisconsin	Republican	1907–1911
Hiram W. Johnson	(1866–1945)	Sacramento, California	Republican	1911–1917
William D. Stephens	(1859–1944)	Eaton, Ohio	Republican	1917–1923
Friend William Richardson	(1869–1943)	Washtenau County, Michigan	Republican	1923–1927
Clement C. Young	(1869–1947)	Lisbon, New Hampshire	Republican	1927–1931
James Rolph, Jr.	(1869–1934)	San Francisco, California	Republican	1931–1934
Frank F. Merriam	(1865–1955)	Hopkinton, Iowa	Republican	1934–1939
Culbert L. Olson	(1876–1962)	Fillmore, Utah	Democratic	1939–1943
Earl Warren	(1891–1974)	Los Angeles, California	Republican	1943–1953
Goodwin J. Knight	(1896–1970)	Provo, Utah	Republican	1953–1959
Edmund G. Brown	(1905–1996)	San Francisco, California	Democratic	1959–1967
Ronald W. Reagan	(1911–)	Tampico, Illinois	Republican	1967–1975
Edmund G. Brown, Jr.	(1938–)	San Francisco, California	Democratic	1975–1983
George Deukmejian	(1928–)	Albany, New York	Republican	1983–1991
Pete Wilson	(1932–)	Lake Forest, Illinois	Republican	1991–1999
Gray Davis	(1942–)	New York City, New York	Democratic	1999–

Some Famous People in California History

This list gives facts about the famous people in California history whom you met in this book. The page number tells where you can read about each person. Also listed are some other famous Californians you might like to know about.

A

Abdul-Jabbar, Kareem *1947–* Basketball star for the University of California at Los Angeles and the Los Angeles Lakers.

Adams, Ansel *1902–1984* Photographer known for his photographs of the West, including the Sierra Nevada. p. 66

Allensworth, Allen *1842–1914* One of the founders of Allensworth, a town settled by African Americans. p. 308

Angelou, Maya *1928–* African American poet, author, and actress; she lived in San Francisco as a teenager.

Anza, Juan Bautista de (AHN•sah, HWAN bow•TEES•tah day) *1735–1788?* Spanish soldier who led settlers to Alta California in 1774 on a new overland route. p. 147

Argüello y Moraga, María de la Concepción Marcela (ar•GWAY•yoh) *1791–1857* California's first native-born nun. She was the daughter of the commander of the presidio at Yerba Buena. p. 126

B

Baca, Judith (BAH•kah) *1946–* Artist who created a mural titled *The Great Wall of Los Angeles* in the 1970s and 1980s. p. 386

Bartleson, John Along with John Bidwell, a leader of the Bidwell-Bartleson expedition. In 1841 this became the first group of American settlers to cross overland into California. p. 208

Beckwourth, James *1798–1867* Trailblazer and trader; he made several overland trips to California in the 1830s and 1840s. Beckwourth Pass is named for him. p. 202

Bidwell, John *1819–1900* Along with John Bartleson, a leader of the Bidwell-Bartleson expedition. In 1841 this became the first group of American settlers to cross overland into California. p. 208

Billy, Susan Pomo basket maker. p. 98

Bono, Sonny *1935–1998* Singer and songwriter who was elected mayor of Palm Springs and later to the United States House of Representatives.

Boxer, Barbara *1940–* United States senator from California; she was elected in 1992. pp. 379, 423

Bradley, Thomas *1917–1998* First African American mayor of Los Angeles; he served from 1973 to 1993. p. 377

Braithwaite-Burke, Yvonne W. *1932–* First African American woman in the California State Assembly, in 1966, and the first African American woman from California in the United States House of Representatives, in 1972. p. 379

Brannan, Samuel *1819–1889* Business person from San Francisco who was the first to announce the discovery of gold in California, in 1848. p. 229

Briones de Miranda, Juana (bree•OH•nays day meer•AHN•dah) *1802?–1889* Owner of Rancho La Purísima Concepción, near San Jose, during the period of Mexican rule. p. 174

Brown, Edmund G. *1905–1996* Governor of California from 1959 to 1967. p. R17

Brown, Edmund G., Jr. *1938–* Governor of California from 1975 to 1983. p. R17

Brown, Willie *1934–* Elected mayor of San Francisco in 1995. He was speaker of the California State Assembly from 1980 to 1995.

Burbank, Luther *1849–1926* Scientist who mixed seeds from different kinds of plants to create new and better kinds of plants. The city of Burbank is named for him. p. 300

Burnett, Peter H. *1807–1895* First governor of California, from 1849 to 1851. pp. 246, R17

Butterfield, John *1801–1869* Founder of the first regular mail service between California and the East. p. 276

C

Cabrillo, Juan Rodríguez (kah•BREE•yoh) *?– 1543* Spanish explorer; he reached San Diego Bay in 1542. p. 133

Carlos III *1716–1788* Spanish king who ordered the settlement of Alta California in the 1760s. p. 142

Carson, Kit *1809–1868* Trailblazer who led John C. Frémont to California. Carson Pass in the Sierra Nevada is named for him. p. 210

Chaffey, George *1848–1932* Engineer of irrigation systems in southern California in the late 1800s and early 1900s. pp. 298, 321

Chaplin, Charlie *1889–1977* Star of many early Hollywood movies; he was known for his comic roles. p. 334

Chávez, César (CHAH•vez, SAY•zar) *1927–1993* Labor leader and organizer of the United Farm Workers. p. 378

Chew, Ng Poon (CHEE•oh, N POON) *1866–1931* Chinese immigrant who established the first Chinese-language daily newspaper in California. p. 306

Chilton, Kevin *1954–* Astronaut from Los Angeles. p. 371

Columbus, Christopher *1451–1506* Italian explorer; he claimed North America for Spain in 1492. p. 131

Cortés, Hernando (kawr•TEZ) *1485–1547* Spanish conquistador; he conquered the Aztecs and claimed Baja California for Spain. pp. 130, 131

Crespi, Juan (KRAYS•pee) *1721–1782* Spanish missionary and explorer; he traveled to California in the late 1760s and early 1770s. p. 144

Crocker, Charles *1822–1888* Member of the "Big Four" who ran the Central Pacific and Southern Pacific railroads in the middle to late 1800s. pp. 282, 288

D

Dana, Richard Henry *1815–1882* Author who wrote about his voyage to California in *Two Years Before the Mast*. p. 180

Davis, Gray *1942–* Elected governor of California in 1998. p. R17

Deukmejian, George (dook•MAY•jee•ihn) *1928–* Governor of California from 1983 to 1991. p. R17

DiMaggio, Joe *1914–1999* Professional baseball player from Martinez; he played for the New York Yankees.

Disney, Walt *1901–1966* Creator of animated movies and popular children's characters and builder of Disneyland in Anaheim in 1955. p. 394

Doheny, Edward (duh•HEE•nee) *1856–1935* Discoverer of oil in Los Angeles in 1893. p. 315

Donner, Eliza *1843–1922* Daughter of George Donner; she traveled with the Donner party to California and later wrote about the journey. p. 212

Donner, George *1784–1847* Leader of an expedition that traveled from Missouri to California in 1846, which became known as the Donner party. p. 211

Doolittle, James *1896–1993* General in the United States Army and Congressional Medal of Honor winner; born in Alameda. p. 349

Douglas, Donald *1892–1981* Founder of an aviation company in Los Angeles in 1920. p. 333

Drake, Francis *1543?–1596* First English explorer to reach the Pacific coast of the Americas and to reach present-day California. p. 134

Durant, Thomas C. *1820–1885* Vice president of the Union Pacific Railroad. p. 288

E

Eastwood, Clint *1930–* Movie actor and director; he served as mayor of Carmel from 1986 to 1988.

Echeandía, José María (eh•chay•ahn•DEE•ah) First governor of California under Mexican rule from 1824 to 1831. p. 201

Eu, March Fong *1927–* First Asian American woman in the California State Assembly; she was elected in 1966. p. 379

F

Feinstein, Dianne *1933–* United States senator from California; she was elected in 1992. She also served as mayor of San Francisco from 1978 to 1988. pp. 379, 423

Frémont, Jessie Ann Benton *1824–1902* Wife of explorer John C. Frémont; she helped him write a popular book about the western United States. p. 210

Frémont, John C. *1813–1890* Explorer of the western United States in the 1840s. Later, he was a leader of the Bear Flag revolt, one of the first two United States senators from California, and a presidential candidate in 1856. pp. 198, 209, 219

Gálvez, José de (GAHL•ves) *1720–1787* Government official of New Spain who sent expeditions to San Diego and Monterey bays in 1769. p. 143

Ghirardelli, Domingo *1817–1894* Founder of the Ghirardelli Chocolate Company in San Francisco.

Giannini, Amadeo Pietro (jee•uh•NEE•nee) *1870–1949* Banker whose Bank of Italy grew into the largest bank in the world, the Bank of America. p. 313

Gibbs, Mifflin *1823–1915* Founder of the *Mirror of the Times*, the first newspaper owned by an African in California. pp. 230, 237

Gilman, Charlotte Perkins *1860–1935* Author and a leader of the movement for women's rights in California. p. 329

Gonzales, David M. (guhn•ZAH•luhs) Congressional Medal of Honor winner from Pacoima. p. 349

Gordon, Laura de Force *1838–1907* A leader of the movement for women's rights in California. p. 329

Grant, Ulysses S. *1822–1885* Eighteenth President of the United States. p. 286

Guerra, Pablo de la *1819–1874* Californio delegate to California's first constitutional convention, and later, a state senator and lieutenant governor. p. 249

Guthrie, Woody *1912–1967* Singer and songwriter who wrote many songs about the Great Depression. p. 337

Gwin, William M. *1805–1885* One of the first two United States senators from California; he served from 1850 to 1855 and from 1857 to 1861. p. 246

H

Hallidie, Andrew Smith (HAL•uh•dee) *1836–1900* Inventor of the cable car. p. 312

Hayakawa, S.I. (hah•yah•KAH•wah) *1906–1992* United States senator; he served from 1977 to 1983.

Hearst, Phoebe Apperson *1842–1919* One of the founders of the National PTA; mother of William Randolph Hearst. p. 385

Hearst, William Randolph *1863–1951* Politician and publisher of a San Francisco newspaper, the *Examiner*.

Hidalgo, Miguel (ee•DAHL•goh, mee•GAYL) *1753–1811* Mexican priest whose 1810 speech, known as the *Grito de Dolores*, marked the beginning of the Mexican War for Independence. p. 166

Hoover, Herbert *1874–1964* Thirty-first President of the United States. p. 421

Hopkins, Mark *1813–1878* Member of the "Big Four" who ran the Central Pacific and Southern Pacific railroads in the middle to late 1800s. p. 282

Hoya, Oscar de la *1973–* Boxer from East Los Angeles who won a gold medal in the 1992 Olympics.

Huerta, Dolores (HWAIR•tah) *1930–* Labor leader and organizer of the United Farm Workers. p. 378

Hughes, Howard *1905–1976* Pilot and business leader active in California aviation.

Huntington, Collis P. *1821–1900* Member of the "Big Four" who ran the Central Pacific and Southern Pacific railroads in the middle to late 1800s. p. 282

Ishi *1861?–1916* Last survivor of the Yahi, a California Indian tribe. p. 306

Jackson, Helen Hunt *1830–1885* Writer who in the 1880s brought attention to the poor treatment of Native Americans by the United States government.

Jackson, Odis African American lawyer who protested when a builder refused to sell him a house in a new Los Angeles suburb in 1963. p. 377

Jobs, Steven *1955–* Computer designer who started Apple Computers with Steven Wozniak in the Silicon Valley in 1976.

Johnson, Hiram *1866–1945* Governor of California from 1911 to 1917 and a United States senator from 1917 to 1945. p. 328

Joyner-Kersee, Jackie *1962–* University of California at Los Angeles graduate and gold medalist in the pentathlon and long jump in the 1988 Olympics and in the heptathlon in the 1992 Olympics.

Judah, Theodore D. *1826–1863* Engineer who founded the Central Pacific Railroad and planned the route of the first transcontinental railroad. pp. 274, 281

K

Kaiser, Henry *1882–1967* Business leader whose shipyards in California built many of the vessels used by the United States armed forces during World War II. p. 345

Kearny, Stephen W. (KAR•nee) *1794–1848* General in the United States Army during the Mexican-American War. p. 219

Kennedy, Anthony *1936–* United States Supreme Court justice from Sacramento. p. 423

Kerouac, Jack *1922–1969* Author who set many of his novels in the San Francisco Bay area.

Kientepoos, Chief Modoc Indian chief; also known as Captain Jack. p. 307

King, Martin Luther, Jr. *1929–1968* African American civil rights leader who worked to end segregation in nonviolent ways. p. 376

Kingston, Maxine Hong *1940–* Chinese American author from Stockton.

L

Lange, Dorothea *1895–1965* Photographer known for her pictures of migrant workers and families, taken during the 1930s.

Leidesdorff, William *1810–1848* African American who built the first hotel and helped found the first school in San Francisco in the 1840s.

Lincoln, Abraham *1809–1865* Sixteenth President of the United States. p. 280

Lockheed, Allan *1889–1969* Along with his brother, Malcolm, and John K. Northrop, he founded an aviation company in California in the early 1900s. p. 333

Lockheed, Malcolm Along with his brother, Allan, and John K. Northrop, he founded an aviation company in California in the early 1900s. p. 333

London, Jack *1876–1916* Author from San Francisco; he wrote adventure stories, including *The Call of the Wild*. p. 311

Lopez, Nancy *1957–* Professional golfer from Torrance.

Marshall, James W. *1810–1885* Carpenter at Sutter's Mill; he claimed to have discovered gold there in 1848, which led to the California gold rush. p. 227

Martin, Glenn *1886–1955* Builder of California's first airplane factory, in Santa Ana in 1909. p. 333

Mason, Biddy *1815–1891* Former slave who became one of the wealthiest African Americans in Los Angeles during the late 1800s. She donated much of her money and time to helping others. p. 252

Maynard, Robert *1937–1993* Owner of the *Oakland Tribune* in the 1980s; he was the first African American to own a major metropolitan newspaper in the United States.

Megquier, Mary Jane (meh•GWEER) Forty-niner who went to California with her husband Thomas in search of gold. pp. 226, 229, 236

Molina, Gloria *1948–* First Hispanic woman in the California State Assembly, in 1982, and on the Los Angeles City Council, in 1987. p. 379

Morrow, Irving One of the designers of the Golden Gate Bridge. p. 341

Morse, Samuel F. B. *1791–1872* One of the inventors of the telegraph and the creator of Morse code. p. 279

Muir, John (MYOOR) *1838–1914* Naturalist and conservation leader. pp. 46, 54, 57, 397

Mulholland, William (muhl•HAH•luhnd) *1855–1935* Engineer of the Los Angeles Aqueduct. p. 322

Nixon, Richard *1913–1994* Thirty-seventh President of the United States. p. 421

Nolan, Mae Ella *1886–1973* First woman from California in the United States House of Representatives; she was elected in 1922. p. 379

Norris, Frank *1870–1902* Author who wrote about California in the late 1800s.

Northrop, John K. *1895–1981* Along with the Lockheed brothers, he founded an aviation company in California in the early 1900s. p. 333

O

Ochoa, Ellen (oh•CHOH•uh) *1958–* Astronaut from Los Angeles; she flew on the space shuttle *Discovery* in 1993. p. 371

Pacheco, Romualdo *1831–1899* Governor of California in 1875.

Famous People

Pattie, James Ohio *1804–1850?* Trailblazer who traveled to California with his father, Sylvester Pattie. p. 202

Pattie, Sylvester Trailblazer who traveled to California with his son, James Ohio Pattie. p. 202

Patton, George *1885–1945* General in the United States Army; born in San Gabriel. p. 349

Phelan, James *1861–1930* San Francisco mayor from 1896 to 1902 and United States senator from 1915 to 1921.

Pickford, Mary *1893–1979* Star of many early Hollywood movies. p. 334

Pico, Andrés *1810–1876* Californio general during the Mexican-American War. p. 220

Pico, Pio *1801–1904* Last governor of Mexican California; he served from 1845 to 1846. Brother of Andrés Pico.

Polk, James K. *1795–1849* Eleventh President of the United States. p. 215

Portolá, Gaspar de (pawr•toh•LAH) *1723?–1784?* Spanish army captain and government official who led a land expedition to Alta California in 1769 to establish settlements. p. 143

R

Reagan, Ronald *1911–* Fortieth President of the United States. He was governor of California from 1967 to 1975. pp. 406, 422, R17

Reed, Patty *1838–1923* One of the survivors of the Donner party. p. 194

Ride, Sally *1951–* Astronaut from Encino; she became the first woman from the United States to fly in space when she flew on the space shuttle *Challenger* in 1983. p. 371

Riordan, Richard *1930–* Elected mayor of Los Angeles in 1993.

Rivera, Diego *1886–1957* Mexican artist known for his murals, including ones he painted for San Francisco's Art Institute and City College. p. 93

Rivera y Moncada, Fernando (ree•VAY•rah ee mohn•KAH•dah) *1711–1782* Spanish army captain who led a land expedition to Alta California in 1769 to establish settlements. p. 144

Robinson, John (Jackie) *1919–1972* University of California at Los Angeles athlete who in 1947 became the first African American to play major league baseball. p. 320

Rodia, Sam (roh•DEE•uh) *1879–1965* Artist who in the 1920s built the sculpture *Watts Towers*, which is located in the Watts neighborhood of Los Angeles. p. 387

Roosevelt, Franklin D. *1882–1945* Thirty-second President of the United States. pp. 339, 344

Roosevelt, Theodore *1858–1919* Twenty-sixth President of the United States. p. 398

Roybal-Allard, Lucille *1941–* First Hispanic woman from California in the United States House of Representatives; she was elected in 1992. p. 379

Ruiz, Bernarda (roo•EES) Californio woman who convinced John C. Frémont not to punish the Californios for fighting the Americans in the Mexican-American War. p. 220

Russell, William H. Founder of the Pony Express. p. 270

Ryan, T. Claude *1898–1982* Builder of the plane, named *Spirit of St. Louis*, that Charles Lindbergh flew across the Atlantic Ocean in 1927. p. 333

S

Sanchez, José *1778–1831* Head of the San Gabriel Mission who welcomed trailblazer Jedediah Strong Smith in the late 1820s. p. 200

Saund, Dalip Singh *1899–1973* First Asian American elected to Congress; he served from 1957 to 1963.

Schmitz, Eugene *1864–1928* Mayor of San Francisco from 1902 to 1907.

Serra, Junípero (SEH•rah, hoo•NEE•pay•roh) *1713–1784* Spanish priest; he founded many of the California missions from 1769 to 1784. pp. 143, 145

Severance, Caroline (SE•vuh•ruhns) *1820–1914* A leader of the movement for women's rights in California. p. 329

Shima, George *1863–1926* Japanese immigrant who became known as the "Potato King" for growing most of California's potato crop in the early 1900s. p. 309

Sloat, John *1781–1867* Officer in the United States Navy during the Mexican-American War. p. 219

Smith, Jedediah Strong *1799–1831* Trailblazer and trader; he traveled overland to California in the late 1820s. p. 200

Stanford, Leland *1824–1893* Member of the "Big Four" who ran the Central Pacific and Southern Pacific railroads in the middle to late 1800s. Governor of California from 1862 to 1863. pp. 282, R17

Stearns, Abel *1789–1871* Early settler of California. p. 206

Steinbeck, John *1902–1968* Author from Salinas; he described the experiences of migrants to California in his novel *The Grapes of Wrath.* p. 338

Stockton, Robert F. *1795–1866* Officer in the United States Army during the Mexican-American War. p. 219

Strauss, Levi *1830–1902* German immigrant to California during the gold rush who made his fortune selling to miners "jeans" made of canvas and, later, denim. p. 237

Strong, Harriet Russell *1844–1929* Californian who worked to improve crops in California. p. 300

Sutter, John Augustus *1803–1880* Swiss immigrant who founded Sutter's Fort in the Central Valley. Gold was discovered near his mill in 1848. p. 206

Tan, Amy *1952–*　Chinese American author from Oakland.

Temple (Black), Shirley *1928–*　Child star of many early Hollywood movies. Later, she became the United States' ambassador to Ghana.

Tibbets, Eliza Orange grower whose seedless oranges sparked California's citrus industry in the late 1800s. Wife of Luther Calvin Tibbets. p. 298

Tibbets, Luther Calvin Orange grower whose seedless oranges sparked California's citrus industry in the late 1800s. Husband of Eliza Tibbets. p. 298

Toypurina (toy•poo•REE•nuh) *1761–1799* Tongva Indian woman who led Indians in a revolt at the San Gabriel Mission. p. 155

Uchida, Yoshiko (oo•chee•dah, yoh•shee•koh) *1921–1992* Japanese American author from Berkeley; she wrote about her experiences in a relocation camp during World War II in *The Invisible Thread.* p. 368

V

Vallejo, Mariano (vah•YAY•hoh, mar•ee•AHN•oh) *1808–1890* Californio rancho owner and Mexican general who surrendered to the Bear Flaggers in 1846. pp. 157, 216

Vizcaíno, Sebastián (vees•kah•EE•noh) *1550?–1616* Spanish explorer; he sailed to Monterey Bay in the early 1600s and recommended establishing Spanish settlements there. p. 136

Vuich, Rose Ann First woman in the California State Senate; she was elected in 1976. p. 379

W

Walker, Joseph Reddeford *1798–1876* Trailblazer who found a route through a mountain pass in the Sierra Nevada in 1834. p. 202

Warren, Earl *1891–1974* Governor of California from 1943 to 1953 and Chief Justice of the United States Supreme Court from 1953 to 1969. p. 423

Watson, Diane E. *1933–*　First African American woman in the California State Senate; she was elected in 1978. p. 379

Weller, John B. *1812–1875* Governor of California from 1858 to 1860; United States senator from 1851 to 1857. pp. 275, R17

Wilson, Pete *1932–*　Served as governor of California from 1991 to 1999; he was a United States senator from 1983 to 1991.

Wimmer, Jennie Cook at Sutter's Mill who was present when James Marshall claimed to have discovered gold in 1848. p. 227

Wong, Anna May *1907–1961* Chinese American star of many early Hollywood movies.

Wozniak, Steven *1950–*　Computer designer who started Apple Computers with Steven Jobs in the Silicon Valley in 1976.

Y

Yamaguchi, Kristi *1971–*　Ice skater from Fremont who won a gold medal in the 1992 Olympics.

Yeager, Chuck (YAY•ger) *1923–*　United States Air Force test pilot; in 1947 he became the first pilot to fly at supersonic speeds, at Edwards Air Force Base in California. p. 370

Young, Ewing *1792?–1841* Trapper and trailblazer, he helped develop the Old Spanish Trail in the early 1830s. p. 202

Gazetteer

The Gazetteer is a geographical dictionary that will help you locate places discussed in this book. The page number tells where each place appears on a map.

Alameda A city built on an island; an important port in the San Francisco Bay area. (38°N, 122°W) p. 305

Alamo River A river in southern California. p. 65

Alcatraz Island (AL•kuh•traz) An island in San Francisco Bay; a former prison; the site of an Indian civil rights protest. (38°N, 122°W) p. 305

Alturas A city in northeastern California; county seat of Modoc County. (41°N, 121°W) p. 383

American River A tributary of the Sacramento River. p. 106

Anacapa Islands A group of islands off the southern coast of California. p. 100

Anaheim A large city in southwestern California. (34°N, 118°W) p. 40

Angel Island State Park A state park in San Francisco Bay. (38°N, 122°W) p. 305

Appalachian Mountains (a•puh•LAY•chee•uhn) A mountain range in the eastern United States. p. 49

Auburn A city in eastern California, northeast of Sacramento; county seat of Placer County. (39°N, 121°W)

Bakersfield A city in the San Joaquin Valley; county seat of Kern County. (35°N, 119°W) p. 35

Barstow A city in southern California. (35°N, 117°W) p. 323

Beckwourth Pass A mountain pass through the Sierra Nevada; named for trailblazer James Beckwourth. (40°N, 120°W) p. 211

Berkeley A city in the San Francisco Bay area; site of the University of California at Berkeley. (38°N, 122°W) p. 305

Big Pine A town in the Owens Valley in California's Desert Region. (37°N, 118°W) p. 323

Bishop A city in eastern California in the Owens Valley. (37°N, 118°W) p. 323

Blythe A city in southeastern California, near the Colorado River. (34°N, 115°W) p. 383

Brawley A city in the Imperial Valley. (33°N, 116°W) p. 322

Bridgeport A village in eastern California; county seat of Mono County. (38°N, 119°W)

Buena Vista Lake A lake in southern California. (35°N, 119°W) p. 107

Burbank A city 10 miles (16 km) north of Los Angeles. (34°N, 118°W) p. 264

Cabrillo National Monument A national monument in southwestern California, where Juan Rodríguez Cabrillo first sighted land in 1542. (33°N, 117°W) p. 398

Cahuenga Pass (cah•HWEN•gah) A pass near what is now Los Angeles; the site where an agreement was reached to end the fighting in California during the Mexican-American War. (34°N, 118°W) p. 221

Calexico A city in southern California, on the Mexican border. (33°N, 116°W) p. 322

Cascade Range A range of mountains that lies north of the Sierra Nevada. p. 57

Central Valley One of the four natural regions in California. p. 57

Channel Islands A group of eight islands off the southern coast of California. p. 57

Channel Islands National Park A national park off the southern coast of California; has examples of volcanic activity. p. 398

Chemehuevi Peak A mountain peak in the Mojave Desert; its elevation is 3,694 feet (1,126 m). (35°N, 115°W) p. 111

Chico A city in northern California, north of Sacramento; home of California State University at Chico. (40°N, 122°W) p. 383

Chocolate Mountains A mountain range in southern California, in the Imperial Valley. p. 322

Clair Engle Lake A lake in northwestern California. (41°N, 123°W) p. 65

Clear Lake A lake in northern California. (39°N, 123°W) p. 65

Coachella A city in southeastern California. (34°N, 116°W) p. 322

Coast Ranges Several small mountain ranges that lie along the California coast and reach north into Oregon and Washington. p. 40

Coastal Region One of the four natural regions in California. p. 57

Coloma A town on the American River. (39°N, 121°W) p. 228

Colorado Desert A desert south of the Mojave Desert. p. 322

Colorado River A river that flows from Colorado to the Gulf of California; part of it forms the border between California and Arizona. p. 65

Colusa A city in north central California on the Sacramento River; county seat of Colusa County. (39°N, 122°W)

Cosumnes River (kuh•SUHM•nuhs) A tributary of the San Joaquin River. p. 106

Crescent City A city on the northwestern coast of California; county seat of Del Norte County. (42°N, 124°W) p. 71

Cuyama River A river in southern California. p. 65

D

Dead Mountains A mountain range in the Mojave Desert. p. 111

Death Valley The lowest point in California and in the Western Hemisphere; at one point, it lies 282 feet (86 m) below sea level. p. 40

Death Valley National Park A national park located in eastern California. p. 326

Desert Region One of the four natural regions in California. p. 57

Devils Postpile National Monument A national monument in Madera County, in central California; it features unusual rock formations that look like piles of fence posts. (38°N, 119°W) p. 398

Diablo Range (dee•AH•bloh) One of the mountain ranges that make up the Coast Ranges. p. 107

Downieville A village in northeastern California, north northeast of Sacramento; county seat of Sierra County. (40°N, 121°W) p. 233

E

Eagle Lake A lake in northern California. (41°N, 121°W) p. 65

Eel River A river in northwestern California. p. 65

El Centro A city in the southeastern corner of California; county seat of Imperial County. (33°N, 116°W) p. 322

Escondido A city in the southwestern corner of California, north of San Diego. (33°N, 117°W) p. 383

Eureka A city on the northwestern coast of California; county seat of Humboldt County. (41°N, 124°W) p. 35

F

Fairfield A city in central California, southwest of Sacramento; county seat of Solano County. (38°N, 122°W)

Farallon Islands (FAIR•uh•lahn) A group of small, rocky islands off the northern coast of California. (38°N, 123°W) p. 57

Feather River A tributary of the Sacramento River. p. 106

Folsom A city in north central California. (39°N, 121°W) p. 284

Folsom Lake A lake in north central California. (39°N, 121°W) p. 65

Fort Ross State Historic Park The site, north of San Francisco, of a fort built in 1812 by Russians. (39°N, 123°W) p. 167

Fremont A city in western California, southeast of Oakland. (37°N, 122°W) p. 325

Fresno A city in the San Joaquin Valley; county seat of Fresno County. (37°N, 120°W) p. 35

G

Golden Gate A narrow body of water that connects the Pacific Ocean and San Francisco Bay. (38°N, 122°W) p. 305

Goose Lake A lake in northeastern California. (42°N, 120°W) p. 65

Great Basin A large basin, or low, bowl-shaped area of land with higher ground all around it, that extends into parts of six western states; includes much of California's Desert Region. p. 202

Gulf of California A part of the Pacific Ocean, located off the northwestern coast of Mexico. p. 136

H

Hanford A city in southwestern central California; county seat of Kings County. (36°N, 120°W)

Healdsburg A city in western California, northwest of Santa Rosa. (39°N, 123°W) p. 167

Hetch Hetchy Aqueduct A water project completed in 1931 that supplies water from the Hetch Hetchy Valley to San Francisco. p. 325

Hetch Hetchy Valley A valley in the Sierra Nevada; located in Yosemite National Park. p. 325

Hollister A city in western California, east of Monterey Bay; county seat of San Benito County. (37°N, 121°W)

Hollywood A district in Los Angeles; center of the movie industry. (34°N, 118°W) p. 40

Holtville A city in the Imperial Valley. (33°N, 115°W) p. 322

Humboldt Bay A natural harbor on the northwestern coast of California. (41°N, 124°W) p. 99

Huntington Beach A city on the coast of southwestern California. (34°N, 118°W) p. 40

Imperial A city in the southeastern corner of California, in the Imperial Valley, north of El Centro. (33°N, 116°W) p. 322

Imperial Valley A valley within the Desert Region of California, near the Mexican border. p. 322

Independence A town in eastern California, east of Fresno; county seat of Inyo County. (37°N, 118°W) p. 323

Indio A city in southeastern California, southeast of San Bernardino. (34°N, 116°W) p. 322

Inyo Mountains A mountain range in Inyo County, in eastern California. p. 326

Isabella Lake A lake in southern California. (36°N, 118°W) p. 65

Jackson A city in central California; county seat of Amador County. (38°N, 121°W)

Joshua Tree National Park A national park located in southern California; known for its unusual desert plants. p. 398

Kern River A river in south central California. p. 65

King City A city in western California, on the Salinas River. (36°N, 121°W) p. 383

Kings Canyon National Park A national park located along the Kings River in south central California, in the Sierra Nevada; known for its unusual canyons. p. 398

Kings River A river in south central California. p. 65

Klamath Mountains (KLA•muhth) One of the mountain ranges that make up the Coast Ranges. p. 99

Klamath River A river in northwestern California. p. 65

Lake Almanor A lake in northeastern California. (40°N, 121°W) p. 65

Lake Berryessa A lake in northern California. (39°N, 122°W) p. 65

Lake McClure A lake in central California. (38°N, 120°W) p. 65

Lake Oroville A lake in northern California. (40°N, 122°W) p. 65

Lake Tahoe (TAH•hoh) One of California's two largest lakes; located in the Sierra Nevada, on the California-Nevada border. (39°N, 120°W) p. 65

Lakeport A city in western California; county seat of Lake County. (39°N, 123°W)

Lassen Peak A mountain peak with an elevation of 10,457 feet (3,187 m); located in the Cascade Range; part of Lassen Volcanic National Park; last erupted in 1921. (40°N, 122°W) p. 57

Lassen Volcanic National Park A national park in northeastern California, in the Cascade Range. p. 398

Lava Beds National Monument A national monument located in northern California; known for its volcanic landscape features. (42°N, 122°W) p. 398

Lompoc A city in southwestern California, near the Pacific Ocean. (35°N, 121°W) p. 383

Long Beach A city in California's Coastal Region; about 20 miles (32 km) south of Los Angeles. (34°N, 118°W) p. 35

Los Altos A city in the Santa Clara Valley, near San Jose. (37°N, 122°W) p. 393

Los Angeles A city in southwestern California; more than 15 million people live in the Los Angeles metropolitan area; county seat of Los Angeles County. (34°N, 118°W) p. 35

Los Angeles Aqueduct An aqueduct that carries water from the Owens River to Los Angeles. p. 323

Los Angeles River A river in Los Angeles; before construction of the Los Angeles Aqueduct it gave Los Angeles most of its water. p. 323

Mariposa An unincorporated settlement in central California; county seat of Mariposa County. (37°N, 120°W) p. 233

Mariposa River A tributary of the San Joaquin River. p. 233

Markleeville A town in eastern California; county seat of Alpine County. (39°N, 120°W)

Martinez A city in western California; county seat of Contra Costa County. (38°N, 122°W)

Marysville A city in north central California; county seat of Yuba County. (39°N, 122°W) p. 233

Merced A city in central California; county seat of Merced County. (37°N, 120°W) p. 313

Merced River A tributary of the San Joaquin River. p. 107

Mill Valley A city in western California, northwest of San Francisco. (38°N, 123°W) p. 305

Modesto A city on the Tuolumne River in central California; county seat of Stanislaus County. (38°N, 121°W) p. 53

Mojave Desert (moh•HAH•vay) A large desert area between the southern Sierra Nevada and the Colorado River. p. 40

Mokelumne River (moh•KEH•luh•mee) A tributary of the San Joaquin River. p. 107

Mono Lake A lake in eastern California, near Nevada. (38°N, 119°W) p. 325

Monterey A historic town located on the coast of California; original state capital of California. (37°N, 122°W) p. 35

Monterey Bay A natural harbor near Monterey. p. 65

Mount Pinos (PEE•nohs) The tallest peak in the Coast Ranges, with an evevation of 8,831 feet (2,692 m). (35°N, 119°W) p. 57

Mount Shasta A mountain peak with an elevation of 14,162 feet (4,317 m); located in the Cascade Range. (41°N, 122°W) p. 57

Mount Whitney The tallest peak in California, with an elevation of 14,495 feet (4,418 m); located in the Sierra Nevada. (37°N, 118°W) p. 40

Mountain Region One of the four natural regions in California. p. 57

Muir Woods National Monument A national monument located 12 miles (19 km) northwest of San Francisco. (38°N, 122°W) p. 398

N

Napa A city in west central California; county seat of Napa County. (38°N, 122°W) p. 383

Napa Valley A valley in the Coast Ranges, located north of San Francisco. p. 40

Nevada City A city in eastern California; county seat of Nevada County. (39°N, 121°W)

New River A river in southern California. p. 322

O

Oakland A large city and port in northern California, on San Francisco Bay opposite San Francisco; county seat of Alameda County. (38°N, 122°W) p. 305

Oceanside A city in the southwestern corner of California. (33°N, 117°W) p. 264

Oroville A city in north central California on the Feather River; county seat of Butte County. (40°N, 122°W)

Owens Lake A lake that gets its water from the Owens River; now nearly dry. (36°N, 118°W) p. 326

Owens River A river that flows through the Sierra Nevada. p. 323

Oxnard A city in southwestern California. (34°N, 119°W) p. 383

P

Pacific Rim A region of the world that includes California and other states and countries that border the Pacific Ocean. p. 51

Palo Alto A city in the Santa Clara Valley; site of Stanford University. (37°N, 122°W) p. 393

Panamint Mountains A mountain range in eastern California, west of Death Valley; highest peak is Telescope Peak, 11,049 feet (3,368 m). p. 326

Pasadena A city northeast of Los Angeles. (34°N, 118°W) p. 264

Petaluma A city in western California, on the Petaluma River, south of Santa Rosa. (38°N, 123°W) p. 167

Pine Flat Reservoir A lake in central California. (37°N, 119°W) p. 65

Pinnacles National Monument A national monument in west central California; it features spirelike rock formations. (36°N, 121°W) p. 398

Pit River A tributary of the Sacramento River. p. 65

Placerville A city in the Central Valley; county seat of El Dorado County. (39°N, 121°W) p. 233

Q

Quincy An unincorporated village in northeastern California; county seat of Plumas County. (40°N, 121°W)

R

Rancho la Brea Tar Pits An archaeological site in Los Angeles. (34°N, 118°W) p. 92

Red Bluff A city in northern California; county seat of Tehama County. (40°N, 122°W) p. 383

Red Mountain A mountain peak with an elevation of 4,265 feet (1,300 m); located in the Siskiyou Mountains in central California. (41°N, 124°W) p. 99

Redding A city in northern California, on the Sacramento River; county seat of Shasta County. (41°N, 122°W) p. 383

Redwood City A city in western California, west of San Francisco Bay; county seat of San Mateo County. (37°N, 122°W)

Redwood National Park A national park located along the northwestern coast of California; its groves of ancient trees include some of the world's tallest. p. 398

Ridgecrest A city in southern California, northeast of Bakersfield. (36°N, 118°W) p. 323

Ring of Fire An area of volcanic activity surrounding the Pacific Ocean. p. 59

Riverside A city in southern California, located east of Los Angeles; county seat of Riverside County. (34°N, 117°W) p. 40

Rocky Mountains A mountain range that extends through the western United States into Canada. p. 49

Russian River A river in northwestern California. p. 65

S

Sacramento A city in the Central Valley; California's state capital; county seat of Sacramento County. (39°N, 121°W) p. 35

Sacramento Mountains A mountain range in the Mojave Desert. p. 111

Sacramento River A river that flows through the Sacramento Valley. p. 65

Sacramento Valley A valley that forms the northern part of the Central Valley. p. 57

Salinas A city in western California; county seat of Monterey County. (37°N, 122°W) p. 374

Salinas River A river in western California. p. 65

Salton Sea One of California's two largest lakes; located in the Imperial Valley. (33°N, 116°W) p. 65

San Andreas A village in central California; county seat of Calaveras County. (38°N, 121°W)

San Andreas Fault (an•DRAY•uhs) A fault more than 600 miles (966 km) long that begins off the coast of northwestern California and runs to the southeast. p. 57

San Bernardino A city located about 55 miles (88 km) east of Los Angeles; county seat of San Bernardino County. (34°N, 117°W) p. 40

San Diego A city located 12 miles (19 km) north of California's border with Mexico; county seat of San Diego County. (33°N, 117°W) p. 35

San Diego Bay A natural harbor near San Diego. p. 65

San Francisco A city in northern California; county seat of San Francisco County. (38°N, 122°W) p. 35

San Francisco Bay A natural harbor near San Francisco. p. 65

San Gabriel A city about 10 miles (16 km) east of Los Angeles. (34°N, 118°W) p. 204

San Jacinto Mountains (san hah•SEEN•toh) A range of mountains southeast of Los Angeles, near the San Bernardino Mountains. p. 147

San Joaquin River (san wah•KEEN) A river that flows through the San Joaquin Valley. p. 65

San Joaquin Valley A valley that forms the southern part of the Central Valley. p. 57

San Jose (san hoh•ZAY) A city in west central California; county seat of Santa Clara County. (37°N, 122°W) p. 35

San Luis Obispo (san LOO•is uh•BIS•poh) A city near the California coast, about halfway between Los Angeles and San Francisco; county seat of San Luis Obispo County. (35°N, 121°W) p. 264

San Luis Reservoir A lake in central California. (37°N, 121°W) p. 65

San Miguel Island One of the eight Channel Islands. (34°N, 120°W) p. 100

San Rafael A city in western California; county seat of Marin County. (38°N, 123°W) p. 374

San Rafael Mountains A mountain range in southwestern California. p. 100

Santa Ana A city in southwestern California; county seat of Orange County. (34°N, 118°W) p. 40

Santa Barbara A city located along the central coast of California; county seat of Santa Barbara County. (34°N, 120°W) p. 40

Santa Barbara Channel A channel off the coast of Santa Barbara County. p. 100

Santa Catalina Island One of the eight Channel Islands. (33°N, 118°W) p. 264

Santa Clara River A river in southern California. p. 65

Santa Cruz A city at the north end of Monterey Bay; county seat of Santa Cruz County. (37°N, 122°W) p. 53

Santa Cruz Island One of the eight Channel Islands. (34°N, 120°W) p. 100

Santa Cruz Mountains One of the mountain ranges that make up the Coast Ranges. p. 393

Santa Maria River A river in southern California. p. 100

Santa Monica A city west of Los Angeles; located on the California coast. (34°N, 119°W) p. 264

Santa Rosa A city 50 miles (80 km) northwest of San Francisco, in the Sonoma Valley; county seat of Sonoma County. (38°N, 123°W) p. 167

Santa Rosa Island One of the eight Channel Islands. (34°N, 120°W) p. 100

Santa Ynez Mountains A mountain range in southern California. p. 100

Santa Ynez River A river in southern California. p. 65

Sausalito A city in western California, on San Francisco Bay; northwest of San Francisco. (38°N, 122°W) p. 305

Sebastopol A city in western California, southwest of Santa Rosa. (38°N, 123°W) p. 167

Sequoia National Park A national park in south central California, in the Sierra Nevada; established in 1890; contains Mount Whitney. p. 398

Shasta Dam A dam built on the Sacramento River, in northern California. (41°N, 122°W) p. 339

Shasta Lake A reservoir in northern California; formed by Shasta Dam. (41°N, 122°W) p. 65

Sierra Madre (see•AIR•ah MAH•dree) A mountain range in southern California. p. 100

Sierra Nevada (see•AIR•ah neh•VAH•dah) California's largest mountain range; it stretches north and south across much of the eastern part of the state. p. 40

Silicon Valley An area in western California, between San Jose and Palo Alto; the name refers to the area's computer industry, which makes and uses silicon chips. p. 393

Siskiyou Mountains (SIS•kee•yoo) A mountain range that extends from northern California to southwestern Oregon. p. 99

Sonoma A city north of San Francisco. (38°N, 122°W) p. 167

Sonora A city in central California; county seat of Tuolumne County. (38°N, 120°W) p. 233

Stanislaus River A tributary of the San Joaquin River. p. 65

Stockton A city in the San Joaquin Valley; county seat of San Joaquin County. (38°N, 121°W) p. 35

Susanville A city in northeastern California; county seat of Lassen County. (40°N, 121°W) p. 383

Sutter's Mill The site at Coloma where gold was found in California in 1848. (39°N, 121°W) p. 228

Tiburon A peninsula north of San Francisco, extending into San Francisco Bay. (38°N, 122°W) p. 305

Trinity River A river in northern California. p. 65

Truckee A city in eastern California, north of Lake Tahoe. (39°N, 120°W) p. 71

Tulare A city in south central California. (36°N, 119°W) p. 313

Tulare Lake A dry lake in southern California. (36°N, 120°W) p. 107

Tuolumne River (too•AH•luh•mee) A tributary of the San Joaquin River; site of a dam that provides water for San Francisco. p. 325

Turtle Mountains A mountain range in the Mojave Desert. p. 111

Ukiah A city in western California, on the Russian River; county seat of Mendocino County. (39°N, 123°W)

Ventura A city in southwestern California; county seat of Ventura County. (34°N, 119°W)

Visalia A city in central California; county seat of Tulare County. (36°N, 119°W) p. 383

Walker Pass A mountain pass through the Sierra Nevada; named for trailblazer Joseph Reddeford Walker. (36°N, 118°W) p. 202

Weaverville An unincorporated settlement in northwestern California; county seat of Trinity County. (41°N, 123°W)

West Region One of the five regions of the United States. p. 49

Western Hemisphere The half of the Earth made up of North and South America and the waters around them. California is in the United States, in North America, in the Western Hemisphere. p. 48

Whipple Mountains A mountain range in the Mojave Desert. p. 111

Willows A city in northern California; county seat of Glenn County. (40°N, 122°W)

Woodland A city in north central California; county seat of Yolo County. (39°N, 122°W)

Yosemite National Park A national park located in the central Sierra Nevada; established in 1890. p. 398

Yreka (wy•REE•kuh) A city in northern California; county seat of Siskiyou County. (42°N, 123°W)

Yuba City A city in north central California, on the Feather River; county seat of Sutter County. (39°N, 122°W)

Yuba River A tributary of the Feather River. p. 106

Glossary

This Glossary contains important social studies terms and their definitions. Each word is respelled as it would be in a dictionary. When you see the stress mark ´ after a syllable, pronounce that syllable with more force than the other syllables. The page number at the end of the definition tells where to find the word in your book.

add, āce, câre, pälm; end, ēqual; it, īce; odd, ōpen, ôrder; tŏŏk, pōōl; up, bûrn; yōō as *u* in *fuse*; oil; pout; ə as *a* in *above, e* in *sicken, i* in p*ossible, o* in *melon, u* in *circus*; **ch**eck; ri**ng**; **th**in; **th**is; **zh** as in *vision*

A

absolute location (ab´sə•lōōt lō•kā´shən) The exact position of a place on the Earth. p. 52

adapt (ə•dapt´) To fit one's ways of living to the land and its resources. p. 110

adobe (ä•dō´bā) A mixture of clay, straw, and water that is dried into bricks. p. 152

advertising (ad´vər•tī•zing) Information that a business provides about its product or service to make people want to buy it. p. 299

aerospace (âr´ō•spās) Having to do with building and testing equipment for air and space travel. p. 371

agriculture (a´grə•kəl•chər) Farming. p. 111

air mass (âr mas) A large, moving body of air. p. 72

amendment (ə•mend´mənt) A change to the state or federal constitution. p. 329

analyze (a´nə•līz) To break something down into its parts. p. 28

ancestor (an´ses•tər) An early family member. p. 102

aqueduct (a´kwə•dukt) A large pipe or canal that carries water from one place to another. p. 323

archaeologist (är•kē•ä´lə•jist) A scientist who studies artifacts to learn about what life was like long ago. p. 91

artifact (är´ti•fakt) Any object made by people in the past. p. 91

aviation (ā•vē•ā´shən) The making and flying of airplanes. p. 332

B

barrier (bar´ē•ər) Something that blocks the way or makes it hard to get from place to place. p. 136

barter (bär´tər) To trade one kind of good for another without using money. p. 180

basin (bā´sən) A low, bowl-shaped land area with higher ground all around it. p. 61

bill (bil) A plan for a new law. p. 409

board of supervisors (bôrd uv sōō´pər•vī•zərz) An elected group of people who govern a county. p. 414

boom (bōōm) A time of fast economic growth. p. 314

boundary (boun´drē) A border; the outside edge of a place. p. 32

boycott (boi´kät) A decision by a group of people not to buy something, as a protest. p. 378

bribe (brīb) Something promised to a person, such as money, a gift, or a favor, to get him or her to do something. p. 328

budget (bə´jət) A written plan for spending money. p. 408

C

Californio (ka•lə•fôr´nē•ō) A name that the Spanish-speaking people of Alta California called themselves. p. 167

canal (kə•nal´) A waterway dug across land. p. 321

canyon (kan´yən) A deep, narrow valley with steep sides. p. 75

cape (kāp) A point of land that reaches out into the ocean. p. 231

capital resources (ka´pə•təl rē´sôr•səz) The money, buildings, machines, and tools needed to run a business. p. 345

cardinal direction (kär´də•nəl də•rek´shən) North, south, east, or west. p. 34

cause (kôz) Something that makes something else happen. p. 103

century (sen´chə•rē) A period of 100 years. p. 150

Glossary

ceremony (ser´ə•mō•nē) A series of actions performed during a special event. p. 101

channel (cha´nəl) A path for a river to flow through. p. 66

citizen (si´tə•zən) A member of a country, a state, or a city or town. p. 19

city manager (si´tē ma´ni•jər) A person hired by a city council to run the city the way the city council wants. p. 417

civil rights (si´vəl rīts) The rights of citizens to equal treatment. p. 376

civil war (si´vəl wôr) A war between groups of people in the same country or in what had been the same country. p. 282

civilization (si•və•lə•zā´shən) A culture that usually has cities and highly developed arts and sciences. p. 92

claim (klām) The area a miner said belonged to him or her. p. 233

classify (kla´sə•fī) To group information. p. 94

climate (klī´mət) The kind of weather a place has most often, year after year. p. 70

clipper ship (kli´pər ship) A fast sailing ship. p. 231

coastal plain (kōs´təl plān) An area of low land that lies along the ocean p. 55

colony (ko´lə•nē) A settlement set up and ruled by a faraway country. p. 137

commission (kə•mi´shən) A group of people chosen to make a decision about a certain problem. p. 249

communication (kə•myōō•nə•kā´shən) The sending and receiving of information. p. 275

compass rose (kum´pəs rōz) The direction marker on a map. p. 34

competition (kom•pə•ti´shən) The contest among companies to get the most customers or sell the most products. p. 314

compromise (kom´prə•mīz) An agreement in which each side in a conflict gives up some of what it wants. p. 247

conquistador (kon•k(w)is´•tə•dôr) A Spanish explorer who claimed large areas of North and South America for Spain. p. 131

consequence (kon´sə•kwens) What happens because of an action. p. 428

conservation (kon•sər•vā´shən) The protection and wise use of natural resources. p. 398

constitution (kon•stə•tōō´shən) A plan of government. p. 245

consumer (kən•sōō´mər) A person who buys a product or a service. p. 238

consumer good (kən•sōō´mər good) A product made for personal use. p. 332

continent (kon´tə•nənt) One of the seven largest land areas on Earth. p. 47

convention (kən•ven´shən) An important meeting. p. 244

cooperate (kō•o´pə•rāt) To work together. p. 108

county seat (koun´tē sēt) A city that is the center of government for a county. p. 414

Creole (krē´ōl) A person of Spanish background who had been born in New Spain. p. 165

crossroads (krôs´rōdz) Any place that connects people, goods, and ideas. p. 51

cross section (krôs sek´shən) A slice or piece cut straight across something. p. 316

cross-section diagram (krôs´sek•shən dī´ə•gram) A drawing that shows what you would see if you could slice through something and then look at the cut surface. p. 316

culture (kul´chər) A way of life. pp. 28, 90

custom (kus´təm) A usual way of doing things. p. 153

D

decade (de´kād) A period of ten years. p. 150

delegate (de´li•gət) A person who is chosen to speak and act for others. p. 244

delta (del´tə) Land built up at a river's mouth. p. 67

demand (di•mand´) A need or a desire for a good or service by people willing to pay for it. p. 199

democracy (di•mo´krə•sē) A form of government in which the people rule by making decisions themselves or by electing leaders to make decisions for them. p. 426

depression (di•presh´ən) A time when there are few jobs and people have little money. p. 335

derrick (der´ik) A tower built over an oil well to hold the machines used for drilling. p. 315

discrimination (dis•kri•mə•nā´shən) The unfair treatment of people because of such things as their religion, their race, or their birthplace. p. 239

diseño (di•sān´yō) A hand-drawn map that showed what the boundaries of a rancho would be. p. 174

diverse economy (di•vûrs´ i•ko´nə•mē) An economy that is based on many kinds of industries. p. 369

division of labor (di•vi´zhən uv lā´bər) Dividing the work among different workers. p. 106

drought (drout) A long time with little or no rain. p. 74

E

economics (e•kə•no´miks *or* ē•kə•no´miks) The study of how people use resources to meet their needs. p. 36

economy (i•ko´nə•mē) The way people in a state, a region, or a country use resources to meet their needs. pp. 36, 168

effect (i•fekt´) What happens as a result of something else happening. p. 103

elevation (e•lə•vā´shən) The height of the land above sea level. p. 62

emissions (ē•mi´shənz) The chemicals put into the air by cars and factories. p. 399

engineer (en•jə•nir´) A person who plans and builds roads, bridges, and railroads. p. 281

entrepreneur (än•trə•prə•nûr´) A person who sets up a new business. p. 237

environment (in•vī´rən•mənt) Surroundings. p. 21

equator (i•kwā´tər) The imaginary line between the Northern Hemisphere and the Southern Hemisphere. p. 47

erosion (i•rō´zhən) The wearing away of the Earth's surface. p. 66

ethnic group (eth´nik grüp) A group of people from the same country, of the same race, or with a shared culture. p. 376

event (i•vent´) Something that happens. p. 22

executive branch (ig•ze´kyə•tiv branch) The branch of government that makes sure that laws made by the legislative branch are carried out. p. 409

expedition (ek•spə•di´shən) A trip made for a special reason, such as to explore a place or find a treasure. p. 133

export (ek´spôrt) A product shipped from one country to be sold in another. p. 391

extinct (ik•stingkt´) Having died out. p. 81

fact (fakt) A statement that can be checked and proved to be true. p. 213

fault (fôlt) A crack in the Earth's surface along which underground layers of rock can move. p. 56

federal government (fe´də•rəl gə´vərn•mənt) The national government. p. 420

fertile (fûr´təl) Good for growing crops. p. 60

festival (fes´tə•vəl) A celebration that takes place every year, usually at the same time of the year. p. 387

fiesta (fē•es´tə) A party. p. 176

floodplain (flud´plān) The low, flat land along a river. p. 66

flow chart (flō chärt) A drawing that shows the order in which things happen. p. 412

food processing (food pro´se•sing) The cooking, canning, drying, and freezing of foods and the preparing of them for market. p. 394

foothill (foot´hil) A low hill at the base of a mountain or a range of mountains. p. 108

forty-niner (fôr´tē•nī´nər) A person who went to California in 1849 to search for gold. p. 229

free enterprise (frē en´tər•prīz) A kind of economy in which people can own and run their own businesses. p. 237

free state (frē stāt) A state in which slavery was outlawed. p. 247

freeway (frē´wā) A wide, divided highway with no cross streets or stoplights. p. 373

frontier (frən•tir´) The land beyond the settled part of a country. p. 208

fuel (fyool) A natural resource used to make heat or energy. p. 77

G

galleon (ga´lē•ən *or* gal´yən) A large Spanish trading ship. p. 134

geographer (jē•o´grə•fər) A person whose work is to study geography. p. 29

geography (jē•o´grə•fē) The study of the Earth's surface and the way people use it. p. 29

glacier (glā´shər) A huge, slow-moving mass of ice. p. 87

gold rush (gōld rush) A huge movement of people trying to find gold. p. 229

government (gə´vərn•mənt) A system for deciding what is best for a group of people, including ways to protect the group members and ways to settle disagreements. The main job of government is to make laws and see that they are carried out. pp. 36, 101

governor (gə´vər•nər) A leader of a colony or a state. p. 201

granary (grā´nə•rē *or* gra´nə•rē) A place for storing acorns and grains. p. 105

Great Migration (grāt mī•grā´shən) The movement after World War II of African Americans from the South to California and to states in the North. p. 347

grid (grid) A pattern of squares on a map formed by lines that cross each other. p. 34

growing season (grō´ing sē´zən) The length of time when the weather is warm enough for crops to grow. p. 77

H

habitat (ha´bə•tat) A place where animals find food and shelter. p. 80

hacienda (ä•sē•en´də) A large estate or house. p. 173

harbor (här´bər) A place on a coast—often in a bay—where ships can dock and be safe from storms. p. 64

hemisphere (he´mə•sfir) A half of the Earth. p. 47

heritage (her´ə•tij) A way of life, a custom, or a belief that has come from the past and continues today. p. 386

high tech (hī tek) Shortened form of the words *high technology*; having to do with computers and other electronic equipment. p. 393

historian (hi•stôr´ē•ən) A person whose work is to study the past. p. 26

history (his´tə•rē) The study of the past. p. 26

human feature (hyōō´mən fē´chər) A feature, such as a building or bridge, that has been made by people. p. 30

human resources (hyōō´mən rē´sôr•səz) Workers. p. 345

humidity (hyōō•mi´də•tē) The amount of moisture in the air. p. 72

hydroelectric power (hī•drō•i•lek´trik pou´ər) Electricity made by using the power of fast-moving water. p. 69

I

immigrant (i´mi•grənt) A person who comes from another place to live in a country. p. 206

import (im´pôrt) A product that is brought into one country from another to be sold. p. 392

independence (in•də•pen´dəns) Freedom. p. 165

industry (in´dəs•trē) All the businesses that make one kind of product or provide one kind of service. p. 236

initiative (i•ni´shə•tiv) A law made directly by voters instead of by a legislature. p. 411

inlet (in´let *or* in´lət) A narrow strip of water leading into the land from a larger body of water. p. 64

inset map (in´set map) A small map within a larger map. p. 34

intermediate direction (in•tər•mē´dē•it də•rek´shən) A direction between the cardinal directions: northeast, southeast, southwest, and northwest. p. 34

international trade (in•tər•na´shə•nəl trād) Trade with other countries. p. 391

Internet (in•tər´net) A network that links computers. p. 393

invest (in•vest´) To buy something, such as a share in a company, in the hope that it will make money in the future. p. 282

irrigation (ir•ə•gā´shən) The use of canals, ditches, or pipes to carry water to dry places. p. 60

isthmus (is´məs) A narrow piece of land that connects two larger land areas. p. 231

J

judicial branch (jōō•di´shəl branch) The branch of government that makes sure laws made by the legislative branch are used fairly and agree with the state or federal constitution. p. 410

jury trial (jŏŏr´ē trī´əl) The examination of a case in which a group of citizens decides whether a person accused of a crime or other wrongdoing should be found guilty or not guilty. p. 415

L

labor (lā´bər) Work. p. 177

labor union (lā´bər yōōn´yən) A group of workers who try to get better working conditions. p. 336

laborer (lā´bər•ər) A worker. p. 285

land grant (land grant) A gift of land given by the government. p. 172

land use (land yōōs) How most of the land in a place is used. p. 82

landform (land´fôrm) One of the shapes that make up the Earth's surface. p. 19

language group (lang´gwij grōōp) A group of languages that are alike in some way. p. 94

lava (lä´və) Hot, melted rock from deep inside the Earth. p. 59

legend (le´jənd) A story handed down over time. p. 90

legislative branch (le´jəs•lā•tiv branch) The branch of government that makes laws. p. 408

levee (le´vē) A high wall made of earth to help control flooding. p. 297

line graph (līn graf) A graph that uses a line to show changes over time. p. 242

lines of latitude (līnz uv la´tə•tōōd) A set of lines drawn on maps and globes that run east and west. p. 52

lines of longitude (līnz uv lon´jə•tōōd) A set of lines drawn on maps and globes that run north and south, from the North Pole to the South Pole. p. 52

location (lō•kā´shən) Where something can be found. p. 29

locator (lō´kā•tər) A small map or globe that shows where the place on the main map is located within a state, a country, or a continent or in the world. p. 34

M

manifest destiny (ma´nə•fest des´tə•nē) The idea that the United States should stretch from the Atlantic Ocean to the Pacific Ocean. p. 215

manufacturing (man•yə•fak´chə•ring) The making of goods. p. 77

map key (map kē) The part of a map that explains what the symbols on the map stand for. p. 33

map scale (map skāl) The part of a map that compares a distance on the map to a distance in the real world. p. 34

map title (map tī´təl) The words that tell you the subject of a map. p. 32

meridians (mə•ri´dē•ənz) Another name for lines of longitude. p. 52

metropolitan area (me•trə•po´lə•tən âr´ē•ə) A large city together with its suburbs. p. 373

migrant worker (mī´grənt wûr´kər) Someone who moves from place to place with the seasons, harvesting crops. p. 338

mileage table (mī´lij tā´bəl) A chart that gives the number of miles between the listed cities. p. 375

mineral (mi´nə•rəl) A natural substance found in rocks. p. 77

mission (mi´shən) A religious settlement. p. 143

missionary (mi´shə•ner•ē) A person who teaches his or her religion to others. p. 143

mountain range (moun´tən rānj) A group of connected mountains. p. 49

municipal (myōō•ni´sə•pəl) Having to do with a city. p. 414

N

nation (nā´shən) A group of people who share land and a common way of life. p. 89

natural region (na´chə•rəl rē´jən) A region made up of places that share the same kinds of physical, or natural, features, such as plains, mountains, valleys, or deserts. p. 54

natural resource (na´chə•rəl rē´sôrs) Something found in nature that people can use. p. 30

naturalized citizen (na´chə•rəl•īzd si´tə•zən) An immigrant who has become a citizen by taking the steps described in the law. p. 424

nomad (nō´mad) A person who keeps moving from place to place. p. 87

nonrenewable resource (non•ri•nōō´ə•bəl rē´sôrs) A resource that cannot be made again by nature or by people. p. 78

O

ocean current (ō´shən kûr´ənt) A stream of water that moves through the ocean. p. 134

opinion (ə•pin´yən) A statement that tells what the person who makes it thinks or believes. p. 213

opportunity cost (o•pər•tōō´nə•tē kôst) What you give up to get something else. p. 419

P

Pacific Rim (pə•si´fik rim) A world region that includes the states and countries that border the Pacific Ocean. p. 51

parallels (par´ə•lelz) Another name for lines of latitudes, because they are always the same distance apart. p. 52

pass (pas) An opening between high mountains. p. 202

peninsula (pə•nin´sə•lə) Land that has water almost all around it. p. 133

petition (pə•ti´shən) A signed request for action. p. 411

petroleum (pə•trō´lē•əm) Another name for oil. p. 77

physical feature (fi´zi•kəl fē´chər) A feature, such as a mountain or river, that has been formed by nature. p. 30

pictograph (pik´tə•graf) A graph that uses symbols to stand for numbers. p. 302

pioneer (pī•ə•nir´) One of the first settlers in a place. p. 208

plateau (pla•tō´) An area of high, flat land. p. 61

plaza (pla´zə) An open square at the center of a pueblo. p. 179

point of view (point uv vyōō) A person's set of beliefs that have been shaped by factors such as whether that person is old or young, male or female, rich or poor. p. 28

pollution (pə•lōō´shən) Anything that makes a natural resource dirty or unsafe to use. p. 397

population (po•pyə•lā´shən) The number of people who live in a place. p. 238

population density (po•pyə•lā´shən den´sə•tē) The number of people who live in an area of a certain size. p. 382

port (pôrt) A trading center where ships are loaded and unloaded. p. 133

precipitation (pri•si•pə•tā´shən) Water that falls to the Earth's surface in the form of rain, sleet, or snow. p. 70

prejudice (pre´jə•dəs) The unfair feeling of hate or dislike for members of a certain group because of their background, race, or religion. p. 305

presidio (pri•sē´dē•ō) A Spanish fort. p. 146

primary source (prī´mer•ē sôrs) Information that gives the real words and views of people who were there when an event took place. p. 342

prime meridian (prīm mə•ri´dē•ən) The starting point for the lines of longitude; passes near London, England. p. 52

product (pro´dəkt) Something that people make or grow, usually to sell. p. 76

professional team (prə•fe´shə•nəl tēm) A team of players who are paid for playing a sport. p. 389

protest (prō´test) To act against something. p. 377

pueblo (pwe´blō) A farming community in Spanish California. p. 148

R

rain shadow (rān sha´dō) The drier side of a mountain. p. 72

rancho (ran´chō) A large cattle ranch. p. 172

rebel (re´bəl) A person who fights against the government. p. 216

recall (ri•kôl´) To remove an official from his or her job. p. 411

recreation (re•krē•ā´shən) An activity that people do for fun. p. 389

recycle (rē•sī´kəl) To reuse. p. 400

referendum (re•fə•ren´dəm) An election in which voters can vote to keep or get rid of a law that exists. p. 411

reform (ri•fôrm´) To change for the better. p. 328

region (rē´jən) A place with at least one feature that makes it different from other places. p. 31

register (re´jə•stər) To sign up. p. 425

relative location (re´lə•tiv lō•kā´shən) Where a place is, as compared to one or more other places on Earth. p. 48

religion (ri•li´jən) A set of beliefs about God or gods. p. 93

relocation camp (rē•lō•kā´shən kamp) Prison-like camps in the West in which Japanese Americans were held following the bombing of Pearl Harbor by Japan during World War II. p. 348

renewable resource (ri•noo´ə•bəl re´sôrs) A resource that can be made again by nature or by people. p. 79

republic (ri•pə´blik) A form of government in which people elect their leaders. p. 217

reservation (re•zər•vā´shən) Land set aside by the government for use by Indians. p. 306

reservoir (re´zər•vwär) A lake made by people to collect and store water. p. 69

resist (ri•zist´) To act against. p. 155

responsibility (ri•spon•sə•bi´lə•tē) Something a person should do; a duty. p. 424

revolt (ri•vōlt´) An action against people in charge. p. 155

right (rīt) A freedom that belongs to a person. p. 219

river system (ri´vər sis´təm) A river and its tributaries. p. 65

rodeo (rō´dē•ō) A yearly cattle roundup. p. 179

route (root) A path. p. 138

S

Santa Ana winds (san´tə a´nə windz) Hot, dry winds that form in the Great Basin and blow westward across southern California. p. 75

scarce (skârs) Limited. p. 112

sea level (sē le´vəl) Land that is level with the surface of the ocean. p. 61

secondary source (se´kən•dər•ē sôrs) Information written at a later time by someone who was not there to see what happened when an event took place. p. 342

segregation (se•gri•gā´shən) Keeping people of one race or culture separate from other people. p. 376

self-sufficient (self•sə•fi´shənt) Being able to produce everything that is needed. p. 177

service (sər´vəs) An activity that someone does for others for pay. p. 179

shaman (shä´mən) A religious leader. p. 97

silicon chip (si´li•kän chip) A tiny device that can store millions of bits of computer information. p. 371

slave (slāv) A person who is owned by another person and made to work. p. 156

slave state (slāv stāt) A state in which slavery was allowed. p. 247

slavery (slā´və•rē) The making of some people the property of other people. p. 246

smog (smog) A layer of dirty, yellow-brown air. p. 398

society (sə•sī´ə•tē) A group of people who live in the same place and have many things in common. p. 168

special district (spe´shəl dis´trikt) An area in which a certain problem, such as flooding, needs to be solved or a certain service, such as libraries, needs to be provided. p. 417

specialize (spe´shə•līz) To work at one kind of job and do it well. p. 107

spring (spring) An opening in the Earth's surface through which water flows from under the ground. p. 111

squatter (skwä´tər) Someone who lives in a place without permission. p. 214

stagecoach (stāj´kōch) An enclosed wagon pulled by a team of horses. p. 276

strait (strāt) A narrow channel that connects two larger bodies of water. p. 132

Glossary

strike (strīk) To stop work. p. 336

suburb (su´bərb) A town or small city built near a large city. p. 372

suffrage (su´frij) The right to vote. p. 329

supply (sə•plī´) An amount of a good or a service that is offered for sale. p. 199

swamp (swämp) A low, wet area, usually covered by shallow water. p. 231

symbol (sim´bəl) Something that stands for something else. p. 33

T

tallow (tal´ō) The purest part of the melted fat from the hides of cattle; used to make soap and candles. p. 179

tax (taks) Money that a government collects from its citizens, usually to pay for services. p. 384

technology (tek•no´lə•jē) The way people use new ideas to make tools or machines. p. 241

telegraph (te´lə•graf) A machine that used electricity to send messages over wires. p. 279

temperature (tem´pər•chər) The measure of how warm or cold something is. p. 70

tenant farmer (te´nənt fär´mər) A farmer who pays rent to use a piece of land. p. 301

territory (te´rə•tôr•ē) A place owned and governed by a country. p. 227

time line (tīm līn) A diagram that shows the order in which events took place and the amount of time that passed between them. p. 27

time zone (tīm zōn) A region in which people use the same time. p. 294

tourism (tŏŏr´i•zəm) The selling of goods and services to tourists. p. 396

trade (trād) The exchanging, or buying and selling, of goods. p. 98

trade-off (trād´ôf) Giving up one thing to get another. p. 419

tradition (trə•di´shən) An idea or a way of doing something that has been handed down from the past. p. 100

trailblazer (trāl•blā´zər) A person who makes a new trail for others to follow. p. 202

transcontinental railroad (trans•kon•tən•en´təl rāl´rōd) A railroad that crosses the North American continent, linking the Atlantic and Pacific coasts. p. 281

transportation (trans•pər•tā´shən) The moving of people and goods from place to place. p. 275

treaty (trē´tē) An agreement between groups or countries. p. 220

tribe (trīb) A Native American group that shares the same language and has the same leaders. p. 89

tributary (tri´byə•te•rē) A smaller river that flows into a larger river. p. 65

U

unemployment (ən•im•ploi´mənt) The number of people without jobs. p. 335

urban growth (ər´bən grōth) The growth of cities. p. 310

urban sprawl (ər´bən sprôl) The spread of urban areas. p. 372

V

vaquero (vä•kä´rō) A cowhand. p. 178

vegetation (ve•jə•tā´shən) Plant life. p. 88

veto (vē´tō) To reject a bill and to try to stop it from becoming law. p. 409

vigilante (vi•jə•lan´tē) A person who takes the law into his or her own hands. p. 239

volcano (vol•kā´nō) An opening in the Earth's surface from which hot gases, ashes, and lava may pour. p. 59

volunteer (vo•lən•tir´) A person who works without pay. p. 426

W

wagon train (wa´gən trān) A group of wagons, each pulled by horses or oxen. p. 209

water project (wô´tər pro´jekt) A system of dams, reservoirs, and water pipes that store water, carry it, and control its flow. p. 321

watershed (wô´tər•shed) The region from which a river drains water. p. 400

wealth (welth) Riches. p. 98

weir (wir) A fence built across a river in order to trap fish. p. 97

wetlands (wet´landz) Low-lying areas in which the water level is always near or above the surface of the land. p. 397

Glossary

Index

Page references for illustrations are set in italic type. An italic *m* indicates a map. Page references set in boldface type indicate the pages on which vocabulary terms are defined.

Index

Index

Q

For permission to translate/reprint copyrighted material, grateful acknowledgment is made to the following sources:

Calicanto Associates, 6416 Valley View Rd., Oakland, CA 94611: From "Oh, California!" in *They Came Singing: Songs from California's History*, compiled, edited and arranged by Karen Arlen, Margaret Batt and Nancie Kester. Lyrics copyright © by Calicanto Associates.

The Caxton Printers, Ltd.: From *Patty Reed's Doll: The Story of the Donner Party* by Rachel Kelley Laurgaard, illustrated by Elizabeth Sykes Michaels, cover design by Diane Wilde. Copyright © 1956 by The Caxton Printers, Ltd.

Chronicle Books, San Francisco, CA: Cover illustration by Sylvia Long from *Fire Race: A Karuk Coyote Tale About How Fire Came to the People*, retold by Jonathan London. Illustration copyright © 1993 by Sylvia Long.

Comstock Bonanza Press: From *Vallejo y las cuatro banderas* by Esther J. Comstock, illustrated by Floyd B. Comstock. Text and cover illustration © 1996 by Esther J. Comstock.

Crabtree Publishing Company: Cover illustration from *Historic Communities: Spanish Missions* by Bobbie Kalman and Greg Nickles. Copyright © 1997 by Crabtree Publishing.

Facts On File, Inc.: Untitled Maidu Indian poem from *The First Americans: California Indians* by C. L. Keyworth. Text copyright © 1991 by International Book Marketing Ltd.

Fithian Press: Cover illustration by Leslie Clark from *Anita of Rancho Del Mar* by Elaine F. O'Brien. Copyright © 1990 by Elaine F. O'Brien.

HarperCollins Publishers: Cover illustration by Wendell Minor from *Sierra* by Diane Siebert. Illustration copyright © 1991 by Wendell Minor.

Henry Holt and Company, Inc.: From *Ten Mile Day and the Building of the Transcontinental Railroad* by Mary Ann Fraser. Copyright © 1993 by Mary Ann Fraser.

Lee & Low Books, New York: Cover illustration from *Dia's Story Cloth: The Hmong People's Journey of Freedom* by Dia Cha. Copyright © 1996 by Denver Museum of Natural History. Cover illustration by Dom Lee from *Baseball Saved Us* by Ken Mochizuki. Illustration copyright © 1993 by Dom Lee.

Little, Brown & Company: Cover illustration by Eric von Schmidt from *By the Great Horn Spoon!* by Sid Fleischman. Copyright © 1963 by Sid Fleischman, Inc.

Ludlow Music, Inc., New York: From "Do Re Mi" by Woody Guthrie. TRO - © copyright 1961 (renewed) and 1963 (renewed) by Ludlow Music, Inc.

Margaret K. McElderry Books, an imprint of Simon & Schuster Children's Publishing Division: From "Mole and the Sun" in *Back in the Beforetime: Tales of the California Indians* by Jane Louise Curry. Text copyright © 1987 by Jane Louise Curry.

The Millbrook Press: Cover photograph from *Our Constitution* by Linda Carlson Johnson. © 1992 by Blackbirch Graphics, Inc. Cover photograph courtesy of National Archives.

Open Hand Publishing Inc.: From "Biddy Mason" in *Women of the Wild West* by Ruth Pelz, cover photograph by Edward S. Curtis. Text copyright © 1995 by Ruth Pelz.

Roberts Rinehart Publishers, 6309 Monarch Park Place, Niwot, Colorado 80503: From *Grandmother Oak* by Rosi Dagit, illustrated by Gretta Allison. Text copyright 1996 by Rosi Dagit; cover illustration copyright 1996 by Gretta Allison.

Scholastic Inc.: Cover illustration by Pat Grant Porter from *...If You Lived at the Time of the Great San Francisco Earthquake* by Ellen Levine. Illustration copyright © 1992 by Scholastic Inc.

Scholastic Press, a division of Scholastic Inc.: From *Pony Express!* by Steven Kroll, illustrated by Dan Andreasen. Text copyright © 1996 by Steven Kroll; illustrations copyright © 1996 by Daniel Andreasen.

Smithsonian Institution University Press: From "My Words are Tied in One," translated by A. L. Kroeber in *Bureau of American Ethnology Bulletin 78*. Copyright © 1925 by The Smithsonian Institution.

Steck-Vaughn Company: From *To Fly with the Swallows: A Story of Old California* by Dana Catharine de Ruiz, cover illustration by Mary Beth Schwark. Text and cover illustration copyright © 1993 by Dialogue Systems, Inc.

Troll Communications L.L.C.: Cover illustration by Marion Krupp from *Jim Beckwourth: Adventures of a Mountain Man* by Louis Sabin. Illustration copyright © 1993 by Marion Krupp.

University of Missouri - Kansas City, University Libraries: "Maps" by Dorothy Brown Thompson.

The University of North Carolina Press: Letter 15. "Our pride isn't all gone" from Mrs. I. H. of Lawndale, CA in *Down and Out in the Great Depression: Letters from the Forgotten Man*, edited by Robert S. McElvaine. Text copyright © 1983 by the University of North Carolina Press.

All maps by GeoSystems

Cover Credits

Design Studio: Mariello Grafico, Inc.
Photography: Ken West Photography

Photo Credits:

Page Placement Key: (t)-top, (c)-center, (b)-bottom, (l)-left, (r)-right, (bg)-background

Cover Photo Credit: (bc) "Vaquero" by James Walker, adapted from the original at the Bancroft Library, UC Berkeley:

Table of Contents:

iii Jeffry Myers/FPG International; iv (t) Photograph courtesy of Colby Memorial Library, Sierra Club; iv (b) Lawrence Migdale/Harcourt Brace & Co.; v (t) The Granger Collection, New York; v (b) Betty J. Bradley/Photo: Corey Warner/Harcourt Brace & Co.; vi (t) National Portrait Gallery, Smithsonian Institution/Art Resource, New York; vi (b) The Bancroft Library, University of California, Zelda Mckay Collection; vii (t) Courtesy of The Oakland Museum of California, Kahn Collection; vii (b) Culver Pictures; viii (t) Lawrence Migdale/Harcourt Brace & Co.; viii (b) Tom Zimberoff/Sygma; ix David Muench/David Muench Photography;

Introduction:

A1 David Wagner/Phototake; 18, 19 (t) Weronica Ankarorn/Harcourt Brace & Co.; 19 (b) Lawrence Migdale/Stock, Boston; 20 (t) Arthur Tilley/FPG International; 20 (bl) Harcourt Brace & Co.; 20 (bc), (br) Weronica Ankarorn/Harcourt Brace & Co.; 21 (t), (c) David Stoecklein/The Stock Market; 21 (b) Renee Lynn/Photo Researchers; 24 Weronica Ankarorn/Harcourt Brace & Co.; 26 (t) Mark Burnett/Stock, Boston; 26 (bl) Stephen Frisch/Stock, Boston; 26 (br) Dilon Ellis; 27 (c) The Granger Collection, New York; 27 (b) California History Section, California State Library; 28 Corbis-Bettmann; 29 (t) Weronica Ankarorn/Harcourt Brace & Co.; 29 (b) David Muench/David Muench Photography; 30 Kevin Schafer/Peter Arnold, Inc.; 31 (t) Chris Sorenson/The Stock Market; 31 (bl) Michael Kevin Daly/The Stock Market; 31 (br) Marc Muench/David Muench Photography; 32 Michio Hoshino/Minden Pictures; 36 (t) William Whitehurst/The Stock Market; 36 (c) Thomas Del Brase/Tony Stone Images; 36 (b) Eddie Hironaka/The Image Bank; 37 Weronica Ankarorn/Harcourt Brace & Co.;

Unit 1:

38-39 Jeff Foott/Panoramic Images; 40 (t) Mark E. Gibson; 40 (b) Michelle Burgess/The Stock Market; 41 (t) Geoff Juckes/The Stock Market; 41 (c) Larry Ulrich/Larry Ulrich Photography; 41 (b) Larry Ulrich/Tony Stone Images; 42 Victoria Bowen/Harcourt Brace & Co.; 46 Photograph courtesy of Colby Memorial Library, Sierra Club; 47 Weronica Ankarorn/Harcourt Brace & Co.; 50 (t) John M. Roberts/The Stock Market; 50-51 (b) David Muench/David Muench Photography; 54 Weronica Ankarorn/Harcourt Brace & Co.; 55 Carroll Seghers/The Stock Market; 56 (b) Chase Swift/Westlight; 56 (inset) Kevin Schafer/Tony Stone Images; 58 Ron Sanford/The Stock Market; 59 Hulton-Deutsch Collection/Corbis; 60-61 Frank S. Balthis/Natural Selection Stock Photography; 61 (t) Mark E. Gibson; 61 (inset) David Muench/David Muench Photography; 62 Chris Cheadle/Tony Stone Images; 64 (t) Cheyenne Rouse/Cheyenne Rouse Photography; 64 (b) Ken Biggs/Tony Stone Images; 66 Roger Ressmeyer/(c) Corbis; 66 (inset) The Ansel Adams Publishing Rights

Unit 4:

266-267 Southern Pacific Photo Archive; 270 Victoria Bowen/Harcourt Brace & Co.; 274 Courtesy of The Oakland Museum of California, Kahn Collection; 275 (t) Wells Fargo Bank; 275 (b) Courtesy of The Oakland Museum of California; 276 Denver Public Library; 277, 278(c) The Granger Collection, New York; 278 (bl) St. Joseph Museum, St. Joseph Missouri; 278 (br) Corbis-Bettmann; 279 Smithsonian Institution; 280 The Granger Collection, New York; 281 Ernest H. Robl; 282(l)(inset), (cl)(inset) California History Section/California State Library; 282(cr)(inset), (r)(inset) The Bancroft Library, University of California; 282 Terry Johnson; 286 Union Pacific Railroad; 287 Stanford University Museum of Art/AAA/Gift of David Hewes; 288 Victoria Bowen/Harcourt Brace & Co.; 294 Dale E. Boyer/Tony Stone Images; 296 (t) Courtesy the Oakland Museum of California; 296 (b) J-C Carton/Bruce Coleman, Inc.; 297 Fine Arts Museums of San Francisco, Gift of Mrs. Harold R. McKinnon and Mrs. Harry L. Brown, 1962.21; 298 (inset) Riverside Municipal Museum, Riverside, CA # A572.2; 298 The Granger Collection, New York; 299 Courtesy of the Oakland Museum of California; 300 UPI/Corbis-Bettmann; 301 The Granger Collection, New York; 302 Mark E. Gibson; 303 (t) V. Aubrey and Irene Neasham Collection, Sacramento Archives and Museum Collection Center; 303 (b) Courtesy of the National Park Service, Statue of Liberty National Monument; 304 The Society of California Pioneers; 305 National Archives; 306, 307 California History Section/California State Library; 308 (inset) California Department of Parks and Recreation Photographic Archives; 308 Mark E. Gibson; 309 Courtesy the Bank of Stockton Photo Collection; 310 (t) The Granger Collection, New York; 310 (b) Corbis-Bettmann; 311 (t) Private Collection, California; 311 (b) Courtesy of the Oakland Museum of California; 312 Mark E. Gibson; 313 Corbis-Bettmann; 314 California History Section/California State Library; 316 David R. Frazier; 319 Harcourt Brace & Co.; 320 Culver Pictures; 321 (t) Weronica Ankarorn/Harcourt Brace & Co.; 321 (b) Betty Crowell/Faraway Places; 322-323 Hearst Newspaper Collection, Special Collections, University of Southern California Library; 323 California Historical Society, Title Insurance and Trust Photo Collection, Department of Special Collections, University of Southern California Library; 324 (t) UPI/Corbis-Bettmann; 324-325 (b) Galen Rowell/Mountain Light; 326-327 Superstock; 327 (inset) Great Basin Unified Air Pollution Control District; 328 The Bancroft Library, University of California; 329 (l)(inset) Smithsonian Institution, #79-1004; 329 (r)(inset) Sophia Smith Collection/Smith College; 329 UPI/Corbis-Bettmann; 330 The National Archives/Corbis; 331 (t) Courtesy of the Oakland Museum of California; 331 (bl)

The Pat Hathaway Collection; 331 (br) David Spindel/Superstock; 332 (inset) H. Armstrong Roberts, Inc.; 332 Underwood & Underwood/Corbis-Bettmann; 333 Culver Pictures; 334 (l) The Granger Collection, New York; 334 (r) Culver Pictures; 335 Security Pacific Collection/Los Angeles Public Library; 336 Library of Congress/Corbis; 337 (l) D. Boone/Westlight; 337(r), 338(t) The Granger Collection, New York; 338 (b) Natioanl Portrait Gallery, Smithsonian Institution, Washington, D.C.; 340 Tibor Bognar/The Stock Market; 341 UPI/Corbis-Bettmann; 342 The Granger Collection, New York; 344 (t) David Weintraub/Stock Boston; 344 (b) The National Archives/Corbis; 345 (inset) UPI/Corbis-Bettmann; 345 The Granger Collection, New York; 346 (t) Superstock; 346 (inset) A.K.G., Berlin/Superstock; 346 (b) The Granger Collection, New York; 347 Library of Congress/Corbis; 348 Culver Pictures, Inc.; 348 (inset) UPI/Corbis-Bettmann; 349 (t) Wide World Photos; 349 (b) The Library of Virginia; 350 Brown Brothers; 351 Alfred Eiserstaedt/Life Magazine (c) Time Inc.; 353 Harcourt Brace & Co.; 354-355 (bg) Ron Watts/Westlight; 355 Michael Newman/PhotoEdit; 359 Weronica Ankarorn/Harcourt Brace & Co.;

Unit 5:

360-361 Chromosohm/Sohm/The Stock Market; 368 Lawrence Migdale/Harcourt Brace & Co.; 369 (t) H.G. Ross/H. Armstrong Roberts, Inc.; 369 (b) American Stock Photography; 370 UPI/Corbis-Bettmann; 371 (t) Roger Du Buisson/The Stock Market; 371 (b) NASA/Media Services Corp.; 372 (inset) Harold M. Lambert/American Stock Photography; 372 Archive Photos; 373 Tom Carroll Photography/PhotoBank, Inc.; 376 (t) Declan Haun/Black Star; 376 (b) Superstock; 377 (t) Security Pacific Collection/Los Angeles Public Library; 377 (b) AP Photo/Nick Ut, Files/Wide World Photos; 378 (l) Wayne State University/Archives of Labor and Urban Affairs; 378(r), 379, 380 UPI/Corbis-Bettmann; 384 (t) Jerry White/Harcourt Brace & Co.; 384 (b) Superstock; 385 (c) The Bancroft Library, University of California; 385 (b) Stephen Derr/The Image Bank; 386 Bill Ross/Westlight; 386 (inset) Michael Newman/PhotoEdit; 387 (t) Betty Crowell/Faraway Places; 387 (b) Michele Burgess; 388 (t) Tony Freeman/PhotoEdit; 388 (b) Betty Crowell/ Faraway Places; 389 (t) Jose Carrillo/PhotoEdit; 389 (b) Deborah Davis/PhotoEdit; 390 Chuck Schmeiser/Unicorn Stock Photos; 391 Jeff Hunter/The Image Bank; 392 Superstock; 393 Ted Horowitz/The Stock Market; 394 Weronica Ankarorn/Harcourt Brace & Co.; 395 Dana White/PhotoEdit; 396 Gary A. Conner/PhotoEdit; 396 (inset) Kenneth W. Fink/Bruce Coleman, Inc.; 397 (t) Anthony Mercieca/Natural Selection Stock Photography; 397 (b) Spencer Grant/PhotoEdit; 398 (t) The Bancroft Library, University of California; 398-399

(b) Ron Sanford/The Stock Market; 399 (t) Gary Moon Photography; 399 (inset) Cindy Charles/PhotoEdit; 400 Will & Deni McIntyre/Photo Researchers, Inc.; 401 William McCoy/Rainbow/PNI; 402 Courtesy of Brian Huse; 402-403 Alan Levenson Photography; 403 (t) Robert Foothorap/Black Star/Harcourt Brace & Co.; 403 (c) Courtesy of Bromwyn Hogan; 405 Harcourt Brace & Co.; 406 Tom Zimberoff/Sygma; 407 Office of the Governor; 408 (inset) Mark E. Gibson; 408 Office of the Governor; 409 (t) Craig Aurness/Westlight; 409 (bl) Audrey Gibson; 409 (bc) Office of Governor; 409 (br) Summer Productions; 410 Judicial Council of California; 411 (inset) Victoria Bowen/Harcourt Brace & Co.; 411 Tom Prettyman/PhotoEdit; 412 Glen Korengold Photography; 414 (t) Larry Angier/Image West; 414 (b) Dick James Stock Photography; 416 (inset) Grantpix/PhotoBank; 416-417 D. Young-Wolff/PhotoEdit; 417 (c) Spencer Grant/PhotoEdit; 417 (bl) (inset) W. Whitehurst/The Stock Market; 417 (br) (inset) Michael Newman/PhotoEdit; 418 Weronica Ankarorn/Harcourt Brace & Co.; 419 Stacy Pick/Stock Boston; 420 (t) Harcourt Brace & Co.; 420 (b) Bill Ross/Westlight; 420 (b)(inset) Printed by permission of the Norman Rockwell Family Trust. © 1960 The Norman Rockwell Family Trust/Curtis Publishing; 421 (t) (inset) The Granger Collection, New York; 421 (t) Stephen L. Saks; 421 (b) Michele Burgess/PhotoBank, Inc.; 422 (t)(inset) Michael Evans/Sygma Photo News; 422 (t) Audrey Gibson/Mark E. Gibson; 422-423 (b) Bill Bachmann/PhotoEdit; 423 (tr) Courtesy of Dianne Feinstein; 423 (tl) Courtesy of Barbara Boxer; 423 (b) Tony Korody/Sygma; 424 Mark E. Gibson; 425 (c) Michael Newman/PhotoEdit; 425 (b) Chromosohm/Sohm/The Stock Market; 426 Michael Newman/PhotoEdit; 427 (inset) Tony Freeman/PhotoEdit; 427 D. Young-Wolff/PhotoEdit; 429 Weronica Ankarorn/Harcourt Brace & Co.; 431 Harcourt Brace & Co.; 432-433 (bg) John Lel/Stock Boston; 433 Michael Newman/PhotoEdit; 437 Weronica Ankarorn/Harcourt Brace & Co.;

Reference:

438 (t) Mark E. Gibson; 438-R1 Craig Aurness/Westlight; R1 (inset) David Muench/David Muench Photography, Inc.; R2 P & F Communications/Harcourt Brace & Co.; R3 Eric Camden/Harcourt Brace & Co.; R7 Weronica Ankarorn/Harcourt Brace & Co.; R8 (t) P & F Communications/Harcourt Brace & Co.; R8 (b) Terry D. Sinclair/Harcourt Brace & Co.; R9 Terry D. Sinclair/Harcourt Brace & Co.; R10 (r) Andy Caulfield/Harcourt Brace & Co.; R10 (l) A.G.E. FotoStock/Westlight; R11 Joe Sohm/The Stock Market; R12 (inset) Office of the Governor; R12-R13 Mick Roessler/PhotoBank, Inc.;